STO

ACPL ITEM
DISCARDED

S0-BKX-469

1·15·79

JUL 3 '73

Real Estate Finance

Maurice A. Unger

Professor of Real Estate and Business Law
University of Colorado

Ronald W. Melicher

Professor of Finance
University of Colorado

Published by

S62   **SOUTH-WESTERN PUBLISHING CO.**

CINCINNATI   WEST CHICAGO, ILL.   DALLAS   PELHAM MANOR, N.Y.   PALO ALTO, CALIF.

Copyright © 1978

by

South-Western Publishing Co.
Cincinnati, Ohio

All Rights Reserved

The text of this publication, or any part thereof, may not be reproduced or transmitted in any form or by any means, electronic or mechanical, including photocopying, recording, storage in an information retrieval system, or otherwise, without the prior written permission of the publisher.

ISBN: 0-538-19620-3

Library of Congress Catalog Card Number: 77-73467

1 2 3 4 5 6 D 3 2 1 0 9 8

Printed in the United States of America

PREFACE

The purpose of this text is to provide the student and real estate professional with a basic understanding of the institutions and instruments important to the financing of real estate. This background knowledge should aid in the handling and solving of a variety of real estate problems.

While the user of this text might choose to change the sequence of chapter materials, it is our belief that the presented sequence is logical and useful to both the student and professional. First, we begin with two chapters designed to identify and describe the two basic instruments — the mortgage and deed of trust — of real estate. This is followed by Chapter 3 which contains compound interest or "time value of money" concepts. The understanding of these concepts is important because of the frequent long-term investment and financing decisions involved in real estate problems. This chapter also provides the student and real estate professional with basic analytical skills important to the real estate decision-making process.   **2049124**

After the three background chapters, the text then focuses directly on a number of real estate financing topics. These include: (1) methods involving seller financing of real property, (2) the use of junior liens, (3) construction financing, (4) tract and special purpose financing, and (5) the use of long-term leases. This portion of the text is followed by a chapter on high ratio or financial leverage financing and a chapter summarizing additional real estate financing methods.

The text's emphasis then shifts in Chapter 11 to institutional structures, practices, and policies as they pertain to the financing of real estate. Sources of real estate funds are discussed first and then are followed by a chapter on factors affecting these sources. Our attention next is directed toward the role of mortgage banking and secondary mortgage market developments. This institutional section of the text is culminated with Chapter 14 on governmental involvement in the financing of real estate.

The final portion of the text (Chapters 15 and 16) focuses first on the practices and procedures involved in loan applications, analysis, and closings before turning to the concepts and procedures involved in foreclosures.

In summary, we wish to express our appreciation and thanks to the many students and real estate professionals who contributed to the development of this book.

Maurice A. Unger
Ronald W. Melicher

2949124

CONTENTS

Chapter	1	Mortgages and Deeds of Trust	1
	2	Mortgages and Deeds of Trust (Concluded)	14
	3	Interest Factors in Real Estate Finance Decisions	44
	4	Seller Financing of Real Property	61
	5	Financing by Junior Liens	77
	6	Construction Financing	89
	7	Tract and Special Purpose Financing	104
	8	Financing by Means of Long-Term Leases	116
	9	High Ratio Financing	131
	10	Some Alternative Financing Methods	145
	11	Sources of Mortgage and Real Estate Investment Funds	159
	12	Factors Affecting Sources of Funds	182
	13	Mortgage Banking and Secondary Mortgage Market Developments	201
	14	Government Real Estate Finance Programs and Activities	223
	15	Loan Application, Loan Analysis, and Loan Closings	242
	16	Mortgage Foreclosures	272
Case	1	Pinckney Street	284
	2	503 Rugby Road	304
Appendix	A	Glossary of Selected Terms	324
	B	Tables	331

Appendix C Major Legislation Affecting Real Estate Finance   346

D Some Special Financing Devices   349

E Suggested Readings By Selected Topics   353

F Current Information on Economic, Monetary,
and Capital Market Developments   361

G FHLMC/FNMA Residential Appraisal Report Form
and Guidelines   362

Mortgages and Deeds of Trust

Chapter 1

The most important instrument in real estate finance is the mortgage. It is the evidence of the pledge of real property, generally for the repayment of a loan.[1] The use of the mortgage in the United States had its origin in early English Law.

In early English law one of the forms of transfer of real property as security for a debt was called *mortuum vadium*. It was so called because under the ancient law the pledgee became entitled to the rents and profits from the land, hence the land was "dead" to the debtor. Another form of pledge was called *vivum vadium*, wherein the profits from the land were applied to the payment of the loan.

Out of these two forms of mortgage there gradually evolved the so-called "common-law mortgage," which, in the final analysis, was a transfer of the property subject to a condition — the condition being that upon the payment of the debt, by a certain time, the estate of the transferee would terminate.

In early law, the condition that the debt had to be paid by a certain time was strictly enforced. The result of this was that the debtor lost the property if the sum due was not paid by the stated time, even though a partial payment may have been made on the debt. To relieve this obvious hardship on the debtor, the courts, about the middle of the seventeenth century, gave the debtor the right to pay off the debt even after it became due. The debtor was given the right to redeem the property, and this right became known as the equity of redemption. This concept in turn worked a hardship on the creditor, who might never receive the money owed. This resulted in placing a time limit on

---

[1]Generally, because a mortgage may be given to assure payment of alimony, for example.

1

the equity of redemption, by a decreee of foreclosure issued by a court. By virtue of the decree of foreclosure, the right to redeem was cut off unless the debt was paid by the time named in the decree.

Nearly all modern real property transfers involve the use of the property itself as security for part of the payment of the purchase price. Often, too, real property is used as security for a debt when no transfer takes place. In all of these transactions where land is given as security for a debt, there are two instruments involved. Sometimes these instruments are, for brevity's sake, combined into one form, but essentially they remain two separate and distinct instruments. These instruments are the bond (or promissory note, which in many states is used in place of the bond) and the mortgage. The details of the mortgage will be discussed later, but for the moment let it suffice that a *mortgage* is the creation of an interest in property as security for the payment of a debt or the fulfillment of some obligation. The two parties to a mortgage are the *mortgagor* (borrower) and the *mortgagee* (lender).

The deed of trust, which will be discussed later, is a deed absolute to secure the payment of a debt. There are three parties to the instrument. The borrower transfers the property to a trustee who holds it for the benefit of the lender. On default by the borrower, proper legal steps are taken by the trustee to insure repayment of the loan to the lender. In the following discussion of the mortgage, one should be aware that much of the information relative to the real property mortgage is also applicable to the deed of trust.

THE THREE THEORIES OF REAL ESTATE MORTGAGES

There are three theories of mortgages used in the United States. These theories are the title theory, the lien theory, and the intermediate theory.

The Title Theory

The basic concept of the *title theory*[2] is that upon making the mortgage, the mortgagor (borrower) passes title to the property, the subject of the mortgage, to the mortgagee (lender) subject to a condition subsequent. This condition subsequent is the payment of the debt. Upon fulfillment of the condition, title to the property divests (reverts) to the mortgagor.

---

[2]The states using the title theory are: Alabama, Arkansas, Connecticut, Maine, Maryland, Massachusetts, New Hampshire, Pennsylvania, Rhode Island, Tennessee, Vermont, Virginia, West Virginia, and The District of Columbia.

For example, A (the mortgagor) mortgages real property to B (the mortgagee) in a title state. Under the terms of the instrument, title passes to B. However, the instrument will state that if A complies with the condition (makes payment), then the instrument will be void.

During the period of the mortgage, by virtue of a provision in the mortgage, A is generally entitled to remain in possession of the property even though title has passed to the mortgagee.

The Lien Theory

The majority of the states use the *lien theory* of mortgages.[3] Under this theory, title remains with the mortgagor, and the mortgage that is placed on the property is a charge on the title. The mortgage instrument says nothing about title, but states: "The mortgagor does hereby mortgage to. . . ." After the recording of the instrument, it becomes a lien on the property described in the mortgage.

The rule regarding the priority of mortgages, whether in title or lien states, is substantially the same rule as that regarding the priority of deeds: the instrument recorded first, in the absence of fraud, is the operative one. For example, A mortgages real property to B on October 15 with the instrument bearing that date. On the following day A mortgages the same property to C. C records the mortgage before B. In the absence of fraud, C has a valid enforceable mortgage. To avoid such circumstances, mortgages should be recorded immediately.

The Intermediate Theory

The *intermediate theory* involves a combination of the title and lien theories.[4] When the mortgage is written it is a lien. If the borrower defaults, title passes to the lender who then proceeds to foreclose.

TYPES OF MORTGAGES

There are three basic types of mortgages: FHA, VA, and conventional, which are discussed in the following paragraphs.

The FHA-Insured Mortgage

The primary feature of the FHA mortgage as far as the lender is concerned is that the loan is insured. A loss as a result of failure of the

---

[3]The states using the lien theory are: Alaska, Arizona, California, Colorado, Delaware, Florida, Georgia, Hawaii, Idaho, Indiana, Iowa, Kansas, Kentucky, Louisiana, Michigan, Minnesota, Missouri, Montana, Nebraska, Nevada, New Mexico, New York, North Dakota, Oklahoma, Oregon, South Carolina, South Dakota, Texas, Utah, Washington, Wisconsin, and Wyoming.

[4]The states using the intermediate theory are: Delaware, Illinois, Mississippi, Missouri, New Jersey, North Carolina, and Vermont.

mortgagor to meet the payments will be covered by the Federal Housing Administration, which was instituted under the National Housing Act of 1934. It is now under the jurisdiction of the Department of Housing and Urban Development. This insurance feature enables lending institutions to lend a higher percentage of the appraised value than they would under ordinary circumstances.

One of the provisions of the Housing and Community Development Act of 1974 increased the maximum FHA loan to $45,000. At the same time the maximum interest rate for FHA-insured loans was set at 9½ percent. Both rates and maximum amounts change periodically.

The Act also provides for an increase in the loan-to-value ratios permitted on FHA-insured loans. The *loan-to-value ratio* is the percentage of loan permitted on the appraised value of the property. For example, if the appraised value of a home is $40,000 and the loan-to-value ratio is 80 percent, then the maximum loan permitted is $32,000.

As of November 1977, the formula for loan-to-value ratios permitted FHA-insured lenders was:

97 percent on the first $25,000 of value
95 percent on the value over $25,000, up to a current maximum loan limit of $60,000.

This formula applies to home loans only.

The VA-Guaranteed Mortgage

The VA mortgage, or the so-called GI mortgage, is a part of the Servicemen's Readjustment Act of 1944 and as amended. The crux of the law pertaining to real property is that the Veterans Administration will guarantee a certain percentage of a mortgage loan to a veteran up to a maximum amount to qualified lenders who lend money on homes purchased by veterans. The amount of the maximum guarantee, the rate of interest, and the length of the loan can be changed by an act of Congress. They have varied in the past and will probably be changed again.

The mortgage is said to be guaranteed because the Veterans Administration will currently guarantee the lending institution, in case of default, 60 percent of the loan or $17,500, whichever is the lesser. The amount of the guarantee also changes from time to time.

In some areas, under changes in the law made by Congress, the Veterans Administration has loaned money directly to veterans. For example, from time to time sums of money have been allotted to various counties to be loaned to veterans within that county who have been unable to obtain a VA loan from a bank or other lending institution. In these cases, the veteran obtains a letter from each of two lending institutions who indicate that they will not lend money to the veteran. After having done this, the veteran makes direct application to the Veterans Administration.

There are five groups of veterans entitled to mortgage loan benefits under the GI Bill:

1. Member of the armed forces during World War II (September 10, 1940–July 25, 1947) for either 90 days or longer or were discharged or released from active duty due to a service incurred disability.
2. Members of the armed forces during the Korean Conflict (June 27, 1950, and January 31, 1955) serving anywhere in the world for 90 days or longer or were discharged or released from active duty due to a service connected disability.
3. "Cold War" veterans who as members of the armed services served 180 days or more in active duty since January, 1955.
4. Unremarried widows of veterans who either died from a service-incurred disability, are missing in action, or were captured or detained by a foreign government or power while performing in the line of duty. The veteran spouse must be missing in action for 90 days or more before eligibility commences.
5. American citizens who during World War II served as members of the armed forces of a government *allied* with the United States and who meet other requirements of the law, including residency in the United States at the time benefits are sought.

The Conventional Mortgage

The term *conventional mortgage* as it is presently used refers to a mortgage that is neither FHA-insured nor VA-guaranteed. In general it can be said that the down payment on the conventional mortgage is higher than either the FHA or VA mortgages. However, since 1972 home buyers have been able to borrow from savings and loan associations up to 95 percent of the value of the home, provided the loan is guaranteed or insured by a mortgage insurance company which is determined to be "a qualified private insurer" by the Federal Home Loan Mortgage Corporation.

The standards for underwriting the privately insured conventional mortgages are established by insurance companies themselves. One of the leading insurance companies, Mortgage Guarantee Insurance Corporation, called "MGIC" suggests the following guidelines for underwriting the insurance:

1. Total monthly house payments must not exceed 25 percent of the borrower's gross monthly income.
2. Total monthly house payments plus total monthly installment obligations (on loans of ten months or more) may not exceed 35 percent of gross monthly income. Other factors such as the borrower's net worth, age, and number of dependents are also considered.

3. The borrower's payment attitude must be assured by the possession of a good credit rating.
4. The borrower must present evidence of job stability or income stability.

On applying for an "insured" conventional loan the prospective borrower must pay an application fee. Furthermore, the borrower, if the insurance is approved, must pay the insurance premiums. Because the companies are in the private sector their premiums vary. To begin with, the entire amount of the loan is not insured; only the top end is. This varies from 20 to 25 percent. For example, assume a loan-to-value ratio of 95 percent and the value of the home is $30,000. The down payment is $1,500 ($30,000 × .05). Assume the insurance insures the top 25 percent of the loan. Then the coverage comes to 25 percent of the 95 percent loan; in this case, 25 percent of $28,500, or $7,125. Put another way, the amount "at risk" for the lender is $21,375. On a $30,000 home this is a substantial cushion in the event of default by the borrower.

Generally premiums amount to 1 percent of the loan for the first year and ¼ of 1 percent of the loan balance in each succeeding year. Another plan might be ½ of 1 percent of the loan balance for three years and ¼ of 1 percent of the loan balance thereafter. Again it depends on the company.

MORTGAGE VARIATIONS

Although "labels" are tacked on and names given as if they were different forms of mortgages, in reality the "other" mortgages are simply variations of the FHA, VA, convention, or conventional-insured mortgage.

Flexible-Payment Mortgage

The Federal Home Loan Bank Board is the regulatory body for the savings and loan associations. In early 1974 the Board gave permission to the savings and loan associations to make flexible-payment mortgages labeled FPM's. The associations can make loans allowing monthly payments below those of a level payment mortgage. Under the rules mortgage payments on home loans of "interest only" for the first five years are permissible. After that time payments on principal and interest must be made.

The purpose of the FPM is to enable a buyer to obtain a higher loan based on current income than could otherwise be obtained. Loans are based on a person's income. A person earning $15,000 would be unable, ordinarily, to buy a home in the same price range as a person earning $30,000 per year. The thinking is that the buyer will earn more in future years; therefore, if "interest only" is paid in the early years of the loan, the buyer can afford a more expensive home.

This technique can be reversed for people approaching retirement. For example, if high payments are made for the first ten years of a 20-year mortgage, lower payments for the next five years, and still lower payments for the final five years, the declining income of retirement-age people would still allow them to meet mortgage payments.

The Graduated Payment Mortgage

The *graduated payment mortgage* or GPM is a variation of the FPM. It is based on two assumptions: (1) that the borrower's income will increase over time and (2) that the mortgaged property will appreciate and protect the lender. For example, let's assume that a 30-year mortgage of $40,000 has a market rate of interest at 9 percent. The borrower is told that a graduate payment loan can be acquired at 6 percent. For the first year, monthly payments of a 30-year, $40,000 loan at 6 percent is $239.83. The difference between the 6 percent and the 9 percent interest is added to the principal.

Each year the payments will increase, and in the thirtieth year monthly payments will reach $624.93. What's more, the unpaid balance would not exceed the original principal until the twentieth year. In addition to the $40,000 principal, the borrower would pay more than $100,000 in interest over thirty years.

With a level payment, 30-year, 9 percent mortgage, the monthly payments would be $321.85. Over the 30-year period the total interest would be $75,886.

The Budget Mortgage

The *budget mortgage* is a further development of the self-amortizing mortgage. The self-amortizing mortgage provides for monthly payments of part interest and part principal to enable the mortgagor to build equity in the property from the beginning of the mortgage. In addition, the budget mortgage includes in the monthly payments one twelfth of the year's taxes, a proportionate amount of the yearly fire insurance premiums, and any other charges which might, if left unpaid, constitute a basis for the foreclosure of the mortgage. Generally, when the mortgagor enters into a budget mortgage, six months' taxes are paid in advance at the title closing in order to provide the lender with a revolving fund. Any surplus in the fund is returnable to the mortgagor when the final payment has been made on the mortgage.

The Package Mortgage

The *package mortgage* is a mortgage that goes a step further than the budget mortgage. Usually, it incorporates all the features of the budget mortgage plus payments for certain mechanical equipment put in the home, e.g., a washer and dryer. In this manner all charges are met in one payment.

The Open Mortgage

The term *open mortgage* refers to a mortgage that has reached the due date but has not yet been paid. The mortgagee in these cases can demand payment at anytime, but if security is good and the mortgagee is receiving a fair return on the investment, the mortgagee may be content to allow the mortgagor to continue paying interest and leave the mortgage "open."

It should be remembered that there is a statute of limitations on mortgages in most states. Thus, if there is no payment of interest or principal for six years, the mortgagor has a defense in the event of a foreclosure action by the mortgagee.

The Blanket Mortgage

A *blanket mortgage* is briefly defined as a mortgage that covers more than one parcel of real property. It is a type of instrument that is often used by builders to cover construction loans.

The *partial release clause* is generally used in conjunction with the blanket mortgage. It is a clause that is inserted in a mortgage stating that upon partial payment on the mortgage, the mortgagee will issue a partial satisfaction piece that releases a particular parcel or lot from the terms of the mortgage. It would be worded substantially as follows:

> The mortgagee agrees to release any lot from the lien of this mortgage upon payment to the mortgagee by the mortgagor or mortgagor's assigns of the sum of $500 per lot upon the lands so released.

The Open-End Mortgage

The *open-end mortgage* is a mortgage in which the borrower is given a limit on the amount which may be borrowed. For example, the loan may be authorized up to $20,000, and the borrower may initially borrow only $15,000; but at a later date the loan may be increased to the maximum authorized, in this case $20,000, without changing the terms of the original agreement.

The Purchase Money Mortgage

The *purchase money mortgage* is a mortgage given as part of the consideration for the sale of real property. This is discussed in further detail in Chapter 4.

The Wraparound Mortgage

The *wraparound mortgage* is a mortgage in which the mortgagor assumes the payment of the existing mortgage and gives a new, increased mortgage to the borrower at a higher interest rate. This is detailed in Chapter 10.

The Variable Rate Mortgage

A highly controversial concept being pushed in some quarters is the variable interest rate. Basically the idea is simple. A home buyer signs a mortgage and, instead of agreeing to pay say 7 percent interest, agrees to pay the going rate, whatever it is. The going rate is tied to a "reference rate." One thought is that the "reference rate" might be the prime rate of a large commercial bank. The prime rate is the rate charged on loans to its best customers by the bank. For example, *A* agrees to pay so many points over the reference rate, e.g., two percentage points. Assume that when *A* signs, the reference rate is the prime rate, e.g., 5.5 percent. This plus the two points would mean 7.5 percent to be paid by the borrower. If the "reference rate" goes to 6 percent, then the borrower pays 8 percent interest. On the other hand, if the reference rate declines, say to 4.75 percent, this plus the 2 percent equals 6.75 percent paid in interest.

Currently variable rates are used by the Federal Land Bank on farm and ranch loans. Periodically the Federal Land Bank floats a bond issue backed by their existing pool of mortgages. The "variable rate" is based on their cost of obtaining funds. In short the "points" charged are added to the cost of capital.

California permits the variable rate mortgage with certain restrictions: (1) rates must be flexible downward as they are upward; (2) rate increases are restricted to one quarter of one percent annually; and (3) the borrower may prepay the mortgage within 90 days of a change in the interest rate without penalty.[5]

---

[5]By order of the Federal Reserve Board, effective October 10, 1977, on home loan mortgages, examples must be provided by lenders showing the effect on the payment amount and/or length of maturity that would be caused by a hypothetical immediate increase in the annual percentage rate of one quarter of one percentage point.

TRANSFERS OF MORTGAGED PROPERTY

Where permitted, a person may purchase a piece of real property and "take over" the mortgage. The buyer either takes the property "subject to" or "assumes" the mortgage. The distinction between these two terms is subtle, but important to understand.

Subject To

When a parcel of property is purchased subject to a mortgage, there is inserted in the *deed* this statement:

> This deed is made subject to the following: a certain first mortgage in the amount of $5,000 and interest to date, made by Harriet Jones to Arthur Brown on January 2, 1969, recorded January 3, 1969, in the office of the Clerk of the County of _____, State of _____, in Liber 2159 of Mortgages at page 5.

This statement means that the purchaser recognizes the *existence* of a mortgage on the property. For example, Buyer moves into a house and makes the payments that are due on the property mortgage. At this point things run smoothly; however, what happens if Buyer fails to meet the payments? Seller, who had the mortgage placed on the property originally, signed either a note or bond along with the original mortgage. When payments are not met the mortgagee will commence foreclosure proceedings. The property will be sold and Buyer will be ousted. Suppose, however, that there is a deficiency of $1,000 due the mortgagee after the foreclosure sale has been completed. The question now is: Who is liable for the deficiency — Seller, the mortgagor, or Buyer, who took the property "subject to" the mortgage? Buyer promised nothing by taking the property "subject to" the mortgage. In effect, Buyer merely recognized the existence of the mortgage. Seller, however, promised to pay the mortgagee by signing either the note or the bond. Therefore, the mortgagee will have recourse to Seller for the $1,000 deficiency.

When the seller sells the property "subject to" a mortgage, the seller may be liable for any deficiency. On the other hand, when the purchaser buys "subject to" the mortgage, the buyer is not liable for any deficiency; and the most that the buyer can lose in the event of foreclosure is any equity that is built up in the property.

Assuming the Mortgage

A quite different situation arises when property is sold on which there is a mortgage and the purchaser "assumes" the mortgage. In this event, there generally is inserted in the deed the following clause:

The conveyance hereunder is subject to a certain mortgage executed by Harriet Jones as mortgagor to Arthur Brown as mortgagee, which mortgage is dated January 2, 19--, and was recorded January 3, 19--, in the office of the Clerk of the County, in Liber 2159 of Mortgages at page 5, and on which mortgage there is now due the sum of $4,000 with interest thereon at the rate of 6 percent per annum from July 1, 19--, and that the grantee hereby assumes and covenants to pay such mortgage debt and interest as a part of the consideration for this conveyance.

Buyer moves into the property and fails to meet the payments on the mortgage. The mortgagee forecloses and there is a deficiency in the amount of $1,000. Primarily liable for the deficiency is the Buyer, who "assumed" the mortgage.[6]

When a mortgage is "assumed," the purchaser covenants and promises to pay the deficiency. In other words, the purchaser has entered into a contract with the seller for the benefit of a third party, the mortgagee. Thus, the mortgagee may collect the deficiency from the purchaser. If the purchaser cannot pay, then the mortgagee seeks payment from the mortgagor on the bond or the note. However, in view of the fact that there is a contract between the mortgagor and the purchaser, the seller (mortgagor) may seek the amount of the deficiency from the purchaser.

Often in practice, when there is an assumption clause in a deed, both the purchaser and the seller sign the deed as contrasted to the normal situation when the grantor signs the deed alone. The reason for this is that by virtue of the assumption clause the parties are entering into what amounts to a written contract in addition to a deed conveying title to the property.

In some states where this is not customarily done, the courts have held that the original contract for the sale of real property wherein the purchaser has agreed to "assume" the mortgage may be entered in evidence as proof to that effect against the purchaser.

In about half the states, purchasers customarily buy "subject to" the mortgage, and in the other half, purchasers usually buy "assuming" the mortgage.

The Non-Assumption Clause

In recent years financial institutions have adopted the practice of inserting a non-assumption clause in conventional mortgages.[7] In

---

[6]In some states there is no obligation on the part of the mortgagee to seek the payment of the deficiency from the purchaser, unless the mortgagee has previously executed an "assumption and release agreement." In other states the mortgagee may seek the deficiency from the mortgagor or the purchaser.

[7]In some states this is called an acceleration clause or a non-alienation clause. Alienation means transfer.

essence, this clause states that the mortgagor cannot sell the property and have the buyer assume the mortgage without the consent of the lender. The reasoning behind this is quite simple from the point of view of the institutional lenders. For example, suppose a mortgage carries 8 percent interest. Suppose further that the interest rate drops to 7 percent. In this case the institution will readily give permission to the mortgagor to sell the property and have the buyer assume the mortgage (carrying 8 percent instead of the new rate of 7 percent). However, if the rate jumps from 8 percent to 9 percent, then the institution will refuse permission to the borrower to sell and have the buyer assume at the old rate. They hope, of course that the property will be refinanced and a new mortgage issued at the 9 percent rate.

It should be noted that the non-assumption clause applies only to conventional mortgages and not to FHA or VA mortgages.

QUESTIONS FOR REVIEW

1. Briefly explain the evolution of the concept of a mortgage.
2. Describe each of the following three theories relating to real estate mortgages: (a) title theory, (b) lien theory, and (c) intermediate theory.
3. Explain the principal differences among an FHA-insured mortgage, a VA-guaranteed mortgage, and a conventional mortgage.
4. There are a number of variations of FHA, VA, and conventional mortgages. Briefly describe some of these variations. Particularly consider: (a) a flexible-payment mortgage, (b) a blanket mortgage, and (c) a variable rate mortgage.
5. What is meant by "assuming" a mortgage? What possible repercussions exist if there are non-assumption clauses in conventional mortgages?

PROBLEMS

1. Mr. Morris wants to obtain an FHA-insured mortgage on a $55,000 home he is interested in purchasing. Based on the current formula for loan-to-value ratios, what is the maxiumum loan he could receive? To what extent is this affected by the current maximum limit established for FHA loans? What would be Mr. Morris' minimum required down payment?

2. The Veterans Administration guarantees VA mortgages in case of default. On an outstanding VA loan of $25,000, what would be the extent of guarantee? What would be the amount of guarantee on a $30,000 VA loan?

3. Insured conventional loans do not involve full coverage of the entire amount of the loan. What amount does the lender have at risk if: (a) the loan-to-value ratio

is 90%; (b) the home is appraised at $40,000; and (c) insurance is on the top 20 percent of the loan.

4. Mrs. White agrees to purchase a parcel of property for $10,000 and "take over" the existing $8,000 mortgage. If she fails to make the required payments, and a Foreclosure sale takes place at $6,500, what would be the implications?

Mortgages and Deeds of Trust (Concluded)

As was briefly discussed in Chapter 1, a mortgage is the creation of an interest in property as security for the payment of a debt or the fulfillment of an obligation. The two parties to a mortgage are the mortgagor (borrower) and mortgagee (lender). The mortgagor is the party pledging the property. The mortgagee is the party to whom the pledge of the property is made. This party is the lender or obligee on the bond or payee on the note.

Property is divided into real property and personal property. By implication, our brief definition of the mortgage suggests that real property and personal property may be mortgaged, and so they can. Both types of mortgages are made by an agreement or contract. Thus, an agreement which creates an interest in personal property as security for the payment of a debt or the fulfillment of an obligation might be said to be a chattel (personal property) mortgage; and an agreement that creates an interest in real property for the payment of a debt or the fulfillment of an obligation might be said to be a real property mortgage.

The mortgage form shown on pages 15–21 is the uniform Federal National Mortgage Association/Federal Home Loan Mortgage Corporation form. The Uniform Note is exactly the same, regardless of the state, except for part of one sentence. In states using the Deed of Trust it reads, "The indebtedness evidenced by this Note is secured by a Deed of Trust. . . ." In states using the mortgage it reads, "The indebtedness evidenced by this Note is secured by a mortgage. . . ." This can be seen in the illustration on page 15.

The Uniform Mortgage form is only "uniform" insofar as the first seventeen clauses are concerned. After clause seventeen, non-uniform covenants may be added and these vary among the states.

MORTGAGE

THIS MORTGAGE is made this .... day of ....
19...., between the Mortgagor, ...
.... (herein "Borrower"), and the Mortgagee, ...
..................................., a corporation organized and existing
under the laws of ...., whose address is ....
.... (herein "Lender").
WHEREAS, Borrower is indebted to Lender in the principal sum of ....
.... Dollars, which indebtedness
is evidenced by Borrower's note dated .... (herein "Note"), providing for monthly installments of principal and interest, with the balance of the
indebtedness, if not sooner paid, due and payable on ....;
To SECURE to Lender (a) the repayment of the indebtedness evidenced by the
Note, with interest thereon, the payment of all other sums, with interest thereon,
advanced in accordance herewith to protect the security of this Mortgage, and the
performance of the covenants and agreements of Borrower herein contained, and
(b) the repayment of any future advances, with interest thereon, made to Borrower
by Lender pursuant to paragraph 21 hereof (herein "Future Advances"), Borrower
does hereby mortgage, grant and convey to Lender the following described property located in the County of ...., State of New
York:

which has the address of ....,........................,
                              [Street]   [City]
.... (herein "Property Address");
[State and Zip Code]

TOGETHER with all the improvements now or hereafter erected on the property,
and all easements, rights, appurtenances, rents, royalties, mineral, oil and gas rights
and profits, water, water rights, and water stock, and all fixtures now or hereafter
attached to the property, and all right, title and interest of Borrower in and to the
land lying in the streets and roads in front of and adjoining the property, all of
which, including replacements and additions thereto, shall be deemed to be and
remain a part of the property covered by this Mortgage; and all of the foregoing,
together with said property (or the leasehold estate if this Mortgage is on a leasehold) are herein referred to as the "Property".

Borrower covenants that Borrower is lawfully seised of the estate hereby conveyed and has the right to mortgage, grant and convey the Property, that the Property is unencumbered, and that Borrower will warrant and defend generally the title
to the Property against all claims and demands, subject to any declarations, easements or restrictions listed in a schedule of exceptions to coverage in any title
insurance policy insuring Lender's interest in the Property.

UNIFORM COVENANTS. Borrower and Lender covenant and agree as follows:

1. Payment of Principal and Interest. Borrower shall promptly pay when due
the principal of and interest on the indebtedness evidenced by the Note, prepayment and late charges as provided in the Note, and the principal of and interest on
any future Advances secured by this Mortgage.

**Figure
2-1** Mortgage (Continued)

2. Funds for Taxes and Insurance. Subject to applicable law or to a written waiver by Lender, Borrower shall pay to Lender on the day monthly installments of principal and interest are payable under the Note, until the Note is paid in full, a sum (herein "Funds") equal to one-twelfth of the yearly taxes and assessments which may attain priority over this Mortgage, and ground rents on the Property, if any, plus one-twelfth of yearly premium installments for hazard insurance, plus one-twelfth of yearly premium installments for mortgage insurance, if any, all as reasonably estimated initially and from time to time by Lender on the basis of assessments and bills and reasonable estimates thereof.

The Funds shall be held in an institution the deposits or accounts of which are insured or guaranteed by a Federal or state agency (including Lender if Lender is such an institution). Lender shall apply the Funds to pay said taxes, assessments, insurance premiums and ground rents. Lender may not charge for so holding and applying the Funds, analyzing said account, or verifying and compiling said assessments and bills, unless Lender pays Borrower interest on the Funds and applicable law permits Lender to make such a charge. Borrower and Lender may agree in writing at the time of execution of this Mortgage that interest on the Funds shall be paid to Borrower, and unless such agreement is made or applicable law requires such interest to be paid, Lender shall not be required to pay Borrower any interest or earnings on the Funds. Lender shall give to Borrower, without charge, an annual accounting of the Funds showing credits and debits to the Funds and the purpose for which each debit to the Funds was made. The funds are pledged as additional security for the sums secured by this Mortgage.

If the amount of the Funds held by Lender, together with the future monthly installments of Funds payable prior to the due dates of taxes, assessments, insurance premiums and ground rents, shall exceed the amount required to pay said taxes, assessments, insurance premiums and ground rents as they fall due, such excess shall be, at Borrower's option, either promptly repaid to Borrower or credited to Borrower on monthly installments of Funds. If the amount of the Funds held by Lender shall not be sufficient to pay taxes, assessments, insurance premiums and ground rents as they fall due, Borrower shall pay to Lender any amount necessary to make up the deficiency within 30 days from the date notice is mailed by Lender to Borrower requesting payment thereof.

Upon payment in full of all sums secured by this Mortgage, Lender shall promptly refund to Borrower any Funds held by Lender. If under paragraph 18 hereof the Property is sold or the Property is otherwise acquired by Lender, Lender shall apply, no later than immediately prior to the sale of the Property or its acquisition by Lender, any Funds held by Lender at the time of application as a credit against the sums secured by this Mortgage.

3. Application of Payments. Unless applicable law provides otherwise, all payments received by Lender under the Note and paragraphs 1 and 2 hereof shall be applied by Lender first in payment of amounts payable to Lender by Borrower under paragraph 2 hereof, then to interest payable on the Note, then to the principal of the Note, and then to interest and principal on any Future Advances.

4. Charges; Liens. Borrower shall pay all taxes, assessments and other charges, fines and impositions attributable to the Property which may attain a priority over this Mortgage, and leasehold payments or ground rents, if any, in the manner provided under paragraph 2 hereof or, if not paid in such manner, by Borrower making payment, when due, directly to the payee thereof. Borrower shall promptly furnish to Lender all notices of amounts due under this paragraph, and in the event Borrower shall make payment directly, Borrower shall promptly furnish to Lender receipts evidencing such payments. Borrower shall promptly discharge any lien

Figure
2-1   Mortgage (Continued)

which has priority over this Mortgage; provided, that Borrower shall not be required to discharge any such lien so long as Borrower shall agree in writing to the payment of the obligation secured by such lien in a manner acceptable to Lender, or shall in good faith contest such lien by, or defend enforcement of such lien in, legal proceedings which operate to prevent the enforcement of the lien or forfeiture of the Property or any part thereof.

5. Hazard Insurance. Borrower shall keep the improvements now existing or hereafter erected on the Property insured against loss by fire, hazards included within the term "extended coverage", and such other hazards as Lender may require and in such amounts and for such periods as Lender may require; provided, that Lender shall not require that the amount of such coverage exceed that amount of coverage required to pay the sums secured by this Mortgage.

The insurance carrier providing the insurance shall be chosen by Borrower subject to approval by Lender; provided, that such approval shall not be unreasonably withheld. All premiums on insurance policies shall be paid in the manner provided under paragraph 2 hereof, or, if not paid in such manner, by Borrower making payment, when due, directly to the insurance carrier.

All insurance policies and renewals thereof shall be in form acceptable to Lender and shall include a standard mortgage clause in favor of and in form acceptable to Lender. Lender shall have the right to hold the policies and renewals thereof, and Borrower shall promptly furnish to Lender all renewal notices and all receipts of paid premiums. In the event of loss, Borrower shall give prompt notice to the insurance carrier and Lender. Lender may make proof of loss if not made promptly by Borrower.

Unless Lender and Borrower otherwise agree in writing, insurance proceeds shall be applied to restoration or repair of the Property damaged, provided such restoration or repair is economically feasible and the security of this Mortgage is not thereby impaired. If such restoration or repair is not economically feasible or if the security of this Mortgage would be impaired, the insurance proceeds shall be applied to the sums secured by this Mortgage, with the excess, if any, paid to Borrower. If the Property is abandoned by Borrower, or if Borrower fails to respond to Lender within 30 days from the date notice is mailed by Lender to Borrower that the insurance carrier offers to settle a claim for insurance benefits, Lender is authorized to collect and apply the insurance proceeds at Lender's option either to restoration or repair of the Property or to the sums secured by this Mortgage.

Unless Lender and Borrower otherwise agree in writing, any such application of proceeds to principal shall not extend or postpone the due date of the monthly installments referred to in paragraphs 1 and 2 hereof or change the amount of such installments. If under paragraph 18 hereof the Property is acquired by Lender, all right, title and interest of Borrower in and to any insurance policies and in and to the proceeds thereof resulting from damage to the Property prior to the sale or acquisition shall pass to Lender to the extent of the sums secured by this Mortgage immediately prior to such sale or acquisition.

Preservation and Maintenance of Property; Leaseholds; Condominiums; Planned Unit Developments. Borrower shall keep the Property in good repair and shall not commit waste or permit impairment or deterioration of the Property and shall comply with the provisions of any lease if this Mortgage is on a leasehold. if this Mortgage is on a unit in a condominium or a planned unit development, Borrower shall perform all of Borrower's obligations under the declaration or covenants creating or governing the condominium or planned unit development, the by-laws and regulations of the condominium or planned unit development, and constituent documents.

Figure
   2-1   Mortgage (Continued)

If a condominium or planned unit development rider is executed by Borrower and recorded together with this Mortgage, the covenants and agreements of such rider shall be incorporated into and shall amend and supplement the covenants and agreements of this Mortgage as if the rider were a part hereof.

7. Protection of Lender's Security. If Borrower fails to perform the covenants and agreements contained in this Mortgage, or if any action or proceeding is commenced which materially affects Lender's interest in the Property, including, but not limited to, eminent domain, insolvency, code enforcement, or arrangements or proceedings involving a bankrupt or decedent, then Lender at Lender's option, upon notice to Borrower, may make such appearances, disburse which sums and take such action as is necessary to protect Lender's interest, including, but not limited to, disbursement of reasonable attorney's fees and entry upon the Property to make repairs. If Lender required mortgage insurance as a condition of making the loan secured by this Mortgage, Borrower shall pay the premiums required to maintain such insurance in effect until such time as the requirement for such insurance terminates in accordance with Borrower's and Lender's written agreement or applicable law. Borrower shall pay the amount of all mortgage insurance premiums in the manner provided under paragraph 2 hereof.

Any amounts disbursed by Lender pursuant to this paragraph 7, with interest thereon, shall become additional indebtedness of Borrower secured by this Mortgage. Unless Borrower and Lender agree to other terms of payment, such amounts shall be payable upon notice from Lender to Borrower requesting payment thereof, and shall bear interest from the date of disbursement at the rate payable from time to time on outstanding principal under the Note unless payment of interest at such rate would be contrary to applicable law, in which event such amounts shall bear interest at the highest rate permissible under applicable law. Nothing contained in this paragraph 7 shall require Lender to incur any expense or take any action hereunder.

8. Inspection. Lender may make or cause to be made reasonable entries upon and inspections of the Property, provided that Lender shall give Borrower notice prior to any such inspection specifying reasonable cause therefor related to Lender's interest in the Property.

9. Condemnation. The proceeds of any award or claim for damages, direct or consequential, in connection with any condemnation or other taking of the Property, or part thereof, or for conveyance in lieu of condemnation, are hereby assigned and shall be paid to Lender.

In the event of a total taking of the Property, the proceeds shall be applied to the sums secured by this Mortgage, with the excess, if any, paid to Borrower. In the event of a partial taking of the property, unless Borrower and Lender otherwise agree in writing, there shall be applied to the sums secured by this Mortgage such proportion of the proceeds as is equal to that proportion which the amount of the sums secured by this Mortgage immediately prior to the date of taking bears to the fair market value of the Property immediately prior to the date of taking, with the balance of the proceeds paid to Borrower.

If the Property is abandoned by Borrower, or if, after notice by Lender to Borrower that the condemnor offers to make an award or settle a claim for damages, Borrower fails to respond to Lender within 30 days after the date such notice is mailed, Lender is authorized to collect and apply the proceeds, at Lender's option, either to restoration or repair of the Property or to the sums secured by this Mortgage.

Unless Lender and Borrower otherwise agree in writing, any such application of proceeds to principal shall not extend or postpone the due date of the monthly

**Figure
  2-1**   Mortgage (Continued)

installments referred to in paragraphs 1 and 2 hereof or change the amount of such installments.

10. Borrower Not Released. Extension of the time for payment or modification of amortization of the sums secured by this Mortgage granted by Lender to any successor in interest of Borrower shall not operate to release, in any manner, the liability of the original Borrower and Borrower's successors in interest. Lender shall not be required to commence proceedings against such successor or refuse to extend time for payment or otherwise modify amortization of the sums secured by this Mortgage by reason of any demand made by the original Borrower and Borrower's successors in interest.

11. Forbearance by Lender Not a Waiver. Any forbearance by Lender in exercising any right or remedy hereunder, or otherwise afforded by applicable law, shall not be a waiver of or preclude the exercise of any such right or remedy. The procurement of insurance or the payment of taxes or other liens or charges by Lender shall not be a waiver of Lender's right to accelerate the maturity of the indebtedness secured by this Mortage.

12. Remedies Cumulative. All remedies provided in this Mortgage are distinct and cumulative to any other right or remedy under this Mortgage or afforded by law or equity, and may be exercised concurrently, independently or successively.

13. Successors and Assigns Bound; Joint and Several Liability; Captions. The covenants and agreements herein contained shall bind, and the rights hereunder shall inure to the respective successors and assigns of Lender and Borrower, subject to the provisions of paragraph 17 hereof. All covenants and agreements of Borrower shall be joint and several. The captions and headings of the paragraphs of this Mortgage are for convenience only and are not to be used to interpret or define the provisions hereof.

14. Notice. Except for any notice required under applicable law to be given in another manner, (a) any notice to Borrower provided for in this Mortgage shall be given by mailing such notice by certified mail addressed to Borrower at the Property Address or at such other address as Borrower may designate by notice to Lender as provided herein, and (b) any notice to Lender shall be given by certified mail, return receipt requested, to Lender's address stated herein or to such other address as Lender may designate by notice to Borrower as provided herein. Any notice provided for in this Mortgage shall be deemed to have been given to Borrower or Lender when given in the manner designated herein.

15. Uniform Mortgage; Governing Law; Severability. This form of mortgage combines uniform covenants for national use and non-uniform covenants with limited variations by jurisdiction to constitute a uniform security instrument covering real property. This Mortgage shall be governed by the law of the jurisdiction in which the Property is located. In the event that any provision or clause of this Mortgage or the Note conflicts with applicable law, such conflict shall not affect other provisions of this mortgage or the Note which can be given effect without the conflicting provision, and to this end the provisions of the Mortgage and the Note are declared to be severable.

16. Borrower's Copy. Borrower shall be furnished a conformed copy of the Note and of this Mortgage at the time of execution or after recordation hereof.

17. Transfer of the Property; Assumption. If all or any part of the Property or an interest therein is sold or transferred by Borrower without Lender's prior written consent, excluding (a) the creation of a lien or encumbrance subordinate to this Mortgage, (b) the creation of a purchase money security interest for household appliances, (c) a transfer by devise, descent or by operation of law upon the death of a joint tenant or (d) the grant of any leasehold interest of three years or less not containing an option to purchase, Lender may, at Lender's option, declare all the

**Figure
2-1** Mortgage (Continued)

sums secured by this Mortgage to be immediately due and payable. Lender shall have waived such option to accelerate if, prior to the sale or transfer, Lender and the person to whom the Property is to be sold or transferred reach agreement in writing that the credit of such person is satisfactory to Lender and that the interest payable on the sums secured by this Mortgage shall be at such rate as Lender shall request. If Lender has waived the option to accelerate provided in this paragraph 17, and if Borrower's successor in interest has executed a written assumption agreement accepted in writing by Lender, Lender shall release Borrower from all obligations under this Mortgage and the Note.

If Lender exercises such option to accelerate. Lender shall mail Borrower notice of acceleration in accordance with paragraph 14 hereof. Such notice shall provide a period of not less than 30 days from the date the notice is mailed within which Borrower may pay the sums declared due. If Borrower fails to pay such sums prior to the expiration of such period, Lender may, without further notice or demand on Borrower, invoke any remedies permitted by paragraph 18 hereof.

NON-UNIFORM COVENANTS. Borrower and Lender further covenant and agree as follows:

18. Acceleration; Remedies. Except as provided in paragraph 17 hereof, upon Borrower's breach of any covenant or agreement of Borrower in this Mortgage, including the covenants to pay when due any sums secured by this Mortgage, Lender prior to acceleration shall mail notice to Borrower as provided in paragraph 14 hereof specifying: (1) the breach; (2) the action required to cure such breach; (3) a date, not less than 30 days from the date the notice is mailed to Borrower, by which such breach must be cured; and (4) that failure to cure such breach on or before the date specified in the notice may result in acceleration of the sums secured by this Mortgage, foreclosure by judicial proceeding and sale of the Property. The notice shall further inform Borrower of the right to reinstate after acceleration and the right to assert in the foreclosure proceeding the non-existence of a default or any other defense of Borrower to acceleration and foreclosure. If the breach is not cured on or before the date specified in the notice, Lender at Lender's option may declare all of the sums secured by this Mortgage to be immediately due and payable without further demand and may foreclose this Mortgage by judicial proceeding. Lender shall be entitled to collect in such proceeding all costs allowed by applicable law.

19. Borrower's Right to Reinstate. Notwithstanding Lender's acceleration of the sums secured by this Mortgage, Borrower shall have the right to have any proceedings begun by Lender to enforce this Mortgage discontinued at any time prior to entry of a judgment enforcing this Mortgage if: (a) Borrower pays Lender all sums which would be then due under this Mortgage, the Note and notes securing Future Advances, if any, had no acceleration occurred, (b) Borrower cures all breaches of any other covenants or agreements of Borrower contained in this Mortgage, (c) Borrower pays all reasonable expenses incurred by Lender in enforcing the covenants and agreements of Borrower contained in this Mortgage and in enforcing Lender's remedies as provided in paragraph 18 hereof, including, but not limited to reasonable attorney's fees, and (d) Borrower takes such action as Lender may reasonably require to assure that the lien of this Mortgage, Lender's interest in the property and Borrower's obligation to pay the sums secured by this Mortgage shall continue unimpaired. Upon such payment and cure by Borrower, this Mortgage and obligations secured hereby shall remain in full force and effect as if no acceleration had occurred.

20. Assignment of Rents; Appointment of Receiver; Lender in Possession. As additional security hereunder, Borrower hereby assigns to Lender the rents of the Property, provided that Borrower shall, prior to acceleration under paragraph 18

Figure
2-1 Mortgage (Continued)

hereof or abandonment of the Property, have the right to collect and retain such rents as they become due and payable.

Upon acceleration under paragraph 18 hereof or abandonment of the Property, Lender, in person, by agent or by judicially appointed receiver, shall be entitled to enter upon, take possession of and manage the Property and to collect the rents of the Property including those past due. All rents collected by Lender or the receiver shall be applied first to payment of the costs of management of the Property and collection of rents, including, but not limited to, receiver's fees, premiums on receiver's bonds and reasonable attorney's fees, and then to the sums secured by this Mortgage. Lender and the receiver shall be liable to account only for those rents actually received.

21. Future Advances. Upon request of Borrower, Lender, at Lender's option prior to release of this Mortgage, may make Future Advances to Borrower. Such Future Advances, with interest thereon, shall be secured by this Mortgage when evidence by promissory notes stating that said notes are secured hereby. At no time shall the principal amount of the indebtedness secured by this Mortgage, not including the sums advanced in accordance herewith to protect the security of this Mortgage, exceed the original amount of the Note plus US $ . . . .

22. Release. Upon payment of all sums secured by this Mortgage, Lender shall discharge this Mortgage without charge to Borrower. Borrower shall pay all costs of recordation, if any.

23. Lien Law. Borrower will receive advances hereunder subject to the trust fund provisions of Section 13 of the Lien Law.

IN WITNESS WHEREOF, Borrower has executed this Mortgage.

Witnesses:

. . . .
—Borrower

. . . .
—Borrower

STATE OF NEW YORK, ...County ss:

On this . . . . day of . . . . , 19. . . . , before me personally came . . . . .to me known and known to me to be the individual(s) described in and who executed the foregoing instrument, and . .he. . duly acknowledged to me that . .he. . executed the same.

. . . .
Notary Public

Figure
2-1   Mortgage (Concluded)

ESSENTIALS OF THE MORTGAGE

A mortgage is a contract. Therefore, the instrument creating the mortgage must embrace the elements of a contract, namely:

1. Competent parties.
2. Offer and acceptance.
3. Consideration.
4. Legality of object.
5. In writing and signed because it is real property and subject to the Statute of Frauds.

SOME MORTGAGE CLAUSES AND THEIR MEANINGS

In general most of the statutory forms of the mortgage require: (1) a date, (2) the names of the parties, (3) the amount of the debt, and (4) a statement that the "mortgagor hereby mortgages to the mortgagee" certain described property.

General Clauses

Following the description of the property, the statutory form of mortgage contains this statement:

And the mortgagor covenants with the mortgagee as follows:

Here follow the general clauses or covenants found in the statutory mortgages in most states. They will vary slightly among the states, but in general they are as described below.

Covenant to Pay Indebtedness. The covenant to pay indebtedness states "that the mortgagor will pay the indebtedness as hereinbefore provided." This is self-explanatory.

Covenant of Insurance. The covenant of insurance is a promise that the premises shall be covered by fire insurance in a stated amount for the benefit of the mortgagee and that the mortgagor will assign and deliver the policies to the mortgagee. Depending upon the location of the property, a statement should be added to the mortgage in regard to an extended coverage endorsement. The reason for this is that the standard fire policy specifically exempts damage from wind and rain. In hurricane or frequent storm areas, this means that the mortgagee has insufficient protection with the fire policy alone because of the possibility that damage might be done by wind and rain.

Covenant Against Removal. The covenant against removal is often included in the statutory form of mortgage and states that the mortgagor will not remove or demolish any building without the consent of the mortgagee. This clause is necessary because the amount generally loaned is based on an appraisal that includes both land and buildings. One case involving this clause arose when a mortgage was given on a farm. The mortgagor, anticipating a possible default and having heard that real property consisted of land and things that were attached to the land, built all of the outbuildings on skids. The mortgagor did default on the mortgage, and then hauled the buildings on the skids off the land. The court held that despite the fact that the buildings were not physically attached to the land, they were still under the terms of the mortgage. Thus, the mortgagee was entitled to the foreclosure on those buildings.

Covenant to Pay Taxes. The covenant to pay taxes is a promise by the mortgagor that the taxes and assessments that might be levied against the property will be paid. Together with this covenant there is generally an acceleration clause stating that if the taxes or assessments are not paid after a certain time has elapsed, the mortgagee has the option to declare the entire amount of principal and interest due. This clause, in effect, gives the mortgagee the right to foreclose after a stated period in the event that the taxes or assessments are not paid.

Acceleration Clause. The mortgage form contains an acceleration clause. This clause specifies that, if the mortgagor fails to keep the covenants or if the title is defective, then the entire debt will become due and collectible at the option of the mortgagee.

In mortgages or deeds of trust containing the "non-assumption" clause, the acceleration clause also states in effect that if the borrower sells the property without the consent of the lender then the balance shall be due and payable.

Warrant of Title. Most statutory forms of mortgage contain a warrant of title clause. It states simply that the mortgagor warrants title to the premises. It means in effect that the mortgagor guarantees the title to the property. This will be discussed in detail later in this chapter.

These six clauses are in general use in nearly every type of simple mortgage in all of the states.

Special Clauses

In addition to the general clauses, there are many other clauses that can be and are inserted into the mortgage form to cover special situations. The most common ones are discussed in the following paragraphs.

Covenant to Pay Attorney's Fees. In some states the mortgagor promises to pay reasonable attorney's fees together with costs and disbursements if the mortgagee finds it necessary to foreclose. Some states do not require a covenant to pay attorney's fees inasmuch as the mortgagee may demand reasonable fees in the event of foreclosure without the statement being included in the instrument.

Receiver Clause. The receiver clause states that in any action to foreclose a mortgage the holder of the mortgage shall be entitled to the appointment of a receiver. The receiver is one who will collect any rents and profits from the property and maintain the property. This clause is intended to protect the mortgagee during the interval between the commencement of the foreclosure action and the final order of the court. If the receiver, after having satisfied the mortgagee's claim, has a net balance, the mortgagor is credited with that balance.

This clause is especially important when the sale concerns a parcel of real property on which there is a business. For example, suppose A sells B real property on which there is a shoe store. B is really purchasing three things: the land and building, the stock in the store, and the goodwill of the store, this often being regarded by business people as having the greatest value. The goodwill is referred to by business as "the key." Suppose that A is going to finance the purchase in part by becoming the mortgagee for part of the purchase price. Commonly it is said that A "takes back" the mortgage. When a person "takes back" a mortgage as part of the purchase price, that person is said to have a *purchase money mortgage*, which will be discussed in detail later.

Assume that B defaults on the payments. A has security for the value of the land in the land itself and has probably been paid for the stock, but what about the goodwill or "key"? This may have given the sale its greatest value. Between the time of default and the time of termination of foreclosure action, B might operate the business in such a way as to destroy the value of the goodwill.

With a receiver clause in the mortgage, A can readily have a receiver appointed who will run the business in a satisfactory manner and thus preserve the value of the goodwill.

Estoppel Clause. The estoppel clause states that upon the request of the mortgagee (lender), the mortgagor (borrower) will furnish a written statement "duly acknowledged of the amount due on this mortgage and whether any offsets or defenses exist against the mortgage debt." In some states this is known as a Certificate of No Defense.

Although it might appear strange for the mortgagee to make a request of the mortgagor of how much the mortgagor owes on the mortgage, the inclusion of this is extremely important in the event the mortgagee desires to sell the mortgage. If the mortgagee decides to sell the mortgage in order to raise capital for a further investment, when the mortgagee approaches a third party to sell the mortgage, the third party will want to know the present value of the mortgage. The third party can demand to see the mortgage, but this will not disclose the present value because part of the face value may have been paid. If the mortgage contains an estoppel clause, the mortgagee can demand an estoppel certificate from the mortgagor indicating the present value of the mortgage. In addition, the mortgagor will certify that there are no defenses up to date in the event of a foreclosure action. After having certified that there are no defenses to a foreclosure, the mortgagor cannot later assert in court that a defense existed as of that time. Technically, the mortgagor is said to be "estopped."

Good Repair Clause. The good repair clause states that if the mortgagor does not keep the premises in "reasonably good repair" or if the owner fails to comply with the requirements of any governmental department within three months, then the mortgagee may foreclose. The test of what is in "reasonably good repair" is that the mortgagee is entitled to foreclose if the security is being impaired.

The inclusion of this clause came about as a result of the condemning of buildings by municipalities as being unfit for human habitation. For example, A is the mortgagee on an apartment building and B the owner and mortgagor. B has tenants in the building and allows the building to deteriorate to such a state of disrepair that the municipality feels it necessary to take action. B abandons the building, leaving A with a worthless building, in the sense of being untenantable. With a "good repair" clause inserted in the action, A could foreclose on the mortgage prior to the time that the municipality takes action and thus protect the security for the debt.

Sale in One Parcel Clause. The sale in one parcel clause is generally written as follows: "that in case of a sale, said premises, or as much thereof as may be affected by this mortgage, may be sold in one parcel." This clause is applicable when more than one lot is covered by the terms of the mortgage. In the event of a foreclosure, the mortgagee must offer the lots for sale one at a time until the amount due under the mortgage is paid. If the mortgagor has sold any of the lots "subject to the mortgage," the mortgagee must sell those lots in inverse order of their sale. In short, those lots still owned by the mortgagor must be sold and then those that the mortgagor has already sold, but in inverse order of their sale, last ones first. After they are sold, if this does not bring in enough money, the mortgagor may sell them in bulk. The sale of the individual lots is tentative until it is ascertained that they have brought sufficient funds to cover the debt.

Owner Rent Clause. The owner rent clause creates a landlord-tenant relationship between the mortgagee and the mortgagor in the event of a foreclosure. By means of this clause the owner agrees to pay a reasonable rent for the premises during the time of possession of the building after the commencement of the foreclosure action. In some states, even if a receiver under the terms of the mortgage has been appointed, the receiver cannot collect any money except that due on property contracts that the owner had. The owner rent clause enables the receiver to collect rent from the owner of the property.

Trust Clause. A trust clause is inserted in the mortgage in some states. In New York State, for example, this clause states:

The mortgagor will, in compliance with Section 13 of the lien law, receive the advances secured hereby and will receive the right to such advances as a trust fund to be applied first for the purpose of paying the cost of the improvement and will apply the same, first to the payment of the cost of the improvement before using any part of the total of the same for any other purpose.

The purpose of this clause is to prevent the owner from improving property before applying for a loan, and then not paying the cost of the improvement. If an owner, for example, hires a painter to paint a house and then obtains a loan without paying the painter, the painter may file a mechanic's lien against the property. A *mechanic's lien* is a species of lien or charge created by statute which exists in favor of persons who have performed work or furnished materials in the erection or repair of a building.

The placing of the lien on the property will involve the mortgagee in legal action. When this clause is included in a mortgage, it puts the burden on the mortgagor to pay for these improvements. If payment is not made, then the mortgagor has breached what amounts to a trust agreement for the benefit of those persons who have improved the property, and the mortgagor by breaching the agreement, will become liable under the penal code.

Prepayment Clause. The prepayment clause is inserted in the mortgage at the request of the mortgagor. It generally states that the mortgagor may pay the entire or stated amounts on the mortgage principal at anytime prior to the due date. The mortgagor could not do this without the insertion of the prepayment clause. Some of the prepayment clauses call for the payment of a penalty by the mortgagor for the privilege of prepayment. This penalty may be inserted in the prepayment clause by stating that the entire amount due on the mortgage may be paid upon ninety days' written notice to the mortgagee and upon "the payment of two months' interest." The two months' interest then is the penalty which is in addition to the interest paid between the time of giving of notice and the prepayment. If a bank is the mortgagee, this penalty helps defray some of the bank's costs of making the mortgage.

Effective May 1, 1972, the FHA suspended loan prepayment penalties. The regulation suspends prepayment penalties to borrowers who pay off their loans before the first ten years of the amortization period have passed. The effect of this regulation is to make the FHA loans more competitive with the VA loans under which no prepayment charges are imposed.

ACKNOWLEDGMENT AND RECORDING

Both the mortgage and deed of trust must be acknowledged. The county clerk,[1] recorder, or some other designated person is required to record and index certain instruments as provided by the statute. The county clerk is not required, however, to record these instruments until they have been properly acknowledged. An acknowledgment is a formal declaration made before some public officer, usually a notary public, by a person who has signed a deed, mortgage, or other instrument stating that the instrument is that person's act and deed. The instrument to be recorded is usually signed in the presence of a notary or other public officer with the acknowledgment attached substantially in the following form:

State of _____, County of _____ ss.:
On this _____ day of _____ 19___ before me came _____, known to me to be the said person(s) described in and who executed the foregoing instrument, and duly acknowledged to me that _(he, she, they)_ executed the same as _(his, her, their)_ free act and deed.

_____, Notary Public
(Seal)

The Satisfaction of Mortgage

The satisfaction of mortgage, or what in some states is called the "release of mortgage," is a receipt signed by the mortgagee stating that the amount due under the mortgage has been paid and may be discharged of record. This means that upon recording, the county clerk will stamp the photostat or typewritten copy of the mortgage as being paid. This instrument is acknowledged and recorded. The effect upon recording is to clear the record of the mortgage.

Many states have statutes imposing criminal penalties upon mortgagees who refuse to deliver the satisfaction when the debt has been paid.

Too much emphasis cannot be placed upon the desirability of immediately recording the satisfaction piece. Without the satisfaction being placed on record, the opportunity presents itself for a fraudulent assignment of the mortgage because a prospective assignee upon examining the record will be led to believe that the mortgage has not been paid and satisfied. Further difficulties are apt to arise if the mortgagor, after having paid a mortgage, fails to record the satisfaction, then attempts to sell the property or to obtain a new mortgage. The

---

[1]In Connecticut instruments are recorded in the office of the town clerk.

record will show the mortgage as not having been paid. In addition, failure to record a satisfaction piece may cause difficulties in the case of death of the mortgagor.

In order to avoid this and to prevent fraudulent assignments, some states require that the mortgage be delivered to the county clerk together with the satisfaction piece in order for the mortgage to be properly discharged of record. The clerk will then efface the original mortgage, which tends to prevent fraudulent negotiation of mortgages which have been paid. To efface the mortgage, the clerk stamps in the margin of a copy of the mortgage filed in the office either "discharged" or "satisfied" and gives also the book and page number where a copy of the satisfaction piece is kept.

Some states, notably New York, prohibit more than one mortgage being discharged by a single satisfaction piece. If there are two mortgages, there must be two satisfaction pieces. In New York, if the mortgage has been assigned, the assignment must be stated in the satisfaction together with the date of each assignment in the chain of title of the persons signing the instrument. The interest assigned and the book and page where each assignment is recorded must be stated. In the event that the mortgage has not been assigned, the satisfaction piece must state it. Furthermore, if the mortgage is held by a fiduciary, including an executor or administrator, the certificate must recite the name of the court and venue of the proceedings.

A satisfaction of mortgage is shown on page 29.

Assignment of Mortgage

The assignment of mortgage or deed of trust is an instrument used by a mortgagee to transfer interest in a mortgage to a third party. The mortgagee, who is the maker of the assignment, is called the assignor. The person to whom the assignment is made is called the assignee. The instrument names the parties and the consideration and states that the assignor "hereby assigns unto the assignee" interest in the mortgage being transferred. The mortgage is identified by giving, among other things, the book and the page number in which the mortgage is recorded in the county clerk's office. In some states the assignment makes provision for the description of the property assigned, which should be verified against the premises described in the recorded mortgage. Some assignments may contain a covenant by the assignor to the effect that there are no defenses to the mortgage in case it becomes necessary to foreclose and the assignor verifies the amount due on the mortgage at the time of the assignment (see Figure 2-3).

The signature of the assignor is acknowledged and the assignment is sent to the office of the county clerk, in the county in which the

SATISFACTION OF MORTGAGE

KNOW ALL PERSONS BY THESE PRESENTS,
that   Charles Cox   , residing at   104 South Wilson Street,
Cincinnati, Ohio

DOES   **HEREBY CERTIFY** that a certain indenture of mortgage, bearing date the
   14th   day of   May   , 19–– , made and executed by   Sharon Jones

to   Charles Cox
to secure payment of the principal sum of   twelve thousand and 00/100
($12,000) –––––––––––Dollars and interest, and duly recorded in the office of
the   Clerk   of the County of   Hamilton   , in Liber   24   of Mortgages, of
Section   20B   , page   70   on the   16th   day of   May   , 19––,

which mortgage has not been further assigned,

IS PAID, and do es   hereby consent that the same be discharged of record.

Dated the   18th   day of   December   , 19––.

In presence of:

/s/ Richard Roe   /s/ Charles Cox

STATE OF OHIO, COUNTY OF   Hamilton   ss.:

On this   18th   day of   December   , 19–– before me came   Charles Cox   ,
known to me to be the said person(s) described in and who executed the foregoing
instrument, and duly acknowledged to me that   he   executed the same as
   his   free act and deed.

/s/ Richard Roe
Notary Public

**Figure
  2-2**   Satisfaction of Mortgage

property is located, to be recorded. The assignment is given a book
number and a page number, is entered in the book, and a photostatic
copy is made. At the same time the county clerk will make a notation
on the margin of the photostat of the assigned mortgage indicating the
book and page where the assignment has been entered. This enables
anyone later searching the records to have notice of the assignment.

A prospective purchaser of a mortgage should have the records
searched to determine whether or not a mortgage has been satisfied,
has been previously assigned, or whether there are any actions pending on the property described in the mortgage being considered.

ASSIGNMENT OF MORTGAGE WITH COVENANT

KNOW THAT   Roberta Weathers   , residing at   2700 E. Seventh Street, New York, New York

, assignor,

in consideration of   four thousand and 00/100 ($4,000)----   dollars, paid by   John Murphy   , residing at   401 Pacific street, New York, New York

, assignee,

hereby assigns unto the assignee

a certain mortgage made by Floyd Butler, residing at   183 Minton Avenue, New York, New York

, given

to secure payment of the sum of   Six Thousand and 00/100 ($6,000)--- -------------------- dollars and interest, dated the   16th day of   April   , 19-- recorded on the   19th   day of   April   , 19-- in the office of the   Registrar   of the County of   Kings   in Liber   21A of Mortgages, of Section   4B   , at page   72   , covering premises

(here insert complete legal description)

TOGETHER with the bond described in said mortgage   , and the moneys due and to grow due thereon with the interest,

TO HAVE AND TO HOLD the same unto the assignee and to the successors, legal representatives and assigns of the assignee forever.

AND the assignor covenants that there is now owing upon said mortgage   , without offset or defense of any kind, the principal sum of   Four Thousand Five Hundred and 00/100 ($4,500) -------------------------dollars, with interest thereon at $7\frac{1}{2}$ per centum per annum from the   18th   day of   January   , nineteen hundred . . . .

IN WITNESS WHEREOF, the assignor has duly executed this assignment the   23rd day of   February   , 19--.

IN PRESENCE OF:

/s/ Richard Roe   /s/ Roberta Weathers

STATE OF NEW YORK, COUNTY OF   Kings   ss.:
On the   23rd   day of   February   , nineteen hundred and . . .
before me personally came   Roberta Weathers   to me known to be the individual described in and who executed the foregoing instrument, and acknowledged that   she executed the same.

/s/ Richard Roe
Notary Public

**Figure
  2-3**   Assignment of Mortgage with Convenant

When mortgages are "packaged" and sold in the secondary market as described in Chapter 13 they are assigned. Sometimes many mortgages or deeds of trust are transferred in the same instrument.

Assignments are sometimes made *with recourse*. This means that if *A* assigns to *B* and the borrower *X* fails to pay, then *B* may go against *A* to collect the debt due. The assignment *with recourse* is accomplished by simply including a covenant to that effect in the assignment.

It is important that actual notice of the assignment be immediately given to the mortgagor. The reason for this is that the recording of the assignment will not protect the new owner of the mortgage against subsequent payments to prior holders of the mortgage.

Furthermore, the assignee must receive the original note or bond and original mortgage at the time of the assignment. The reason for this is due to the fact that when the loan is paid off the borrower may insist on receiving both instruments.

THE DEED OF TRUST

A *deed of trust* is a deed absolute to secure the payment of a debt.[2] There are three parties to the deed of trust: the trustor (borrower), the beneficiary (lender), and the trustee. The loan is given to the trustor who in turn transfers the trust deed to the trustee for the benefit of the beneficiary (lender). In the event of default by the trustor, the trustee forecloses for the benefit of the beneficiary.

In most instances in financing real estate there are two instruments signed by the borrower: a note and a mortgage or deed of trust. There are a number of states that use a deed of trust (or trust deed or trust indenture, as it is sometimes called) in the nature of a mortgage.[3] In many of these states the lender is given a choice of using either a mortgage or a deed of trust as the security for a real property loan.

In an ordinary mortgage transaction there are usually only two parties: the mortgagor and mortgagee. In the deed of trust, however, there are three parties to the transaction. The borrower executes the deed of trust which conveys the property to a third person known as the trustee who receives from the conveyance sufficient title to carry out the trust. This trustee holds for the benefit of the owner of the note or bond executed by the borrower at the time of the transaction. The

---

[2]In Georgia neither a mortgage or deed of trust is used. There a Security Deed is used. Basically, the deed secures payment of a debt, grants power of attorney to sell the property upon default, and payment of the debt cancels the deed.

[3]Alabama, Alaska, California, Colorado, Delaware, District of Columbia, Illinois, Mississippi, Missouri, Nevada, New Mexico, Tennessee, Texas, Utah, Virginia, and West Virginia. The Small Tract Financing Act (Sec. 52-401 et. seq. Revised Code of Montana) provides for a Deed of Trust, but "only for parcels not exceeding three (3) acres." The 1957 Act of Idaho provides a deed of trust for 20 acres or less.

note or the bond is the evidence of the debt. If the borrower defaults, the property is either transferred to the lender, after proper legal proceedings have been completed, or disposed of at a public sale at which the trustee transfers title to the purchaser.

Depending upon state law, the trustee is either a private trustee whose only qualification is the possession of contractual capacity, or the trustee is a public trustee. Generally speaking, the public trustee is either the county clerk or an individual apppointed by the governor of the state. The public trustee in these states is bonded and handles all of the trust deeds recorded in the state.

The deed of trust is also used as security for some corporate bond issues. A corporation, for example, will sell bonds and at the same time deliver a deed of trust to a third person as security for the payment of the money due on the bonds. If the corporation defaults on its payments, the trustee, after proper legal proceedings, will sell the property and pay the proceeds to the bondholders up to the extent of the indebtedness.

DEED OF TRUST

THIS DEED OF TRUST is made this ....day of ....,
19...., among the Grantor,...
....(herein "Borrower"), the Public Trustee of
....County (herein "Trustee"), and the Beneficiary,
...., a corporation
organized and existing under the laws of ....,
whose address is ....
(herein "Lender").

BORROWER, in consideration of the indebtedness herein recited and the trust herein created, irrevocably grants and conveys to Trustee, in trust, with power of sale, the following described property located in the County of ....,
State of Colorado:

which has the address of ...., ...,
                                    [Street]   [City]
....(herein "Property Address");
        [State and Zip Code]

**Figure
2-4** Deed of Trust (Continued)

TOGETHER with all the improvements now or hereafter erected on the property, and all easements, rights, appurtenances, rents (subject however to the rights and authorities given herein to Lender to collect and apply such rents), royalties, mineral, oil and gas rights and profits, water, water rights, and water stock, and all fixtures now or hereafter attached to the property, all of which, including replacements and additions thereto, shall be deemed to be and remain a part of the property covered by this Deed of Trust; and all of the foregoing, together with said property (or the leasehold estate if this Deed of Trust is on a leasehold) are herein referred to as the "Property";

To SECURE TO LENDER (a) the repayment of the indebtedness evidenced by Borrower's note dated . . . . .herein "Note"), in the principal sum of . . . . .Dollars, with interest thereon, providing for monthly installments of principal and interest, with the balance of the indebtedness, if not sooner paid, due and payable on . . . .; the payment of all other sums, with interest thereon, advanced in accordance herewith to protect the security of this Deed of Trust; and the performance of the covenants and agreements of Borrower herein contained; and (b) the repayment of any future advances, with interest thereon, made to Borrower by Lender pursuant to paragraph 21 hereof (herein "Future Advances").

Borrower covenants that Borrower is lawfully seised of the estate hereby conveyed and has the right to grant and convey the Property, that the Property is unencumbered, and that Borrower will warrant and defend generally the title to the Property against all claims and demands, subject to any declarations, easements or restrictions listed in a schedule of exceptions to coverage in any title insurance policy insuring Lender's interest in the Property.

UNIFORM COVENANTS. Borrower and Lender covenant and agree as follows:
1. Payment of Principal and Interest. Borrower shall promptly pay when due the principal of and interest on the indebtedness evidenced by the Note, prepayment and late charges as provided in the Note, and the principal of and interest on any Future Advances secured by this Deed of Trust.
2. Funds for Taxes and Insurance. Subject to applicable law or to a written waiver by Lender, Borrower shall pay to Lender on the day monthly installments of principal and interest are payable under the Note, until the Note is paid in full, a sum (herein "Funds") equal to one-twelfth of the yearly taxes and assessments which may attain priority over this Deed of Trust, and ground rents on the Property, if any, plus one-twelfth of yearly premium installments for hazard insurance, plus one-twelfth of yearly premium installments for mortgage insurance, if any, all as reasonably estimated initially and from time to time by Lender on the basis of assessments and bills and reasonable estimates thereof.
The Funds shall be held in an institution the deposits or accounts of which are insured or guaranteed by a Federal or state agency (including Lender if Lender is such an institution). Lender shall apply the Funds to pay said taxes, assessments insurance premiums and ground rents. Lender may not charge for so holding and applying the Funds, analyzing said account or verifying and compiling said assessments and bills, unless Lender pays Borrower interest on the Funds and applicable law permits Lender to make such a charge. Borrower and Lender may agree in writing at the time of execution of this Deed of Trust that interest on the Funds shall be paid to Borrower, and unless such agreement is made or applicable law requires such interest to be paid, Lender shall not be required to pay Borrower any interest or earnings on the Funds. Lender shall give to Borrower, without charge,

Figure
2-4 Deed of Trust (Continued)

an annual accounting of the Funds showing credits and debits to the Funds and the purpose for which each debit to the Funds was made. The Funds are pledged as additional security for the sums secured by this Deed of Trust.

If the amount of the Funds held by Lender, together with the future monthly installments of Funds payable prior to the due dates of taxes, assessments, insurance premiums and ground rents, shall exceed the amount required to pay said taxes, assessments, insurance premiums and ground rents as they fall due, such excess shall be, at Borrower's option, either promptly repaid to Borrower or credited to Borrower on monthly installments of Funds. If the amount of the Funds held by Lender shall not be sufficient to pay taxes, assessments, insurance premiums and ground rents as they fall due, Borrower shall pay to Lender any amount necessary to make up the deficiency within 30 days from the date notice is mailed by Lender to Borrower requesting payment thereof.

Upon payment in full of all sums secured by this Deed of Trust, Lender shall promptly refund to Borrower any Funds held by Lender. If under paragraph 18 hereof the Property is sold or the Property is otherwise acquired by Lender, Lender shall apply, no later than immediately prior to the sale of the Property or its acquisition by Lender, any Funds held by Lender at the time of application as a credit against the sums secured by this Deed of Trust.

3. Application of Payments. Unless applicable law provides otherwise, all payments received by Lender under the Note and paragraphs 1 and 2 hereof shall be applied by Lender first in payment of amounts payable to Lender by Borrower under paragraph 2 hereof, then to interest payable on the Note, then to the principal of the Note, and then to interest and principal on any Future Advances.

4. Charges; Liens. Borrower shall pay all taxes, assessments and other charges, fines and impositions attributable to the Property which may attain a priority over this Deed of Trust, and leasehold payments or ground rents, if any, in the manner provided under paragraph 2 hereof or, if not paid in such manner, by Borrower making payment, when due, directly to the payee thereof. Borrower shall promptly furnish to Lender all notices of amounts due under this paragraph, and in the event Borrower shall make payment directly, Borrower shall promptly furnish to Lender receipts evidencing such payments. Borrower shall promptly discharge any lien which has priority over this Deed of Trust; provided, that Borrower shall not be required to discharge any such lien so long as Borrower shall agree in writing to the payment of the obligation secured by such lien in a manner acceptable to Lender, or shall in good faith contest such lien by, or defend enforcement of such lien in, legal proceedings which operate to prevent the enforcement of the lien or forfeiture of the Property or any part thereof.

5. Hazard Insurance. Borrower shall keep the improvements now existing or hereafter erected on the Property insured against loss by fire, hazards included within the term "extended coverage", and such other hazards as Lender may require and in such amounts and for such periods as Lender may require; provided, that Lender shall not require that the amount of such coverage exceed that amount of coverage required to pay the sums secured by this Deed of Trust.

The insurance carrier providing the insurance shall be chosen by Borrower subject to approval by Lender; provided, that such approval shall not be unreasonably withheld. All premiums on insurance policies shall be paid in the manner provided under paragraph 2 hereof or, if not paid in such manner, by Borrower making payment, when due, directly to the insurance carrier.

All insurance policies and renewals thereof shall be in form acceptable to Lender and shall include a standard mortgage clause in favor of and in form acceptable to Lender. Lender shall have the right to hold the policies and renewals thereof, and Borrower shall promptly furnish to Lender all renewal notices and all

**Figure
2-4** Deed of Trust (Continued)

receipts of paid premiums. In the event of loss, Borrower shall give prompt notice to the insurance carrier and Lender. Lender may make proof of loss if not made promptly by Borrower.

Unless Lender and Borrower otherwise agree in writing, insurance proceeds shall be applied to restoration or repair of the Property damaged, provided such restoration or repair is economically feasible and the security of this Deed of Trust is not thereby impaired. If such restoration or repair is not economically feasible or if the security of this Deed of Trust would be impaired, the insurance proceeds shall be applied to the sums secured by this Deed of Trust, with the excess, if any paid to Borrower. If the Property is abandoned by Borrower, or if Borrower fails to respond to Lender within 30 days from the date notice is mailed by Lender to Borrower that the insurance carrier offers to settle a claim for insurance benefits, Lender is authorized to collect and apply the insurance proceeds at Lender's option either to restoration or repair of the Property or to the sums secured by this Deed of Trust.

Unless Lender and Borrower otherwise agree in writing, any such application of proceeds to principal shall not extend or postpone the due date of the monthly installments referred to in paragraphs 1 and 2 hereof or change the amount of such installments. If under paragraph 18 hereof the Property is acquired by Lender, all right, title and interest of Borrower in and to any insurance policies and in and to the proceeds thereof resulting from damage to the Property prior to the sale or acquisition shall pass to Lender to the extent of the sums secured by this Deed of Trust immediately prior to such sale or acquisition.

6. Preservation and Maintenance of Property; Leaseholds; Condominiums; Planned Unit Developments. Borrower shall keep the Property in good repair and shall not commit waste or permit impairment or deterioration of the Property and shall comply with the provisions of any lease if this Deed of Trust is on a leasehold. If this Deed of Trust is on a unit in a condominium or a planned unit development, Borrower shall perform all of Borrower's obligations under the declaration of covenants creating or governing the condominium or planned unit development, the by-laws and regulations of the condominium or planned unit development, and constituent documents. If a condominium or planned unit development rider is executed by Borrower and recorded together with this Deed of Trust, the covenants and agreements of such rider shall be incorporated into and shall amend and supplement the covenants and agreements of this Deed of Trust as if the rider were a part hereof.

7. Protection of Lender's Security. If Borrower fails to perform the covenants and agreements contained in this Deed of Trust, or if any action or proceeding is commenced which materially affects Lender's interest in the Property, including, but not limited to, eminent domain, insolvency, code enforcement, or arrangements or proceeds involving a bankrupt or decedent, then Lender at Lender's option, upon notice to Borrower, may make such appearances, disburse such sums and take such action as is necessary to protect Lender's interest, including, but not limited to, disbursement of reasonable attorney's fees and entry upon the Property to make repairs. If Lender required mortgage insurance as a condition of making the loan secured by this Deed of Trust, Borrower shall pay the premiums required to maintain such insurance in effect until such time as the requirement for such insurance terminates in accordance with Borrower's and Lender's written agreement or applicable law. Borrower shall pay the amount of all mortgage insurance premiums in the manner provided under paragraph 2 hereof.

Any amounts disbursed by Lender pursuant to this paragraph 7, with interest thereon, shall become additional indebtedness of Borrower secured by this Deed of Trust. Unless Borrower and Lender agree to other terms of payment, such amounts

**Figure
2-4** Deed of Trust (Continued)

shall be payable upon notice from Lender to Borrower requesting payment thereof, and shall bear interest from the date of disbursement at the rate payable from time to time on outstanding principal under the Note unless payment of interest at such rate would be contrary to applicable law, in which event such amounts shall bear interest at the highest rate permissible under applicable law. Nothing contained in this paragraph 7 shall require Lender to incur any expense or take any action hereunder.

8. Inspection. Lender may make or cause to be made reasonable entries upon and inspections of the Property, provided that Lender shall give Borrower notice prior to any such inspection specifying reasonable cause therefor related to Lender's interest in the Property.

9. Condemnation. The proceeds of any award or claim for damages, direct or consequential, in connection with any condemnation or other taking of the Property, or part thereof, or for conveyance in lieu of condemnation, are hereby assigned and shall be paid to Lender.

In the event of a total taking of the Property, the proceeds shall be applied to the sums secured by this Deed of Trust, with the excess, if any, paid to Borrower. In the event of a partial taking of the Property, unless Borrower and Lender otherwise agree in writing, there shall be applied to the sums secured by this Deed of Trust such proportion of the proceeds as is equal to that proportion which the amount of the sums secured by this Deed of Trust immediately prior to the date of taking bears to the fair market value of the property immediately prior to the date of taking, with the balance of the proceeds paid to Borrower.

If the Property is abandoned by Borrower, or if, after notice by Lender to Borrower that the condemnor offers to make an award or settle a claim for damages, Borrower fails to respond to Lender within 30 days after the date such notice is mailed, Lender is authorized to collect and apply the proceeds, at Lender's option, either to restoration or repair of the Property or to the sums secured by this Deed of Trust.

Unless Lender and Borrower otherwise agree in writing, any such application of proceeds to principal shall not extend or postpone the due date of the monthly installments referred to in paragraphs 1 and 2 hereof or change the amount of such installments.

10. Borrower Not Released. Extension of the time for payment or modification of amortization of the sums secured by this Deed of Trust granted by Lender to any successor in interest of Borrower shall not operate to release, in any manner, the liability of the original Borrower and Borrower's successors in interest. Lender shall not be required to commence proceedings against such successor or refuse to extend time for payment or otherwise modify amortization of the sums secured by this Deed of Trust by reason of any demand made by the original Borrower and Borrower's successors in interest.

11. Forbearance by Lender Not a Waiver. Any forbearance by Lender in exercising any right or remedy hereunder, or otherwise afforded by applicable law, shall not be a waiver of or preclude the exercise of any such right or remedy. The procurement of insurance or the payment of taxes or other liens or charges by Lender shall not be a waiver of Lender's right to accelerate the maturity of the indebtedness secured by this Deed of Trust.

12. Remedies Cumulative. All remedies provided in this Deed of Trust are distinct and cumulative to any other right or remedy under this Deed of Trust or afforded by law or equity, and may be exercised concurrently, independently or successively.

13. Successors and Assigns Bound; Joint and Several Liability; Captions. The covenants and agreements herein contained shall bind, and the rights hereunder

Figure
2-4 Deed of Trust (Continued)

shall inure to, the respective successors and assigns of Lender and Borrower, subject to the provisions of paragraph 17 hereof. All covenants and agreements of Borrower shall be joint and several. The captions and headings of the paragraphs of this Deed of Trust are for convenience only and are not to be used to interpret or define the provisions hereof.

14. Notice. Except for any notice required under applicable law to be given in another manner, (a) any notice to Borrower provided for in this Deed of Trust shall be given by mailing such notice by certified mail addressed to Borrower at the Property Address or at such other address as Borrower may designate by notice to Lender as provided herein, and (b) any notice to Lender shall be given by certified mail, return receipt requested, to Lender's address stated herein or to such other address as Lender may designate by notice to Borrower as provided herein. Any notice provided for in this Deed of Trust shall be deemed to have been given to Borrower or Lender when given in the manner designated herein.

15. Uniform Deed of Trust; Governing Law; Severability. This form of deed of trust combines uniform covenants for national use and non-uniform covenants with limited variations by jurisdiction to constitute a uniform security instrument covering real property. This Deed of Trust shall be governed by the law of the jurisdiction in which the Property is located. In the event that any provision or clause of this Deed of Trust or the Note conflicts with applicable law, such conflict shall not affect other provisions of this Deed of Trust or the Note which can be given effect without the conflicting provision, and to this end the provisions of the Deed of Trust and the Note are declared to be severable.

16. Borrower's Copy. Borrower shall be furnished a conformed copy of the Note and of this Deed of Trust at the time of execution or after recordation hereof.

17. Transfer of the Property; Assumption. If all or any part of the Property or an interest therein is sold or transferred by Borrower without Lender's prior written consent, excluding (a) the creation of a lien or encumbrance subordinate to this Deed of Trust, (b) the creation of a purchase money security interest for household appliances, (c) a transfer by devise, descent or by operation of law upon the death of a joint tenant or (d) the grant of any leasehold interest of three years or less not containing an option to purchase, Lender may, at Lender's option, declare all the sums secured by this Deed of Trust to be immediately due and payable. Lender shall have waived such option to accelerate if, prior to the sale or transfer, Lender and the person to whom the Property is to be sold or transferred reach agreement in writing that the credit of such person is satisfactory to Lender and that the interest payable on the sums secured by this Deed of Trust shall be at such rate as Lender shall request. If Lender has waived the option to accelerate provided in this paragraph 17, and if Borrower's successor in interest has executed a written assumption agreement accepted in writing by Lender, Lender shall release Borrower from all obligations under this Deed of Trust and the Note.

If Lender exercises such option to accelerate, Lender shall mail Borrower notice of acceleration in accordance with paragraph 14 hereof. Such notice shall provide a period of not less than 30 days from the date the notice is mailed within which Borrower may pay the sums declared due. If Borrower fails to pay such sums prior to the expiration of such period, Lender may, without further notice or demand on Borrower, invoke any remedies permitted by paragraph 18 hereof.

Non-Uniform Covenants. Borrower and lender further covenant and agree as follows:

18. Acceleration; Remedies. Except as provided in paragraph 17 hereof, upon Borrower's breach of any covenant or agreement of Borrower in this Deed of Trust, including the covenants to pay when due any sums secured by this Deed of Trust,

Figure
2-4 Deed of Trust (Continued)

Lender prior to acceleration shall mail notice to Borrower as provided in paragraph 14 hereof specifying: (1) the breach; (2) the action required to cure such breach; (3) a date, not less than 30 days from the date the notice is mailed to Borrower, by which such breach must be cured; and (4) that failure to cure such breach on or before the date specified in the notice may result in acceleration of the sums secured by this Deed of Trust and sale of the property. The notice shall further inform Borrower of the right to reinstate after acceleration and the right to assert in the foreclosure proceeding the non-existence of a default or any other defense of Borrower to acceleration and sale. If the breach is not cured on or before the date specified in the notice, Lender at Lender's option may declare all of the sums secured by this Deed of Trust to be immediately due and payable without further demand and may invoke the power of sale and any other remedies permitted by applicable law. Lender shall be entitled to collect all reasonable costs and expenses incurred in pursuing the remedies provided in this paragraph 18, including, but not limited to, reasonable attorney's fees.

If Lender invokes the power of sale, Lender shall give written notice to Trustee of the occurrence of an event of default and of Lender's election to cause the property to be sold. Lender shall mail a copy of such notice to Borrower as provided in paragraph 14 hereof. Trustee shall record a copy of such notice in the county in which the property is located. Trustee shall publish a notice of sale for the time and in the manner provided by applicable law and shall mail copies of such notice of sale in the manner prescribed by applicable law to Borrower and to the other persons prescribed by applicable law. After the lapse of such time as may be required by applicable law, Trustee, without demand on Borrower, shall sell the Property at public auction to the highest bidder for cash at the time and place and under the terms designated in the notice of sale in one or more parcels and in such order as Trustee may determine. Trustee may postpone sale of all or any parcel of the property by public announcement at the time and place of any previously scheduled sale. Lender or lender's designee may purchase the Property at any sale.

Trustee shall deliver to the purchaser Trustee's certificate describing the property and the time when the purchaser will be entitled to Trustee's deed thereto. The recitals in Trustee's deed shall be prima facie evidence of the truth of the statements made therein. Trustee shall apply the proceeds of the sale in the following order: (a) to all reasonable costs and expenses of the sale, including, but not limited to, reasonable trustee's and attorney's fees and costs of title evidence; (b) to all sums secured by this Deed of Trust; and (c) the excess, if any, to the person or persons legally entitled thereto.

19. Borrower's Right to Reinstate. Notwithstanding Lender's acceleration of the sums secured by this Deed of Trust, Borrower shall have the right to have any proceedings begun by Lender to enforce this Deed of Trust discontinued at any time prior to the earlier to occur of (i) the fifth day before sale of the property pursuant to the power of sale contained in this Deed of Trust or (ii) entry of a judgment enforcing this Deed of Trust if: (a) Borrower pays Lender all sums which would be then due under this Deed of Trust, the Note and notes securing Future Advances, if any, had no acceleration occurred; (b) Borrower cures all breaches of any other covenants or agreements of Borrower contained in this Deed of Trust; (c) Borrower pays all reasonable expenses incurred by Lender and Trustee in enforcing the covenants and agreements of Borrower contained in this Deed of Trust and in enforcing Lender's and Trustee's remedies as provided in paragraph 18 hereof, including, but not limited to, reasonable attorney's fees and Trustee's expenses and withdrawal fee; and (d) Borrower takes such action as Lender may reasonably require to assure that the lien of this Deed of Trust, Lender's interest in the Property and Borrower's obligation to pay the sums secured by this Deed of Trust shall

Figure
2-4 Deed of Trust (Continued)

continue unimpaired. Upon such payment and cure by Borrower, this Deed of Trust and the obligations secured hereby shall remain in full force and effect as if no acceleration had occurred.

20. Assignment of Rents; Appointment of Receiver; Lender in Possession. As additional security hereunder, Borrower hereby assigns to Lender the rents of the Property, provided that Borrower shall, prior to acceleration under paragraph 18 hereof or abandonment of the property, have the right to collect and retain such rents as they become due and payable.

Upon acceleration under paragraph 18 hereof or abandonment of the property, Lender, in person, by agent or by judicially appointed receiver, shall be entitled to enter upon, take possession of and manage the Property and to collect the rents of the property including those past due. All rents collected by Lender or the receiver shall be applied first to payment of the costs of management of the property and collection of rents, including, but not limited to, receiver's fees, premiums on receiver's bonds and reasonable attorney's fees, and then to the sums secured by this Deed of Trust. Lender and the receiver shall be liable to account only for those rents actually received.

21. Future Advances. Upon request of Borrower, Lender, at Lender's option prior to release of this Deed of Trust, may make Future Advances to Borrower. Such Future Advances, with interest thereon, shall be secured by this Deed of Trust when evidenced by promissory notes stating that said notes are secured hereby.

22. Release. Upon payment of all sums secured by this Deed of Trust, Lender shall request Trustee to release this Deed of Trust and shall produce for Trustee duly cancelled all notes evidencing indebtedness secured by this Deed of Trust. Trustee shall release this Deed of Trust without further inquiry or liability. Borrower shall pay all costs of recordation, if any, and shall pay the statutory Trustee's fees.

23. Waiver of Homestead. Borrower hereby waives all right of homestead exemption in the Property.

IN WITNESS WHEREOF, Borrower has executed this Deed of Trust.

....
— Borrower

....
— Borrower

STATE OF COLORADO ....County ss:

The foregoing instrument was acknowledged before me this ..day of ...., 19...., by ....

Witness my hand and official seal.

My commission expires:

....
Notary Public

**Figure
2-4** Deed of Trust (Concluded)

Action on Payment of the Indebtedness

Depending on the laws of a particular state, either one of two things happen upon the payment of the indebtedness under the terms of the trust deed. In one case an instrument called a reconveyance is used to release the security (the land and improvements) from the trust. There are two types of reconveyance. One is a full reconveyance which is made by the trustee and evidences satisfaction in full and release of the security. Secondly, there is a partial reconveyance which is made by the trustee and evidences satisfaction in part and the release of a portion of the security.[4] Both full and partial reconveyances must describe the deed of trust accurately and in detail, and a partial reconveyance must contain the legal description of the security being released.

The other way the deed of trust is handled upon payment of the indebtedness is as follows. The beneficiary under the trust deed signs an instrument known as a Request for Release of Deed of Trust. This is then presented either to the private, or in most cases, to the public, trustee together with the canceled note and the deed of trust. The trustee then signs a Release of Deed of Trust. As in the case of the mortgage, this release may be complete or partial. The Release of Deed of Trust is then recorded in the office of the County Clerk or Recorder of the county in which the property is located.

Trustor's Right of Reinstatement

In most states using the deed of trust a defaulting trustor has a time period within which to reinstate the obligation.[5] To do so the trustor must (a) pay all sums in arrears, (b) pay any additional costs incurred by the beneficiary, and (c) pay a small fee to the trustee.

THE NOTE

The bond is not used with a mortgage or deed of trust as evidence of the debt in all states. Instead, a promissory note is employed, the real property being used as collateral security for the note. A *promissory note* is defined as a written promise by one person to pay money to another. The note often is made in the form shown in Figure 2-5. This is a standard Federal National Mortgage Association, Federal Home Loan Mortgage Corporation Uniform Instrument. Although

---

[4]Some states use a "marginal release," Tennessee and Maryland, for example. A marginal entry is made on the record in the office where the mortgage is recorded, or a release of mortgage is written on the original and then filed in the office where the mortgage is recorded. C.f. Md. Code, Art. 21, Secs. 38–44.

[5]In California, for example, the time period is 3 months.

much more will be said about FNMA and FHLMC later, for the moment they can be thought of as institutions that purchase mortgages. This form is exactly the same in states using either deeds of trust or mortgages except for the one sentence previously mentioned.

NOTE

US $ ...., Colorado
                                                    City

                              ...., 19....

FOR VALUE RECEIVED, the undersigned ("Borrower") promise(s) to pay
....or order, the principal
sum of ....Dollars, with
interest on the unpaid principal balance from the date of this Note, until paid, at the
rate of ....percent per annum. Principal and interest
shall be payable at ....
or such other place as the Note holder may designate, in consecutive monthly
installments of ....Dollars
(US $ ....), on the ....day of each month
beginning ...., 19..... Such monthly installments
shall continue until the entire indebtedness evidenced by this Note is fully paid,
except that any remaining indebtedness, if not sooner paid, shall be due and
payable on ....
   If any monthly installment under this Note is not paid when due and remains
unpaid after a date specified by a notice to Borrower, the entire principal amount
outstanding and accrued interest thereon shall at once become due and payable at
the option of the Note holder. The date specified shall not be less than thirty days
from the date such notice is mailed. The Note holder may exercise this option to
accelerate during any default by Borrower regardless of any prior forbearance. If
suit is brought to collect this Note, the Note holder shall be entitled to collect all
reasonable costs and expenses of suit, including, but not limited to, reasonable
attorney's fees.
   Borrower shall pay to the Note holder a late charge of ....percent
of any monthly installment not received by the Note holder within ....days
after the installment is due.
   Borrower may prepay the principal amount outstanding in whole or in part.
The Note holder may require that any partial prepayments (i) be made on the date
monthly installments are due and (ii) be in the amount of that part of one or more
monthly installments which would be applicable to principal. Any partial prepayment shall be applied against the principal amount outstanding and shall not postpone the due date of any subsequent monthly installments or change the amount of
such installments, unless the Note holder shall otherwise agree in writing. If, within
five years from the date of this Note, Borrower make(s) any prepayments in any
twelve month period beginning with the date of this Note or anniversary dates
thereof ("loan year") with money lent to Borrower by a lender other than the Note
holder, Borrower shall pay the Note holder (a) during each of the first three loan
years ....percent of the amount by which the sum of prepayments made in any such loan year exceeds twenty percent of the original principal

Figure
   2-5   Promissory Note (Continued)

Chapter 2 / Mortgages and Deeds of Trust (Concluded)   **41** amount of this Note and (b) during the fourth and fifth loan years...................percent of the amount by which the sum of prepayments made in any such loan year exceeds twenty percent of the original principal amount of this Note.

Presentment, notice of dishonor, and protest are hereby waived by all makers, sureties, guarantors and endorsers hereof. This Note shall be the joint and several obligation of all makers, sureties, guarantors and endorsers, and shall be binding upon them and their successors and assigns.

Any notice to Borrower provided for in this Note shall be given by mailing such notice by certified mail addressed to Borrower at the Property Address stated below, or to such other address as Borrower may designate by notice to the Note holder. Any notice to the Note holder shall be given by mailing such notice by certified mail, return receipt requested, to the Note holder at the address stated in the first paragraph of this Note, or at such other address as may have been designated by notice to Borrower.

The indebtedness evidenced by this Note is secured by a Deed of Trust, dated ...., and reference is made to the Deed of Trust for rights as to acceleration of the indebtedness evidenced by this Note.

....

....

....
                      Property Address
                                                        (Execute Original Only)

**Figure
  2-5** Promissory Note (Concluded)

THE BOND

In order for there to be a valid mortgage, there must usually be a debt; and there must also exist evidence of this debt. In some states the bond is employed almost exclusively as the evidence of the debt; in other states the promissory note is used as the evidence of the debt. A *bond* is a sealed agreement in writing in which an obligor (a borrower) promises to pay under stated terms a sum certain to an obligee (a lender). Both parties to a bond must have contractual capacity. To be valid, the bond must embrace the following:

1. A writing.
2. An obligor with contractual ability.
3. An obligee with contractual ability.
4. A promise or covenant by the obligor to pay a sum certain.
5. Terms of payment.
6. Default clause including mortgage covenants by reference.

7. Proper execution.
8. Voluntary delivery and acceptance.

The bond, which embodies the debt, is the primary instrument, while the mortgage is merely a secondary or collateral instrument.

QUESTIONS FOR REVIEW

1. A number of general clauses or covenants are usually found in statutory mortgages. Briefly explain each of the following general clauses: (a) covenant of insurance, (b) covenant against removal, (c) covenant to pay taxes, and (d) acceleration clause. Describe some additional general clauses.
2. A number of special clauses may be inserted into the mortgage form. Briefly describe each of the following clauses designed to cover special situations: (a) receiver clause, (b) estoppel clause, (c) good repair clause, and (d) prepayment clause. What are some additional special clauses?
3. Explain the major or principal differences between a mortgage and a deed of trust.
4. Explain what is meant by acknowledgement and recording of mortgages and deeds of trust.
5. Explain what happens upon the payment of the indebtedness under the terms of a deed of trust.
6. Describe the difference between (a) the note, and (b) the bond.

PROBLEMS

1. Assume that you are the mortgagee on a piece of property valued at $100,000. The mortgagor purchased the property from you at $90,000 and added portable buildings worth $10,000. You agreed to a mortgage of $80,000 to be paid over 20 years at a 10 percent interest rate. After making only a couple of payments, the mortgagor has missed the most recent payment date.

(a) What will happen if the mortgage contains only the six general clauses found in nearly every type of simple mortgage?

(b) What kind of special mortgage clauses might be important to this problem? Describe briefly.

Interest Factors in Real Estate Finance Decisions

Because of the frequent long-term nature of real estate investments and corresponding financing requirements, it is necessary to consider and understand the concept of compound interest. This also is sometimes referred to as the "math of finance." Some people are inclined to simply avoid considering compound interest because of an unfounded belief that the subject is very difficult and complex. This is simply not the case. Furthermore, erroneous financing decisions may be made if there is a failure to consider the "time value of money." The old adage that a "dollar today is worth more than a dollar tomorrow" reflects the fact that the value of money depends upon when it is received —thus the term *time value of money*.

COMPOUND INTEREST OR FUTURE VALUE

Compounding involves the determination of the future worth or value of an investment made now; that is, a current investment "growing" at some rate will increase in value over time. This is the basic concept of compounding or *compound interest*.

Now, assume that you deposit $1,000 in a savings and loan association. You can earn 6 percent interest on your savings each year. At the end of 1 year your savings or investment will be worth $1,060. This is because you receive your original principal (P_0), or beginning amount, of $1,000 plus an *interest* (i) return of 6 percent of the principal or $60. This also may be expressed as $P_0(1 + i)$, which gives the compound or future value at the end of one year (P_1). In this example, $1,000(1.06) = $1,060. Thus, a $1,000 savings growing at 6 percent per year has a future value of $1,060 one year from now.

44

But what if you decide to leave your savings in the savings and loan association for two years before withdrawing the initial principal and accumulated interest. What is the future value of your investment? This involves *compounding* since you will earn "interest on interest" as well as interest on the principal. Assuming annual compounding, this can be expressed as $P_2 = P_0(1 + i)(1 + i)$. In our example, $P_2 = \$1{,}000(1.06)(1.06)$ or $\$1{,}060(1.06)$. Thus, the future worth two years from now of $1,000 growing at 6 percent per year is $1,124.

While it is possible to calculate future values for each problem, standardized tables are available to reduce the amount of necessary calculations. A partial "compound sum of $1" table is illustrated as Table 3-1. A more comprehensive table is presented in Appendix B. As can be seen, a "compound sum of $1" table contains *interest factors* corresponding to various interest rates and time periods or years. For example, the interest factor (IF) for 1 year at 6 percent is 1.060. Future value is determined by multiplying the interest factor by the principal or beginning amount. The interest factor for a two-year period at 6 percent is 1.124. An initial savings of $1,000 would "grow" to $1,124 in two years, i.e., $\$1{,}000(1.124) = \$1{,}124$. In other words, the 1.124 interest factor is the same as $(1.06)(1.06)$ or $(1.06)^2$.

Table 3-1   Compound Sum of $1

Year n	1%	2%	3%	4%	5%	6%	7%
1	1.010	1.020	1.030	1.040	1.050	1.060	1.070
2	1.020	1.040	1.061	1.082	1.102	1.124	1.145
3	1.030	1.061	1.093	1.125	1.158	1.191	1.225
4	1.041	1.082	1.126	1.170	1.216	1.262	1.311
5	1.051	1.104	1.159	1.217	1.276	1.338	1.403
6	1.062	1.126	1.194	1.265	1.340	1.419	1.501
7	1.072	1.149	1.230	1.316	1.407	1.504	1.606
8	1.083	1.172	1.267	1.369	1.477	1.594	1.718
9	1.094	1.195	1.305	1.423	1.551	1.689	1.838
10	1.105	1.219	1.344	1.480	1.629	1.791	1.967
11	1.116	1.243	1.384	1.539	1.710	1.898	2.105
12	1.127	1.268	1.426	1.601	1.796	2.012	2.252
13	1.138	1.294	1.469	1.665	1.886	2.133	2.410
14	1.149	1.319	1.513	1.732	1.980	2.261	2.579
15	1.161	1.346	1.558	1.801	2.079	2.397	2.759

BASIC COMPOUND INTEREST PROBLEMS

There are a number of problems involving compound interest concepts that can be solved. We need to know only two of the three characteristics contained in the "compound sum of $1" table in order to find the third characteristic. This can easily be seen in terms of the following compound interest formula:

$$P_n = P_0(1 + i)^n$$

where
P_n = future value at the end of n years
P_0 = principal or initial amount at year 0
i = annual interest rate
n = number of years.

As we saw earlier, the $(1 + i)^n$ is calculated as the interest factor (IF) for a given interest rate and time period — with a large number of different combinations being used to construct a standardized table.

Determining Future Values

This is determined in the same manner as earlier problems. What is the compound amount or future value of a $500 investment made for 15 years at a 7 percent per year interest rate? The solution is found by multiplying the interest factor at 7 percent for 15 years (i.e., 2.759 as shown in Table 3-1) times the $500 initial investment which equals $1,379.50.

Determining Investment Time Periods

How long will it take for $1,000 to grow to a future value of $1,477 if the annual compound interest rate is 5 percent? The solution is, first, to divide the future amount by the initial amount to get the interest factor (i.e., $1,477/$1,000 = 1.477). Next, find the 5 percent interest rate column in Table 3-1 and read down the column until the 1.477 interest factor is found. This corresponds with the eighth year in the end-of-year rows. Thus, it will take 8 years for a $1,000 investment to grow to $1,477 assuming a 5 percent interest rate.

Determining Rates of Return

A $200 investment now is expected to be $246 at the end of 7 years. What is the annual compound rate of return? The solution is to divide the future value ($246) by the initial investment ($200) to obtain a 1.230 investment factor. In Table 3-1, read across at the 7-year row until the 1.230 factor is found. This occurs at the 3 percent interest rate column indicating a 3 percent annual compound rate of return over the 7-year period.

PRESENT WORTH OR VALUE

Most real estate and other finance problems involve making decisions now during the current or present time period. At the same time it is still necessary to forecast and estimate future values. However, since decisions are made in the present time period, future values are "brought back" or *discounted* so as to represent their present worth or value. In essence, present value is just the opposite of compound interest or future value. It is the worth today of an amount to be received (or paid) in the future.

Assume that you need $1,060 at the end of one year from now. If you can earn 6 percent interest on your investment, how much would you have to invest now? Certainly, the required investment would be less than $1,060. In order to answer this question, we need to "bring back" or *discount* the future value to the present time period. It may be recalled that in compounding, the initial principal or current amount is multiplied by the sum of one plus the interest rate to arrive at next year's future value. In a similar fashion, the present value can be found by dividing the future value by the sum of one plus the interest rate. Present value in our example is determined as: $1,060/1.06 = $1,000.

Now, what is the present worth of $1,124 to be received in two years if the interest or discount rate is 6 percent? Since this is the reverse of compounding, we divide $1,124 by (1.06)(1.06) or 1.124. Thus, the present worth is $1,000. In other words, one would be indifferent between receiving $1,000 now or $1,124 two years from now if one's objective was to invest at a 6 percent interest rate.

Standardized tables for finding present values, like compound interest tables, are available to reduce the amount of needed calculations. A partial "present worth of $1" table is presented as Table 3-2 with a more comprehensive table contained in the Appendix. Since this is the reverse of the "compound sum of $1" table, the present value interest factors are found by taking the reciprocal of the compound sum interest factors; that is, by dividing the compound sum interest factor into 1. For example, the present value interest factor for 1 year at 6 percent would be: 1/1.06 = .943. For two years at 6 percent, the present value interest factor would be: 1/1.124 = .890. It now should be apparent that the interest factors for a given interest rate and time period are interchangeable between compound sum (Table 3-1) and present worth (Table 3-2) tables.

Table 3-2 Present Worth of $1

Year n	1%	2%	3%	4%	5%	6%	7%	8%	9%	10%
1	.990	.980	.971	.962	.952	.943	.935	.926	.917	.909
2	.980	.961	.943	.925	.907	.890	.873	.857	.842	.826
3	.971	.942	.915	.889	.864	.840	.816	.794	.772	.751
4	.961	.924	.889	.855	.823	.792	.763	.735	.708	.683
5	.951	.906	.863	.822	.784	.747	.713	.681	.650	.621
6	.942	.888	.838	.790	.746	.705	.666	.630	.596	.564
7	.933	.871	.813	.760	.711	.665	.623	.583	.547	.513
8	.923	.853	.789	.731	.677	.627	.582	.540	.502	.467
9	.914	.837	.766	.703	.645	.592	.544	.500	.460	.424
10	.905	.820	.744	.676	.614	.558	.508	.463	.422	.386
11	.896	.804	.722	.650	.585	.527	.475	.429	.388	.350
12	.887	.788	.701	.625	.557	.497	.444	.397	.356	.319
13	.879	.773	.681	.601	.530	.469	.415	.368	.326	.290
14	.870	.758	.661	.577	.505	.442	.388	.340	.299	.263
15	.861	.743	.642	.555	.481	.417	.362	.315	.275	.239

BASIC PRESENT VALUE PROBLEMS

Problems similar to those involving compound interest concepts can be viewed in a present value context. A look at the basic present value formula makes it easier to understand the kinds of present value problems. The previously presented compound interest formula, $P_n = P_0(1 + i)^n$, can be rewritten as

$$P_0 = P_n/(1 + i)^n.$$

This means that the present value (P_0) of an investment is equal to the future value (P_n) divided by the present value interest factor (PVIF) for a specific interest rate (i) and time period (n). However, in order to standardize present worth tables, the right side of the formula is rewritten as P_n times $1/(1 + i)^n$. Thus, any future value amount is multiplied times the present value interest factor for $1 for a specified interest rate and time period. This is similar to the use of compound interest tables.

Determining Present Values

Assume that you require a 7 percent annual rate of return on investments. You are offered $1,500 payable at the end of 15 years. What is the present worth of this future amount if a 7 percent discount rate is used? The present worth is found by multiplying the present value interest factor at 7 percent for 15 years (i.e., .362 as shown in Table

48

3-2) times the $1,500. This results in a present value of $543. Thus, in a strict investment sense you are indifferent between $543 now or $1,500 fifteen years from now if you could earn a 7 percent compound rate of return on your investments.

A practical application of this principle comes about when a lease is being appraised. One thing to be considered in a leasehold appraisal is the value of the reversion. For example, if you are the landlord of a commercial lease having 10 years to run, you are entitled to the reversion or to get back the property at the end of 10 years. Assume the value of the property today is $100,000. You expect the property also to be worth $100,000 10 years from now. The discount rate (also sometimes called the "capitalization" rate) is 10 percent. The question is: What is the value of the reversion 10 years from now?

From Table 3-2, 10 percent for 10 years indicates a factor of .386; thus, $100,000 × .386 = $38,600, the value of the reversion today.

Determining Investment Time Periods

A $1,000 investment growing at a 5 percent compound rate will reach $1,477. How long will it take? To solve this problem using present value concepts, divide the initial amount by the future amount to get the present value interest factor (i.e., $1,000/$1,477 = .677). Next, find the 5 percent discount rate column in Table 3-2 and read down the column until the .677 present value interest factor is found. This corresponds with the end-of-year-eight row. Thus, 8 years are required.

Determining Rates of Return

A $200 investment is expected to double over the next 12 years. What will be the rate of return on this investment? To use the "present worth of $1" table to solve this problem, divide the initial amount ($200) by the future amount ($400 since the initial amount will double) which results in a .500 present value interest factor. Read across the 12-year row in Table 3-2 until the .497 factor (which is approximately .500) is found. This indicates that the rate of return is approximately 6 percent.

VALUE OF AN ANNUITY

An annuity is a fixed amount payable each year for a number of years. It is possible to use Tables 3-1 or 3-2 to solve annuity problems. However, the number of calculations can be reduced substantially through the use of "compound sum of a $1 annuity" and "present worth of a $1 annuity" tables. These tables allow us to handle the same types of problems — future values, present values, time periods, and rates of return — discussed earlier in this chapter involving only initial and terminal amounts.

Table 3-3 allows us to work future value problems involving annuities. If you invest $1,000 each year beginning one year from now at 5 percent interest, how much will you have at the end of the 4th year? That is, what is the future value of a $1,000, 4-year annuity earning 5 percent per year? The solution is to multiply the annuity interest factor at 5 percent for 4 years (i.e., 4.310 as shown in Table 3-3) times the $1,000 annuity investment. Thus, the future value of the annuity is $4,310. The compound value of an annuity can be easily expressed in formula form as

$$S_n = PP(AIF).$$

In essence, the compound sum of an annuity (S) for a number of periods (n) is equal to the constant or periodic payment (PP) times the appropriate annuity interest factor (AIF) for a specific interest rate and time period.

It also is possible to calculate the present value of an annuity. This can be easily done with the aid of Table 3-4. More complete versions of Tables 3-3 and 3-4 are presented in Appendix B. What is the present value or worth of a 4-year, $1,000 annuity invested at a 5 percent annual interest rate? The solution is to multiply the periodic payment ($1,000) times the present value annuity interest factor at 5 percent for 4 years (3.546 as shown in Table 3-4). Thus, the present value of the annuity is $3,546.

Table 3-3 Compound Sum of a $1 Annuity

Year n	1%	2%	3%	4%	5%	6%	7%
1	1.000	1.000	1.000	1.000	1.000	1.000	1.000
2	2.010	2.020	2.030	2.040	2.050	2.060	2.070
3	3.030	3.060	3.091	3.122	3.152	3.184	3.215
4	4.060	4.122	4.184	4.246	4.310	4.375	4.440
5	5.101	5.204	5.309	5.416	5.526	5.637	5.751
6	6.152	6.308	6.468	6.633	6.802	6.975	7.153
7	7.214	7.434	7.662	7.898	8.142	8.394	8.654
8	8.286	8.583	8.892	9.214	9.549	9.897	10.260
9	9.369	9.755	10.159	10.583	11.027	11.491	11.978
10	10.462	10.950	11.464	12.006	12.578	13.181	13.816
11	11.567	12.169	12.808	13.486	14.207	14.972	15.784
12	12.683	13.412	14.192	15.026	15.917	16.870	17.888
13	13.809	14.680	15.618	16.627	17.713	18.882	20.141
14	14.947	15.974	17.086	18.292	19.599	21.051	22.550
15	16.097	17.293	18.599	20.024	21.579	23.276	25.129

A basic present value of an annuity formula can be expressed as

$$A_n = PP(AIF).$$

This means that the present value of an annuity (A) for a number of periods (n) is equal to the constant or periodic payment (PP) times the present value annuity interest factor (AIF) for a specific interest rate and n periods. This formula, along with the one for a compound value of annuity, allows us to solve other types of annuity problems as we will show next. At this time, the reader should note that the interest factor for the *sum* of an annuity *always is larger* than the length or the number of periods the annuity covers. The *present value* of an annuity *always is less* than the number of periods.

BASIC ANNUITY PROBLEMS

Problems involving the determination of future values and present values of annuities were discussed above. It also is possible to determine the number of years required for an annuity invested at a specific interest rate to grow to a future sum. For example, how long will it take for a $1,000 annuity earning 5 percent interest per year to grow to $11,000? To solve, divide the future sum of the annuity ($11,000) by the periodic payment ($1,000) to find the compound sum interest factor (11.000). Then, find the 5 percent interest rate column in Table 3-3 and read down the column until a factor close to 11.000 is found. This occurs approximately at the 9-year row. Thus, slightly less than 9 years are required for the annuity to reach $11,000.

Table 3-4 Present Worth of a $1 Annuity

Year n	1%	2%	3%	4%	5%	6%	7%	8%	9%	10%
1	0.990	0.980	0.971	0.962	0.952	0.943	0.935	0.926	0.917	0.909
2	1.970	1.942	1.913	1.886	1.859	1.833	1.808	1.783	1.759	1.736
3	2.941	2.884	2.829	2.775	2.723	2.673	2.624	2.577	2.531	2.487
4	3.902	3.808	3.717	3.630	3.546	3.465	3.387	3.312	3.240	3.170
5	4.853	4.713	4.580	4.452	4.329	4.212	4.100	3.993	3.890	3.791
6	5.795	5.601	5.417	5.242	5.076	4.917	4.767	4.623	4.486	4.355
7	6.728	6.472	6.230	6.002	5.786	5.582	5.389	5.206	5.033	4.868
8	7.652	7.325	7.020	6.733	6.463	6.210	5.971	5.747	5.535	5.335
9	8.566	8.162	7.786	7.435	7.108	6.802	6.515	6.247	5.995	5.759
10	9.471	8.983	8.530	8.111	7.722	7.360	7.024	6.710	6.418	6.145
11	10.368	9.787	9.253	8.760	8.306	7.887	7.499	7.139	6.805	6.495
12	11.255	10.575	9.954	9.385	8.863	8.384	7.943	7.536	7.161	6.814
13	12.134	11.348	10.635	9.986	9.394	8.853	8.358	7.904	7.487	7.103
14	13.004	12.106	11.296	10.563	9.899	9.295	8.745	8.244	7.786	7.367
15	13.865	12.849	11.938	11.118	10.380	9.712	9.108	8.559	8.060	7.606

Another place where this has practical application in the area of real estate is in the appraisal of a lease. Again, one of the problems to be answered is what is the present value of a future stream of income. Suppose that the rent under a lease is $1,200 per year, the remaining term of the lease is 10 years, and the discount or capitalization rate is 10 percent. What is the value of the stream of income?

From Table 3-4 the factor for 10 percent for 10 years is 6.145. The total of the stream of income of $1,200 for 10 years is $1,200 × 6.145 = $7,374, the present worth of a stream of income of $1,200 per year for 10 years.

Determining Annual Payments or Amounts

A frequent type of annuity problem involves determining periodic payments or amounts. Included are savings and amortization repayment problems. For example, how much would we have to deposit annually at a 6 percent interest rate in order to retire a $10,000 debt obligation 7 years from now? This problem can be solved by using the "compound sum of a $1 annuity" table. The basic compound value of an annuity formula can be rewritten as $PP = S_n/AIF$ to illustrate how the problem is solved. Divide the future sum of the annuity ($10,000) by the annuity interest factor for 6 percent and 7 years (8.394 as shown in Table 3-3). This results in an annual payment of $1,191.33.

The "present worth of a $1 annuity" table also can be used for problems involving annual amounts. Assume that you want to retire a $10,000 loan in five annual payments. If the interest rate being charged on the loan is 7 percent on the unpaid balance, how much will you have to pay each year? This problem can be illustrated by rewriting the present value of annuity formula as $PP = A_n/AIF$. In essence, divide the present value of the annuity ($10,000) by the present value annuity interest factor for 7 percent and 5 years (4.100 as shown in Table 3-4). Thus, the necessary annual payment will be $2,439.02.

Determining Rates of Return

Interest rates or rates of return also can be estimated for problems involving annuities if you know either the present value or future value of the annuity and the periodic cash flows. For example, if you invest $1,000 per year and have a worth of $7,153 at the end of 6 years, what annual compound interest rate or rate of return would you have earned? To solve, divide the future worth of the annuity ($7,153) by the periodic investment ($1,000) to find the compound sum annuity interest factor (7.153). Then in Table 3-3 read across at the 6-year row until the 7.153 factor is found. This shows the rate of return to be 7 percent.

52

Now, assume that you are in the process of making a loan for $3,890 from a bank. If the bank requires you to pay $1,000 at the end of each year for the next 5 years, what interest rate are you being charged? This present value problem can be solved using the "present worth of a $1 annuity" table. In essence, we first find the present value annuity interest factor by dividing the present value of the annuity ($3,890) by the annual payment ($1,000). This can be illustrated by rewriting the present value of an annuity formula as: $AIF = A_n/PP$. Looking across the 5-year row in Table 3-4, the factor 3.890 is found under the 9 percent column indicating that the cost of borrowing is 9 percent on the loan.

INVESTMENT EVALUATION METHODS

The time value of money concepts discussed earlier in this chapter are important in making real estate financing and investment decisions. There are two basic investment evaluation methods that take account of the time value of money by discounting future cash flows. These are the "net present value" method and the "internal rate of return" method.

Net Present Value Method

This method involves the comparison of future cash benefits or inflows, adjusted for the time value of money, against the initial investment or cost outlay. A discount rate must be specified under this method. Such a discount rate should reflect the cost of financing or a required rate of return.

Table 3-5 on page 54 illustrates the use of a worksheet for calculating the net present value method. The initial property investment or cost outlay is $8,500, with the minimum required rate of return being set at 10 percent. Cash benefits or inflows will occur for 5 years. However, since the yearly cash inflows are uneven, annual discount factors are taken from a "present worth of $1" table such as Table 3-2. The sum or total of the yearly cash flows discounted at a 10 percent rate equals $8,993.20 and is referred to as the present value of the cash inflows. Subtracting the investment or cost of $8,500.00 results in a difference or net present value of $493.20. A positive net present value implies that the rate of return is greater than 10 percent.

The net present value method does not usually permit the determination of interest rates or rates of return. In general, once a discount rate has been specified, this method allows us to say whether the rate of return is higher than the discount rate (a positive net present value)

Table 3-5 Net Present Value Method Worksheet

Date _____

Name _____   Property _____

Investment or Cost _____$8,500.00_____   _____

End of Year	Cash Flow	Discount at _10_ %		Discount at ___%		Discount at ___%	
		P.V. of $1	Amount	P.V. of $1	Amount	P.V. of $1	Amount
1	$2,000	.909	$1,818.00				
2	$2,400	.826	1,982.40				
3	$2,400	.751	1,802.40				
4	$2,600	.683	1,775.80				
5	$2,600	.621	1,614.60				
6							
7							
8							
9							
10							
Total			$8,993.20				
Less Cost			−8,500.00				
Net P.V.			$ 493.20				

or lower than the discount rate (a negative net present value). Negative net present values occur when the investment or cost is greater than the present value of the cash inflows. Of course, if the cost is exactly equal to the present value of the cash flows, then the rate of return equals the discount rate.

Internal Rate of Return Method

The internal rate of return method is directly related to the net present value method. However, instead of beginning with a specified discount rate, this method seeks to find the interest rate that makes the present value of cash inflows exactly equal to the initial investment or cost. That is, through a trial and error process we find the interest rate or discount rate that will result in a zero net present value.

The internal rate of return method can be illustrated by use of the same problem developed in Table 3-5. Assume that you can make an investment of $8,500 which will produce cash benefits or flows of $12,000 over the next five years. The individual end-of-year flows will be: year 1 ($2,000), year 2 ($2,400), year 3 ($2,400), year 4 ($2,600), and year 5 ($2,600). What interest rate or rate of return will you earn on the investment?

Table 3-6 illustrates the use of a worksheet for solving problems involving the use of the internal rate of return method. We begin by selecting what seems to be a reasonable discount rate. Let us assume that our first choice was 10 percent. This, of course, produces the same results as the net present value method since a 10 percent discount rate was specified in that example. We know that the interest rate or rate of return on the project is greater than 10 percent because of the $493.20 positive net present value. But how much greater?

In our trial and error process, we must now select a higher rate of discount. Assume that we decided to try 14 percent. The results for discounting at 14 percent, as shown in the middle of Table 3-6, indicate a *negative* net present value of $391.80. This indicates that the correct interest rate is between 10 percent and 14 percent. Working the problem with a 12 percent discount rate results in a net present value close to zero indicating that the rate of return is slightly greater than 12 percent.

Table 3-6   Internal Rate of Return Method Worksheet

Date _____

Name _____   Property _____

Investment or Cost _____   _____

End of Year	Cash Flow	Discount at 10 % P.V. of $1	Amount	Discount at 14 % P.V. of $1	Amount	Discount at 12 % P.V. of $1	Amount
1	$2,000	.909	$1,818.00	.877	$1,754.00	.893	$1,786.00
2	$2,400	.826	1,982.40	.769	1,845.60	.797	1,912.80
3	$2,400	.751	1,802.40	.675	1,620.00	.712	1,708.80
4	$2,600	.683	1,775.80	.592	1,539.20	.636	1,653.60
5	$2,600	.621	1,614.60	.519	1,349.40	.567	1,474.20
6							
7							
8							
9							
10							
Total			$8,993.20		$8,108.20		$8,535.40
Less Cost			−8,500.00		−8,500.00		−8,500.00
Net P.V.			$ 493.00		$ −391.80		$ 35.40

A more accurate measure of the internal rate of return can be gotten through the process of interpolation. Table 3-6 indicates that the return is between 12 and 14 percent and we interpolate as follows:

	Percentage Rate	P.V. of Cash Flows	Net P.V. for Smaller Discount Rate
Smaller	12.00	$8,535.40	
Larger	14.00	$8,108.20	
Absolute Difference	(2.00 ÷	$427.20) = .00468	× $35.40 = .17%

Adding the .17 percent to the 12 percent discount factor (i.e., the lower factor with a positive net present value) results in an internal rate of return of 12.17 percent.

REAL ESTATE FINANCE PROBLEMS AND TABLES

As can be seen from the previous discussion, a basic understanding of compound interest and discounting concepts permits calculation of a variety of different kinds of problems. In fact it is possible to develop standardized tables for handling specific real estate financing and investing problems. Following are some examples of standard real estate problems along with excerpts of several different tables.

Loan Amortization Payments

A common real estate finance problem involves determining periodic payments necessary to amortize or retire a loan over a given time period. For example, assume that you make an $8,200 loan at a 7 percent interest rate and want to pay it off in five annual payments. This is a present value of an annuity problem and it is like the one worked earlier in the chapter. We find the annual payment by dividing the $8,200 annuity by the present value annuity interest factor for 7 percent and 5 years (4.100 as shown in Table 3-4). This results in an annual payment of $2,000.

The annual payment involves principal (or amortization repayment) and interest components. And, since interest is paid on the unpaid balance, the mix between interest and principal changes over the life of the loan. A loan repayment schedule is illustrated in Table 3-7. The total annual payment is $2,000. Interest for the first year is $574 (i.e., $8,200 times .07) with the principal or amortization repayment being $1,426. Interest payments decline, while payments of principal increase, as the remaining balance declines toward zero. This, of course, illustrates the procedure for handling loans involving constant periodic cash flows.

Table 3-7 Loan Repayment Schedule

Year	Total Payment	Interest*	Amortization Repayment	Remaining Balance
1	$2,000	$ 574	$1,426	$6,774
2	2,000	474	1,526	5,248
3	2,000	367	1,633	3,615
4	2,000	253	1,747	1,868
5	2,000	132	1,868	0
Total	$10,000	$1,800	$8,200	

*Interest for the first year is 0.07 × $8,200 = 574, for the second year, 0.07 × $6,744 = 474, and so on.

Many loans require monthly rather than annual payments. While it is possible to calculate the monthly periodic payment, it often is easier to find the payment directly from monthly loan amortization payment tables. Table 3-8 is a partial table showing the monthly payments necessary to amortize a loan at 8 percent interest. For example, a $25,000 loan at 8 percent interest made for a 25-year period would require a monthly payment of $192.96. Table 5 in Appendix B contains monthly payments needed to amortize a $1,000 loan. It can be used to work this same problem. A slight rounding error from the use of Table 5 results in an estimated monthly payment of $193.00.

Table 3-8 Monthly Payments Necessary to Amortize a Loan at 8%

Amount	Term					
	5 Years	10 Years	15 Years	20 Years	25 Years	30 Years
$16,000	324.46	194.14	152.92	133.84	123.50	117.41
17,000	344.74	206.28	162.47	142.20	131.21	124.74
18,000	365.02	218.41	172.03	150.57	138.93	132.08
19,000	385.30	230.54	181.59	158.93	146.65	139.42
20,000	405.58	242.68	191.15	167.30	154.37	146.76
21,000	425.86	254.81	200.70	175.66	162.09	154.10
22,000	446.13	266.95	210.26	184.03	169.81	161.43
23,000	466.41	279.08	219.82	192.39	177.53	168.77
24,000	486.69	291.21	229.37	200.76	185.24	176.11
25,000	506.97	303.35	238.93	209.12	192.96	183.45
26,000	527.25	315.48	248.49	217.49	200.68	190.79
27,000	547.53	327.62	258.05	225.85	208.40	198.12
28,000	567.81	339.75	267.60	234.22	216.12	205.46
29,000	588.09	351.88	277.16	242.58	223.84	212.80
30,000	608.36	364.02	286.72	250.95	231.56	220.14

Annual Constant Concepts

An *annual constant* is defined as the sum of 12 monthly payments expressed as a percentage of a principal loan amount. For example, it takes a monthly payment of $12.13 to amortize a $1,000 loan for 10 years at 8 percent interest (this is calculated in Table 5 of Appendix B). Twelve times $12.13 equals $145.56 per year which is 14.56 percent of $1,000. Thus, the annual constant percentage is 14.56.

The basic formula for calculating annual constant percentages is:

Annual Constant = (12 × Monthly Payment × 100)/Loan Amount.

The 100 factor is used to express the annual constant in percentage form. As in other problems, we can solve for any of the three factors as long as we know the other two. For example, assume that you have $200 available for monthly payments. What is the maximum amount that can be borrowed for 10 years at an 8 percent interest rate? Table 3-9 is an abbreviated "constant annual percentage" table. We find the annual constant of 14.56 within the table at 10 years and 8 percent. Rearranging the annual constant formula results in (12 × $200 × 100)/14.56, indicating a maximum loan amount of $16,483.52. Annual constant percentages are provided in Table 6 in Appendix B.

Table 3-9 Annual Constant Percentages

Year	6%	7%	8%	9%	10%
1	103.30	103.84	104.39	104.95	105.50
2	53.19	53.73	54.28	54.82	55.37
3	36.51	37.06	37.61	38.16	38.72
4	28.19	28.74	29.30	29.86	30.44
5	23.20	23.76	24.33	24.91	25.50
6	19.89	20.46	21.04	21.63	22.23
7	17.53	18.11	18.70	19.31	19.92
8	15.77	16.36	16.96	17.58	18.21
9	14.41	15.01	15.62	16.25	16.89
10	13.32	13.93	14.56	15.20	15.86

Let us try another problem involving the use of annual constant percentage tables. Assume that you want to amortize a $10,000 loan over 9 years by making equal monthly payments of $125. What would be the interest rate on the loan? Using the annual constant formula we have: (12 × $125 × 100)/$10,000 = 15.00. Then we search for the 15.00 annual constant factor in Table 3-9. Looking at the 9-year row, read across until an annual constant close to 15.00 is found. This occurs at the 7 percent column which is the interest rate on the loan.

Remaining Loan Balances

In a variety of real estate finance problems it is important to know the remaining balance on a loan that has been outstanding for a period of time. For example, the problem described in Table 3-7 requires an annual payment of interest and principal of $2,000 over five years to pay off an $8,200, 7 percent loan. At the end of one year the remaining loan balance is $6,774 because of a payment of principal (amortization repayment) totaling $1,426. The remaining loan balance as a percentage of the original loan amount after one year is 82.6 percent (6,774/$8,200). The percentage relationship at the end of two years is 64.0 percent ($5,248/$8,200). This greater drop in the remaining balance is due to the declining interest payments over the life of the loan.

While the remaining balance on a specific loan could be calculated by preparing a loan repayment schedule similar to the one presented in Table 3-7, standardized (i.e., stated as a percentage of the original loan amount) remaining loan balances are available. Table 7 in Appendix B contains remaining loan balances for selected interest rates, loan lives, and loan ages involving monthly fixed payments. For example, let's assume that you want to know the remaining balance on a $10,000, 9 percent, 20-year mortgage loan requiring monthly payments; the loan has been outstanding for five years. The appropriate percentage factor from Table 6 in Appendix B is 88.7 percent. Thus, the remaining balance on the $10,000 mortgage loan after five years would be $8,870.

Other Problems

A number of additional problems will be introduced throughout this text. However, the understanding of these later problems should be made easier now that basic compounding and discounting concepts have been identified and discussed. Knowledge of investment evaluation methods and available real estate finance tables also will be useful in future chapters.

QUESTIONS FOR REVIEW

1. (a) Explain what is meant by compounding an investment made now. Be sure to include the relevant variables and what they mean.
   (b) Explain what is meant by determining the present worth of a future value. Be sure to include the relevant variables and what they mean.
   (c) What is an annuity and how is it compounded and discounted?
2. What is the mathematical relationship between the present value and the compound value?

3. Explain the use of the following investment evaluation techniques and state exactly what each one tells you: (a) net present value method, (b) internal rate of return method.
4. What do the annual loan amortization payments include and what is the relative relation between these elements as the remaining balance declines?
5. What is an annual constant and how is it determined?

PROBLEMS

1. How many years will it take $600 invested now at 6% to reach $1,200? Determine by using (a) the present value relation, and (b) the compound value relation.
2. What is the present value of $1,120 to be received 6 years from now with an interest of 7%? Can you determine this from the compound sum table?
3. What would be the annual payments necessary to amortize a $20,000 mortgage in 15 years at 7% interest?
4. As an investor in real estate you have an option to buy one of two properties. Property A costs $50,000 and expects to have cash inflows for the next five years of $15,000, $23,000, $15,000, $5,000, and $5,000. Property B also costs $50,000 and expects five-year cash inflows of $5,000, $15,000, $15,000, $20,000, and $20,000. If you require a 10% rate of return, which, if either, investment would you choose? Determine first by the net present value method. What are the actual rates of return on these investments?

Seller Financing of Real Property

Chapter 4

In many cases, it may not only be convenient for the seller to do the financing, but it may be necessary. The need for the seller to do the financing most often arises because financial institutions may shy away from the deal due to a lack of good credit on the part of the buyer or because of a "tight" money situation. In addition, there may be legal restrictions placed on the institutions for that particular type loan. Often a seller may decide to do the financing simply to earn the interest to be paid by the buyer.

THE PURCHASE MONEY MORTGAGE (OR DEED OF TRUST)

In a simple transaction assume a seller agrees to sell property to a buyer for $30,000 with the buyer paying $5,000 and the seller "taking back" a mortgage or deed of trust for $25,000. This is done by means of a purchase money mortgage (purchase money deed of trust).

A *purchase money mortgage* is a mortgage that is given as part of the consideration for the sale of real property. The seller is really financing or partially financing the transaction. In this case the seller receives $5,000 from the buyer, and "takes back" a mortgage in the amount of $25,000. It should be remembered that a purchase money mortgage becomes a purchase money mortgage because it is created by spelling it out in the mortgage instrument. In short, a statement that it is a purchase money mortgage must be written into the instrument. It is sometimes called colloquially a "P.M." mortgage.

The Purchase Money Clause

A clause spelling out the existence of the P.M. mortgage and the method of payment is added after the property description:

Being the same premises which were conveyed by the mortgagor by deed dated March 13, 19–– and delivered and intended to be recorded simultaneously herewith, this mortgage being given to secure a portion of the purchase money or consideration for which the said conveyance was made.

Need for Delivery of Deed

In the clause above note that it states that the mortgage was given and a deed delivered *simultaneously*. The reason for this is that in order to effectuate a purchase money mortgage a crucial condition must be met; namely, that the mortgage is given at the same time the property is acquired and as a *part* of the entire transaction.

Priority of the Purchase Money Mortgage

The real reason for the simultaneous delivery of deed and the mortgaging is due to the P.M. mortgage's superiority in the priority of liens. Ordinarily it takes preference over all other existing and subsequent claims and liens against and through the borrower. This is because the mortgage is really a limitation on the borrower's title rather than a limitation on the land.[1]

Warrant of Title Clause in the Purchase Money Mortgage

All the forms of mortgage previously discussed contain a clause warranting title. This states in effect that the mortgagor warrants title to the premises and that the title is good. This means that the property is free from encumbrances according to the mortgagor's declarations. When the seller "takes back" the purchase money mortgage, the seller signs and delivers the deed to the purchaser, who is the mortgagor. The mortgagor delivers such cash as is being paid to the seller and at the same time signs and delivers the purchase money mortgage to the seller, who is the mortgagee. This exchange raises the question of what should be done with the "warrant of title clause" in the mortgage. Conceivably, the mortgagee (who is the seller in this case) may have a defective title which may be transferred over to the mortgagor (the purchaser); now the purchaser is placed in the position of the warrantor of title as a result of the clause in the mortgage. To avoid this situation, the warrant of title clause should be supplanted with a clause stating that the mortgagor warrants only such title as has been conveyed by the mortgagee. The net effect of this is that the burden of

---

[1]Many states provide for the purchase money mortgagee's priority over liens by statute. In New York, for example, the statute makes the P.M. mortgage superior to the lien of a previous judgment against the mortgagor.

"good title" has been passed back to the seller (mortgagee), who is the logical defender of the title.

Use of the Purchase Money Mortgage By Builders

Often a combination blanket purchase money mortgage containing a partial release clause is the favorite instrument of the builder who operates with little cash and who can't afford to tie up capital in land. For example, A is a builder and B has 100 lots for sale. A arranges a transaction with B that requires very little cash down. After A has gone to a bank and has received a tentative commitment for a construction loan, A approaches B and offers $1,000 per lot. A proposes to B to pay $100 cash down for each of the lots and to give B a blanket purchase money mortgage covering $900.00 per lot for the balance due. This is accepted by B. A insists that the mortgage contain a partial release clause to the effect that upon the payment of $900, B will release from the terms of the mortgage any one of the lots that A desires. B agrees to all of this, and A pays out only 10 percent cash at this point, begins building, and obtains a commitment from a bank. When A has built enough of the house to satisfy the bank appraiser, B is paid for one lot (the $900 due), and A receives cash from the bank, finishes the building, and sells it for a profit.

This hypothetical problem is, of course, an oversimplification, but not completely. The only variations in the figures given would depend upon the bargaining position of the parties. A, the builder, might have to put down more than 10 percent cash, but, in the final analysis, it can be done with very little money.

The practitioner will recognize at once that there are "two sides to every coin." If the seller and the builder do make a deal as far as a price is concerned, should the seller draw up the partial release clause releasing one lot for the payment of the balance due on that one lot? It is thought that it might offer more protection to the seller to have A, the builder and mortgagee, pay off, let us say, $1,000 on each lot released, the extra $100 to be applied toward the payment of the principal on the balance of the mortgage. This would mean that the entire balance would be completely paid after which the remainder of the lots would be released from the terms of the mortgage. It might be stated here that the seller should take another precautionary measure in the transaction outlined above.

As all practitioners know, different lots in a block have a different value as a general rule; hence, the partial release clause should be drawn in terms of at least two lots being paid for in full by the purchaser and released at the same time. One lot will be considered to be of greater value than the other. This will effectively avoid the seller's being "stuck" with the poorer lots in the event the builder becomes financially embarrassed before the mortgage has been completely paid.

The Partial Release

The *partial release* is the instrument that is employed to release part of the mortgaged premises from the terms of the mortgage. It simply recites the mortgage, the amount paid for the release, and a description of the part of the mortgaged premises that has been released. The instrument is acknowledged and recorded in the office of the county clerk in the county in which the property is located.[2] The effect of this instrument is that part of the property so released is no longer subject to the mortgage. The owner may then, if desired, obtain a new mortgage on the parcel so released.

A partial release is shown on page 65.

THE INSTALLMENT LAND CONTRACT

The *installment land contract* was historically used in the sale of vacant lots, generally with a small down payment and small monthly payments until the balance was paid. After the final payment a deed is delivered to the buyer. Under such an agreement the seller retains title to the property. In this sense it differs from the purchase money mortgage where title is delivered to the buyer at the time of the execution of the agreement.

Over time the installment land contract began to be used to finance homes, vacant land, and particularly farms and ranches. In practice the instrument began to be called "contract for deed," "land contract," and even "real estate contract." This sort of careless usage often confused it with the simple Contract for the Sale of Real Property or Purchase Agrement.

An installment land contract is shown on pages 66–67.

The Installment Land Contract Must be a Valid Contract

An installment land contract is governed by the law of contract. It is an agreement resulting from an offer and acceptance. The parties must be identified and competent. There must be genuine assent (this means no fraud, duress, undue influence, or mistake). The subject matter must be identified and the terms definite and certain. There must be consideration. Because it is a contract for the sale of land the Statute of Frauds must be satisfied.

---

[2]In Connecticut the instrument is recorded in the office of the Town Clerk.

RELEASE OF PART OF MORTGAGED PREMISES

WHEREAS Joan Mortgagor, by indenture of mortgage, bearing date the 1st day of June, 19--, and recorded in the office of the clerk of the County of   Brown   in Liber 1414 in Mortgages page 567 on the 3rd day of June, 19-- , for the consideration therein mentioned, and to secure the payment of the money therein specified, did mortgage certain lands and tenements of which the lands hereinafter described are part, unto
Richard Mortgagee,

This indenture made the 16th day of March, nineteen hundred and . . . between Richard Mortgagee party of the first part and Joan Mortgagor party of the second part,

AND WHEREAS, the party of the first part, at the request of the party of the second part, has agreed to give up and surrender the lands hereinafter described unto the party of the second part, and to hold and retain the residue of the mortgaged lands as security for the money remaining due on said mortgage.

NOW THIS INDENTURE WITNESSETH, that the party of the first part in pursuance of said agreement, and in consideration of   One Hundred Fifty and 00/100 ($150) - - - - - - - - - Dollars, lawful money of the United States, paid by the party of the second part, does grant, release and quitclaim unto the party of the second part, all that part of said mortgaged lands described as follows:

Lots number 1 and number 2, of the Map of Security Acres Development Company, surveyed by James Jones April 3, 1964, and Filed in the office of the Clerk of the County of Brown, August 7, 1964.

Together with the hereditaments and appurtenances thereunto belonging and all the right, title and interest of the party of the first part, of, in and to the same, to the intent that the lands hereby released may be discharged from said mortgage, and that the rest of the land in said mortgage specified may remain mortgaged to the party of the first part as heretofore.

To have and to hold the lands and premises hereby released and quitclaimed by the party of the second part, his heirs and assigns to his and their own proper use, benefit and behoof forever, free, clear and discharged of and from all lien and claim under and by virtue of the indenture of mortgage aforesaid.

IN WITNESS WHEREOF, the party of the first part has signed and sealed these presents the day and year first above written.

IN PRESENCE OF:

/s/ Richard Roe   /s/ Richard Mortgagee

STATE OF   Ohio   **, COUNTY OF**   Brown
ss.:

On the 16th day of March, 19-- , before me personally came   Richard Mortgagee   to me known to be the individual described in and who executed the foregoing instrument, and acknowledged that   he   executed the same.

/s/ Richard Roe
Notary Public

**Figure
4-1**   Release of Part of Mortgaged Premises

The following is a simplified form of Contract For Deed or Installment Land Contract. It can, of course, be more complex than the illustration. In all cases an attorney should be consulted and actually prepare the contract.

CONTRACT FOR DEED

This contract for deed entered into this   3rd   day of   June , 19-- by and between Jane Doe, residing at   1411 Mason Ct, Dayton, Ohio   , party of the first part, and J. J. DeFoe, party of the second part residing at   501 Marycrest Lane, Dayton, Ohio

Witnesseth:

That for and in consideration of the payments hereinafter agreed to be made and the mutual covenants hereinafter set forth, the party of the first part agrees to sell and convey to the party of the second part, by good and sufficient warranty deed, the following described property to wit:

(Property description goes here).

The party of the second part agrees to purchase the above described property for the sum of   Twenty Thousand Dollars ($20,000.00)   , said amount to be paid in the following manner:

The sum of Six Thousand Dollars ($6,000.00) on signing of this agreement, receipt of which is hereby acknowledged.

The sum of One Thousand Dollars ($1,000.00) on or before November 1, 19--.

The balance of Thirteen Thousand Dollars ($13,000.00) to be paid in annual installments of Twenty-four Hundred Dollars ($2,400.00) each, the first installment to be paid on the 1st day of November, 19-- and the 1st day of November each year thereafter. It is agreed that the annual payment shall include interest at 8 percent per annum.

It is agreed that the party of the second part is to have the privilege of prepaying any part of the unpaid balance at any time during the contract period without penalty.

It is agreed that the party of the second part shall have possession of the above described property from and after the date hereof.

It is agreed that the party of the second part is to pay all taxes levied upon said property prior to delinquency.

It is understood that the party of the first part has executed a good and sufficient Warranty Deed granting and conveying the above described property to the party of the second part and that said deed, a copy of this contract, and the Abstract of Title to the above premises, continued to date and showing merchantable title to the premises to be vested in the party of the first part free of encumbrances will be placed in escrow (name of escrow agent) and that said escrow agent acting as agent for both parties is instructed to deliver said deed and abstract to the party of the second part upon receipt of final payment as recited herein. It is further agreed that the second party shall have the right to examine said abstract at any time within ninety days after the date hereof and should said examination disclose any defect the first party shall take immediate steps to correct such defect or defects.

In the event the party of the second part shall default in the performance of any of the terms, convenants, conditions or obligations of this agreement assumed by

Figure 4-2   Installment Land Contract (Continued)

the party of the second part, the parties agree that the party of the first part shall have the option to declare all deferred balances due and payable. Said option shall be exercisable by giving to the party of the second part at his address in   Dayton, Ohio , by certified mail, thirty days written notice of the nature of such default. In the event of the failure of the party of the first part to cure such default within such thirty-day period, then all such deferred balances shall be due and payable at the end of such thirty-day period, the parties of the first part shall have the right to retake possession of the property described above and to retain all payments made by the party of the second part and all improvements made by them in the premises as liquidated damages for the breach of this agreement, accurate damages being incapable of ascertainment.

It is mutually agreed by and between the parties hereto that time of payment shall be an essential part of this agreement and that all the covenants and agreements herein contained shall be binding on the heirs, executors, administrators, and assigns of the respective parties.

In witness whereof, both parties have hereunto set their hands and seals the day and year first above written.

_____/s/ Jane Doe_____ L.S.

_____/s/ J. J. DeFoe_____ L.S.

(Acknowledgment)

Figure 4-2 Installment Land Contract (Concluded)

The Statute of Frauds

The _Statute of Frauds_ involves contracts which must be in writing to be enforceable. One section of the statute requires that contracts relating to real property must be in writing in order to be enforceable. If A agrees with B to purchase a lead pencil for the price of $1 and A agrees orally to deliver the pencil and then fails to do so, B may bring an action against A for any damages suffered.

If the same situation takes place, except that the oral agreement contemplates the transfer of _real property_ rather than personal property, and A fails to keep the bargain, B will be unable to bring a successful action against A, for oral contracts concerning many real estate transactions are void under the Statute of Frauds.

For example, Section 259 of the New York Real Property Law is as follows:

> A contract for the leasing for a longer period than one year, or for the sale of any real property or an interest therein, is void unless the contract, or some note or memorandum thereof, expressing the consideration, is in writing, subscribed by the party to be charged, or by his lawful agent, thereunto authorized in writing.

The other states' statutes are substantially the same.

Of what then must this memorandum in writing consist to render a contract for the sale of real property enforceable? There are four things that must be done to bring the contract for the sale of real property into compliance with the Statute of Frauds. The memorandum must have a date, the terms of payment, a description of the property, and it must bear the signature of the party to be charged. The party to be *charged* is the person against whom the suit is brought. In practice both parties generally sign because no one knows ahead of time who is going to sue whom if it comes to that.

Uses of the Installment Land Contract

The installment land contract is used by builders in one of three ways: (1) to finance a subdivision; (2) to finance the sale of homes; and (3) for additional financing.

In the first instance, a builder will buy developed vacant lots from a subdivider under a blanket land contract. The down payment is generally minimal. The builder who has a line of credit with a commercial bank borrows most of the construction costs, builds the home, and then sells it. At the time of the sale the improved lot is paid for and is released from the terms of the contract. In this way the builder avoids having to have the money with which to buy the vacant land and the money necessary to put in roads, sewers, and so forth.

Builders and individual sellers often use the installment land contract to finance the sale of homes. For example, A desires to purchase a home and has insufficient funds for the down payment satisfactory to a financial institution. The builder or owner may enter into an installment contract with A providing that, when enough has been paid on the contract to satisfy a lending institution, the balance of the purchase price will be financed by an FHA loan or other suitable loan.

The question is why would a builder or individual seller do this? Obviously most builders would prefer to have the buyer pay the down payment and have an instituion lend the buyer the balance. In the above case the builder would be "out" the money. If a builder has failed to arrange for permanent financing and a tight money situation arises, the builder may be unable to arrange for a financial institution loan. At the same time the builder has to pay interest on the construction loan on the property, and paying this sort of interest can be a disaster to a builder. The builder reasons that if sales cannot be made on a contract, at least the interest paid on the contract by the buyer will be enough to pay the interest on the construction loan.

In the last case, builders sometimes use contracts for additional financing. Although some builders have a strong line of credit with financial institutions, many do not. Thus, the installment land contract is used as collateral for personal notes; i.e., a builder may borrow additional sums by pledging installment land contracts in a portfolio.

Installment Contract Used to Defer Taxes

Some individuals may use the installment land contract for tax purposes. The sale may qualify under the IRS regulations as an "installment sale" if two requirements are met: (1) there is no down payment in the year of the sale (other than the original down payment); and (2) payments in the year of the sale do not exceed 30 percent of the selling price and payments are made in two or more installments.

Installment Contract Used in the Sale of Farms and Ranches

Financial institutions, for the most part, tend to shy away from farm and ranch financing. What little farm and ranch financing is done by institutions is hardly ever done with greater than a 60 percent loan-to-value ratio. For example, a 100-cow ranch, by a very rough rule of thumb appraisal, is worth $120,000. With a 60 percent loan-to-value ratio this means institutions are reluctant to lend more than $72,000, requiring a substantial down payment of $48,000. This makes the property difficult to sell. Furthermore, many ranches on today's market were bought by "old timers" who would rather sell on an installment sale for tax purposes. This results in the extensive use of the installment land contract in farm and ranch sales with its smaller down payment, interest to the seller, and a tax advantage to the seller.

COMMON CLAUSES IN AN INSTALLMENT LAND CONTRACT

The clauses in an installment land contract are much the same as in the mortgage. For example, the buyer promises to pay the indebtedness, taxes, and insurance; keep the premises in good repair; and not commit waste.

Furthermore, the buyer agrees that upon default all payments previously made are forfeited. Because of the severity of this penalty, many states prohibit strict forfeiture. This topic is discussed in greater detail in Chapter 16.

The Mortgage Clause

This clause permits the seller to mortgage the property for an amount not to exceed the contract balance, in which case the mortgage is given priority over the contract. For example, the buyer owes the seller $50,000 on the contract. The seller may mortgage this for $50,000. If the seller defaults, the argument is that the buyer will not be hurt because the buyer can pay off the $50,000 due the seller on the mortgage.

Escrow Provision

Most installment land contracts should contain an escrow provision. *Escrow* may be defined as a scroll, writing, or deed delivered by the grantor into the hands of a third person to be held by the latter until the happening of a contingency or the performance of a condition, and then delivered by the third person to a grantee.[3]

The escrow clause in the contract states:

> The seller within . . . days from the date of this contract will deposit in escrow with . . . (the name of the escrowee is entered here), a good and sufficient deed together with an executed copy of this contract and such other documents including abstract of title or title insurance policy and fire insurance policies which shall pertain to this contract, to be by such escrow agent held in escrow until the terms of this contract shall be completely executed, or until default is made under the same. The terms of such deposit in escrow shall be given by separate escrow agreement to be at the said time executed.

The escrow agent, who is usually a bank or the escrow department of a brokerage firm or title insurance firm, is paid a fee for holding the instruments in escrow. The agent collects the monthly or annual payments on the contract from the purchaser and turns the receipts over to the seller.

From the viewpoint of the buyer it is most important that the deed signed by both husband and wife (if the sellers are married) be placed in escrow. There are three main reasons for this: (1) in case of divorce either or both parties may refuse to sign the deed, which can result in costly and time-consuming litigation; (2) in the event of the death of the seller or sellers the property can be tied up in an estate settlement; and (3) if one of the sellers is a wife, she may refuse to release her dower interests, if any, after final payment has been made.

Once an escrow agent is decided upon, the installment land contract, together with a deed, is sent to the escrow agent. This is done by means of a Letter of Transmittal which is shown in Figure 4-3.

Recording of Installment Land Contracts

An instrument affecting the title to land may be recorded in all states. In so doing notice is given to the "world" of the existence of the contract. In order to record the contract it must be acknowledged; that

---

[3]Like the term "contract" or "agreement to purchase," the word *escrow* has many meanings. In California and Nevada, in addition to the escrow provision in an installment land contract, escrow means something quite different. In those two states it is a step in a real estate transaction. Once a binding contract exists the parties "open an escrow." The escrow agent has the transfer documents drawn, cash is impounded for future delivery, demands are made on existing loans, title is examined, and if necessary cleared, and prorations are calculated. Finally the deal is closed by transfer of title.

LETTER OF TRANSMITTAL

To _____ Date _____

_____ Net Escrow $_____

_____

_____ as SELLERS,

whose address is _____ and

_____ as BUYERS,

whose address is _____

hereby employ the organization named above to act as Escrow Agent.

We hand you herewith the following papers and documents as checked:

_____ Warranty Deed	_____ Mortgage
_____ Quit Claim Deed	_____ Release of Mortgage
_____ Contract for Deed	_____ Bill of Sale
_____ Abstract	_____ Insurance Policy
_____ Note	_____ Misc. Papers (Itemize Below)

_____

_____

Description of Property _____
(Full Legal Not Necessary)

_____

Terms of Sale: Gross Sale Price $_____; Down Payment $_____;

Unpaid Balance $_____; Interest Starts: _____;

Manner of Payment: _____

_____

_____

Special Provisions: (If any) _____

_____

Proceeds to be _____

BUYER and SELLER agree to pay herewith an Escrow Fee of $_____ and SELLER agrees to pay $_____ per payment thereafter until fully paid and authorize Escrow Agent to deduct this amount from proceeds.

SELLER agrees that the escrow agent is authorized to affix revenue stamps in the sum of $_____ and deduct same from the last payment before delivery of deed.

BUYER and SELLER agree that "The escrow agent's sole responsibilities hereunder are to keep safely the documents entrusted to it and to account for and remit moneys paid to it less its agreed fee. The escrow agent shall not be responsible for:

(a) Payment of taxes;
(b) Payment of liability or hazard insurance;
(c) Giving notice of nonpayment to any party;

Figure 4-3   Letter of Transmittal (Continued)

(d) Safekeeping of abstract removed at request of either party;
(e) Recording of contract."

BUYER _____   SELLER _____
BUYER _____   SELLER _____

Receipt of above papers and escrow fee of $ _____
acknowledged this _____ day of _____ 19_____.

_____
_____
Authorized Signature

Figure
4-3 Letter of Transmittal (Concluded)

is, the signature of the seller and buyer must be done before a notary public or other authorized official.

From the viewpoint of the buyer it should be recorded because it provides a greater degree of protection.

Effect of Judgments on Installment Land Contracts

Naturally any judgment of record against the seller prior to the contract is a lien upon any land held by the seller. However, any judgment filed after the contract does not become a lien on the buyer's real estate even though legal title is still in the name of the seller. This is especially true after the contract has been recorded.

The argument is that the judgment creditor can be paid through court action as the buyer makes payments to the seller.

"Interest Only" Land Contracts

Such a contract is often used in the sale of vacant land where the seller finances the transaction either with a land contract or a purchase money mortgage (deed of trust).

Suppose, for example, you have 20 acres of raw land and you are really not hurting for cash. You advertise the property, "no down payment, interest only." To begin with, because there is no down payment, you can probably charge an interest rate somewhat higher than the market rate. In addition, you may be able to charge somewhat higher than the going price for the land.

In these cases, most of the buyers are speculators who hope to sell to developers in the near future. Say you want $5,000 per acre and "interest only" for three years at 9 percent. Then the selling price is $100,000 covered by a mortgage and interest at $9,000 per year. Your buyer during the three-year period attempts to sell the land at a profit. If the buyer fails to do so, or fails to pay the interest, you may foreclose.

As a practical matter, this sort of buyer will probably give you a deed in lieu of foreclosure to avoid the additional expense of foreclosure.

The Option As a Seller's Financing Method

Simply put, an *option* is a contract to keep an offer open. Because an option is a contract a seller cannot withdraw an offer until after the time stipulated in the contract. An option is shown on page 74.

Use of Option by Builders

Frequently a small builder will operate by means of an option taken on a relatively small number of lots. The builder will do this when uncertain whether the houses will sell readily and when the builder wishes or needs to remain in a financially liquid position. For example, if there are ten lots in which a builder is interested, one lot can be purchased outright and an option obtained from the seller on the other nine. After the first house is built and sold the builder may, if the first house was profitable, exercise the option on the other nine lots.

In a situation of this type, the seller should, depending upon bargaining position, insist that the builder exercise the option on at least two lots at a time. If the lots vary in their price because some are more valuable than others, the owner might examine the possibility of the optionee's exercising the option on a high-priced lot and a low-priced lot at the same time. Otherwise, the builder might just exercise the option on the choice lots and leave the seller with the poorer lots. This is particularly applicable in a situation where there is a flat price per lot. If the purchaser exercises the option only on the choice lots, the seller would be left in an unprofitable position if the builder discontinues the operation.

The Rolling Option

Many of the larger developers and subdividers use what they have labeled "the rolling option." It is simply a device to free capital and minimize risk. For example, a subdivider may have in mind to subdivide 150 acres. The subdivider may choose to purchase the 150 acres and subdivide it all at one time. However, if this is done, a large amount of capital is tied up and the subdivider faces a risk of loss in the event the project fails. Consequently, to avoid this risk the subdivider simply enters into an option agreement with the seller of the land which could be substantially as follows: 50 acres are purchased

OPTION TO PURCHASE

THIS INDENTURE, made the 10th day of July , 19-- , between John Smith , residing at 4250 Maple Blvd., Denver, Colorado , party of the first part, and William Jones , residing at 923 Austin Drive, Denver, Colorado , party of the second part,

WITNESSETH:

IN CONSIDERATION of the sum of $5,000 paid by the party of the second part to the party of the first part, receipt whereof is hereby acknowledged, the party of the first part hereby grants, bargains, and sells to the party of the second part his heirs, executors, administrators, successors and assigns, the exclusive option to purchase the premises known as 109 Broadway, Denver, Colorado , more particularly described in the form of agreement hereto annexed and made a part hereof,[1]

UPON THE FOLLOWING TERMS AND CONDITIONS:

FIRST: This option and all rights and privileges hereunder shall expire on the 10th day of August , 19-- , at 5 o'clock P.M.

SECOND: This option is to be exercised by the party of the second part by written notice subscribed by the party of the second part, sent by registered mail, within the time set herein for the exercise of this option, to the address of the party of the first part above set forth.

THIRD: The total purchase price shall be the sum of $5,000 to be paid by the party of the second part, if this option is exercised, as provided in the said annexed form of agreement the sum paid for this option shall be credited on account of the cash payment to be made on closing title as provided in the said annexed form of agreement.

FOURTH: In the event that the party of the second part does not exercise this option as herein provided the said sum of $5,000 shall be retained by the party of the first part free of all claim of the party of the second part and neither party shall have any further rights or claims against the other.

FIFTH: In the event that this option is exercised as herein provided, the party of the first part and the party of the second part will respectively as Seller and Purchaser, perform the obligations stated in the annexed form of agreement to be performed by the Seller and Purchaser therein.

SIXTH: This option and all rights hereunder shall be freely assignable, and if assigned by the party of the second part, any and all acts performable by him hereunder (including the execution and delivery of the purchase money bond and mortgage) may be performed by any assignee, whether such assignment be before or after the exercise of this option.

IN WITNESS WHEREOF the party of the first part has signed and sealed this indenture the day and year first above written.

/s/ John Smith L.S.

In the presence of

/s/ Janet Nathan

(ACKNOWLEDGMENT)

[1]A contract for sale of real property, complete except for execution, is annexed to the option.

**Figure
4-4** Option to Purchase

outright and an option is given to buy the second 50 within a stated time; then the subdivider has a further option to buy the third 50-acre tract within a stated time. Thus, if the subdivider fails on the first 50-acre tract project, there is no obligation to buy the second or third 50-acre tracts. If things go well, the whole tract will be subdivided, with options exercised as needed.

Use of Option by Speculators

Speculators frequently use an option. For example, suppose you see a property you believe to be underpriced. Say it's $20,000 and you really think you can resell it for $30,000. Instead of buying it for $20,000 and freezing that much capital you can get an option on the property. If you succeed, you then may get a buyer for $30,000. In this case you simply assign the option to the buyer and the buyer exercises the option. The buyer pays you $10,000 and pays the optioner $20,000 totaling $30,000 in return for a deed. Your profit is $10,000 minus the cost of the option.

As a general rule the longer the option the more you have to pay for it.

Lease with Option to Buy

Often, when a tenant erects a building upon the premises owned by the landlord, the lease contains an option giving the tenant the right to purchase the improvement and the land at the end of the term. The option may state a price to be paid for the property, or the option may provide that if the lessor and the lessee are unable to negotiate a price, then the lessor and the lessee shall each appoint an appraiser. The appraisers shall then appoint an umpire. Each of the appraisers and the umpire appraise the property. In general, the lease states that the decision of any two appraisers (one of whom is the umpire) as to the price shall be binding on the parties. In the event that the third party then refuses to accept the decision of the other two, it has been held in most states that the proper remedy for the enforcement of the option to purchase at an appraised valuation is by specific performance.

The lease with option to buy is sometimes used as a financing device in the purchase of a residence. For example, the price of the home is agreed upon at $25,000. The tenant moves in under a lease and is given an option to buy the home at the $25,000, provided the option is exercised within a stated time. The tenant also agrees to pay rent. More often than not an agreed percentage of the rent is applied to the $25,000 purchase price.

QUESTIONS FOR REVIEW

1. What is a purchase money mortgage? Briefly describe some of the important characteristics of such a mortgage.
2. Describe how builders make use of the purchase money mortgage.
3. How does an installment land contract differ from a mortgage and from a deed of trust?
4. The installment land contract can be used by builders in three basic ways. Discuss.
5. A number of clauses are contained in an installment land contract. Briefly explain (a) the mortgage clause, and (b) the escrow provision.
6. Briefly describe (a) an "interest only" land contract, and (b) the concept of an option.

PROBLEMS

1. Assume that you sell property valued at $40,000. The buyer makes a down payment of $10,000 and you "take back" a mortgage for $30,000. How should this be handled? Draw the clause necessary to spell out such an arrangement.

2. Mr. Richards is a builder, who like many other smaller builders, has limited cash resources. Ms. Williams has 20 lots for sale at $4,000 per lot. However, Mr. Richards has only $12,000 available for the purchase of land. What can Mr. Richards do or propose in order to begin constructing homes?

3. Farm and ranch financing is often difficult to obtain. In addition, loan-to-value ratios tend to be much lower than those for financing homes. If a loan-to-value ratio is set at 60 percent, how could a ranch appraised at $150,000 be purchased? Could you purchase the ranch with a $40,000 down payment? Why might the seller be interested in entering into an installment land contract?

Financing by Junior Liens

The general rule regarding the priority of liens is "first in time, first in right." This refers to time of recording the instrument, not the length of time of the instrument. For example, if *A* gives a mortgage to *B* today and another to *C* tomorrow, if *C* records prior to *B*, then *C* has the first lien. Subsequent recording by *B* gives *B* the second or junior lien. In the absence of fraud, *C* will win over *B*. *B*, of course, may have a legal cause of action against *A*.

THE JUNIOR LIEN AS A FINANCING DEVICE

The junior or second mortgage (deed of trust, or second land contract) is used as a financing device in both residential and commercial real property transactions.

Use in Residential Transactions

Where financing is difficult because of a tight money situation, the seller might take a second mortgage. In this sort of situation, interest rates shoot up and money is hard to obtain.

Suppose a seller purchased a home for $30,000 some years ago with a 7¾ percent loan. The balance due on the loan has been reduced to $25,000. In the meantime, the home has increased in value to $37,500. This means a prospective buyer has to put down $12,500 ($37,500 purchase price — $25,000 indebtedness) if the first mortgage is assumable. Even if the buyer could obtain institutional financing, the interest rate could be as high as 9.5 percent in addition to, say, 10 percent down, or $3,750.

The seller could permit the buyer to make a $3,750 down payment (or more if possible) and take back a second purchase money mortgage for five years. A further stipulation could be that at the end of the five-year period, the buyer would refinance the property and pay off the second mortgage. The second mortgage is also often used where the property does not meet the lending requirements of a particular financial institution.

The seller in this type situation often is able to convert the profit on the home sale into an installment sale for tax purposes. This may be more financially advantageous than paying a long-term capital gains tax.

It would be naive not to realize that where a seller uses a junior lien, the price of the home frequently is "jacked up." For example, rather than sell the home in the example above at the $37,500 fair market value, the seller may price it at $38,000. The seller would argue that this is justified because the buyer is saving interest on the 7¾ percent loan assumption rather than paying 9.5 percent on a new loan. It could be further argued that in order to "cash out" on the transaction the seller would be forced to discount "the second mortgage."

Discounting

There are several meanings to the term "discounting." To avoid confusion, it would seem appropriate to discuss them here. In one sense a *discount* is an amount deducted in advance from a principal sum before the borrower is given the use of the principal. The problem arises from having a fixed rate of interest on some "paper" being offered investors in a market where "the" interest rate is over the fixed rate. For example, suppose the fixed rate on an FHA-insured mortgage is 8 percent and the market rate is 9 percent. Assume A has a home eligible for a $25,000 FHA mortgage. If the market rate is 9 percent, an institution will refuse to make a loan at 8 percent. Consequently, the seller, A, in order to sell the home, must be willing to discount the mortgage to obtain the FHA mortgage for B, the buyer. Assume the discount rate is 3 points or 3 percent. Then at the sale, (1) A receives $24,250 from the loan proceeds ($25,000 − $750 discount); (2) B pays back the entire $25,000 plus interest; and (3) the institution receives $750 it actually did not lend out, plus interest on the $750, plus $24,250 it did lend out, plus interest on the $24,250.

In the final analysis, this part of discount tends to equate the 8 percent final yield with the 9 percent market yield. And it is, in this situation, paid by the seller.

In dealing with second mortgages, the term "discount" can be thought of in the sense of discounting almost anything — a percentage "off the top" as it were. I own a bicycle worth $100. I offer it to you at a 10 percent discount or $90. And so it is with second mortgages.

For example, A is the owner of a second mortgage bearing a face value of $10,000 with interest at 8 percent for 10 years. A offers the mortgage for sale to B at $9,000. Put another way, it is offered for sale at a discount off the face value of 10 percent, more commonly referred to as a "10-point" discount. If it were discounted at 5 percent, it would be called a "5-point" discount, and so forth.

Yields

This raises the question of the effective rate of interest or yield. In the case above, A's mortgagor is paying $10,000 with interest at 8 percent for 10 years. B, upon buying the indebtedness, has only paid $9,000 for the instrument but the mortgagor has to pay B back $10,000 with 8 percent figured on the $10,000.

The following formula is used to calculate an aproximation of the effective rate of return or yield where discounts are involved:

$$Y = \frac{Pr + \dfrac{d}{n}}{P - d/2}$$

where,

Y = yield or annual percentage rate
P = principal amount in dollars
r = the interest rate expressed decimally
d = discount or charge expressed in dollars
n = number of years or fraction thereof to maturity.

Then, in the case above:

$$Y = \frac{(\$10,000 \times .08) + \dfrac{\$1,000}{10}}{\$10,000 - \$1,000/2}$$

$$Y = \frac{\$900}{\$9,500}$$

Y = .095 or 9.5 percent approximate effective rate of return.

Discounting a First Mortgage and Creating a Second Mortgage

Investors frequently buy first mortgages at a discount as well as second mortgages. Generally the amount of the discount is less on a first mortgage than on a second mortgage. However, the discount rate will vary with the money markets. Often to obtain cash, the purchaser of a first mortgage will create a junior or second position. For example, suppose *A* purchases a mortgage with a face value of $10,000 on a home valued at $20,000. Assume it bears a rate of 9 percent interest. *A* pays, say, $8,500 for the mortgage. If the market rate is currently 8 percent, the 9 percent loan may be attractive to an institutional investor (industrial savings banks will often do this sort of thing).

A arranges for an industrial savings bank to participate as senior investor in the $10,000 face value mortgage. The industrial savings bank agrees to purchase a *senior* participation for, say, $7,000. *A* agrees to become a *junior* owner in the $10,000 mortgage for which *A* paid only $8,500. At this point *A* receives $7,000 cash from the savings bank and signs an ownership agreement agreeing to be in second place. *A*'s equity in the $10,000 mortgage is $3,000 and the bank's first right is for $7,000. *A* now owns a $3,000 piece of the $10,000 mortgage for which $8,500 was paid, or at a 15 percent discount. Now *A* has "at risk" $1,500 for a return of $3,000, or what amounts to a 50 percent discount together with an increase in the effective yield.

For example, prior to *A* being placed in a junior position, *A*'s income was $900 ($10,000 × .09), with a yield of 10.6 percent ($900 ÷ $8,500). After the participation *A*'s income is $270 ($3,000 × .09). The yield on the $1,500 now at risk is 18 percent or $270 ÷ $1,500.

The specific clause creating the senior participation is written as follows:

> The ownership of the party of the second part (in this case the industrial bank or other investor) in said note and mortgage is $7,000 and interest thereon at the rate of nine percent per annum from July 1 ... and the party of the first part (*A* in this case) is the owner of the balance of said debt amounting to $3,000; but the ownership of the party of the second part is superior to that of the party of the first part, as if the party of the second part held a first mortgage for said sum of $7,000 and interest thereon as aforesaid, and the party of the first part held a second and subordinate mortgage, to secure the interest of the party of the first part in said mortgage debt.

Participations are more fully discussed in Chapter 10.

Use of the Second Mortgage by Home Builders

One reason why home builders may use the second mortgage is to sell out subdivisions as fast as possible. It may be to their advantage even though the builders have to discount the mortgage.

Recall that home building is basically a two-step financing transaction. First is the construction loan (interim financing), which is to be replaced by a first mortgage (typically from an institution, the permanent financing). This is a simple case which may become more complex, as will be pointed out in Chapter 13 (Mortgage Banking and Secondary Market Developments).

The thorn in the side of the builder is the interest or carrying charge that must be paid on the construction loan prior to the permanent loan. Suppose a builder's permanent financing commitment is for conventional mortgages with an 80 percent loan-to-value ratio. This means a home buyer must put down 20 percent. If there is a turndown in the economy, prospects with the necessary 20 percent decline. To increase the rate of sales, a builder might offer a home with 90 percent financing, 80 percent from the institution with the builder "taking" back a purchase money second mortgage for 10 percent of the purchase price. The builder will then discount these. This provides fast working capital for other prospects, as well as no further responsibility for carrying charges.

Use of Second Mortgage to Increase Leverage

Leverage is the use of borrowed money to increase gains. For example, suppose you have $20,000 to invest on which you can earn 10 percent or $2,000 per year. Suppose you can borrow another $20,000 at 8 percent. You then invest the $40,000 (your $20,000 plus the borrowed $20,000 at 10 percent). The gross income is $4,000 per year. Out of this you pay interest of $1,600, netting $2,400. Your rate of return on your equity of $20,000 is then $\frac{\$2,400}{\$20,000}$, or 12 percent, a gain of 2 percent as a result of the leverage.

This sort of thing frequently arises in commercial or apartment-type ventures, the reason being that most institutional lenders will only lend between 60–75 percent of the appraised value. Assume the cost of a small apartment complex is $150,000 and a lender agrees to lend two thirds, or $100,000. Consequently, an investor may look to a second mortgage as a means of raising more money. Let's suppose a second mortgage can be obtained for $20,000. Then the amount of equity needed by the investor is reduced from $50,000 to $30,000, thereby increasing the leverage.

Furthermore, this could make the property easier to sell. If the owner of the property is a "builder-developer" rather than an "investor," in the sense of a person seeking income from the property, the "builder-developer" will attempt to sell to an "investor" for $150,000. Typically, it is easier to sell the property with $30,000 cash down as opposed to $50,000 cash down.

Debt Service

Debt service is the dollar amount of periodic payments needed to pay off the mortgage or mortgages. With a second mortgage there must be enough income to pay the first mortgage as well as the second mortgage and other operating expenses. Most loans are of the *direct reduction* type. This means that the debt service consists of fixed periodic payments of principal and interest during the term of the loan. The interest is paid on the reduced principal balance. Consequently, as each payment is made the interest paid declines while the amount of principal due is reduced. Put another way, as the interest paid declines, the amount paid in the principal increases.

Another method of amortizing a loan used by some savings and loan associations is called the *sinking fund plan*. Here an account is opened in the name of the borrower and each month the home payments are deposited in the account. The association pays interest on the account, say 5 percent. The mortgage loan is not reduced during the term of the loan. Consequently the borrower pays full interest on the loan, say 8 percent. As a result, the borrower pays more than the 8 percent stated on the loan because the principal is never reduced during the term. The excess rate paid is roughly one half the difference between the loan rate and the rate paid the borrower, in this case, 1½ percent (8 − 5 = 3/2 = 1½). The total paid then is 9½ percent.

There are to two basic ways that the debt service is expressed: by a monthly amortization amount or by an annual constant.

The Monthly Amortization. This simply indicates the amount of monthly payments necessary to amortize a loan of $1,000 at a given rate for a given period of time. Thus, given a $10,000 loan at 8 percent for 25 years, the payback is $7.72 per thousand per month. Then for a $100,000 loan, monthly payment is $772 ($100,000 × $7.72), or $9,264 annually. (See Table 5 in Appendix B for the monthly amortization schedule for a $1,000 loan.)

The Annual Constant. The mortgage constant is a way to estimate how much money it takes on an annual basis to amortize a mortgage. The annual constant is calculated by multiplying the monthly payments including principal and interest by 12.

For example, assume a 20-year mortgage of $100,000 at 8½ percent interest. From Table 5 in Appendix B, it takes a monthly payment of $8.68 to amortize a $1,000 loan at 8½ percent over 20 years. This means it takes $104.16 annually to pay off $1,000 over 20 years. To pay off $100,000 over 20 years at $8.68 monthly per $1,000, it takes $868 per month, or $10,416 annually.

The annual constant as a ratio of annual payment to the original mortgage is expressed as a percentage. Thus,

$$\frac{\$10,416}{\$100,000} = 10.4\%$$

In this case the annual constant is equal to $8.68 per $1,000 borrowed. What difference does it make? It's a rapid method of calculating the amount needed to pay off the loan annually. For example, if the property nets $9,800 per year (not including principal and interest payments), it can be quickly calculated that $10,416 is needed annually to pay off the loan. You'd be coming up short. In this case it might be feasible to lengthen the loan and lower the constant. For example, if the length were increased to 25 years, it would take $8.05 per $1,000 per month, or $805 per month for the $100,000 loan, or $9,660 per year. The constant would then be $9,660/$100,000 = 9.660 percent annual constant. Then, with an income of $9,800, the project would be feasible, the payment being $9,660 annually. (Table 6 in Appendix B contains some selected annual constant percentages.)

Use of Second Mortgage in Land Purchases

This is a device used by builder-developers in conjunction with a subordination clause in a mortgage. For example, A (a builder-developer) can buy 40 acres for a subdivision at $2,500 per acre. The seller agrees to sell it for 10 percent down or $10,000 cash down. The seller agrees to take back a first blanket purchase money mortgage containing partial release clauses as previously discussed.

The problem created is this: When a construction loan is sought, the builder-developer will be turned down. Why? Because there is an existing first mortgage held by the seller. Therefore the buyer-builder insists on a subordination clause in the seller's first mortgage. This states that the seller's first mortgage agrees to move into number two position in order for the buyer to obtain a *first* construction loan.

Briefly, the clause in the seller's first mortgage will state:

> The mortgagor shall have the right to substitute other mortgages for a prior mortgage or mortgages now in the mortgaged premises. Such substituted mortgage shall have the same priority with reference to this mortgage. The mortgagee hereby agrees to execute all necessary instruments to effectuate any substitution above described.

When the buyer is about to obtain the construction loan, the seller and the buyer enter into a Subordination Agreement. This is the instrument mentioned in the clause. The Subordination Agreement is recorded, at which time the seller's first purchase money mortgage is moved to a second. A subordination agreement is shown on page 84.

Generally sellers of vacant land will go along with this sort of transaction because it's easier to sell the vacant land. Furthermore, the original mortgage generally contains a sliding interest rate. For example, the mortgage might state that so long as the mortgage is a first, the rate will be 8 percent and once a Subordination Agreement, if any, is recorded, the rate shall be 10 percent as long as it is in second place.

SUBORDINATION AGREEMENT

AGREEMENT, made the   24th   day of   October   nineteen hundred and . . .

BETWEEN William Thomas , residing at   2210 Beech Street, Cincinnati, Ohio , party of the first part, and   Teresa Perez , residing at   8490 Woodbind Drive, Cincinnati, Ohio
party of the second part,

WITNESSETH:

WHEREAS, the said party of the first part now owns and holds a certain mortgage and the bond secured thereby, which mortgage is dated the   16th   day of   June , 19-- , and made by   Teresa Perez   to   William Thomas   to secure the principal sum of   Seven Thousand and 00/100 ($7,000)-------- dollars and interest and recorded in the office of the Register of the County of   Clermont   in Liber   1410   of the Mortgages at page   69 , and covers premises hereinafter mentioned as a part thereof, and

WHEREAS
the present owner of the premises hereinafter mentioned is about to execute and deliver to said party of the second part, a mortgage to secure the principal sum of   Twenty Thousand and 00/100 ($20,000)------- dollars and interest, covering premises
(here follows complete legal description)
and more fully described in said mortgage, and

WHEREAS, said party of the second part has refused to accept said mortgage   unless said mortgage   held by the party of the first part be subordinated in the manner hereinafter mentioned.

NOW THEREFORE, in consideration of the premises and to induce said party of the second part to accept said mortgage   and also in consideration of   one dollar   paid to the party of the first part, the receipt whereof is hereby acknowledged, the said party of the first part hereby covenants and agrees with said party of the second part that said mortgage   held by said party of the first part be and shall continue to be subject and subordinate in lien to the lien of said mortgage   for   Twenty Thousand and 00/100 ($20,000)------- dollars and interest about to be delivered to the party of the second part hereto, and to all advances heretofore made or which hereafter may be made thereon (including but not limited to all sums advanced for the purpose of paying brokerage commissions, mortgage recording tax, documentary stamps, fee for examination of title, surveys, and any other disbursements and charges in connection therewith) to the extent of the last mentioned amount and interest, and all such advances may be made without notice of extensions, renewals and modifications thereof.

THIS AGREEMENT shall be binding on and enure to the benefit of the respective heirs, personal representatives, successors and assigns of the parties hereto.

IN WITNESS WHEREOF, the said party of the first part has duly executed this agreement.

IN PRESENCE OF:

    /s/ James Mason

(ACKNOWLEDGMENT)

Figure
5-1   Subordination Agreement

Use of Second Mortgages for Home Improvement Loans

FHA, Title I, provides insurance for home modernization loans up to $5,000. The maximum term of the loan is seven years and 32 days. Basically this is a "credit" loan. Most individuals who apply for this type of loan own a home with an existing first mortgage. Consequently, lenders have to look to the "credit" of the borrower. However, many lenders insist on a second mortgage for additional security.

In recent years the volume of Title I loans has declined. Most lenders are giving conventional loans with a second mortgage. There are two reasons for this trend: (1) the interest rates that can be charged on the conventional loan are higher than those permitted under the FHA loan; and (2) under the Housing and Community Development Act of 1974, real estate loans by national banks have been liberalized. This of course means greater participation by commercial banks in the mortgage market. Specifically the Act provides that loans secured by other than first mortgages may be granted provided the total lien does not exceed the permissable loan-to-value ratio. For example, suppose there is a loan-to-value ratio of 80 percent. A owns a home valued at $30,000. The loan-to-value ratio is $24,000 ($30,000 × .80). Suppose A has an existing first mortgage of $18,000. Under the Act, A may borrow on a second mortgage from a commercial bank a maximum of $6,000 for home improvement. Loans of this type are limited to 20 percent of the bank's capital and surplus. For the most part the maximum term of this type loan is 10 years.

While many of these loans are to individuals, banks do accept the "paper" from contractors. For example, a contractor may specialize in home modernization. An arrangement is made with a bank to buy the contractor's paper. This means that the note is signed by the individual with the contractor as payee. The contractor endorses the note over to the bank and receives the money. The home owner then pays the bank. If the home owner defaults on the note, the bank then looks to the contractor for their money as well as to the home owner.

Where banks buy the paper from the contractor, the banks require a Completion Certificate. This Certificate is signed by both home owner and contractor certifying that the improvement has been completed according to specification.

The Call Second Mortgage

The *call second mortgage* is merely a second mortgage giving the lender the right to "call" it at a time prior to its termination date. At the time of the call, the borrower has to agree to refinance the entire loan into a first mortgage and to pay off the second mortgage. For example, assume an institutional lender has committed an 80 percent loan-to-value ratio on a development home. In order to expedite sales, the builder-developer may offer the property with 10 percent down and agree to take back a second mortgage for 15 years with a call, at the developer's option, in 5 years.

Assume the sales price is	$34,000
An 80% first mortgage for	
30 years at 8% is	27,200
	$ 6,800
Assume a $3,400 second with a 5-year	
call at 9% for 180 months (15 years)	3,400
The 10% down is	$3,400

Payments for principal and interest on the first	
mortgage are ($7.34 per $1,000 times 27.2)	$199.65. per month
Payments for principal and interest on the second	
mortgage are ($10.14 per $1,000 times 3.4)	34.48 per month
Total monthly payments	$234.13 per month

The monthly payments were, of course, arrived at by using Table 5 in Appendix B. In addition, Table 7 in Appendix B is useful in determining the remaining loan balances.

At the end of the "call" period, five years in this case:

Balance due on first mortgage is (95.1% times $27,200)	$25,867
Balance due on second mortgage is (80.1% times $3,400)	2,723
Total due	$28,590

The basic assumption is that the property will appreciate during the five-year period, thus making the "call" feasible. Assume a compound rate of growth or appreciation of 3 percent per year (i.e., a compound interest factor of 1.159 is obtained from Table 1 in Appendix B). Then, 1.159 × $34,000 = $39,406, the value of property at the end of five years. With a new 80 percent mortgage of $31,525 (.80 × $34,000), the original first and second mortgages could be retired for $28,590. This would result in a surplus to the owner less expenses of $2,935 ($31,525 − $28,590).

MAJOR SOURCES OF JUNIOR LIEN FUNDS

When first organized in 1910, industrial banks specialized in making loans to industrial workers; hence, the name industrial bank. In addition to making loans to business firms and individuals, they also make first- and second-mortgage loans. Typically they charge a high rate of interest, about 18.5 percent. In addition, they frequently buy portfolios of second mortgages (at a discount) held by builder-developers.

Individual lenders are a large source of second mortgage money. Generally such lenders will lend only on short-term loans, five years or less. Typically interest rates are high. In addition, like most lenders, "points" are charged (as much as the traffic will bear).

Under the Housing and Community Development Act of 1974, commercial banks are rapidly entering the field of the second mortgage. Recently, too, savings and loan associations have begun giving second mortgages based on the rapid increase in appreciation of many homes.

QUESTIONS FOR REVIEW

1. Under what conditions might a second mortgage be used to finance the purchase of a residential property? How is such an arrangement advantageous to the buyer? To the seller?
2. Why is it sometimes necessary to discount a mortgage in order to "cash out," and also to get financing for the buyer? Give an example.
3. Describe the procedure for discounting a first mortgage and creating a second. What are the respective advantages or gains for the senior and junior owners in such an arrangement?
4. How might a builder use a second mortgage to sell out a subdivision rapidly and provide fast working capital?
5. Explain the use of a second mortgage in creating leverage for an investor. What would be the effect if the return on the investment was less than the interest rate paid for the second mortgage?
6. Describe the direct reduction and sinking fund types of loan amortization. Which is more expensive?
7. What are the two basic ways by which debt service is expressed? Describe them.
8. What is the purpose of a Subordination Agreement in a builder's purchase money mortgage with the seller?
9. What is a call second mortgage and what are its provisions?
10. What are the major sources of junior lien funds?

PROBLEMS

1. If you sell a mortgage for $11,000 with terms of $12,000 with interest of 8% for 8 years, what is the effective yield to the buyer?
2. On a 10-year face value $15,000 mortgage paying 9%, as compared to the current market of 8%, a mutual savings bank agrees to take a senior participation for $10,000. The junior owner originally paid $13,000 for the mortgage. As a result of this arrangement, what does the junior owner have at risk, how much does the junior owner

expect to receive in return, and what is the effective yield?

3. What is the monthly amortization rate on a loan of $50,000 at 9% for 20 years? What is the annual constant for this same loan?

4. An institutional lender has committed an 80% loan-to-value ratio on the development of a home. The price of the home is $30,000, and the interest rate on the lender's loan is 8% and the mortgage is for 25 years. The developer offers to take 10% down and give you a 10-year second mortgage at 10% for the remainder with a call in 5 years. The property is expected to appreciate at 5% per year not compounded. What is the owner's surplus, if any, after the call?

Construction Financing

Chapter 6

Construction financing is a two-stage procedure consisting of interim financing and permanent financing. *Interim financing* is relatively short-term financing involving a loan designed to finance the building during the construction period. *Permanent financing* takes place after the building is completed and is designed to cover the long term. The construction loan is paid off by the permanent loan and the buyer of the house or improvement pays off the permanent loan. For example, suppose a house is sold for $50,000, the construction loan is $40,000, and a buyer puts $5,000 down and obtains a long-term mortgage for $45,000. The long-term lender pays off the construction loan of $40,000 and gives the builder $5,000 and this, together with the $5,000 down payment, presumably is the builder's profit.

Although not always, the construction loan and the permanent financing are generally handled by two different financial institutions. For example, a commercial bank may make the construction loan while a savings and loan association places the so-called permanent loan. There may be many variations of this, as shown in Table 6-1 on page 90.

Construction loans can be used for three types of site improvements:

1. One- to four-family residential dwellings.
2. Multi-family residential dwellings.
3. Other commercial improvements; e.g., a shopping center.

While the basic principles are the same in all these instances, there are some slight differences with regard to the institutions employed.

89

Table
6-1 Variations in Construction Financing

Construction Loan (Interim)	Permanent (Long-Term Mortgage/ Deed of Trust)
1. Commercial bank	Mortgage banker, who may intend to sell the mortgage at a later date.[1]
2. Savings and loan association	Savings and loan association, which may hold the mortgage or sell it at a later date to the Federal Home Loan Mortgage Corporation or another participating savings and loan association.[2]
3. Commercial bank	Mortgage banker with an advance commitment from the Federal National Mortgage Association.[3]
4. Commercial bank	Savings and loan association, which may either hold the mortgage or sell it.
5. Commercial bank	Mortgage banker with an advance commitment from either a life insurance company or a mutual savings bank.
6. Mortgage banker (who is in effect a subsidiary of a commercial bank)	Commercial bank, which may keep the mortgage or, most likely, sell it to another institution. The mortgage banker may sell directly to another institution such as a savings and loan association.

Notes: [1]A mortgage banker is defined as any person, firm, or corporation engaged in the business of lending money on the security of improved real estate or who is an investor in real estate securities or is the recognized agent of an insurance company or the direct purchaser of first mortgage real estate securities for investment only. The mortgage banker's activities are discussed in further detail in Chapter 13.

[2]The Federal Home Loan Mortgage Corporation's activities are outlined in Chapter 14.

[3]The Federal National Mortgage Association is discussed in Chapter 13. The term "advance commitment," as used above, means that the Federal National Mortgage Association has agreed to buy the mortgages when the builder has sold the homes. To obtain the "advance commitment" the mortgage banker has to pay a sum of money. The mortgage banker is then said to have "bought" money. These costs are, in turn, paid for by the builder-developer. The idea of "buying" money is discussed on page 91.

THE PRELIMINARY LENDING PROCEDURE

Assume a builder-developer, developing one- to four-family residential houses, makes a decision to approach a mortgage banker for financing and that the mortgage banker is a subsidiary (or, as they prefer to be called, a separate entity) of a commercial bank. The builder-developer hopes to obtain construction financing from the mortgage banker and permanent financing from the parent bank.

In essence, what the builder-developer is doing is "buying" money, or seeking an advance commitment. Of course, like buying anything else, the money has its price, as will be pointed out later.

Assume further that the builder-developer has the necessary zoning, water tap permits, and any other necessary permissions. In addition, the builder-developer has land or an option on land for, say, 100 homes and asks for a commitment for a construction loan for this number of homes. Unless the builder-developer has an absolute triple A credit rating, this proposal will be rejected.

In most cases, the mortgage banker will insist that off-site improvements be made on a maximum of 20 lots. Then, and only then, will the mortgage banker make a commitment for a construction loan. In all probability, the commitment will be made on four units at a time. Four is the chosen number because both the builder-developer and the mortgage banker know that the construction costs for building four homes at a time are much less than building one home at a time. For example, if a backhoe or bulldozer is being used to dig basements, it's less expensive to have four basements done at one time than one at a time, and so on with other costs.

THE COST OF MONEY

If the builder-developer decides to go along with the building of four homes at a time, the discussion will turn to the cost of money.

There are three "costs" of buying money:

1. The cost of the construction commitment.
2. The cost of the advance commitment (permanent financing).
3. The cost of the construction loan itself.

The Cost of the Construction Commitment and the Advance Commitment

The cost of the construction commitment and the advance commitment is expressed in "points" — one point being equal to one percent of the face amount of the loan. Suppose, for example, that both loans are to be $200,000. The commitment fee on the construction loan is 2 points, and 3 points on the permanent financing. The cost, then, is $4,000 for the construction financing ($200,000 × .02 = $4,000), plus $6,000 for the permanent financing ($200,000 × .03 = $6,000), or a total of $10,000. This amount ($10,000) cannot be borrowed as part of the loan but must be paid by the borrower at the time the loan is made.

Admittedly, 2 points and 3 points is high. The range is from 1 to 3 points. The amount depends on the availability of money: if money is "easy," the lower figure will prevail; if money is "tight," the higher figure will prevail.

The Cost of the Construction Loan

The cost of the construction loan is the interest that must be paid on the construction loan during the time of building or until the building is sold. This rate is either a "fixed" or a "floating" rate.

The Fixed Rate. By definition this rate is a stated rate that does not vary during the period of the loan. In short, the rate is set by contract in the construction loan agreement (called a "building loan agreement" in some states). For example, the agreement may state that 8 percent interest will be paid on the amount of money advanced for the construction loan.

The Floating Rate. The floating rate amounts to a variable interest rate. For example, the agreement may read to the effect that the builder-developer must pay interest of, say, two points above the prime rate. The *prime rate* is the rate of interest charged by large banks to their most credit-worthy customers. The prime rate of a particular bank is chosen as a reference point; for example, the Continental Bank and Trust Company of Chicago. Assume their prime rate at the time of signing the agreement is 7 percent. Then initially the borrower must pay 7 + 2, or 9 percent. The rate "floats" because it is adjusted either monthly or quarterly — depending on the agreement. If the prime rate goes to, say, 6 percent, then the builder-developer pays 8 percent until the next adjustment period. If at the following adjustment period the prime rate has risen to 9 percent, then the builder-developer pays 11 percent.

In general, builders dislike floating rates because they cannot easily calculate their costs, and because the cost of money is a rather large portion of the total cost of construction.

Why are floating rates used? Lenders will insist on floating rates, particularly in a market where interest rates are rising rapidly. When interest rates are firm or thought to be firm, fixed rates are most likely to be used.

THE BUILDER'S FORM OF BUSINESS ENTERPRISE

Sooner or later, the builder's form of business enterprise will be raised by the mortgage banker. Is the builder a corporation, a partnership, or a single proprietorship? Most builder-developers are corporations. The reason for this is to enable the builder-developer to hide behind the corporate veil; but only if the builder-developer is an exceedingly strong corporation financially will the lender permit the builder-developer to sign any legal document as a corporation only. The lender will insist that the builder-developer sign the documents both as the corporate entity and individually as a guarantor. This is to protect the lender in the event of bankruptcy by the corporation. If bankruptcy should occur, and if it is necessary, then the lender can possibly seize corporate assets as well as individual assets.

THE PROPOSED SITE

At this point, the lender of the construction loan will raise the question as to whether or not the four (or perhaps more) lots are encumbered. The construction loan, after all, is a mortgage or deed of trust and the lender will insist on having a first lien against the property. If the land is free and clear, there is no problem. However, if the builder-developer purchased the land and gave the seller a blanket purchase money mortgage, then one of two things must be done.

1. If the blanket purchase money mortgage or deed of trust contained a partial release clause, then the four (or more) lots must be paid off. A partial release of the lots proposed for development is obtained from the mortgagee. The partial release is then recorded, thereby rendering the lots free and clear.
2. Any mortgage or deed of trust in existence on the proposed building sites must be made subordinate to the construction loan. In order for this to be done a clause to this effect must have been included in the blanket purchase money mortgage or deed of trust that had been entered into by the builder-developer and the seller. In this case, the seller enters into a subordination agreement, such as that shown in Chapter 5, making the purchase money mortgage or deed of trust subordinate to the proposed construction loan. This subordination agreement will contain a clause to the effect that the builder-developer's seller will be paid a certain amount as each home is sold.

Many builder-developers prefer the latter to a partial release. The reason for this is that it enables the builder-developer to operate using less out-of-pocket cash.

FINALIZING THE LOAN

There are many steps to be taken before the loan is finally approved. After the preliminary discussions, as outlined above, the builder-developer must submit an application for the construction loan. This will be discussed in Chapter 15. In essence, the application contains a list of assets and liabilities to reveal the builder-developer's net worth. At this point, unless the builder-developer is well known, a credit check is made to ascertain credit-worthiness. Next, a title insurance policy, or abstract of title, is ordered to determine if the title to the proposed development site is clear.

The builder-developer may have to submit a feasibility study to determine the marketability of the proposed project. In any event, the lender, if familiar with the location of the project, will attempt to analyze the marketability of the proposed project.

Assuming the builder-developer's credit rating is satisfactory and the homes appear to be marketable, then a number of other steps are taken:

1. Plans, specifications, and cost estimates are submitted to the lender. The plans and specifications must be complete, clear, and accurate. Costs must be accurately estimated. This sounds like a truism. However, an experienced lender will check subcontractors' bids when analyzing the overall builder's cost estimates. Subcontractors' bids which are either "too low" or "too high" in the lender's opinion constitute a red flag to the lender. For example, if the subcontractors' bid is "too low" under local conditions, it may mean that the builder cannot complete the job without obtaining additional funds. If the subcontractors' bid is "too high" this may cause the price of the home to be out of the market.

2. An appraisal is made by the lender on the basis of the lot, plans and specifications. Assume, for the purposes of illustration, that the proposed construction loan is to be $40,000 and the builder-developer has placed an exaggerated selling price of $75,000 on the proposed home. Obviously, the construction lender won't go along with this because the home won't appraise out to this amount and consequently won't sell under current market conditions.

3. At this point, the Construction Loan Agreement will be entered into. In those states using the mortgage, it will be in the form of a blanket mortgage on, say, four lots. In those states using the Deed of Trust, the agreement will take the form of a blanket deed of trust. An example of a construction loan agreement is shown in Figure 6-1.

CONSTRUCTION LOAN CONTRACT

THIS AGREEMENT, made the   day of
nineteen hundred and

BETWEEN

hereinafter referred to as the borrower, and

hereinafter referred to as the lender.

WHEREAS, the borrower has applied to the lender for a loan of
                                        Dollars to be advanced as
hereinafter provided and to be evidenced by the note of the borrower for the payment of said sum, or so much thereof as shall at any time be advanced thereon, on

---

**Figure
6-1**   Construction Loan Agreement (Continued)

the day of   nineteen hundred and   with interest
upon each amount so advanced from the date of such advance at the rate of
per centum per annum to be paid on the   day of
and quarter annually thereafter; said   note to be secured by a
                        on the premises described as follows:

(here follows complete legal description)

TOGETHER will all fixtures and articles of personal property now or hereafter
attached to, or contained in and used in connection with said premises, including
but not limited to all apparatus, machinery, fittings, gas ranges, ice boxes, mechanical refrigerators, awnings, shades, screens, storm sashes, plants and shrubbery.

WHEREAS the lender agrees to make said loan upon the terms, convenants and
conditions hereinafter set forth and the borrower agrees to take said loan and expressly covenants to comply with and perform all of the terms, covenants and conditions of this agreement.

NOW, THEREFORE, it is agreed between the parties as follows:

1. The borrower expressly covenants to make on said premises the improvement
described below in accordance with the plans and specifications therefor, which,
before the making of the first advance hereunder, the borrower agrees to file with
all governmental authorities having jurisdiction and to obtain all necessary approv-
als of said plans and specifications and all necessary building permits from said
authorities. The said plans and specifications shall first be submitted to and approved by the lender in writing; and no changes or amendments thereto shall be
made without first obtaining the written approval of the lender. The said improvements to be made shall be as follows:

(here follow plans and specifications)

2. Said loan is to be advanced at such times and in such amounts as the lender may
approve, but substantially in accordance with the following schedule:

(a schedule of payments follows here)

                                    /s/ Ace Realty Corporation, Inc.,
(Corporate Seal)   by George Ace, President

                                    /s/ Fourth National Bank of Mineola, N.Y.
(Corporate Seal)   by Frances Jones, Cashier

Acknowledgment
STATE OF NEW YORK, COUNTY OF   s.s.:

                                    being duly sworn, deposes and says:

I am at No.   . I am the   , the borrower mentioned
in the within building loan contract. The consideration paid or to be paid by the
borrower to the lender for the loan described therein is   Dollars

Figure
6-1   Construction Loan Agreement (Continued)

($), and that all other expenses incurred, or to be incurred, in connection with said loan are as follows:*

Broker's commission $_____

Examination and insurance of title and recording fees $_____

Mortgage tax $_____

Architect's, engineer's, and surveyor's fees $_____

Inspections $_____

Appraisals $_____

Conveyancing $_____

Building loan service fees $_____

Sums paid to take by assignment prior existing mortgages which are consolidated with building loan mortgages and also the interest charges on such mortgages $_____

Sums paid to discharge or reduce the indebtedness under mortgages and accrued interest thereon and other prior existing encumbrances $_____

Sums paid to discharge building loan mortgages whenever recorded $_____

Taxes, assessments, water rents and sewer rents paid (existing prior to the commencement of improvement) $_____

and that the net sum available to the said borrower for the improvement is   Dollars ($) less such amounts as may become due or payable for insurance premiums, interest on building loan mortgages, ground rent, taxes, assessments, water rents and sewer rents accruing during the making of the improvement.

SWORN TO before me this   day of   , 19   .

/s/_____   /s/_____
    Notary Public
    (Seal)

    *This is the statement regarding the fee for the loan commitment. For example, assume the total loan is to be $160,000 and the borrower is to pay one point, or 1 percent. This equals $1,600 and is mentioned here and paid immediately.

Figure
6-1   Construction Loan Agreement (Concluded)

    The schedule of payments mentioned in the preceding loan agreement can be made substantially in accordance with the building loan inspection report shown in Figure 6-2. This payment schedule can be set up in five, four, or any number of payments. Sometimes the schedule is set up in percentages which are spelled out in the agreement. The percentages may be substantially as shown in Table 6-2.

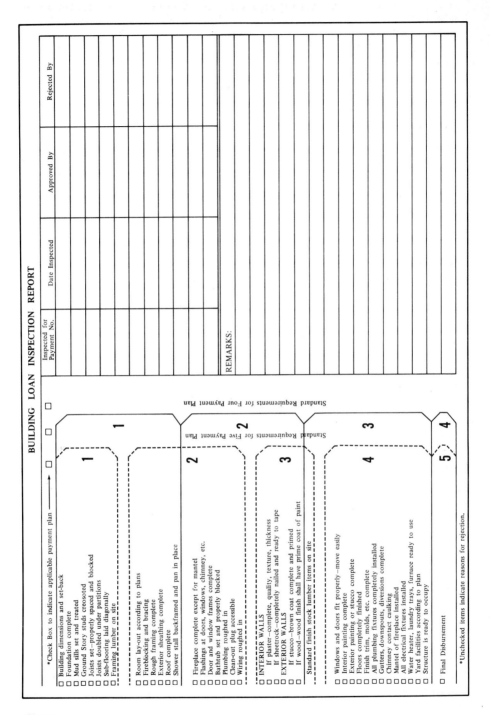

Figure 6-2 Building Loan Inspection Report

Table
6-2 Schedule of Payments Using Percentages

	Six Payouts	Five Payouts	Four Payouts	Three Payouts	Three Payouts
Foundation & rough grading / First floor laid	15%	25%	25%	50%	30%
Framing complete & sub-flooring / Roof sheathing and chimney / Window frames set	15%				
Rough plbg., heating, wiring	10%	15%	25%		
Exterior finish / Lath & plaster or dry wall	20%	20%		25%	30%
Basement floor & htg. plant / Interior finish, except flooring	20%	20%	25%		
All finish flooring / Ready for occupancy	20%	20%	25%	25%	40%

MECHANICS' LIENS

The *mechanic's lien*, created solely by statute, gives the right of lien to those persons who have furnished work or materials for the improvement of real property. The persons who are entitled to the lien include contractors, subcontractors, laborers, material suppliers, engineers, and architects.

The underlying basis of the right of lien lies in the fact that, as a result of the work done or materials furnished, the property is improved. *Improvement* means generally the erection, alteration, or repair of any structure upon, connected with, or beneath the surface of any real property. It also includes any work done or materials furnished for the structure's permanent improvements.

Because the lien is based on the idea of improvement, it can be placed only against the property. For example, *A* owns two parcels of property. *B* works on one of them and is not paid. *B*'s right to a lien exists only against the property on which *B* has actually worked. The right of lien does not exist against both parcels of property.

Time in Which to File the Mechanic's Lien

The lien laws contain a statement regarding the time in which to file. Generally it states "that four months have not elapsed dating from the last item of work performed and dating from the last items of materials furnished. . . ."

The purpose of this statement is to show compliance with the statute when, for example, the statute states that the notice must be filed within four months after the last work or last items of material are furnished. Although most state statutes require that the lien be filed within four months, the requirements vary among states. They may also vary with regard to the time in which the material supplier has a right to file, and the time in which the laborer has a right to file. For example, in Idaho and Oregon the material supplier must file within sixty days after the last items of materials are furnished; the laborer must file within ninety days after the completion of the work.

Priority of Liens

The problem concerning the priority of liens may be divided into two parts: (1) between various mechanics' liens and (2) between the mechanic's lien and the mortgage.

Rights Between Mechanics' Liens. The priority that establishes the rights between the various mechanics' liens that may be placed against a property is fixed by the time of recording. When the notice of lien reaches the county clerk's office, the date and time of the recording are stamped on the notice of lien; and a note indicating the time of recording is entered in the proper index. This establishes the priority. The first notice of mechanic's lien filed has the prior right over subsequently filed notices of liens.

In some states the lien of the mechanic is attached when work begins. The date of priority is not dependent upon the actual filing of the notice, although, without any filing within the requisite period, the lien may be lost. In these states a number of situations may arise. For example, the lender has a mortgage on the property and *A* commences work. In this case, the rights of the lender are superior to those of *A*. But if *A* begins work and then the lender obtains a mortgage on the property, *A*'s lien will be superior to the mortgage, even though a notice has not yet been filed.

Another situation that can arise in these states is when there is no mortgage and *A* commences work. The lender then places a mortgage on the property, and *A* hires *B*. In this case, the right of *A* is superior to that of the lender. But the lender's right is superior to that of *B*, who began working after the mortgage was recorded.

Rights Between Mechanic's Lien and Mortgage. The rights of the mechanic's lien over the rights of a lender vary among the states. In New York, for example, if the mechanic's lien is filed before the mortgage is recorded, the rights of the *lienor*, the holder of the lien, are superior to the rights of the lender. On the other hand, if the mortgage is recorded prior to the filing of the lien, the lender's rights are superior. The reason for this is that the lien does not attach until it is actually filed. The states following this rule are said to operate under the "New York System" of mechanics' liens.

In most states the lien will date back to the day of the beginning of the job by the prime contractor. For example, a builder orders materials delivered to the job on July 1. On August 1 the lender places a mortgage on the property and records it. On August 15 the material supplier files a lien. In those states following the Pennsylvania System the lumberyard or material supplier will have a lien against the premises superior to that of the lender, the former's time relating back to the day of delivery of materials for the job, which was July 1.[1]

PROTECTION AGAINST LIENS

Most states are concerned with the serious question continually being raised by construction lenders concerning methods by which they might have protection against liens that are placed against their properties. In some states, New York, for example, there is no serious question as far as lenders are concerned. If the mortgage is filed prior to mechanics' liens, then it has priority over such liens. However, what can be done in the other states? In some states there is the so-called "no lien contract." This is a contract between the builder-developer and the construction lender wherein the builder-developer agrees that no liens can be placed against the property. This contract is then recorded. By virtue of the recording, there is constructive notice to the world. Therefore, subcontractors become bound by the terms of the contract and cannot file effective liens against the property.

---

[1]In Arizona, Arkansas, California, Colorado, Connecticut, District of Columbia, Georgia, Idaho, Iowa, Kansas, Louisiana, Michigan, Minnesota, Montana, Nebraska, Nevada, New Hampshire, New Mexico, Ohio, Oklahoma, Rhode Island, Tennessee, Utah, Washington, West Virginia, and Wisconsin mechanics' liens growing out of a particular job relate back to the beginning of the job. In Illinois and Maine a mechanic's lien attaches to the land on the date on which the owner contracted for improvements.

Waiver of Lien

This instrument waives the right of subcontractors to file any liens against the premises. Sometimes this is signed by the subcontractors when final payment is made or the instrument may be executed prior to beginning work on the premises. In the event the subcontractors enter into this type of agreement, they are bound by its terms not to file liens. However, in some states, although the subcontractor cannot file a lien in the event of non-payment, the subcontractor may still obtain a personal judgment against the builder-developer.

Completion Bond

Another means of protection against liens is to have the contractor obtain a *completion bond*, a type of surety bond, prior to commencing a job. In the event that any parties remain unpaid, they will be taken care of under the terms of the bond and no liens will be attached to the property.

Holding Funds

Holding funds can be utilized effectively to thwart mechanics' liens. The construction lender merely holds back part of the contract price until the period for the filing of the mechanics' liens has passed. After this period, the balance due to the contractor is paid.

In those states where the lien relates back to the commencement of the job, another method of holding back funds is employed. The construction loan agreement is executed by the builder-developer and is recorded. After the recording the contractor starts the job. In this case no actual cash is delivered to the builder-developer at the time of execution of the mortgage but is turned over as the job progresses. The construction loan agreement is recorded prior to the beginning of the job and thus is prior in right to any subsequent mechanics' liens.

To further make certain of this, a lot inspection is done by the construction lender. The lot is physically inspected to determine that no work has been done or material delivered to the job. A report is made attesting to this fact. Often, in addition to the written report, photos are taken of the lot as additional substantiation.

Another way a lending institution may attempt to protect itself against liens is to pay the contractors' bills itself. The contractor lists monies owed on the form shown in Figure 6-3 and the institution pays the bills and charges such payment against the construction loan.

Some institutions will also insist upon a pre-construction *affidavit*, which is a sworn statement. To swear falsely puts the affiant in a position subject to criminal penalties. A pre-construction affidavit is shown in Figure 6-4.

CONSTRUCTION LOAN DRAW REQUEST

TO SAVINGS, BUILDING AND LOAN ASSOCIATION

LOAN NO._____   DATE_____

LOAN IN NAME OF:_____

PROPERTY ADDRESS: _____

LEGAL DESCRIPTION: _____

PLEASE PAY THE FOLLOWING BILLS:

NAME OF PERSON, SUPPLIER, OR SUB-CONTRACTOR	FOR	NET AMOUNT (AFTER DISCOUNT)
		$

(Paid bills and/or invoices and/or labor list for the above are enclosed herewith)   Total $

_____
Authorized Signature

Remarks:

**Figure
6-3**   Construction Loan Draw Request

STATE OF   ) ss
COUNTY OF   )

The undersigned, first being duly sworn, deposes and says that your affiant is about to commence construction on the premises known as _____ which has been mortgaged to (the interim lender) _____ to secure a construction loan for the erection of _____ buildings on said premises. Affiant further states that a true itemization of said construction costs is furnished at this time, same to be used for labor and materials on said premises.

Affiant further states that no labor or materials, prefabricated or otherwise, have been used or prepared for use on said premises to this date.

Further affiant sayeth naught.

_____
Contractor

SWORN TO before me this _____ day of _____, 19____.

/s/ _____
Notary Public

Figure 6-4   Pre-Construction Affidavit

QUESTIONS FOR REVIEW

1. What is meant by the statement that construction financing is a two-stage procedure?
2. List and explain the three costs in "buying" construction money.
3. What is a floating rate on a construction loan?
4. Explain the "New York System" of mechanic's lien and other mechanic's liens.
5. How do lending institutions protect themselves against mechanics' liens?
6. What does the pre-construction affidavit attempt to do?

PROBLEMS

1. Assume that a construction loan for $45,000 is obtained from a commercial bank with permanent financing to be provided by a savings and loan association. The builder sells the house for $60,000 and the savings and loan will make a mortgage loan for 80 percent of the purchase price. Explain what will happen.

2. Money has a "cost" or "price." For example, a builder often is faced with costs for a construction loan commitment and the advance commitment or permanent financing. The builder also must pay interest on the construction loan itself. Using the data in problem 1 above, calculate the builder's cost of money if 2 points are charged on each of the construction and advance commitments. Also, the interest cost on the construction loan is 8 percent with the building time expected to last 6 months. What is the total cost of buying the construction money?

Tract and Special Purpose Financing

Chapter 7

Because most real estate development begins with the land or tract, as it is sometimes called, we will discuss this area first.

TRACT OR LAND DEVELOPMENT LOANS

A *tract* or *land development loan* is a loan given to a developer or subdivider to put in streets and utilities after the acquisition of raw land. Most land development loans by institutions are made on land to be used for residential purposes.

The amount of the loan can be as much as 75 to 80 percent of the appraised valuation of the finished lots. Sometimes due to inaccurate appraisals or even accurate appraisals (in a rapidly rising market) the subdivider with an 80 percent loan frequently winds up with a sum greater than the cost of the land plus the site improvements.

A financial institution, as security for the development loan, places a blanket mortgage containing a partial release clause on the lots. The loan is, of course, a lump sum loan on the tract, but for purposes of the partial release a part of the total amount loaned is attributed to each lot.

In practice a schedule of release prices is established. The prices of the individual building sites to be allocated against the total mortgage are determined by value. For example, Lot #20 might be given a retail price of $5,000 while Lot #5 is given a retail price of $7,500. Furthermore, a premium ranging between 15 to 20 percent is added to the release price. Thus, assume the retail price of Lot #20 is $5,000 and a 20 percent premium is added. To release the lot $6,000 is paid to the lender. The extra $1,000 reduces the blanket mortgage by that amount.

The principal payments are thus accelerated and the lender will not be in the position of having released the best lots and being "stuck" with the undesirable lots.

HOW A LENDING INSTITUTION LOOKS AT TRACT LOANS

Before a well-managed financial institution will lend on a tract to be developed they will make a careful appraisal of the tract. Primarily the institution is interested in the completion time estimate for the development. Therefore, Revenues or Sales − Expenses = Profit is not the only consideration; also of primary concern is Income − Expenses over time = Profit.

If enough time is not allocated for the development sales program, the developer may be in trouble. This dilemma would be founded in the continual increase of the amount of interest the developer must pay on the loan, which could result in disaster. Consequently, lenders are vitally concerned with a realistic appraisal of the value of the raw land.

For example, assume that a developer could purchase a tract of land, subdivide it into 100 lots, and sell each lot after improvements for $5,000, or $500,000 in total. Assume further that all calculations of interest, income, and expenses occur at the end of each year. (In practice these monies flow throughout the year as the project progresses.)

In addition, an off-site improvement of a storm sewer requires an immediate expense of $50,000. Estimate lot property taxes at $30 per year. Estimate a three-year sales program. There are zero sales in the current year, 30 sales in the first year, 45 sales the second year, and 25 sales the third year. On-site improvement costs amount to $50,000 per year and financing costs or carrying charges (on both raw land purchase and development loans) are 10 percent interest per year. The developer anticipates a 15 percent profit on raw land. Income tax factors are not considered for purposes of simplification. First, a time-line schedule is created which is shown in Table 7-1 on page 106.

Looking at the table, several conclusions can be reached: (1) expenses that are paid during these four years plus the value of the raw land equal the capital investment; (2) the return on the investment plus profits comes from future sales; (3) these sales must generate profit plus carrying (interest) charges.

Again, a glance at this table reveals a net subdivision income of $244,150. One might initially (but erroneously) conclude that the developer could pay up to $244,150 for the raw land and still break even. (In actual practice the income figures would be reduced by the developer's estimated income tax rate.) Financing costs or carrying charges,

Table
7-1   Time-Line Schedule

					Total
Lots sold	0	30	45	25	100
Years	0	1	2	3	0–3
Off-site expense	(50,000)				(50,000)
On-site expense	(50,000)	(50,000)	(50,000)	(50,000)	(200,000)
Lot tax expense	(3,000)	(2,100)	(750)		(5,850)
Lot sales income		150,000	225,000	125,000	500,000
Net subdivision income	$−103,000	$ 97,900	$174,250	$75,000	$244,150

however, must be worked into the figures because both the raw land value and cost (in this case) and real profits will be affected. Failure to create a realistic time-line schedule and to take the carrying charges into account have in recent years caused the downfall of many lenders as well as developers.

To calculate carrying charges, net sales income is applied to present worth discount factors. These factors are taken from Appendix B (Table 2, Present Worth of $1) for interest at 10 percent. The net annual income and expense factors are multiplied times the present worth discount factors to determine the present value of the raw land and developer's profits, if any. To do this, Table 7-2 is constructed.

Table
7-2   Calculation of Impact of Carrying Charges

	Net Income Projection	×	Discount Factor	=	Present Worth
Date of value — 0 — starting date	($103,000) ×		1.000	=	($103,000)
1	97,900 ×		.909	=	88,991
2	174,250 ×		.826	=	143,930
3	75,000 ×		.751	=	56,325
Present worth of land + profit				=	$186,246
Estimated value of raw land ($186,246 ÷ 115%)*				=	161,953
Developer's profit estimate as 15% of raw land				=	$ 24,293

*Note that in this table and in Table 7-3 the 15 percent Profit on Raw Land is given as $24,293. This is not 15 percent of $186,246, the Profit + Raw Land. The $24,293 is arrived at by "pulling out" the profit from the total $186,246. To arrive at this figure, the $186,246 is divided by 115%. Thus,

$$\frac{\$186,246}{1.15} = \$161,953, \text{ the estimated value of raw land.}$$

Then,

$$
\begin{array}{ll}
\$186,246 & \text{Profit + Raw Land} \\
-\ 161,953 & \text{Raw Land} \\
\hline
\$\ 24,293 & \text{Profit}
\end{array}
$$

106

From Table 7-2 the present worth of Land + Profit = $186,246. What about the so-called net subdivisions income of $244,150 from Table 7-1? In reality the difference between $186,246 and $244,150 represents carrying charges (interest). This amounts to a startling $57,904 over four years. A summary of the computations is shown in Table 7-3.

Table 7-3 Summary

Sales income	$500,000
Development expenses:	
Off-site $ 50,000	
On-site 200,000	
Taxes 5,850	
$255,850	−255,850
Raw land + carrying charges + profit	$244,150
Minus carrying charges	− 57,904
Profit + raw land	$186,246
Minus profit (15% of raw land)	− 24,293
Estimated value of raw land	$161,953

An alternative way of working the above problem would be to discount the cash flows in Table 7-2 at the developer's 15 percent desired rate of return. This would result in a raw land value of $163,256, which presumably would include a profit to the developer. (This figure differs from the originally calculated $161,953 because the initial method for calculating a 15 percent profit did not explicitly consider the time value of money.) One could then rework Table 7-3. The implications, however, will not change. If the developer is earning a 15 percent return on the raw land and its development, and financing costs or carrying charges amount to 10 percent, the net result will leave little margin for error.

In analyzing this example, it would appear that the proposed tract development is a "bad deal" both from the viewpoint of the lender and the developer. To begin with, a projected profit of $24,293 on a $500,000 development is rather small. In the event of even a slight downturn in the economy, with a concomitant slowdown in sales, the profit can disappear in additional carrying charges, possibly resulting in foreclosure. The implication is that $161,953 is too high a price for the raw land and/or the proposed selling price of the lots is too low. Given the risk, a higher return expectation on the land and its development relative to the cost of financing seems warranted. Of course, if the developer has substantial equity capital to invest, the dollar amount of carrying charges could be reduced.

Furthermore, the prospective developer might think in terms of *opportunity cost*. That is, consideration should be given to other investments which might provide a higher net return or yield. The difference between yields on alternative investments is the opportunity cost or loss of investing in the lower yielding alternative.

To minimize carrying charges and opportunity costs, developers have made increasing use of the rolling option, which was discussed on pages 73 and 75 of Chapter 4.

TRACT ACCOUNTING PROCEDURES

In recent years the accounting practices and procedures used by many land development companies have led to financial problems and disasters for both stockholders and involved financial institutions.

Typically the properties are sold on a land installment contract with a minimum down payment. The company holds the contract, which is unenforceable by specific performance. If the buyer defaults, all interest in the lot and in all payments made by the buyers is lost (unless the contract has reached a point where such loss of payments will be declared a forfeiture either by state statutes or the courts).

Upon the "sale" of a lot on an installment land contract, many companies recorded the purchase price called for in the contract as if it were a completed sale that had been paid for in full. The contract itself was treated as a receivable. For example, suppose a lot is valued at $5,000, its cost is $1,000, and it is sold "on contract" with $100 down. The balance due of $4,900 is a receivable and the "sale" is credited for $5,000 with a profit of $4,000 ($5,000 − $1,000). This "profit" essentially presented a false picture to the corporate shareholders simply because the lot was not paid for. What's worse, the cash flow in this instance amounts to only $100.

To counter this practice, the American Institute of Certified Public Accountants, Committee on Land Development Companies, issued somewhat feeble guidelines. These are contained in *Accounting for Retail Land Sales* (New York: AICPA, 1973).

Basically the Committee recommends that recognition of a sale be deferred until certain conditions are met that indicate that (1) the customer seriously intends to complete the contract, and (2) the company is capable of fulfilling its obligations under the contract so that the customer cannot later demand and receive refunds for failure to deliver. Retail land contracts should be recorded as sales only when all the following conditions are met:

1. The customer has made the down payment and each regularly required subsequent payment until the period of cancellation with refund has expired.

2. The aggregate payments (including interest) equal or exceed 10 percent of the contract sales price.
3. The selling company is clearly capable of providing both land improvements and off-site facilities promised in the contract and of meeting all other representations it has made.[1]

Until all conditions have been met, monies collected should be recorded as deposits and the transactions accounted for under the deposit method. Under this method, all collections (including interest) should be recorded as deposits until the contracts qualify to be recorded as sales.

COOPERATIVES AND CONDOMINIUMS

A *cooperative* dwelling is one in which a tenant purchases stock in the corporation that owns the building rather than renting an individual unit in the building. Thus, tenant-stockholders own a portion of the building's equity. Tenants pay rent, which includes a portion of the cost of operation, plus interest and amortization of the mortgage, if any.

In such a building 100 percent of the ownership of the building is allocated to the various units. For example, if there are 100 identical units in the project, then each shareholder owns one one-hundredth of the building. When tenant-stockholders purchase stock it covers their proportionate share of the equity over and above the amount of the outstanding mortgage. As the mortgage is amortized, the equity in the tenant-stockholder's unit increases. In addition to stock, a tenant-stockholder is given a *proprietary lease* which is a long-term lease. The lease also gives a tenant-stockholder a restricted right to sell to a third party during the term of the lease. Under the lease restriction a tenant-stockholder often must obtain the consent of a majority of the other stockholders to sell a unit. In some cases the tenant-stockholder must obtain the consent of the Board of Directors of the corporation in order to sell his or her unit.

Sometimes this method of tenant-ownership is in the form of a trust. In these cases a certificate of beneficial interest is given the tenant instead of a stock certificate.

Financing the Cooperative

The financing of the cooperative is similar to the financing of any commercial property. First the developer obtains a construction loan and a commitment for permanent conventional financing. Like most

---

[1]AICPA Committee on Land Development Companies, *Accounting for Retail Land Sales* (New York: AICPA, 1973), p. 6.

commercial financing the loan maximum is about 75 percent of the appraised value. The corporate mortgage covers all of the apartments. Stock is then sold and the proprietary lease executed. For example, suppose a particular apartment is valued at $30,000. Assume the pro rata share of the mortgage is $20,000. The stock is then sold for $10,000 with the purchasers liable for their share of the payments on $20,000 plus maintenance costs, a pro rata share of the taxes, and so forth.

Because of the initial low loan-to-value ratio (66⅔ percent in this example) the buyer of the cooperative must put down a substantial down payment. This makes the units difficult to sell. Furthermore, a lender cannot take a second mortgage on an "individual" apartment. The reason obviously is that there is no way in the cooperative building for a holder of a second mortgage to foreclose against a single unit. Any borrowing done by a prospective purchaser of a unit must be done on a personal basis; for example, a prospect with only $5,000 in cash who needs a total of $10,000 must borrow the additional $5,000 on a personal note. This means it will probably have to be paid off at a faster rate than the underlying mortgage.

This leads to another difficulty with the cooperative. Suppose that A buys a cooperative apartment for $30,000 and it appreciates to $40,000. There is no way that A's individual unit can be refinanced because of the underlying blanket corporation mortgage. In addition, suppose A purchased a single family home for $30,000 and its value is now $40,000. If A needs money for family responsibilities such as a child's education, the loan can be entirely refinanced or a second mortgage placed on the property. This cannot be done with the cooperative apartment.

Another problem arises when a prospective tenant wishes to pay all cash for a unit. In this case the unit still bears a pro rata share of the entire blanket corporate mortgage. If the neighbors fail to make their payments, and a foreclosure takes place, the individual's apartment is lost with the rest. In some parts of the country, title companies have issued policies against this sort of loss.

Cooperative Loan Procedure. The cooperative loan procedure is not unlike any other loan. There are, however, a few minor variations within the mortgage instrument. For example, any subsequent transaction is subject to the terms of the executed mortgage. If A owns a unit and sells it to B, the executed mortgage is made a part of the conveyance. Further, in case of default the lender is immediately given the power of attorney to collect all rents and profits of the mortgaged property. In addition the mortgage contains a clause specifically stat-

ing that no individual unit will be released to an individual cooperative owner until the underlying mortgage is paid in full.

FHA Cooperative Financing. The FHA cooperative insurance program provides for two basic types: (1) the sales type project and (2) the
management type project.

The Sales Type Project. Here a cooperative corporation is organized
and each individual member is a stockholder. It should be noted that
the sales type cooperative involves new construction. Consequently an
FHA-insured blanket mortgage is placed by the lender on the project
while it is being built. After the sale of the individual units an FHA
mortgage is given to the individual purchasers with the proceeds going
to pay off the blanket mortgage. Title to common spaces remains in
the name of the cooperative.

The Management Type Cooperative. Here a nonprofit cooperative
corporation or trust is organized. The purpose is to build permanent
cooperative housing for its stockholders. The management type project
is covered by a blanket mortgage. The shareholders do not receive title
to their individual units, but have the right to occupy individual units.
They do, however, share both in the management of the project and
have a share interest in the entire project. The interest paid is the FHA
maximum rate plus one half of one percent on the unpaid balance of
the mortgage as the insurance premium.

Condominium Financing

Some housing authorities predict that by the year 2025 over 50
percent of the nation's population will be housed in condominiums.
What is a condominium? *Webster's Third New International Dictionary*
defines a condominium as:

> Common ownership by two or more persons holding undivided frac-
> tional shares in the same property and having the right to alienate
> their shares resembling tenancy in common in Anglo-American law
> rather than joint tenancy with its right of survivorship.

Briefly, the condominium is an ownership in fee simple by an individual of a single unit in a multi-unit structure, coupled with ownership of an undivided interest in the land and other elements of the
structure held in common with other unit owners of the building. The
fee simple ownership of the single unit generally applies to the air-
space between the walls and between the floors and ceilings. If the
walls are for the support of the building or are in common with another unit, they belong in the category called "common elements."
Generally, the common elements consist of the land beneath the

buildings, yards, service installations, and community entrances and exits. In the final analysis, individuals own their own units in a fee and are co-owners with others in the common elements.

Most condominiums are found in the area of residential housing. However, the condominium form of ownership is growing in the area of office buildings, industrial property, and even shopping centers.

There are four basic documents to establish a condominium:

1. The declaration (sometimes called a master deed). The declaration places the property under the condominium statutes.
2. The plot plan or architects' drawing showing the division into apartments.
3. The by-laws which control and govern the internal organization of the condominium.
4. The deed conveying the apartment and rights in common areas to purchasers.

Why the Condominium? Logically the question arises as to the reason why condominiums have taken over from the cooperatives. There are a number of reasons:

1. The cooperative tenant does not own an individual apartment. The cooperative corporation owns it. The shareholder-tenant merely has a proprietary lease.
2. The building has a *single* mortgage on the entire structure. Shareholders are responsible not only for their individual payments on interest and taxes, but also are collectively responsible if one shareholder fails to meet the payments.
3. In the condominium, each person has an individual mortgage and is responsible for taxes on that unit and is thus personally liable.
4. In the cooperative, an individual shareholder can increase equity through amortization of the loan, through appreciation in the value of the unit, or both. However, if the shareholder wants to sell, the buyer must be able to put down a large amount in cash. In the case of the condominium, the individual unit can be refinanced or the owner can take back a second mortgage.

The FHA and Condominiums. Although there has been a form of condominium ownership in Puerto Rico since 1958, the major impetus for this form of ownership is to be found in Section 234 of the Housing Act of 1961. This Act provided for FHA financing and insurance. Two conditions had to be met by the individual states:

1. Historically, assessors levied taxes on the value of the land plus the structure as a single unit. Basically they were limited to a two-dimensional concept. Because FHA financing was and is available only if the states permitted taxes to be levied on a three-dimensional concept, the states hurried to comply. Thus, taxes are now levied on the individual apartment plus a proportion of the value of the common spaces.

2. One other requirement was necessary which follows from the above FHA requirement. That is, the states also had to provide for the recording of title to the condominium as a three-dimensional unit. This, too, the states have done.

Although the FHA gave the first real impetus to the growth of condominium financing, not too many condominiums are FHA financed. The red tape is formidable. For example, a sponsor-owner can apply for a 90 percent construction loan. The amount of the loan is based on 90 percent of replacement value of the total value of the proposed project, or 90 percent of the total unit sales price. However, 80 percent of the units must be pre-sold to FHA-approved buyers by the time the construction loan is closed; otherwise, the construction loan will be reduced to 80 percent of the value.

In reality, the value on which the 80 percent loan is figured is *less* than replacement cost. The basis of the loan is determined by figuring the value of the pre-sold units plus estimating the value of the unsold units as if they were sold to a single investor who resells to individual investors. For example, suppose that 20 units have a total selling price of $20,000 per unit, or $400,000. Assume the value of the pre-sold units to be $200,000 and the gross sales of the remaining 10 units to be $200,000 less holding costs, plus a discount factor of 10 percent. Then:

	Sold Within One Year	
Dollar value of units		$200,000
Less sales costs	$10,000	
Less monthly charges (interest)	12,000	
Less real estate taxes	3,000	25,000
		$175,000

Discount factor @ 10% = $175,000 × .909
Present worth   = $157,500

Then, the value on which the loan is based is $157,500 + $200,000 = $357,500, with a loan-to-value ratio of 80 percent, or $357,500 × .80 = $286,000 as compared to a straight 80 percent loan on $400,000 of $320,000 ($400,000 × .08).

When the construction loan is closed it becomes a permanent, insured blanket loan. The sponsor-owner then has two years within which to sell 80 percent of the value of the units to FHA-approved buyers and other buyers (this can mean cash buyers). When a sale is made, the unit is released from the blanket. If the owner cannot sell 80 percent of the value of the units within the two-year time period, then the Federal National Mortgage Association buys the loan. The project then becomes an apartment rental project with a 40-year loan.

Condominium Conventional Financing. Although the availability of FHA financing gave impetus to condominiums through expediting the state statutes providing for real property taxes on individual units, relatively little FHA financing was done. Most of the condominiums were and are built with conventional financing. However, it is conventional financing with a difference.

First, a construction loan is obtained. Typically in condominiums the interim lender agrees to place the permanent financing. A frequent source of money for the interim financing is the real estate investment trust. At yearend 1975, such financing accounted for 34.8 percent of the investment trusts total loans. The length of the construction loan ranges from 1 to 3 years with the maturity matched with the expected time of completion of the project.

Second, each unit is financed by means of a permanent loan. It is here that it becomes conventional financing with a difference. The reason is that many state statutes provide that the individual unit cannot be sold subject to the construction loan. Consequently the developer must pre-sell enough units to pay off the construction loan. In cases like this the developer retains the right to call off the condominium if an insufficient number of units are pre-sold. In this case the project will revert to a unit rental situation.

Converting Rentals to Condominiums

Frequently existing rental apartments are converted to condominiums. For a successful conversion, in addition to the usual feasibility studies, there are several rules of thumb:

1. At least 25 percent of the existing tenants must indicate a willingness to purchase their units.
2. New units should be selling for at least 30 percent higher than the price of the existing units if the building was sold as one unit.
3. As a developer, you should earn 20 percent more than the market value for your efforts.

"Bridge" Financing

The name given to the financing of conversions is called *bridge financing*. The developer or converter approaches a lender who agrees to pay off any existing mortgage, plus any sums for upgrading. In addition, the same lender agrees to place the permanent financing as the units are sold. Typically, the permanent loan is 80 percent of the value of each unit.

QUESTIONS FOR REVIEW

1. What is a land development loan? How is it secured? How is it generally paid off?
2. Describe the tract accounting procedures that have proven disastrous to land development companies in the past few years. What recommendations did the AICPA make regarding these practices?
3. Why is the tenant of a cooperative actually a tenant-stockholder? What privileges, responsibilities, and relations exist for tenant-stockholders?
4. What are the financing difficulties and disadvantages of a tenant in a cooperative?
5. Explain the difference between the sales type cooperative project and the management type cooperative.
6. What are the advantages of a condominium over a cooperative?
7. How did the availability of FHA financing pave the way for the condominium boom? What is the present status of FHA financing in condominiums? Why is this so?
8. Explain the statement that most condominium financing is by "conventional financing with a difference"?
9. What are the stipulations in converting rentals to condominiums?

PROBLEMS

1. A tract development problem was illustrated early in the chapter. Tables 7-1 through 7-3 show a procedure for analyzing the problem.
   A. Rework the problem (including the three tables) under the assumption that each of the 100 lots could be sold for $6,000. How would this affect your analysis and decision?
   B. In the original problem, what would be the impact of financing costs or carrying charges of 8 percent (instead of 10 percent) on the estimated value of the raw land?

   Show the necessary calculations.

2. Calculate the "value" on which an FHA condominium construction loan would be based given the following conditions. Assume a 30-unit condominium complex is to be constructed with a selling price of $20,000 per unit. Twenty units are pre-sold. Costs associated with selling the additional units are expected to be $30,000. It is estimated that the additional units will require on the average one year to sell. The cost of funds or discount factor will be 10 percent.

Financing by Means of Long Term Leases

A *lease* is a contract creating a landlord and tenant relationship. The landlord is called the *lessor*, and the tenant, the *lessee*. The contract between the two parties conveys the right of possession of the leased premises to the tenant, in return for which the tenant pays the landlord rent. The term *rent* is defined as the compensation, whether money, provisions, chattels, or labor, received by the owner of the soil or buildings from the occupant thereof.

A lease may be thought of primarily as a contract; and as a general rule, the parties to a contract may agree to almost anything in a lease.[1] However, they cannot agree to things which are said to be against public policy.

As in all contracts, a lease must be entered into by persons having contractual ability. There must be a consideration, a delivery, and an acceptance. In addition, to validate a lease there must be a description that locates the premises with reasonable certainty. A lease should contain the term or the duration of the lease. The lease should also have a definite beginning and a certain ending. The following example illustrates the problems of a lease that is not properly executed:

> A written lease stating that the tenant's occupation was for the term of "one year, two years, three years" was sent to the landlord, who was to strike out all except one of the terms mentioned and then execute the lease. The landlord, however, executed the lease without striking out any of its terms. The court held there was no meeting of the minds, and consequently the lease was ruled invalid.[2]

---

[1]Actually the lease is both a contract and a conveyance.
[2]*Sayles v. Lienhardt*, 119 Misc. 851, 198 NY Supp. 337.

A lease must also contain an agreement, technically called "an agreement to let and take," although the words "let and take" rarely appear in the lease. The lease generally will state that the lessor "grants, demises, and lets unto the lessee." This is considered to be the agreement to let and take. These words give the tenant the right of possession, and also, in the event that someone appears later who has a better title to the premises than the landlord, give the tenant the right to proceed against the landlord for damages.

Finally, the lease must be executed in accordance with the statute. Some statutes state that the lease must be acknowledged, while others do not contain this provision. As a practical matter, it is a good procedure to have the lease acknowledged in order to enable the lease to be recorded, if the occasion arises.

CLASSIFICATION OF LEASES

Leases are generally classified in one of two ways: (1) by method of payment, or (2) by term, which is by length of the lease.

Lease Classified by Method of Payment

In classifying by method of payment the most common lease is the gross, or flat, lease. Several other leases are also classified by this method and will be discussed in the following paragraphs.

The Gross Lease or Flat Lease. The *gross*, or *flat, lease* is a type of lease in which the premises are rented at a fixed rate. The rent is paid to the landlord by the tenant, and the landlord, in turn, agrees to pay the taxes, insurance, and any other expenses that might be incurred in the operation of the premises. The possible exception to this is that the tenant would pay ordinary repairs if they were called for under the terms of the lease.

The Net Lease. The *net lease* is the type of lease in which the tenant pays the taxes, assessments, and all operating expenses in connection with the use of the premises. The landlord receives a net figure.

Most long-term leases are net leases. The net lease has become increasingly popular with owners of investment properties. Many owners do not wish to sell the property, but hope to obtain a steady income from the property without incurring any of the headaches of supervising the premises. The owner may lease the property and receive a flat rental from the lessee. The lease will provide that the lessee pay all of the expenses of maintaining and managing the property. In this type of lease the lessee hopes to make a profit out of the rents that will be received from the building.

Where the tenant pays 100 percent of all costs, the lease is sometimes called a *net-net-net* lease.

The Percentage Lease. The *percentage lease* is a type of lease in which the rental is based either on a flat fee plus a percentage of the gross or on the net income received by a tenant doing business on the premises.

There are several factors of importance that must be considered in the percentage lease. Suppose, for example, that the rental is based upon a small flat fee plus a percentage of the gross. *A* goes into possession as the tenant and does a gross business that by far exceeds expectations; consequently, *A*'s rent is high. Across the street from *A* there is a vacant property that is available for a flat or gross rental. *A* acquires this property and proceeds to open another store at that location. In effect, *A* enters into competition with the original store by drawing some of the patronage away from that store. This results in a reduction of *A*'s gross receipts in the store where the percentage base is in effect. To guard against this, the landlord should insert in the percentage lease a clause to the effect that tenants may not enter into competition with themselves either in the city, if it is a small city, or within a stated number of blocks of the leased premises if it is a large city.

If the percentage lease is to be based upon a net profit, the definition of net profit must be made clear. Is the flat rental to be a deduction from the gross profit in determining net profit? Are repairs and alterations to be deducted? Who is to pay the taxes? These are but a few of the many questions that must be spelled out in the lease in order to avoid any later misunderstanding.

The lease should contain a clause giving the lessor the right at anytime during the demised term to examine all the books of account and any other records that might reflect the operations of the lessee.

The parties also might consider the feasibility of inserting a recapture clause. A *recapture clause* gives the right to the landlord to take back the demised premises in the event that the tenant's business does not reach a certain gross. The clause may also give the right to the tenant to surrender the premises in the event that business does not reach a stated gross.

Other Methods of Payment. There are other sorts of subclassification of leases as to payment, such as the escalator lease, the index lease, and the revaluation lease.

Escalator or Step-Up Leases. In a long-term lease one of the problems to be considered by the landlord is changes in taxes, insurance, and operating costs over time. Although the precise changes in these amounts are at best a guess, rents are stepped up in long-term leases. A schedule is generally included in the lease showing changes in rent over time.

Index Leases. The *index lease* provides for rental changes in accordance with changes in a price index. The index could be the consumer price index, the wholesale price index, or even the construction cost index. Obviously the purpose of the index lease is to guard against inflation and declines in the purchasing power of the dollar.

Suppose, for example, the rents are linked with the consumer price index and the index rises 20 percent; the rents also must be raised 20 percent. It is 20 percent even though when prices rise the decrease in the value of the dollar is less than the increase in prices. If prices rise 100 percent, the value of your dollar cannot fall 100 percent to zero. It is still worth something. The formula is:

$$\frac{\text{Base year prices (currently 1967)}}{\text{Prices this year}} = \frac{\text{Value of dollar in current year}}{\text{Value of dollar in base year}}$$

Thus,

$$\frac{100}{120} = \frac{X}{100} \text{ or } 120X = 10,000 \text{ or } X = 83.33$$

Then, $100 - 83.33 = 16.67\%$ decline in dollar value.

Revaluation Leases. A *revaluation lease* calls for the lessor to select an appraiser and the lessee to select an appraiser. The two appraisers then select a third appraiser and among them they re-evaluate the long-term lease. The three then set the rent for another time period, after which the rents may again be revalued.

Leases Classified by Term

Leases are generally referred to as short-term or long-term leases. Generally short-term leases are thought to be those of less than 21 years. Leases that are over 21 years are regarded as long-term leases.

THE STATUTE OF FRAUDS AND LEASES

The statute of frauds enters the picture regarding leases much in the same manner as it does in other types of real property contracts. Owners may lease their property for as long a period as they want, but in most states only a lease for less than one year's duration may be oral. Leases for over one year under the statute of frauds must be in writing.

If the state law requires a lease to be in writing and the parties have failed to comply with this, or if the lease fails for any reason to meet the statutory requirements, then the lease cannot be enforced. If the lease cannot be enforced and the tenant has not yet gone into possession, the landlord may refuse the tenant the possession. If the tenant is already in possession under a lease that should have been written, but was not, the lease may be terminated at anytime by the landlord. On the other hand, the tenant may refuse to take possession, without any liability, under an unenforceable lease. If possession has taken place, however, the tenant is liable for "use and occupancy" during the period of occupancy of the premises.

A written lease may be recorded. In New York, for example, a lease for more than three years may be recorded. This is not to imply that a lease must be recorded; it is merely better practice to record long-term leases. The recording gives notice to the world of the rights of the tenant in the property, although in many cases actual possession of the premises is sufficient to give such notice.

REASONS FOR USING LEASES FOR FINANCING

The major reasons leases are often used as financing devices are for tax purposes or as an alternative to mortgage financing which may tend to tie up needed capital.

Obtaining Financing Through a Lease

Suppose A, a small manufacturer, has the opportunity to increase business, but needs more factory space. Assume further that A can get a building built for $200,000. The land cost is $40,000 and the improvements $160,000. A has two alternatives: (1) obtain a mortgage and build the building, or (2) lease the building from an investor. Assume a mortgage can be acquired in the amount of $132,000. This means A has to put up $68,000 in cash. By doing this A will be strapped for working capital; thus, A is forced to lease the property. However, as a tenant the rent is a tax deduction for A. Perhaps more important, though, is the freeing of capital to increase the factory operation that is made possible if the property is leased.

Deferring Taxes Through Leasing

Suppose you own a parcel of land with a current value of $40,000. The property was originally purchased for $10,000. If sold, the property will be subject to a long-term capital gains tax. If developed and leased, the rental income will be taxable, but the long-term gain will be deferred.

Increasing Marketability Through Leasing

With a tenant of good reputation the marketability of the property may be enhanced. If there is a good cash flow and proper tax advantages, the property becomes more readily saleable.

THE GROUND LEASE

In the previous example the owner simply had a vacant land developed and rented it to a tenant. The ground lease situation is quite different. A *ground lease* is a device permitting the ground and the improvements to be owned by different persons. For example, in an oversimplified form, suppose *A* owns land and *B* rents the land and builds a home on it. *A* still owns the land, but *B* owns the home.

If *B* seeks and obtains a loan, the loan is on the improvement, not on the land. Actually the lender has a secondary lien, because the lease (or right to lease) is prior. A leasehold mortgage differs from the fee mortgage in the sense that the security for the leasehold mortgage is a defeasible estate (the lease).

However, in the commercial lease things can become quite complicated. Suppose an owner has property valued again at $40,000. *X*, a developer, borrows $160,000 from Acme Insurance Company, leases the $40,000 vacant land, and builds a small apartment complex. If the developer defaults on the leasehold mortgage (discussed in Chapter 9), the lender can take over the leasehold (thus winding up with the improvement), but must still pay rent to the owner. This type of situation is an *unsubordinated leasehold mortgage*. Note that in this case the owner has first claim to rents because they are due under the terms of the ground lease. As a result, it is difficult for developers to get this rather shaky loan from a lender. Most lenders require that the ground lease be subordinated to the loan.

The Subordinated Ground Lease

Subordinated means to make inferior; consequently, in order for a developer to obtain a loan on a ground lease, the owner (lessor of the ground lease) must agree to subordinate to a mortgagee. For example, assume again that an owner has land worth $40,000 and the developer borrows $160,000. The lender (mortgagee) then places the $160,000 mortgage on the fee plus improvements. Because it is a ground lease, the owner is fully aware that the developer will seek a loan. The owner also knows that the probabilities of the developer obtaining such a loan are slim if the developer's lease is unsubordinated. Consequently, a clause will be put in the ground lease similar to the following:

> The Lessor (the owner in our case) hereby agrees that his/her rights under this lease are subordinate to any and all mortgages hereafter placed from time to time on the said premises and if the Lessee (the developer in this case) or the mortgagee so desire, the Lessor agrees to execute any instruments or instrument to evidence such subordination.

At the time the loan is actually made the owner will execute a subordination agreement making the lease inferior to the mortgage. This will be recorded, thus permitting the lender to move to a number one position. In short, as security for the $160,000 loan the lender has $200,000 worth of security after the improvement has been constructed. Furthermore, and this is most important, the property has been developed with 100 percent financing. In effect, the developer has used the owner-lessor's $40,000 piece of vacant land as a down payment.

An agreement for subordination of a lease begins below.

**CONSULT YOUR LAWYER BEFORE SIGNING THIS INSTRUMENT —
THIS INSTRUMENT SHOULD BE USED BY LAWYERS ONLY.**

AGREEMENT, made the   day of   nineteen hundred and

BETWEEN

party of the first part, and

party of the second part,

WITNESSETH:

WHEREAS, the said party of the first part now owns and holds the following lease   :

Lease dated the   day of   , 19   made by

to

and recorded in (Liber) (Record Liber) (Reel)   of section
of Conveyances, page   , in the office of the
of the

**Figure
8-1**   Subordination Agreement (Continued)

122   *Real Estate Finance* covering premises hereinafter mentioned or a part thereof, and

WHEREAS,

the present owner of the premises hereinafter mentioned is about to execute and deliver to said party of the second part, a mortgage to secure the principal sum of   dollars and interest, covering premises

and more fully described in said mortgage, and

WHEREAS, said party of the second part has refused to accept said mortgage
              unless said lease   held by the party of the first part be subordinated in the manner hereinafter mentioned,

NOW THEREFORE, in consideration of the premises and to induce said party of the second part to accept said   mortgage
and also in consideration of one dollar paid to the party of the first part, the receipt whereof is hereby acknowledged, the said party of the first part hereby covenants and agrees with said party of the second part that said lease   and any and all rights, options, liens and charges therein contained or created thereunder held by said party of the first part be and shall continue to be subject and subordinate in lien to the lien of said   mortgage
              for   dollars and interest about to be delivered to the party of the second part hereto, and to all advances heretofore made or which hereafter may be made thereon (including but not limited to all sums advanced for the purpose of paying brokerage commissions, consideration paid for making the loan, mortgage recording tax, documentary stamps, fee for examination of title, surveys, and any other disbursements and charges in connection therewith) to the extent of the last mentioned amount and interest, and all such advances may be made without notice to the party of the first part, and to any extensions, renewals and modifications thereof.

This agreement may not be changed or terminated orally. This agreement shall bind and enure to the benefit of the parties hereto, their respective heirs, personal representatives, successors and assigns. The word "party" shall be construed as if it read "parties" whenever the sense of this agreement so requires.

IN WITNESS WHEREOF, the said party of the first part has duly executed this agreement the day and year first above written.

IN PRESENCE OF:

Figure
8-1   Subordination Agreement (Concluded)

The Residential Ground Lease

Most leasehold financing is done on commercial properties; however, some is done on residential property. For example, it has long been the custom to build homes on 99-year leased land. The homeowner pays the ground rent and taxes directly to the lender, who distributes the rent to the owner, and the lender pays the taxes directly. There has been some residential leasehold financing in Missouri, Ohio, Pennsylvania, New York, Hawaii, and Maryland.

Lending institutions have gradually come to accept this form of loan because of FHA, Title II, Sec. 203. This provision provides insurance for loans on 1- to 4-family homes held by the borrower under renewable leases. The stipulation is that the lease must not be longer than 99 years nor less than 50 years from the date of the mortgage.

INSURED LEASES

One recent development has been the advent of private mortgage insurance companies. For the most part they insure conventional mortgages. However, they have recently begun insuring rents which facilitate financing. For example, if a builder is going to build a factory for a "triple A" rated tenant, the builder need only take the tentative lease to an institution and the financing will be readily available. However, if the prospective tenant is not rated triple A, a private mortgage insurance company must step in to insure the rent. If the private insurance mortgage company agrees to insure the rent, then the financial institution will lend the money knowing that if the tenant defaults it will be paid the money due under the terms of the mortgage.

SOME COMMON LEASE TERMS

Although real estate brokers are the prime negotiators of commercial leases, they should never attempt to draw the lease. This must be left to competent lawyers. However, one should be familiar with some of the more common aspects of the lease. Aside from such terms as the rent payments, insurance provisions, and terms of length of the lease some of the problems that arise are discussed in the following paragraphs.

Option to Purchase

Usually, when a tenant erects a building upon the premises of the landlord, the lease contains an option giving the tenant the right to purchase the improvement and the land at the end of the term. The option may state a price to be paid for the property, or the option may provide that if the lessor and the lessee are unable to negotiate a price, then the lessor and the lessee shall each appoint an appraiser. The appraisers shall then appoint an umpire. Each of the appraisers and the umpire appraise the property. In general, the lease states that the decision of any two appraisers (one of whom is the umpire) as to the price shall be binding on the parties. In the event that the third party then refuses to accept the decision of the other two, it has been held in most states that the proper remedy for the enforcement of the option to purchase at an appraised valuation is by specific performance. When such a clause exists, the proper procedure for its enforcement is by a suit for specific performance in a court of equity.

Often a lump sum for the option is paid to the lessor at the beginning of the lease. It sometimes is stipulated that this sum will be used as part of the purchase price if the option is exercised. Sometimes only part of this sum is applied to the purchase price. Frequently, all or part of the sum given for the option is applied to the last year's rent, if the option is not exercised.

The lease with option to buy is sometimes used as a financing device in the purchase of a residence. For example, the price of the home is agreed upon at $25,000. The tenant moves in under a lease and is given an option to buy the home at the $25,000, provided the option is exercised within a stated time. The tenant also agrees to pay rent. More often than not an agreed percentage of the rent is applied to the $25,000 purchase price.

Option to Renew

Often a lease contains an option to renew the lease. The option must usually be exercised within a stated time prior to the expiration of the lease. The right to renew may be either for a definite renewal period or for an automatic renewal. There may be included in this covenant granting the option to renew a different amount to be paid as rent for the renewal term.

In the first instance, the option gives a right to the lessee to notify the lessor within a stated time, prior to the end of the term of the lease, that the lessee desires to renew the lease for a stated period under the same terms and conditions as the old lease. The option to renew in the original lease states further that the old lease will be renewed as is, except for the deletion of the clause granting the option to renew. This suggests, then, that the lease may not be renewed under the option a second time.

The automatic renewal is slightly different in that it gives either party the right to notify the other within a stated period that a renewal is not wanted. In the ordinary option to renew, the right is given only to the lessee, but here both parties have the right to refuse to renew. It is different, too, from the option to renew for a definite period in that the option states that the renewal shall be in accordance with all of the provisions of the old lease "including this covenant." This suggests then that after the first renewal of the lease, the lease may again be renewed at the option of both parties to the original lease.

Covenant Not to Sublet or Assign

In the absence of a provision to the contrary, a tenant has a right to assign the lease or to sublet the premises. An *assignment* is the transfer of the entire term of the lease by the tenant; a *subletting* is, in effect, the making of a new lease in which the original tenant is the lessor and the subtenant the lessee. In the former case, the assignee steps into the shoes of the tenant and is generally liable for the payment of the rent to the original landlord. In the latter case, the subtenant is generally not liable for the rent or other obligations to the original landlord. However, the assignor may also be held for the failure of an assignee to live up to terms and conditions of the lease.

One distinction between a sublet and an assignment lies in the period of time involved. For example, if a lease was drawn for a term running from January 1 to July 15 and the tenant delivered the premises to another person until July 14, this would be a sublease. However, if the premises were occupied by another person from January 1 to July 15, which is the end of the term, then this would be construed as an assignment regardless of what the transaction was called. A second distinction is that a sublease may convey a portion of the premises.

To prevent the subletting or assignment of leased property, the landlord will usually insist that the lease contain a covenant in which the tenant agrees not to sublet or assign without the written consent of the landlord. The covenant will generally provide that the lease may be terminated if the tenant violates this covenant. Many landlords specifically insert a clause both to keep out undesirable tenants and to receive a bonus from the tenant in the event a tenant desires to sell a business opportunity.

The distinction between sublet and assign has some serious tax implications. Suppose A has a lease which B wants, with $10,000 to be paid monthly over the rental to be paid the landlord. A sublets to B one day short of the term. The monthly rental paid A over the rent due the landlord is taxable as ordinary income. If *A* assigns to *B*, then the $10,000 paid monthly over the sum paid the landlord is a long-term capital gain.

Use of the Premises

When a property is leased, the landlord receives the right to the rent, and the tenant receives the right of possession. In a sense, the tenant is the owner of the premises during the period of the lease. The tenant may use this possession in any legal manner, in the absence of any covenants to the contrary, and the landlord may not prevent the tenant from so doing. There is, however, one restriction by implication on all tenants; that is, the tenant cannot do anything that will injure or diminish the value of the landlord's interest. Any improper use of the premises by the tenant that does injure or diminish the value of the landlord's reversion is known as waste. In the event the tenant does injure the value of the reversion, the landlord may bring an action for damages, or an injunction which may result in a court order restraining the tenant from committing waste, or both. The lease may also provide that such breach by the tenant gives the landlord the right to terminate the lease upon the occasion of such breach.

It is customary in modern leases to limit the use of the premises. This is done by inserting a covenant in the lease stating what the premises are to be used for and including the words "only" or "no other." For example, the lease may state: "For use as a grocery store and for no other purpose."The words "only" or "no other" will limit the use of the premises to that which is specifically stated in the lease. The absence of these words may prevent the use of the premises from being effectively limited. In many states there are statutes providing for the termination of a lease if the lessee makes illegal use of the premises. A lease under these statutes is declared void.

Condemnation

Eminent domain is the right of the government to take private property for public use provided just compensation is made. The legal proceeding to take property under eminent domain is called a *condemnation proceeding*.

Lessee's Right to Make Payments on Mortgage

In long-term leases the lessee may have almost as much at stake in a property as the lessor-mortgagor. Consequently, one of the important clauses gives the lessee the right to make the mortgage payments if the lessor-mortgagor defaults on the mortgage. The clause is substantially as follows:

In the event that the Lessor should at any time fail to pay an installment of principal or interest under any mortgage now or hereafter placed on the demised premises, or any other sum therein provided to be paid by the Lessor, the failure of which payment or payments would constitute a default under the terms of said mortgage or mortgages, so as to permit a foreclosure thereof, the Lessee shall have the right forthwith to pay such principal, interest, or other sums, with respect to which the Lessor may be in default as aforesaid, and to deduct the amount of such payment, and the cost or expense attaching or incurred on account of such nonpayment by the Lessor, with interest thereon at the rate of (six) per cent per annum, from the successive installments of rental then due or thereafter falling due until the Lessee shall have been fully reimbursed for any and all such payments, cost, expenses and interest as aforesaid.

Ordinarily when a leased property is condemned, the tenant has no right to seek any damages that may have been suffered from the landlord.[3] To avoid any possible legal entanglements that might arise on this account, the lease will contain a clause that in the event of condemnation ". . . the lesee shall not be entitled to any part of the award as damages, or otherwise for such condemnation, and the lessor is to receive the full amount of such award. . . ."

Suppose, for example, that A rents space in a building for a garage. Over a period of time, A builds up goodwill which gives value to the business over and above the fixtures and equipment. Assume that the equipment is worth $1,000, but that the business, because of the goodwill, is worth $5,000. A sells the business to B, in return for which A receives $5,000. If the property is then condemned, the landlord will receive compensation for the property, but B will be forced to move out of the premises taking only the $1,000 worth of equipment. B will thus suffer the loss of the $4,000 that was paid A for the goodwill of the business. If A had not sold the business, the value of the goodwill that had been developed would have been lost by A.

It is therefore important, from the viewpoint of the lessee, to insist upon a clause in the lease stipulating payment to the lessee in the event of condemnation. This clause generally states, in effect, that if the property is condemned before a certain date, the lessee is to receive a stated sum. Other dates are generally inserted with other sums stated, and the clause also contains a final date after which the tenant is not entitled to any part of the condemnation award.

For example, in the event of condemnation, the clause will state:

The lessee shall receive the following amounts and none other as the agreed share of the award for such condemnation when, as and if it is paid.

---

[3]Sometimes in extremely rare cases the tenant may seek damages from the firm or political subdivision that condemned the property.

If such final order of condemnation is entered before April 1, 1974, the sum of $6,000; if between April 1, 1974, and April 1, 1977, the sum of $4,000; if between April 1, 1977, and April 1, 1979, the sum of $2,000; if thereafter, no award or share whatsoever.

Destruction of the Premises

Under the common law, the tenant is held liable for rent in the event that the premises are destroyed. By statute in several states, however, a complete destruction of the premises terminates the lease and relieves the tenant from any liability for further rents.[4]

THE SALE OF LEASEHOLDS

In one sense a lease consists of two parts: (1) a stream of income, and (2) the reversion, which is the right to the property after the termination of a lease.

The owner of a lease then has the stream of income, plus the reversion. If the owner has a need for money, both the income stream and the reversion could be sold; i.e., the fee subject to the lien of the mortgage could be sold in the case of a ground lease. The owner of the lease can also sell the stream of income. How much is it worth?

Suppose 10 years remain on the lease and the rental is $10,000 per year totaling $100,000 over the 10-year period. Clearly the income stream is not worth $100,000 because there is a 10-year waiting period. Assume that the "going rate is 9 percent." Then, using a 9 percent discount rate, the factor is 6.418 (the present worth of an annual income of $1 for 10 years discounted at 9 percent — see Table 4, Appendix B, Present Worth of a $1 Annuity). Then $10,000 × 6.418 = $64,180 the present worth of the $100,000 stream of income.

Whether this can be sold for this sum is another matter considering bargaining power, risk factor of the tenant, and relative nonliquidity.

QUESTIONS FOR REVIEW

1. Briefly describe the concept or meaning of the term lease.
2. Leases may be described by method of payment. Explain the differences among: (a) gross or flat lease, (b) net lease, and (c) percentage lease. Identify some additional methods relating to the payment of leases.
3. Discuss some of the reasons why leases are used for financing purposes.
4. What is meant by a ground lease?

---

[4]These states are: Arizona, Connecticut, Kentucky, Maryland, Michigan, Minnesota, Mississippi, New Jersey, New York, North Carolina, Ohio, Virginia, West Virginia, and Wisconsin.

5. Leases are characterized by a number of common terms. Briefly describe the following terms: (a) option to purchase, (b) option to renew, (c) covenant not to sublet or assign, and (d) use of the premises.
6. The concept of condemnation is important to lease arrangements. Discuss.
7. In discussing the possible sale of leaseholds, what is meant by the reversion?

PROBLEMS

1. Assume that you have entered into an index lease and your rental payments are tied to the consumer price index. Recently, the consumer price index rose from 150 to 180. When the index was at 150 your monthly rent was $300. How much will your rent be raised? What percentage increase does this represent? What would have happened if the consumer price index had dropped from 150 to 120 instead of rising?

2. It is sometimes said that a tenant may obtain 100 percent financing from a lease. Explain this statement in terms of the following information. Assume that you want to expand your manufacturing plant capacity. Additional land requirements will cost $50,000 with plant costs amounting to $100,000. What factors would be important in deciding whether to obtain a mortgage and build the building or lease the building from an investor?

3. You have the opportunity to purchase an existing lease. The lease is for 7 remaining years and will produce a stream of income (i.e., cash inflows in the form of rental payments) of $15,000 per year. If you desire a 10 percent return on your investment, how much would you be willing to pay to own the lease? In other words, what is the present worth of this lease arrangement to you?

High Ratio Financing

Chapter 9

High ratio financing involves a high loan-to-value ratio. That is, there is low or no cash equity by a promoter-developer in a project. In this sense the financing involves leverage.

LEVERAGE

Leverage is the use of borrowed money — hopefully to increase gains. It is based on the assumption that the borrower can earn more from the borrowed money than the amount paid in interest for the use of the borrowed money.

For example, A borrows money at 7 percent and lends the money out at 11 percent for a gross gain of 4 percent. Basically this is what the small loan companies do. The problem comes when A borrows at 7 percent, but can only lend at 5 percent, thereby losing 2 percent.

How Leverage Works

Assume an investor has $100,000 equity capital to invest. It is estimated that a 12 percent return is feasible, or $12,000 per year. Assume further that $100,000 can be borrowed at 10 percent and invested at 12 percent, together with the original $100,000. Then,

Amount borrowed	= $100,000
	.10
Cost at 10%	= $ 10,000
Total investment	= $200,000
	.12
Earnings at 12%	= $ 24,000

The effect of the leverage is thus

$$
\begin{aligned}
\text{Gross income} &= \$24{,}000 \\
\text{Less cost of borrowing} &= \underline{10{,}000} \\
\text{Net earnings} &= \$14{,}000
\end{aligned}
$$

As a result of the leverage $14,000, or 14 percent, has been earned on the equity capital of $100,000. In short, the ratio of earnings to equity $= \dfrac{14{,}000}{100{,}000}$, or 14 percent on the $100,000 equity.

The preceding example is of a one-to-one ratio. The ratio can be one to two, one to three, or whatever. Assume that on a one-to-four ratio (which is not at all unusual) you borrow four times the equity, or $400,000, at 10 percent hoping to earn 12 percent. Then,

$$
\begin{aligned}
\text{Amount borrowed} &= \$400{,}000 \\
& \underline{.10} \\
\text{Cost at 10\%} &= \$\ \ 40{,}000 \\
\text{Total investment} &= \$500{,}000 \\
& \underline{.12} \\
\text{Earnings at 12\%} &= \$\ \ 60{,}000
\end{aligned}
$$

The effect of leverage is thus

$$
\begin{aligned}
\text{Gross income} &= \$60{,}000 \\
\text{Less cost of borrowing} &= \underline{40{,}000} \\
\text{Net earnings} &= \$20{,}000
\end{aligned}
$$

The ratio of earnings to equity $= \dfrac{\$20{,}000}{\$100{,}000}$, or 20 percent on the $100,000 equity.

Reverse Effect of Leverage

In high ratio financing the ratio can be as high as one to 50 percent or even 100 percent borrowed money. However, the problem in high ratio financing is that the leverage may work in reverse. For example, assume a one-to-fifty ratio where $5,000,000 is borrowed at 10 percent. Assume further that as a result of a miscalculation or economic recession only 9 percent is earned on the $5,000,000. Then,

$$
\begin{aligned}
\text{Amount borrowed} &= \$5{,}000{,}000 \\
& \underline{.10} \\
\text{Cost at 10\%} &= \$\ \ 500{,}000 \\
\text{Total investment} &= \$5{,}100{,}000 \\
& \underline{.09} \\
\text{Earnings at 9\%} &= \$\ \ 459{,}000
\end{aligned}
$$

Real Estate Finance

The effect of leverage is thus,

$$
\begin{aligned}
\text{Gross income} &= \$459,000 \\
\text{Less cost of borrowing} &= \underline{-500,000} \\
\text{Net loss} &= \$\ 41,000
\end{aligned}
$$

SALE-LEASEBACK AS HIGH RATIO FINANCING

A *sale-leaseback* is a transaction in which a seller sells real property to a buyer who, as part of the transaction, leases the property back to the seller, usually for a long period of time.

Originally the sale-leaseback was termed a "purchase-leaseback" deal. As far back as 1882 a sale-leaseback was reported in England, but very little was known of the technique in the United States until 1942.

Prior to that time only five states permitted domiciled life insurance companies to buy real property for purposes other than their own use. It should be noted here that since 1942 life insurance companies were and are probably the largest source of funds as "buyers" in sale-leaseback transactions, the reason being that in 1942 the State of Virginia permitted insurance companies to invest up to 5 percent of their admitted assets in commercial real property. Other states followed Virginia's lead. Recently Connecticut permitted insurance companies to invest up to 5 percent of their admitted assets in loans or investments either not permitted by statute or by charter. Other states followed with the percentage of permitted investment in income-producing real estate ranging from 3 to as high as 20 percent.

This type of investment by a life insurance company received the label of "basket loan."[1] A *basket loan* is defined as a loan made as a result of a provision in the regulatory acts governing investments by insurance companies allowing for a percentage of total assets to be placed in otherwise unauthorized or illegal investments.

Types of Sale-Leaseback

There are a number of types of sale-leasebacks. The earliest type, still in use, is simply an institutional investor assuming the role of buyer-lessor with, more often than not, a department store assuming the role of seller-lessee. Both the terms of the sale and the lease are designed to fit the parties' requirements, particularly the lessee's

---

[1]New York and several other states permit mutual savings banks to invest in land or to engage in this type of investment as a joint participant.

credit rating. The leases are for an initial fixed term at a net rental designed to give the buyer an adequate return on the investment, plus a rate designed to retire the investment over the term of the lease. For example, a seller-lessee builds a building for $100,000. The building is sold to an investor, the buyer-lessor. It is leased back to the seller-lessee for 20 years. The rent is calculated to net out at 10 percent over the 20 years or $10,000 per year. Five percent is used to amortize the loan over the 20-year period, or $5,000 per year ($5,000 × 20 years = $100,000 cost of investment). The other 5 percent per year, or $5,000 per year, is considered an adequate return on the investment.

Since its early beginnings many other forms of sale-leaseback have been created. Many of these forms are based on fragmenting interests, such as in the sale and leaseback of land and partial financing by sale-leaseback.

Sale-Leaseback of Land. This agreement provides that the tenant is to erect a building financed by a leasehold mortgage. An example of a mortgage on a lease is shown in Figure 9-1 on pages 136–37.

For example, *A* owns land valued at $300,000 and sells it to *B* with a leaseback of $30,000 rent per year for 20 years. *A*, now the tenant, builds an office building for $1 million financed by Life Insurance Company, *C. C* obtains the mortgage on the lease, which makes the lease of *A* subordinate to the mortgage. *A* rents the offices and pays *B* $30,000 rent per year. *A* pays on the mortgage and presumably has money left over as profit. In the event of default, *C* (Life Insurance Company) forecloses on the lease, pays *B* the $30,000 per year, and rents out the building.

The property is thus 100 percent financed as far as *A* is concerned. As you recall, it was sold to *B* for $300,000, presumably at a profit. The label put on this sort of transaction is "land-sale-leaseback and leasehold mortgage." It should be noted that lenders will often require a participation in the income.

In addition to the profit from rents, *A* has a tax shelter through the use of depreciation, as well as the rental payments to *B*, greater than if *A* had had a straight mortgage.

Partial Financing by Sale-Leaseback. In this situation the object is to reduce the amount of equity which would be obtained through "normal" or conventional financing.

For example, *A* (or a syndicate) buys an existing building and land (typically an office building) for $1,500,000. Simultaneously the property is sold to a life insurance company for $1,350,000, or 10 percent off the purchase price. Then the property is leased back to the group under a very long-term lease at a rental of $100,000 per year. Space is leased out by group A, which hopes to receive more than the $100,000 rental per year.

1. A has $150,000 invested ($1,500,000 purchase price − $1,350,000 selling price = $150,000).
2. If A had used conventional financing on this older building, the best loan-to-value ratio it could hope for would be a 75 percent loan, or in this case .75 × $1,500,000 = $1,125,000. This means that A would have to put down $375,000 in cash. Thus, A reduced the needed cash by $225,000: $375,000 cash by conventional financing − $150,000 cash by the sale-leaseback = $225,000 less cash than needed by conventional mortgage financing.

Advantages and Disadvantages of the Sale-Leaseback

Before becoming involved in a sale-leaseback, both the buyer-lessor and the seller-lessee should analyze the advantages and disadvantages of such a transaction.

Advantages to the Buyer-Lessor. The advantages to the buyer-lessor are:

1. The rents would probably yield a higher rate of return than would a mortgage investment.
2. The buyer-lessor is the owner and thus has direct control rather than the indirect control of a mortgagee.
3. The transaction is set up so that much of the cost is amortized over the term of the first lease. Consequently, the buyer-lessor can cash in on the sale or lease of the remainder.
4. While rental income is taxable as income, depreciation is permitted within IRS limitations, thereby reducing the taxable income of the buyer-lessor.

Disadvantages to the Buyer-Lessor. The disadvantages to the buyer-lessor are:

1. The risk is greater than it would be if the investment were a mortgage because presumably there would be a down payment which would serve as a "cushion."
2. The buyer-lessor becomes tied to both the management and the credit of the seller-lessee. In case of bankruptcy, the Chandler Act limits the buyer-lessor's claim to one year's rent in case of general bankruptcy, but three years' rent in case of reorganization.
3. Because a portion of the rent is set aside to amortize the investment, the actual net income is lowest in the early years when the investment is the highest and the risk is the greatest.

In some states statutes require that the "basket" loan made by insurance companies be amortized according to statute. For example, in

MORTGAGE ON A LEASE

This indenture made this   day of   , One thousand nine hundred and   , by and between   , party of the first part and   , party of the second part.

WHEREAS   , did, by a certain indenture of lease, bearing date the   day of   , in the year One thousand nine hundred and   , demise, lease, and farm-let unto   , and to its successors and assigns, all and singular the premises hereinafter mentioned and described together with their appurtenances;

TO HAVE AND TO HOLD THE SAME unto said   , and its successors and assigns, for and during and until the full end and term of   years, from the   day of   One thousand nine hundred and   , fully to be completed and ended, yielding and paying therefor unto the said   , and to its heirs successors and assigns, the yearly rent or sum of   ; and

WHEREAS the said party of the first part is justly indebted to the said party of the   part in the sum of   secured to be paid by a certain note bearing even date herewith conditioned for the payment of the said sum of   on the   day of   , One thousand nine hundred and   (   ), and the interest thereon to be computed from (the date thereof) at the rate of 10 per centum per annum and to be paid monthly on the   day of   and monthly thereafter on the first day of each and every month thereafter.

IT BEING THEREBY EXPRESSLY AGREED that the whole of the said principal sum shall become due at the option of the mortgagee after default in the payment of interest, taxes or assessments of rents as hereinafter provided.

NOW THIS INDENTURE WITNESSETH that the said party of the second part, for the better securing the payment of the said sum of money mentioned in the condition of the said note, with interest thereon, and also for and in consideration of the sum of *one dollar*, paid by the said party of the first part, the receipt whereof is hereby acknowledged, doth grant and release, assign, transfer and set over unto said party of the second part, and to its heirs and assigns forever:

(Description of the Lease)

TOGETHER with the apurtenances and all the estate and rights of the party of the first part of and in and to said premises under and by virtue of the aforesaid indenture of lease.

TO HAVE AND TO HOLD the said indenture of lease and renewal thereof, if any, and the above granted premises, unto said party of the second part, its heirs, and assigns for and during all of the rest, residue and remainder of said term of years yet to come and unexpired in said indenture of lease and in the renewals therein provided for; subject, nevertheless, to the rents, covenants, conditions and provisions in the said indenture of lease above mentioned.

Figure
9-1   Mortgage on a Lease (Continued)

Provided always that if the said party of the first part shall pay unto the said party of the second part, the said sum of money mentioned in the condition of the said note and all the interest thereon, at the time and in the manner mentioned in the said condition, that then these presents and the estate hereby granted shall cease, determine and be void.

And the said party of the first part covenant(s) with the said party of the , part as follows:

FIRST: That the party of the first part will pay the indebtedness herein-before provided. And if default shall be made in the payment of any part thereof, the said party of the second part shall have power to sell the premises therein described according to law.

SECOND: That the said premises now are free and clear of all incumbrances whatsoever, and that the party of the first part has good right and lawful authority to convey the same in manner and form hereby conveyed.

THIRD: That the party of the first part will keep the building on the said premises insured against loss by fire, for the benefit of the mortgagee.

FOURTH: And it is hereby expressly agreed that the whole of the said principal sum shall become due at the option of the said mortgagee after default in the payment of any installment of principal, or after default in the payment of interest for (20) days, or after default in the payment of any rent or other charge made payable by said indenture for (40) days or after default in the payment of any tax or assessment for (20) days after notice and demand.

AND THAT IN CASE OF ANY DEFAULT, Whereby the right of foreclosure occurs hereunder, the said party of the second part or the holder of said note shall at once become entitled to the possession, use and enjoyment of the property aforesaid, and to the rents, issues and profits thereof, from the accruing of such right and during the pendency of foreclosure proceedings and the period of redemption, if any there be; and such possession shall at once be delivered to the said party of the second part or the holder of said note on request and on refusal, the delivery of such possession may be enforced by the said party of the second part or the holder of said note by any appropriate civil suit or proceeding, and the said party of the second part, or the holder of said note, or any thereof, shall be entitled to a Receiver for said property, and of the rents, issues and profits thereof, after such default, including the time covered by foreclosure proceedings and the period of redemption, if any there be, and shall be entitled thereto as a matter of right without regard to the solvency or insolvency of the party of the second part, without regard to the value thereof, and such Receiver may be appointed by any court of competent jurisdiction upon ex parte application and without notice — notice being hereby expressly waived — and all rents, issues and profits, income and revenue therefrom shall be applied by such Receiver to the payment of the indebtedness hereby secured, according to law and the orders and directions of the court.

IN WITNESS WHEREOF, the said party of the first part to these presents has hereunto set hand and seal the day and year first above written.

Sealed and delivered in the presence of   /s/   A Inc.,   (L.S.)

(JOHN DOE)

(Acknowledgment)

Figure
9-1   Mortgage on a Lease (Concluded)

New York the cost must be amortized at not less than two percent per annum and all income over four percent must be used to amortize the cost. In Pennsylvania improvements, not the cost of the land, must be amortized at two percent per year.

Advantages to the Seller-Lessee. Advantages to the seller-lessee are:

1. The seller-lessee frees up cash.
2. The financing constitutes 100 percent financing.
3. Rent is deductible for tax purposes.
4. The seller-lessee has a chance for a long-term capital gain if the sale is made with a profit.

Disadvantages to the Seller-Lessee. The disadvantages to the seller-lessee are:

1. Rents are higher than mortgage payments because the property is being amortized. Furthermore, mortgage payments stop after the debt is repaid, while the rent continues in the event the lease is renewed.
2. The remainder value is lost to the seller-lessee.
3. The seller-lessee is not permitted to take any depreciation.

SALE-BUYBACK

The basic idea of the sale-buyback is quite simple. A lending institution buys the property and sells it back to the builder-developer. The instrument used is a Contract for Deed (discussed in Chapter 4).

While the concept of a sale-buyback is simple, the contract executing it may be rather complex. An institution will agree to pay between 80 and 90 percent of the market value of the project, which is designed to equal 100 percent of the developer's cost. For example, assume the market value of the proposed project is $1,000,000, which the lender-institution buys for $850,000. The builder-developer receives a Contract for Deed to buy it back in installments at that price. At this point legal title is in the lending institution and equitable title is with the developer.

The developer is entitled to a tax shelter income by depreciating the property because the developer has equitable title. For example, the project has a remaining economic life of 30 years on the $1,000,000 thus the developer may shelter $33,333 per year on a straight-line basis. Furthermore, the developer-buyer has received 100 percent financing. The contract provides first for a 15-year "lock-in" prohibiting the developer-buyer from paying off the contract for 15 years. During this time the builder-developer shelters the cash flow. For the balance of the term of the contract, there may be termination options at 5-year intervals.

The question arises at this point as to why an institution would get involved in this type of transaction. After all, the institution could buy the property from the developer and lease it back, offsetting rental income against depreciation. The answer is more money for the lender. In a normal loan with a mortgage, as each payment is made the amount paid on principal increases while the amount paid as interest declines. In the case of the sale-buyback the amount paid on principal remains the same and the amount of interest remains the same over the term of the contract.

For example, a 35-year contract has a loan of $850,000. To amortize this loan on an annual basis the annual amortization is determined by dividing the total amount ($850,000) paid off over the years the property is held by the number of years (35). Thus: $\frac{\$850,000}{35} =$ $24,285.71. As a percentage of $850,000 this amounts to $\frac{\$24,286}{\$850,000} =$ 2.857%. In short, the principal is being paid off at the rate of 2.857 percent per year. Obviously the institution has to be paid a rate of interest on top of that, say 6 percent. In terms of dollars per year, 6 percent of $850,000 = $51,000. This is the interest paid. The total payment then is interest of 6 percent plus 2.857 percent, or a constant of 8.857 percent. The annual payments on the $850,000 sales price amount to $850,000 × .08857 = $75,284.50 (or $75,285 rounded off).

Assume that the net income generated on the property will be $100,000. This income will be split as follows:

Net income	= $100,000
Less installment payment at 8.857% =	75,285
Remaining cash flow	= $ 24,715

Split as follows (subject to negotiation):

Lender-seller @ 25%	= $ 6,178.75
Developer-owner @ 75%	= 18,536.25
	$24,715.00

Thus, the lender-seller not only receives payments of interest and principal, but also shares in the net income. The developer-owner gets a write-off of $33,333 per year from depreciation, thus the $18,536.25 received in net income is tax free. The balance of the depreciation is carried over to "other income." In addition, the interest of $51,000 per year can also be written off against "other income."

If this same loan were set up as a mortgage loan rather than a sale-buyback, the lender would also receive monthly payments of principal and interest but the interest payments would decline over the life of the loan. The total annual payments required under the two arrangements are shown in Tables 9-1 and 9-2. You have already seen how the total annual payment is derived for the sale-buyback. To determine the mortgage payment, the loan amount ($850,000) is divided by the present value annuity interest factor for 35 years at 6% interest, which is 14.498. Thus,

$$\frac{\$850,000}{14.498} = \$58,629 \text{ annual payment.}$$

Of this amount, $51,000 is interest in the first annual payment. Thereafter the interest declines while the amortization payments increase. This compares to a $75,285 annual payment under the sale-buyback, of which $51,000 is also the amount of interest paid the first year. However, the interest does not decrease each year under the sale-buyback and the lender is thus repaid a larger amount than under a mortgage arrangement.

Table 9-1   MORTGAGE LOAN

Year	Total Payment	Interest	Amortization Repayment	Remaining Balance
1	$58,629	$51,000	$7,629	$842,371
2	58,629	50,542	8,087	834,284
3	58 629	50,057	8,572	825,712
.	.	.	.	.
.	.	.	.	.
.	.	.	.	.
35	.	.	.	.

Table 9-2   SALE-BUYBACK

Year	Total Payment	Interest	Amortization Repayment	Remaining Balance
1	$75,285	$51,000	$24,285	$825,715
2	75,285	51,000	24,285	801,430
3	75,285	51,000	24,285	777,145
.	.	.	.	.
.	.	.	.	.
.	.	.	.	.
35	.	.	.	.

Under the sale-buyback the effective interest rate may be fairly high. The formula for determining effective interest cost is

$$\frac{2 \times M \times D}{N(P + 1)}$$

where

M = number of payments per year
D = total interest
N = principal
P = total number of payments.

In this case the total interest is found by multiplying the annual interest cost of $51,000 by 35 years, which results in $1,785,000 total interest. The effective interest rate for this loan is thus

$$\frac{2 \times M \times D}{N(P + 1)} = \frac{2 \times 1 \times \$1,785,000}{\$850,000 (35 + 1)}$$

$$= \frac{\$3,570,000}{\$30,600,000}$$

$$= 11.7\% \text{ interest.}$$

FRONT MONEY DEALS

Front money financing is another form of high ratio real estate financing. It takes the form of a joint venture with the lender supplying the money and the developer supplying land plus development skills. Because the lender becomes a participant in the project, the lender cannot be charged with *usury*, which is charging interest in an amount greater than the legal rate. Furthermore, the risk of losing equity capital is shared between the lender and the developer, which brings up the old adage "where risk is shared there's a partnership." By giving the lender a share of the profits, the developer can reduce the risk involved and is further able to increase the size of the project.

The Organizational Form

Assume a lender and a developer agree to enter into a joint venture. Generally the first step is for the lender and the developer to form subsidiary corporations in order to limit their liability. If the lender is an insurance company or a mutual savings bank, it is legally required to form a corporation. After having formed the corporation, it must then be approved by the state insurance commissioner or another regulatory body.

The second step is for the two corporations to enter into either a general partnership or a limited partnership (see Chapter 10).

The typical arrangement may be shown as follows:

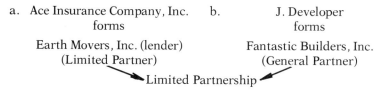

a. Ace Insurance Company, Inc.   b.   J. Developer
                forms   forms

        Earth Movers, Inc. (lender)   Fantastic Builders, Inc.
          (Limited Partner)   (General Partner)

                        Limited Partnership

Typically Ace Insurance Company will provide both the interim and permanent financing for the project with the money being filtered through its subsidiary, Earth Movers, Inc., allowing Ace Insurance Company to receive interest on both type loans. Furthermore, Earth Movers, Inc., and Fantastic Builders agree that Earth Movers, Inc., will participate in the net income (usually 50–50), with this money filtering upward to Ace Insurance Company from Earth Movers, Inc.

For example, suppose J. Developer, through its subisdiary Fantastic Builders, Inc., purchases a piece of land for $125,000. J. Developer approaches Ace Insurance Company with a proposal for a $5,000,000 project on which the development cost is $4,875,000. Ace agrees to the deal and forms Earth Movers, Inc., which enters into the limited partnership. Then the project financing may appear as follows:

Lender provides 100% of development cost	$4,875,000
Developer provides land cost	125,000
Total cost	$5,000,000

It is projected that the cash flow will be 10 percent of cost per year, or $500,000. Each corporation is to receive an 8 percent return on its cash outlay or investment. Thus, Earth Movers, Inc., receives 8 percent of $4,875,000, or $390,000 per year. Fantastic Builders receives 8 percent of $125,000, or $10,000 per year. Since the 8 percent return to each partner amounts to $400,000, the balance of the cash flow ($100,000) is split 50-50, with Earth Movers, Inc., receiving $50,000 and Fantastic Builders receiving $50,000. The total return for each corporation is then

Earth Movers	$390,000
	50,000
	$440,000 per year
Fantastic Builders	$10,000
	50,000
	$60,000 per year.

Fantastic Builders thus receives a return on the money paid down of 48% ($60,000 ÷ $125,000 = 48%), which is an excellent rate of return.

There are other variations of this type of financing. For example, a developer wants to build a project costing $1,000,000, of which the land is to cost $100,000. Construction financing will be at an 80 percent loan-to-value ratio, or $800,000. It is estimated that on completion the project will sell for $1,225,000. The developer approaches an investor who agrees to put up $100,000 and the developer puts up $100,000 to make up the difference between the $800,000 loan and the $1,000,000 project cost. For tax purposes the investor and the developer form a limited partnership. Assume a 10 percent loan is obtained on the $800,000 construction cost. The interest is $80,000 (in real life this would be less because the $800,000 is not all borrowed at once). If the building is sold after a time lapse necessary to qualify it as a long-term capital gain, the results are as follows:

Sale price	$1,225,000
Less construction loan plus interest	880,000
	$ 345,000
Less investor loan plus 10% interest	110,000
	$ 235,000
Less developer's investment	100,000
	$ 135,000

The balance of $135,000 is divided 50-50, so the developer has earned on the cash paid down:

$$\frac{\$67,500}{\$100,000} = 67.5 \text{ percent, again a high rate of return.}$$

This return is in addition to any tax savings the developer may have had during the construction of the building.

Another variation is where the investor puts up the entire $200,000 with the net proceeds being split 50-50. Ownership of the land prior to the sale is in the name of the investor. When the project is sold, the $1,225,000 is divided as follows:

Sale price	$1,225,000
Less construction loan plus interest	880,000
	$ 345,000
Less investor's loan plus 10% interest	220,000
	$ 125,000

The balance of $125,000 is split 50-50 with the developer receiving $62,500 without having to pay any money down.

QUESTIONS FOR REVIEW

1. High ratio financing uses leverage. Explain how leverage can work in reverse.
2. In a sale and leaseback of land the lender obtains security for the loan often by means of a mortgage on a lease. Explain exactly what the lender receives in the event of foreclosure.
3. What is a basket loan?
4. What limitations are imposed on a buyer-lessor under the Chandler Act?
5. Differentiate between a sale-leaseback and a sale-buyback.
6. What are the steps involved in establishing front money financing?
7. How is risk divided in front money deals?

PROBLEMS

1. What is the return on a 1 to 25 ratio with the equity portion being $1,000,000? The cost of the borrowed money is 10 percent and the expected return is 12 percent.

2. Syndicate A buys a building for $1,000,000 and immediately sells it to an insurance company for $900,000. The property is then rented back to the syndicate at $50,000 per year. What is the syndicate's reduction of equity financing if the best loan-to-value ratio they could obtain is 75 percent?

3. Using examples, explain how and where leverage manifests itself in the sale-leaseback, sale-buyback, and front money deals.

Some Alternative Financing Methods

Chapter 10

There are numerous alternative financing methods. Some of these methods are characteristically used in smaller dollar amount transactions, while others involve greater sums. One should become familiar with these methods as they are important means of alternative financing.

THE WRAPAROUND MORTGAGE OR KICKER

Strictly speaking, the *wraparound mortgage* is not a mortgage at all, but rather it is a covenant contained within a mortgage. This covenant is used to entice sellers of commercial-type properties to sell to a buyer with a relatively small down payment, and it is often used during periods of high interest rates. For example, suppose a seller has an older apartment house on which there is an existing first mortgage of $20,000 that was placed some years ago at a rate of 4 percent interest. This property has appreciated and is now worth $100,000. The seller is approached by a buyer who has only $10,000 for a down payment. The seller agrees to take back a purchase money mortgage in the amount of $70,000, which in reality is a second purchase money mortgage, at 8 percent, and the buyer is to assume the $20,000 mortgage. The enticement is this: the buyer agrees not only to assume the $20,000 mortgage and pay the lender 4 percent on the mortgage, but also agrees to pay an additional 4 percent on the old $20,000 mortgage to the seller. The net effect of this is to increase the effective yield to the seller on the $70,000 mortgage.

This same sort of thing has been used effectively in the sale of farms and ranches where installment land contracts are involved. For example, A sells B a ranch on a installment land contract for $100,000. B pays $35,000 down, leaving $65,000 owed to A at 8 percent interest. B then sells the ranch to C for $150,000 with $50,000 down. C effectively owes A $65,000 and B $35,000, totaling $100,000. B may require an 8½ percent interest rate. This means that C is paying 8½ percent on the $65,000 owed to A; consequently, B pockets the ½ percent interest on the $65,000 (the difference between what B agreed to pay A and what C is paying B). In addition, B receives the entire 8½ percent on the remaining $35,000.

PARTICIPATIONS

There are two situations covered by the broad term "participation." One is participation in a loan. The second is participation in the security for a loan.

Participation in the Loan

Participation or sharing in the loan can be done either by an individual or an institution. For example, A and B agree to lend C $20,000 on a first mortgage. A is to put up $10,000 and B is to put up $10,000. In short, they will share equally. The borrower signs the note and mortgage in the amount of $20,000. The mortgage is then recorded. The two individuals (A and B) sign a participation agreement (in some states called an ownership agreement).

The *participation agreement* is the instrument used to define the ownership or shares that two or more persons may have in the same mortgage. It states the terms upon which the parties to the instrument agree to share in the mortgage. Generally, if both of the parties share equally in a single mortgage, they appear as co-owners on the face of the original mortgage. If they do not share equally in the mortgage, one of the parties will be junior to the other. The participation agreement indicates the extent to which one party is to hold a prior interest and the extent to which the other party is to hold a junior interest in the existing mortgage. It authorizes one of the parties to collect the interest and defines the method of distribution of principal and interest. It also recites the respective rights of the parties in the event of need to foreclose the mortgage.

This instrument is acknowledged but is generally not recorded. It may, however, be recorded in the event that it is subsequently necessary to bring any action under the terms of the instrument.

Basically, loan participations by institutions amount to the same thing. They came about as the result of an unusual law involving savings and loan associations. For many years savings and loan associations were permitted to buy and sell FHA and VA mortgages nationwide. However, they were restricted to making loans within a 50-mile radius "lending area." This meant they could not buy or sell conventional mortgages over the 50-mile limit. Consequently, to be able to operate outside the 50-mile radius with conventional loans, the Federal Home Loan Bank Board in 1957 amended the law, which already permitted participation in loans within the 50-mile area, to allow participations beyond the 50-mile area. As a result, institutions may share or *participate* outside the 50-mile area in mortgage loans. A participation agreement is shown in Figure 10-1 on pages 148–49.

Participation in the Security

A participation in the security is used by lenders in tight money situations. They will agree to lend on a commercial property only if they can participate in the income, capital appreciation, or both, of the property. One form of participation is in the income. For example, in order to obtain a loan on an apartment building, an investor may be forced to agree to permit the lender to participate in the gross rent, often as high as 15 percent.

Another form of participation is where the borrower has to agree to give the lender a percentage of the appreciation if the building is sold. For example, a building is sold for $50,000 over cost. The borrower may have to give the lender as high as 50 percent of the gain. Often the participations combine both forms. Needless to say, there are no prepayment clauses in this type of mortgage because the lender does not want the borrower to refinance in case mortgage rates drop.

BALLOON NOTE OR BALLOON MORTGAGE

The balloon note or mortgage provides for periodic mortgage payments that do not amortize the loan by the date of its termination, leaving the balance due to be paid in a lump sum. Generally, this type of financing is used in connection with an assumption of a first mortgage and a second purchase money mortgage or deed of trust. For example, suppose a property is for sale for $23,000. The terms are $3,000 down, an assumable mortgage of $15,000 and a second purchase money mortgage of $5,000 for 5 years payable at $50 a month (assume no interest for purpose of illustration). Obviously, then, the $50 per month payments, or $600 per year, will only amount to $3,000 at the end of 5 years ($600 × 5 = $3,000). This leaves a balance of $2,000 due at that time. The note and mortgage will call for a $2,000 payment at the end of the 5 years. This is the "balloon."

Sometimes the lender will renew the note and extend the final balloon; however, the lender is not legally obligated to renew the note and if the "balloon" is not paid foreclosure proceedings may be initiated.

PARTICIPATION OR OWNERSHIP AGREEMENT*

AGREEMENT, made this _____ day of _____, one thousand nine hundred and _____,
between _____
hereinafter designated as the party of the first part and _____

hereinafter designated as the party of the second part, **WITNESSETH** that **WHEREAS**, the party of the second part holds a certain indenture of mortgage and the note (or bond) which it secures made by _____
to _____
to secure the principal sum of _____ dollars,
and interest, dated _____, and
recorded in the office of the Register of the County of _____, _____
in Liber of Mortgages _____, page _____ covering premises in the City
of _____, County of _____ State of _____ and
WHEREAS, the party of the first part has an interest in said note (or bond) and mortgage, to the extent only as hereinafter set forth, and **WHEREAS**, the parties hereto desire to declare the terms upon which said note (or bond) and mortgage are held by the party of the second part.
NOW, THEREFORE, the parties hereto mutually certify and agree: —
FIRST. — The ownership of the party of the second part in said note (or bond) and mortgage is now to the extent of _____ dollars and interest thereon at the rate of per centum per annum from _____,
and the party of the first part is the owner of the balance of said mortgage debt remaining; but the ownership of the party of the second part is superior to that of the party of the first part, as if the party of the second part held a first note (or bond) and mortgage for said sum of _____ dollars and interest thereon as aforesaid, and the party of the first part held a second and subordinate and mortgage to secure the interest of the party of the first part in said mortgage debt.
SECOND. — The party of the second part is authorized to collect all the interest which is secured by said note (or bond) and mortgage and shall retain therefrom a sum equal to the interest then accrued upon the share of said note (or bond) and mortgage owned by the party of the second part, and then remit to the party of the first part any balance of interest remaining.
THIRD. — The party of the second part or any assignee of the interest of the party of the second part in said note (or bond) and mortgage is authorized to accept payment of said note (or bond) and mortgage and to execute the proper satisfaction therefor, and the holder so satisfying said note (or bond) and mortgage shall account to the party of the first part for all money received in excess of the ownership in said note (or bond) and mortgage of said party of the second part of such assignee.
FOURTH. — The party of the second part shall have all the rights of any holder of said note (or bond) and mortgage including the right to foreclose the same and to receive the proceeds of sale from the referee, but the party of the first part shall in

---

Figure
10-1 Participation or Ownership Agreement (Continued)

any and every event, have the right to an accounting for all money received by the party of the second part or any assignee of the interest of the party of the second part in said note (or bond) and mortgage in excess of the ownership of the party of the second part in said note (or bond) and mortgage. In case of foreclosure the party of the second part shall be under no obligation to protect the interests of the party of the first part upon a sale of the mortgaged premises.

FIFTH. — All rights and authority given to the party of the second part under this agreement are irrevocable so long as the party of the second part, or any assignee of the party of the second part has any interest in said note (or bond) and mortgage and shall pass to and apply to the party of the second part and to any assignee of interest of the party of the second part in said note (or bond) and mortgage.

SIXTH. — The interest of the party of the first part under this agreement in said note (or bond) or mortgage or mortgage debt is not assignable as against the party of the second part except by an instrument duly executed in the manner required for the execution of a deed of real property and endorsed upon or attached to this instrument; no assignee of the interest of the party of the first part in said note (or bond) and mortgage shall have any rights under this agreement, nor be entitled to any payment thereunder until such assignment shall have been exhibited to the party of the second part and a copy thereof shall have been filed with the party of the second part, and the receipt of such copy shall have been noted by the party of the second part on this agreement. Whenever the proceeds of the ownership of the party of the first part in said note (or bond) and mortgage shall be paid to the holder thereof, this agreement and all assignments thereof shall be surrendered to the party of the second part. The interest of the party of the second part is assignable to any person or corporation, without liability on the part of the party of the second part, but the interest of any such assignee shall be subject to this agreement.

SEVENTH. — This agreement shall be binding upon and inure to the benefit of the successors, legal representatives and assigns of the parties hereto.

IN WITNESS WHEREOF, the said parties have signed and sealed these presents, the day and year first above written.

IN PRESENCE OF:

(Acknowledgment)

*In the states using the Deed of Trust, the term Deed of Trust is substituted each time the word "mortgage" is used in the above form.

Figure
10-1   Participation or Ownership Agreement (Concluded)

TRUTH IN LENDING AND PROMISSORY NOTES

The Truth in Lending Act, effective July 1, 1969, requires creditors to make clear the exact amount of finance charges to be paid for credit. The rules and regulations are spelled out by the Federal Reserve in Regulation Z, which essentially enables borrowers to shop for money. Not only balloon notes but all notes are governed by this regulation.

Under Regulation Z, both finance charges and the annual average percentage rate (based on a 365 day year rather than a 360 day year) must be spelled out. Finance charges, stated in dollars and cents, include such things as price-time differential; discounts; service, transaction, activity, or carrying charges; loan fees; discount points; finder's fees; appraisal fees; and premiums for credit life insurance. Calculation of these fees is shown in Table 10-1 on pages 150–51.

Table 10-1 Sample Page from Table for Computing Annual Percentage Rate for Level Monthly Payment Plans

EXAMPLE

Finance charge = $35.00; Total amount financed = $200; Number of monthly payments = 24.

SOLUTION

Step 1 — Divide the finance charge by the total amount financed and multiply by $100. This gives the finance charge per $100 of amount financed. That is, $35.00 ÷ $200 = .1750 × $100 = $17.50.

Step 2 — Follow down the left hand column of the table to the line for 24 months. Follow across this line until you find the nearest number to $17.50. In this example $17.51 is closest to $17.50. Reading up the column of figures shows an annual percentage rate of 16%.

NUMBER—ANNUAL PERCENTAGE RATE OF

(FINANCE CHARGE PER $100 OF AMOUNT FINANCED)

PAYMENTS	14.00%	14.25%	14.50%	14.75%	15.00%	15.25%	15.50%	15.75%	16.00%	16.25%	16.50%	16.75%	17.00%	17.25%	17.50%	17.75%
1	1.17	1.19	1.21	1.23	1.25	1.27	1.29	1.31	1.33	1.35	1.37	1.40	1.42	1.44	1.46	1.48
2	1.75	1.78	1.82	1.85	1.88	1.91	1.94	1.97	2.00	2.04	2.07	2.10	2.13	2.16	2.19	2.22
3	2.34	2.38	2.43	2.47	2.51	2.55	2.59	2.64	2.68	2.72	2.76	2.80	2.85	2.89	2.93	2.97
4	2.93	2.99	3.04	3.09	3.14	3.20	3.25	3.30	3.36	3.41	3.46	3.51	3.57	3.62	3.67	3.73
5	3.53	3.59	3.65	3.72	3.78	3.84	3.91	3.97	4.04	4.10	4.16	4.23	4.29	4.35	4.42	4.48
6	4.12	4.20	4.27	4.35	4.42	4.49	4.57	4.64	4.72	4.79	4.87	4.94	5.02	5.09	5.17	5.24
7	4.72	4.81	4.89	4.98	5.06	5.15	5.23	5.32	5.40	5.49	5.58	5.66	5.75	5.83	5.92	6.00
8	5.32	5.42	5.51	5.61	5.71	5.80	5.90	6.00	6.09	6.19	6.29	6.38	6.48	6.58	6.67	6.77
9	5.92	6.03	6.14	6.25	6.35	6.46	6.57	6.68	6.78	6.89	7.00	7.11	7.22	7.32	7.43	7.54
10	6.53	6.65	6.77	6.88	7.00	7.12	7.24	7.36	7.48	7.60	7.72	7.84	7.96	8.08	8.19	8.31
11	7.14	7.27	7.40	7.53	7.66	7.79	7.92	8.05	8.18	8.31	8.44	8.57	8.70	8.83	8.96	9.09
12	7.74	7.89	8.03	8.17	8.31	8.45	8.59	8.74	8.88	9.02	9.16	9.30	9.45	9.59	9.73	9.87
13	8.36	8.51	8.66	8.81	8.97	9.12	9.27	9.43	9.58	9.73	9.89	10.04	10.20	10.35	10.50	10.66
14	8.97	9.13	9.30	9.46	9.63	9.79	9.96	10.12	10.29	10.45	10.62	10.78	10.95	11.11	11.28	11.45
15	9.59	9.76	9.94	10.11	10.29	10.47	10.64	10.82	11.00	11.17	11.35	11.53	11.71	11.88	12.06	12.24
16	10.20	10.39	10.58	10.77	10.95	11.14	11.33	11.52	11.71	11.90	12.09	12.28	12.46	12.65	12.84	13.03
17	10.82	11.02	11.22	11.42	11.62	11.82	12.02	12.22	12.42	12.62	12.83	13.03	13.23	13.43	13.63	13.83
18	11.45	11.66	11.87	12.08	12.29	12.50	12.72	12.93	13.14	13.35	13.57	13.78	13.99	14.21	14.42	14.64
19	12.07	12.30	12.52	12.74	12.97	13.19	13.41	13.64	13.86	14.09	14.31	14.54	14.76	14.99	15.22	15.44
20	12.70	12.93	13.17	13.41	13.64	13.88	14.11	14.35	14.59	14.82	15.06	15.30	15.54	15.77	16.01	16.25
21	13.33	13.58	13.82	14.07	14.32	14.57	14.82	15.06	15.31	15.56	15.81	16.06	16.31	16.56	16.81	17.07
22	13.96	14.22	14.48	14.74	15.00	15.26	15.52	15.78	16.04	16.30	16.57	16.83	17.09	17.36	17.62	17.88
23	14.59	14.87	15.14	15.41	15.68	15.96	16.23	16.50	16.78	17.05	17.32	17.60	17.88	18.15	18.43	18.70
24	15.23	15.51	15.80	16.08	16.37	16.65	16.94	17.22	17.51	17.80	18.09	18.37	18.66	18.95	19.24	19.53
25	15.87	16.17	16.46	16.76	17.06	17.35	17.65	17.95	18.25	18.55	18.85	19.15	19.45	19.75	20.05	20.36

26	16.51	16.82	17.13	17.44	17.75	18.06	18.37	18.68	18.99	19.30	19.62	19.93	20.24	20.56	20.87	21.19
27	17.15	17.47	17.80	18.12	18.44	18.76	19.09	19.41	19.74	20.06	20.39	20.71	21.04	21.37	21.69	22.02
28	17.80	18.13	18.47	18.80	19.14	19.47	19.81	20.15	20.48	20.82	21.16	21.50	21.84	22.18	22.52	22.86
29	18.45	18.79	19.14	19.49	19.83	20.18	20.53	20.88	21.23	21.58	21.94	22.29	22.64	22.99	23.35	23.70
30	19.10	19.45	19.81	20.17	20.54	20.90	21.26	21.62	21.99	22.35	22.72	23.08	23.45	23.81	24.18	24.55
31	19.75	20.12	20.49	20.87	21.24	21.61	21.99	22.37	22.74	23.12	23.50	23.88	24.26	24.64	25.02	25.40
32	20.40	20.79	21.17	21.56	21.95	22.33	22.72	23.11	23.50	23.89	24.28	24.68	25.07	25.46	25.86	26.25
33	21.06	21.46	21.85	22.25	22.65	23.06	23.46	23.86	24.26	24.67	25.07	25.48	25.88	26.29	26.70	27.11
34	21.72	22.13	22.54	22.95	23.37	23.78	24.19	24.61	25.03	25.44	25.86	26.28	26.70	27.12	27.54	27.97
35	22.38	22.80	23.23	23.65	24.08	24.51	24.94	25.36	25.79	26.23	26.66	27.09	27.52	27.96	28.39	28.83
36	23.04	23.48	23.92	24.35	24.80	25.24	25.68	26.12	26.57	27.01	27.46	27.90	28.35	28.80	29.25	29.70
37	23.70	24.16	24.61	25.06	25.51	25.97	26.42	26.88	27.34	27.80	28.26	28.72	29.18	29.64	30.10	30.57
38	24.37	24.84	25.30	25.77	26.24	26.70	27.17	27.64	28.11	28.59	29.06	29.53	30.01	30.49	30.96	31.44
39	25.04	25.52	26.00	26.48	26.96	27.44	27.92	28.41	28.89	29.38	29.87	30.36	30.85	31.34	31.83	32.32
40	25.71	26.20	26.70	27.19	27.69	28.18	28.68	29.18	29.68	30.18	30.68	31.18	31.68	32.19	32.69	33.20
41	26.39	26.89	27.40	27.91	28.41	28.92	29.44	29.95	30.46	30.97	31.49	32.01	32.52	33.04	33.56	34.08
42	27.06	27.58	28.10	28.62	29.15	29.67	30.19	30.72	31.25	31.78	32.31	32.84	33.37	33.90	34.44	34.97
43	27.74	28.27	28.81	29.34	29.88	30.42	30.96	31.50	32.04	32.59	33.13	33.67	34.22	34.76	35.31	35.86
44	28.42	28.97	29.52	30.07	30.62	31.17	31.72	32.28	32.83	33.39	33.95	34.51	35.07	35.63	36.19	36.76
45	29.11	29.67	30.23	30.79	31.36	31.92	32.49	33.06	33.63	34.20	34.77	35.35	35.92	36.50	37.08	37.66
46	29.79	30.36	30.94	31.52	32.10	32.68	33.26	33.84	34.43	35.01	35.60	36.19	36.78	37.37	37.96	38.56
47	30.48	31.07	31.66	32.25	32.84	33.44	34.03	34.63	35.23	35.83	36.43	37.04	37.64	38.25	38.86	39.46
48	31.17	31.77	32.37	32.98	33.59	34.20	34.81	35.42	36.03	36.65	37.27	37.88	38.50	39.13	39.75	40.37
49	31.86	32.48	33.09	33.71	34.34	34.96	35.59	36.21	36.84	37.47	38.10	38.74	39.37	40.01	40.65	41.29
50	32.55	33.18	33.82	34.45	35.09	35.73	36.37	37.01	37.65	38.30	38.94	39.59	40.24	40.89	41.55	42.20
51	33.25	33.89	34.54	35.19	35.84	36.49	37.15	37.81	38.46	39.12	39.79	40.45	41.11	41.78	42.45	43.12
52	33.95	34.61	35.27	35.93	36.60	37.27	37.94	38.61	39.28	39.96	40.63	41.31	41.99	42.67	43.36	44.04
53	34.65	35.32	36.00	36.68	37.36	38.04	38.72	39.41	40.10	40.79	41.48	42.17	42.87	43.57	44.27	44.97
54	35.35	36.04	36.73	37.42	38.12	38.82	39.52	40.22	40.92	41.63	42.33	43.04	43.75	44.47	45.18	45.90
55	36.05	36.76	37.46	38.17	38.88	39.60	40.31	41.03	41.74	42.47	43.19	43.91	44.64	45.37	46.10	46.83
56	36.76	37.48	38.20	38.92	39.65	40.38	41.11	41.84	42.57	43.31	44.05	44.79	45.53	46.27	47.02	47.77
57	37.47	38.20	38.94	39.68	40.42	41.16	41.91	42.65	43.40	44.15	44.91	45.66	46.42	47.18	47.94	48.71
58	38.18	38.93	39.68	40.43	41.19	41.95	42.71	43.47	44.23	45.00	45.77	46.54	47.32	48.09	48.87	49.65
59	38.89	39.66	40.42	41.19	41.96	42.74	43.51	44.29	45.07	45.85	46.64	47.42	48.21	49.01	49.80	50.60
60	39.61	40.39	41.17	41.95	42.74	43.53	44.32	45.11	45.91	46.71	47.51	48.31	49.12	49.92	50.73	51.55

Source: Board of Governors of the Federal Reserve System, Exhibit G — "Truth in Lending — Consumer Credit Cost Disclosure."

THE MORTGAGE ON A LEASE

Although the Mortgage on a Lease was discussed in Chapter 9 another use of it exists in the sale of a business opportunity without the sale of the real property. For example, *B* has leased a store from *A*, and *B* has permission from the landlord, *A*, to assign and mortgage the lease. *B* has a drycleaning establishment with fixtures valued at $1,000, but has built up the business and it is now worth $5,000. Because of an urgent need for money, *B* consents to sell the business to *C*, who has only $1,000 in cash. *B* may take the cash and a note and a security agreement as provided for by the Uniform Commercial Code for $1,000 on the fixtures and *C*'s notes with no other security for the balance of the indebtedness. However, in situations of this sort, in order to secure *C*'s notes, a mortgage on the lease, or leasehold mortgage as it is sometimes called, would seem to be in order. This mortgage is drawn and designed to give *B* the possession of the business in the event *C* defaults on the payment of the notes. The mortgage on the lease, even in those lien theory states like New York, is drawn in the same manner as the ordinary mortgage in title theory states. *D* assigns the lease to *C*. The lease, under the terms of the mortgage, is transferred back to *B* upon the condition that if *C* pays the notes, then the instrument will be void; and if *C* does not pay, then *B* is entitled to the possession of the premises.

MORTGAGE BONDS

This is a device sometimes used by corporations to finance specific real property ventures. A *bond* is evidence of a debt wherein the issuer promises to pay the indebtedness at a specific time together with periodic payments of interest. While most corporate bonds are secured by the assets of a corporation, the mortgage bond is secured by a specific asset.

There are three parties to a mortgage bond: the issuing company, a trustee, and the bondholder (the lender, consequently creditor).[1] The property is mortgaged to the trustee who holds it for the benefit of the bondholder. In the event of default the trustee files a notice that the bonds are due and payable. The trustee may enter the property, exclude the borrower, and manage the property while proceeding with a foreclosure or sale for the bondholder. Generally, the mortgagor has the right prior to sale or foreclosure to make up the default. If this is done the default is considered to have been "cured."

---

[1] It is from mortgage bonds issued by corporations that the deed of trust as commonly used on residences and other typical real estate transactions developed. In short, the borrower conveys to a trustee who holds for the benefit of the lender.

THE CROP MORTGAGE

This is a highly specialized form of financing, but should be mentioned. The *crop mortgage* is a mortgage often given by a farmer, as mortgagor, on growing crops to secure a loan. The crop mortgage usually follows the title theory, even in lien theory states. It states that the mortgagor does "grant, bargain, and sell" to the mortgagee the crops growing or to be grown in a certain year at a certain described place. If the mortgagor pays the debt secured by the crops, the mortgage shall be void. This mortgage usually contains a clause stating that the mortgagor covenants to take proper care of the crops. If the mortgagor fails "to properly harvest, thresh, and care for the same in a proper manner and at the proper season," then the mortgagee shall have the right to sell the crops. In addition, there is a clause covering attorney's fees and costs in the event of foreclosure, together with a covenant by the mortgagor that the crops are free and clear from all encumbrances and that the mortgagor will forever warrant and defend against the lawful claims of any person or persons.

This form of mortgage is employed quite extensively in farm states as security for short-term farm loans.

JOINT VENTURE

A *joint venture* is a form of partnership by two or more people formed for only one or two ventures rather than a continuing business. Thus, even though they are treated as partnerships for tax purposes, they differ from the partnership because it is a special association for a special project.

The joint venture may be entered into between individuals, partnerships, corporations, or any combination of these. More often than not, the group will want to be treated as a partnership for tax purposes. If this is done, losses can be written off by the individual partners.

REAL ESTATE SYNDICATES AND LIMITED PARTNERSHIPS

The syndicate or limited partnership is both an investment vehicle for small investors and a source of funds for a builder-developer. The partnership consists of a general partner and limited partners who are the equity investors. The purchases and/or operations of the partnership can take many forms. For example, a broker may form a limited partnership for the purpose of buying and holding a piece of land for future resale. In this case a limited partnership may be formed with contributions ranging upward from $1,000. Generally, the agreement incorporates a stipulation that the general partner will share any capital appreciation with the limited partners. This may be as high as 50 percent of the gain.

Often the limited partnership takes place where a builder-developer is involved. The builder-developer acts as the general partner, agreeing to sell the land to the partnership, build at a predetermined price, and manage the property. The agreement provides for sharing of profits, losses, and cash flow. In this case, the general partner usually receives 5 percent and the limited partners share 95 percent. There is also a provision for the sharing of any capital appreciation if the property is resold. Often the percentage of the capital appreciation is on a 50-50 basis after the limited partners have received the return of their equity investment.

In most cases, if the project is an apartment house, or even a shopping center, the limited partners contribute one third on the signing of the agreement, one third on completion of construction, and one third when occupancy reaches 95 percent. The form of payment may vary with the agreement.

The tax advantage to the limited partners is the same as if they had been individual investors. They share pro rata in any tax loss that can be written off against other income. In case of resale, their pro rata shares are subject to long-term capital gains.

The Regulation of Limited Partnerships

The offerings of limited partners have been ruled as security offerings and subject to federal and state regulations. Unless the offering is "private," it must be registered under the Securities Act of 1933. Although never statutorily defined, a private offering has been presumed to be a sale to fewer than 25 persons. It should be noted, however, that even a private offering does not exempt the seller from the fraud provisions of the Act. There must be a full disclosure to proposed investors of all facts, circumstances, and risks involved in the investment. Furthermore, state laws have recently tightened up, which may affect the offering of limited partnership shares.

The Risks of the Limited Partnership

As in any investment, there are risks in the limited partnership which are listed as follows:

1. Rents may be lower than projected and operating expenses may be higher.
2. A partnership interest is not readily saleable; consequently, there is a high degree of liquidity risk.

3. It is conceivable that a future Congress may reduce or even repeal liberal depreciation allowances.

Tax Effects of a Limited Partnership

Not only is the Securities and Exchange Commission interested in the limited partnership, but the Internal Revenue Service also looks over the shoulder of the investors. Unless the agreement is properly drawn, the IRS will construe the limited partnership as a corporation. In this case, losses and other tax advantages cannot flow through to the investor. The IRS Code Section 7701 and its regulations provide that a partnership shall be classified as an association taxable as a corporation if its major characteristics more closely resemble those of a corporation than those of any other type of business organization.

The criteria used by the IRS to test for a corporation are as follows:

1. Is it an association?
2. Is there an intention to do business for a profit?
3. Does it have continuity of life?
4. Is there centralization of management?
5. Does it have free transferability of interests?
6. Is there limitation to the organization's property of liability for the organization's debts?

For a limited partnership to be classified as a corporation by the IRS, it must meet more than two of the above criteria. Since the first two criteria are common to all forms of business organization, they are excluded from consideration by the IRS in determining corporate form. Under the Uniform Partnership Act the general partner can dissolve the partnership at any time, or the partnership agreement may contain a terminal date. If the agreement is set up along these lines, the third criterion would not classify the limited partnership as a corporation. Most limited partnerships do have centralization of management, so criterion number four would apply. As to free transferability of interests, a properly drawn agreement would contain a clause requiring permission of the general partner or other partners before an interest could be transferred. Since the IRS regulations state that this interferes with free transferability, the fifth criterion would be eliminated. As for the sixth criteria, "limitation to the organization's property of liability for the organization's debts," the general partner has unlimited liability for the partnership debts, so this criterion also is eliminated. Thus, the limited partnership can be set up so that only one criterion, centralization of management, classifies it as a corporation for tax purposes. If necessary, the limited partnership agreement can even be drawn more loosely and permit free transfers, for example, without losing the tax advantage of the limited partnership.

"GAP" FINANCING

"Gap" financing is usually done on very large projects and can sometimes be financially disastrous. When a developer proposes a project to a lender, among other things the developer submits a pro forma income and expense statement projecting the amount of rental income for the project. For any number of reasons (doubtful economic conditions or a feeling that the developer was overly optimistic on rental projections) the lender may refrain from committing the full amount of the permanent loan requested.

For example, a developer requests a $1,000,000 construction loan. Further, the developer needs a $1,000,000 permanent loan to pay off the construction loan. In the normal course of events the developer receives the $1,000,000 construction loan, which is supplanted by the $1,000,000 permanent loan upon completion of the project. However, if in this situation the lender doubts the project's income projection, the lender may say to the developer, "Sorry, but we will hold back 20 percent of the loan and lend you only $800,000." Because the developer needs $1,000,000 to construct the project, $200,000 is still needed. At this point the developer goes to an intermediate lender who agrees to put up the $200,000 on a second mortgage. The mortgage is actually made by the borrower to the lender for $1,000,000. Then the lender and the "gap" lender enter into a participation agreement showing the lender's share of $800,000 and the gap lender's share of $200,000.

These second mortgages (gap mortgages) usually run from six months to three years, during which time the developer hopes to be fully rented. The cost of this type of second mortgage is high. Initially the cost is about 5 percent plus interest or about 15 percent per annum. The prime risk in this type of financing is that during the time of the second mortgage, debt service must be made on both the first and the second mortgages. Obviously, with rental income not up to projection these payments could be difficult for the developer to meet.

COLLATERAL LOAN

Although this type of loan is used infrequently it should be mentioned. It is sometimes used when the buyer is "assuming," or taking "subject to," a mortgage and doesn't have enough cash to pay the difference between the selling price and the mortgage. An additional prerequisite is that the seller doesn't need the cash and does not want to get involved in a second mortgage.

The seller and lender enter into an agreement whereby the seller agrees to put a certain sum from the proceeds of the sale into a savings account. The existing first mortgage is then increased by this amount. When the new buyer reduces the mortgage to the amount approved by the lender, the savings account is released. It should be noted that the savings account carries with it a rate of interest which is paid to the seller.

For example, the seller has a parcel of property priced at $25,000 and there is an assumable mortgage of $15,000. A buyer comes up with $5,000 cash down. Thus, $5,000 cash plus $15,000 mortgage equals $20,000, or $5,000 short of the purchase price. The seller puts the $5,000 received over the mortgage from the buyer into a savings account. The lender raises the mortgage from $15,000 to $20,000. When the buyer reduces the mortgage to $15,000, the savings account plus the additional $5,000 paid by the lender into the account is released to the seller. Therefore, the seller received $10,000, the $5,000 cash down + the $5,000 paid by the lender into the account, at the time the mortgage was raised from $15,000 to $20,000.

GUARANTEED TRADE-IN

This situation arises where an individual wishes to purchase a new home. The individual owns an older home and if it is sold the equity can be used as cash down on a newer home. If the home fails to sell the new purchase is impossible. As a result an agreement is entered into with a broker giving the broker an exclusive right to sell the property at a specified price at a specified time. The agreement states in effect that if the home fails to sell at the owner's price during that time, the broker will buy the home at the owner's option.

The "guaranteed" price is below the owner's original price. The broker attempts to sell it at the guaranteed price for a stated time. If this fails the broker gives the owner the guaranteed price. This gives the owner sufficient equity to put cash down on the newer home.

QUESTIONS FOR REVIEW

1. What is a wraparound mortgage? What are its advantages to the seller? To the buyer?
2. What sorts of provisions are stated in the loan participation agreement? In participation in the security?
3. What do you see as the advantages and disadvantages to both the lender and borrower of a balloon mortgage?
4. What are the relations and priorities of payment in a leasehold mortgage between an owner of the property, the seller of a business on that property, and the buyer of the property?
5. How does a mortgage bond differ from most corporate bonds?

6. In a real-estate syndicate, what generally is at risk for the general partner and for the limited partners? What does each stand to gain? What protections do the limited partners have?
7. Under what circumstances is "gap financing" usually undertaken? What are the risks involved?

PROBLEMS

1. A seller owns a building presently worth $50,000 with an existing first mortgage of $15,000 at 5%. Could a buyer with $5,000 to put down use a wraparound mortgage to finance this purchase? How?

2. You are a developer with a tentative $100,000 construction loan for an apartment complex. However, a permanent lender will only lend $85,000 permanent financing subject to your fully renting the apartments. How could you obtain the remaining $15,000 that is necessary to complete the apartment complex?

Sources of Mortgage and Real Estate Investment Funds

Savings are the basic source of funds supplied to the money and capital markets. Savings are provided by individuals, corporations, and governments. Individuals and corporations "save" when current income exceeds tax payments plus other current expenditures, whereas governments save when their revenues exceed expenditures.

Savings are the accumulation of cash, savings accounts, and corporate securities. Additional forms of savings include insurance policies, pension plans, and government securities. Individual or personal savings account for more than three fourths of all savings in the United States. A major portion of savings by individuals is in financial institutions or intermediaries which include commercial banks, *thrift* institutions (savings and loan associations, mutual savings banks, and credit unions), pension funds, and insurance companies.

In addition to the level of savings, the supply of funds available for investment is dependent upon the size of the money supply relative to the demand for money. Monetary policy actions by the Federal Reserve System affect the availability of credit and the price, or interest rate, for the use of money. The implications of these relationships will be examined in Chapter 12.

SOURCES AND USES OF FUNDS

Real estate financing represents only one of many possible uses of funds supplied by the money and capital markets. As a result, mortgages and other real estate investment funds must compete for available funds. Table 11-1 indicates how sources of funds have been used for financing purposes since the beginning of the 1970s.

Available funds are channeled into three broad categories or uses: (1) short-term funds; (2) investment funds; and (3) federal government and federal agency securities. Short-term financing takes place in the money markets and involves securities and loans with maturities of one year or less. Included are commercial paper, trade credit, and short-term bank loans. Federal government and agency securities compete for funds supplied to both the money and capital markets. Capital markets include intermediate-term and long-term funds, and thus involve investment funds financing. Approximately 20 percent of fund sources are projected for short-term uses in 1977 with 22 percent of sources projected to meet federal government and agency needs.

Investment funds are expected to continue to be the dominant use of funds. Here real estate mortgages compete directly against corporate stocks and bonds, state and local government securities, and commercial bank term loans for money. The importance of competition for funds is further signified by the fact that real estate mortgages represent the largest annual use of investment funds.

Table 11-1 Summary of Financing — Total Funds
(In Billions of Dollars)

	1971	1972	1973	1974	1975	1976 (est.)	1977 (proj.)
FUNDS RAISED							
Investment funds*	104.6	123.5	123.1	118.3	123.8	142.2	159.9
Short-term funds	22.7	43.9	66.9	57.6	—	39.4	55.7
U.S. Government and budget agency securities, privately held	16.7	20.5	-.4	10.2	78.1	59.4	62.2
Total uses	144.0	187.9	189.6	186.1	202.0	241.0	277.8
*Investment funds breakdown							
Corporate securities							
Bonds	18.7	12.6	9.2	19.7	27.2	24.4	20.0
Stocks	11.9	10.1	6.9	3.6	11.0	10.8	12.0
Total	30.6	22.8	16.1	23.3	38.2	35.2	32.0
State and local securities	17.9	15.7	16.9	20.2	17.5	18.6	20.4
Real estate mortgages	52.5	76.8	79.9	60.5	59.0	78.8	94.3
Foreign securities	1.0	.6	.8	2.0	6.5	8.8	8.3
Term loans							
Commercial banks	2.6	7.6	9.3	12.0	2.3	.6	4.7
Banks for cooperatives	.1	.1	.1	.3	.3	.2	.2
Total	2.7	7.7	9.4	12.3	2.6	.8	4.9
Total	104.6	123.5	123.1	118.3	123.8	142.2	159.9

Source: Bankers Trust Company, *Credit and Capital Markets 1977*, pp. T1–T2.

Table 11-2 shows the amount of funds provided for mortgages in recent years. Residential mortgages, particularly home or 1- to 4-family mortgages, dominate the use of mortgage funds. Home mortgages comprise over 50 percent of all funds invested in mortgages.

The sources or supply of funds for mortgages come largely from savings and loan associations. Mutual savings banks, in the thrift institutions category, also put funds in mortgages. Behind thrift institutions, commercial banks are the next most important supplier of

Table 11-2 Total Mortgages
(In billions of Dollars)

	1971	1972	1973	1974	1975	1976 (est.)	1977 (proj.)
FUNDS RAISED							
Residential mortgages							
Home	30.6	43.7	44.9	33.2	42.7	59.0	70.5
Multifamily	9.7	12.7	10.4	7.0	—	1.5	3.5
Total	40.3	56.4	55.3	40.2	42.7	60.5	74.0
Commercial mortgages	9.9	16.8	19.1	15.2	11.1	12.0	13.5
Farm mortgages	2.4	3.6	5.5	5.1	5.2	6.3	6 8
Total	52.5	76.8	79.9	60.5	59.0	78.8	94.3
FUNDS SUPPLIED							
Insurance companies and pension funds							
Life insurance companies	1.3	1.8	4.5	4.9	2.9	2.0	3.2
Private noninsured pension funds	−.5	−.8	.4	.7	1.5	1.8	2.0
State and local retirement funds	.4	−.3	.1	−.7	.5	.6	.5
Total	1.2	.7	5.0	4.9	4.9	4.4	5.7
Thrift institutions							
Savings and loan associations	25.4	32.9	26.0	18.8	30.9	46.0	51.5
Mutual savings banks	4.8	6.2	6.1	2.6	3.5	6.1	7.9
Credit unions	.5	.5	.5	.2	.6	1.1	.5
Total	30.7	39.6	32.6	21.6	35.0	53.2	59.9
Other financial intermediaries							
Finance companies	1.5	1.7	.9	−.8	−.6	.6	.5
Real estate investment trusts	2.3	4.1	5.6	.2	−4.9	−3.0	−2.5
Total	3.8	5.8	6.5	−.6	−5.5	−2.4	−2.0
Commercial banks	9.8	16.8	20.0	13.1	4.5	11.0	13.5
Government							
U.S. Government	−.4	−.7	−.6	3.9	6.2	−.4	3.0
Nonbudget agencies	3.6	4.0	7.2	10.1	5.5	3.0	4.2
State and local general funds	1.1	1.4	1.7	2.5	1.6	1.0	1.3
Total	4.3	4.7	8.3	16.5	13.3	3.6	8.5
Individuals and others	2.6	9.2	7.5	5.1	6.8	9.0	8.7
Total	52.5	76.8	79.9	60.5	59.0	78.8	94.3

Source: Bankers Trust Company, *Credit and Capital Markets 1977*, p. T10.

mortgage money. Life insurance companies are also significant suppliers of funds for mortgages. Involvement in mortgages by private non-insured pension funds and credit unions has been rather limited. On the other hand, federal government and agency involvement has been very important in supplying funds for mortgages.

Financial Institutions or Intermediaries

Financial institutions play an important role in supplying funds for investment and other uses through the accumulation of savings. This important function is necessary to "bridge the gap" between savers, primarily individuals, and the demand for investment and other funds. Often the financing (use of funds) is not totally compatible with the public's savings objectives. Financial institutions thus act as intermediaries by offering savers attributes such as liquidity, safety of principal, and their willingness to accept savings in small amounts.

The process of accumulating savings in financial institutions and then lending or investing (supplying) funds is called *intermediation*. Financial institutions through the intermediation process bring together or "match" savings (sources of funds) and investments (uses of funds). Intermediation is particularly important in directing accumulated savings into real estate mortgages because direct investment is generally inconsistent with individual saver objectives.

When individuals choose to withdraw savings and/or not accumulate new savings in institutions, the opposite of intermediation, or *disintermediation*, occurs. This bypassing of financial institutions generally develops when other high quality investments such as corporate bonds and government securities provide proportionately higher yields or returns. Savings accounts are then bypassed for direct investments in these securities. The disintermediation severely affects mortgage investment funds because savings diverted from financial institutions rarely go into mortgages.

The effects of disintermediation are shown in Figure 11-1. Significant disintermediation occurred during 1969 and also during 1973 and 1974. The reasons for these developments will be examined in Chapter 12. However, the impact of disintermediation is readily apparent in terms of the corresponding reduction in the amount of outstanding mortgage commitments. Financial institutions depend upon continuing savings inflows to maintain or increase their investment levels. Changes in savings flows directly affect funds available for mortgages.

Financing Residential Mortgages

The mortgage market can be viewed or divided in several ways. For example, there are primary and secondary mortgage markets. The *primary* market involves the creating or issuing of new mortgages. Mortgages often are originated and directly held by financial institutions. In some instances, institutions engage primarily in the origination of the loans or mortgages and have commitments to resell the mortgages to other investors. The term "mortgage market" traditionally has been used to refer to the primary market. Institutions and other financial intermediaries are largely involved in this market.

The *secondary* market provides a vehicle or mechanism for transferring ownership of outstanding mortgages from old investors to new investors. Liquidity and marketability of mortgages is the prime benefit to investors. Secondary markets for other investment securities such as stocks and bonds are, of course, well developed. Certain federal agencies participate and deal primarily in the secondary mortgage market as will be discussed in Chapter 13.

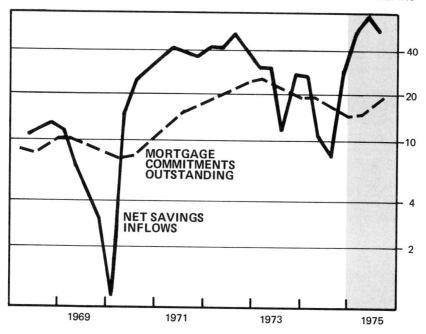

Source: *Federal Reserve Bulletin* (November, 1975), p. 711.

"Net savings inflows" are quarterly averages for savings and loan associations and mutual savings banks at seasonally adjusted annual rates. "Mortgage commitments outstanding," which are mainly residential, are seasonally adjusted end-of-quarter totals for all savings and loan associations and for New York mutual savings banks. Commitments data include loans in process. Latest data, Q3, preliminary.

Figure
11-1   Savings Flows and Residential Mortgage Commitments

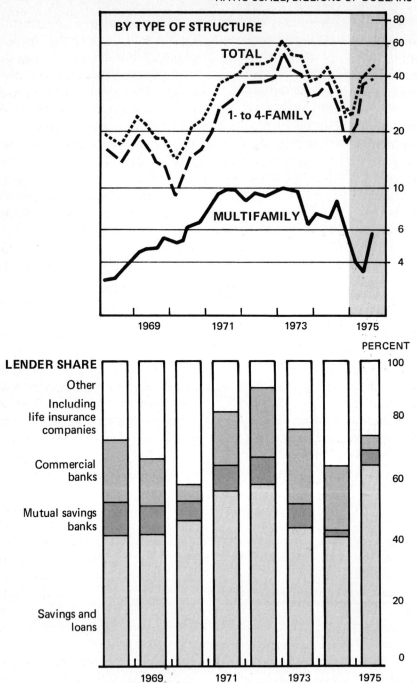

RATIO SCALE, BILLIONS OF DOLLARS

BY TYPE OF STRUCTURE

TOTAL

1- to 4-FAMILY

MULTIFAMILY

1969   1971   1973   1975

PERCENT

LENDER SHARE

Other
Including
life insurance
companies

Commercial
banks

Mutual savings
banks

Savings and
loans

1969   1971   1973   1975

Source: *Federal Reserve Bulletin* (November, 1975), p. 719.

Figure
11-2   Net Change in Residential Mortgage Debt

As previously noted, the majority of funds raised annually for mortgages are directed toward residential mortgages. Changes in residential mortgage debt fluctuate with changes in economic conditions. The upper portion of Figure 11-2 illustrates these fluctuations. Economic downturns or recessions developed during the 1969–70 and 1973–74 period. These also were periods of tight money as reflected in high interest rates and the lack of available credit. Disintermediation also increased during these periods. The substantial economic recovery of 1971–72 brought an easing of money and credit conditions, intermediation, rapid growth in new housing starts, and major increases in residential mortgage debt. Recovery from the most recent recession also is depicted. These interrelationships are examined more fully in Chapter 12.

Residential mortgages are supplied largely by financial institutions operating in the primary market. Institutions involved primarily in the secondary markets will be discussed in detail in Chapter 13. Savings and loan associations continue to be the dominant supplier or lender of funds for residential mortgages. However, there have been significant shifts in market share of residential mortgage debt held by this type of lending institution. These changes or shifts relate to changes in economic conditions and are shown in the lower portion of Figure 11-2. During the 1969 disintermediation period, savings and loan associations were able to maintain their market share. Market share increased with the economic recovery and intermediation. Market share declined in the troubled 1973–74 period of tight money and disintermediation. Mutual savings banks were particularly hard hit in terms of market share during periods when savers bypassed thrift institutions.

The commercial bank market share of residential mortgage debt also has fluctuated dramatically. The 1969–70 tight money period of high interest rates and limited credit resulted in a reduction in the share of the market for commercial banks. Market share was reasonably well maintained during the 1973–74 period. However, commercial bank involvement in residential mortgage debt was severely limited in 1975. Liquidity problems, loan defaults, and continued concern over loans outstanding to real estate investment trusts contributed to their lack of involvement.

It is apparent that during tight money and disintermediation periods traditional lenders (savings and loan associations, mutual savings banks, and commercial banks) reduce their market share of residential mortgage debt. Consequently, other lending sources provide a significantly larger market share of the mortgage funds being raised. These lending sources thus contribute some stability to the primary mortgage market; included are insurance companies, pension funds, credit unions, finance companies, real estate investment trusts, and individuals.

SAVINGS AND LOAN ASSOCIATIONS

The origin of savings and loan associations can be traced back to 1831 when the first "building" association was formed. In some states, savings and loan associations continue to be referred to as "cooperative banks" or "homestead associations." Savings and loan associations traditionally have specialized in home financing and thus have sought to encourage home ownership. Association members were offered liquidity, safety of principal, and a return for saving in these thrift institutions. Funds "pooled" from a number of savers were lent to other members who needed financing for homes.

Structure and Operation

All of the early savings and loan associations were chartered by the states within which they operated. Beginning in 1933, however, the Home Owners' Loan Act provided for federal chartering of savings and loan associations. There are about 5,000 savings and loan associations in operation today. Approximately 40 percent are federally-chartered associations. They control over 55 percent of all association assets which were slightly about $338 billion at the end of 1975.

Federally-chartered associations were initially required to organize as depositor-owned or *mutual* associations. That is, they did not sell stock in the associations and thus they did not have stockholders. However, in recent years a number of federally-chartered mutual associations have been permitted to convert to *stock* associations in order to raise capital by selling stock to shareholders. State-chartered associations also may be mutual or stock associations since approximately one-half of the states permit their chartered associations to issue shares of stock. More than 85 percent of the savings and loan associations continue to operate as mutuals.

Mutual associations are further characterized by the fact that both savers and borrowers are members. Savings represent shares of ownership and thus payments on savings are technically dividends rather than interest. However, with the passage of the Housing and Urban Development Act of 1968, federally-chartered savings and loan associations were permitted to refer to savings accounts as deposits and be classified as deposit institutions. Some state-chartered mutual associations also were permitted similar classifications.

Regulation and Control

Prior to the Depression of the 1930s, savings and loan associations were loosely regulated. Only individual state regulations existed. In 1932 the Home Loan Bank Act was passed. The act provided for the creation of the Federal Home Loan Bank System with organizational characteristics similar to those of the Federal Reserve System. The FHLB System consists of the Federal Home Loan Bank Board, 12 regional Banks, and the financial institutions who are members of the System. All federal savings and loan associations must belong to the FHLB System.

State-chartered savings and loan associations, along with other qualified financial institutions involved in home mortgage loans, may become members of the system. Approximately 70 percent of state-chartered savings and loan associations belong and, together with the federally-chartered members, control approximately 98 percent of the assets held by all savings and loan associations. However, aside from savings and loan association members, only 70 mutual savings banks and two life insurance companies belong to the FHLB System.[1]

The Federal Home Loan Bank System, through its role as a central credit facility, assists member institutions by providing: (1) secondary liquidity to meet withdrawal demands; (2) funds to reduce seasonal differences between savings flows and mortgage loan demands; and (3) a mechanism for shifting funds between geographical areas where imbalances exist between savings supply and mortgage loan demand.[2] The FHLB System has been particularly active in attempting to provide stability in residential financing during periods of disintermediation.

The Federal Savings and Loan Insurance Corporation was created under the National Housing Act of 1934. Insurance is provided for savings accounts held at savings and loan associations. Currently, savings accounts are insured up to $40,000 each. All federal savings and loan associations must belong to the FSLIC and are subject to annual audits.

State-chartered savings and loan associations may apply for insurance under the FSLIC. Only approximately 70 percent of the state-chartered associations are FSLIC-insured.[3] However, over 97 percent of all savings and loan association assets are FSLIC-insured.[4]

---

[1]*1976 Savings and Loan Fact Book* (Chicago, Ill.: United States Savings and Loan League, 1976), p. 96.

[2]*Ibid.*, p. 94.

[3]*Ibid.*, p. 50. Four states, Massachusetts, Ohio, Maryland, and North Carolina, provide insuring organizations for their own state-charatered savings and loan associations.

[4]*Ibid.*, p. 107.

Importance of Savings Flows

Savings and loan associations are dependent upon the savings deposits of their shareholders as their principal source of funds. Table 11-3 shows that the dollar amount of savings has grown rapidly since the mid-1960s. In 1966, with the passage of the Interest Rate Adjustment Act, the Federal Home Loan Bank Board was authorized to set maximum interest rates on savings and loan association passbook accounts and savings certificates. The FHLB Board also was permitted to authorize new forms of savings accounts and certificates under the Housing and Urban Development Act of 1968, for example, certificates of deposit.

The significance of savings flows is made clear by the fact that over 80 percent of total savings and loan association liabilities are in the form of savings balances. Mortgage lending and other investment decisions thus are heavily dependent on the level and changes in savings flows. Advances from the Federal Home Loan Bank System and the net worth of savings and loan associations provide only a partial cushion against the volatility of savings flows.

Table 11-3   Liabilities of Savings and Loan Associations
(In Billions of Dollars)

	1965		1970		1975	
	Amount	Percent	Amount	Percent	Amount	Percent
Savings balances	110.4	85.2	146.4	83.1	286.0	84.5
FHLB advances	6.4	4.9	10.9	6.2	20.7	6.1
Loans in process	2.2	1.7	3.1	1.8	5.2	1.5
Other liabilities	1.9	1.5	3.4	1.9	6.7	2.0
Net worth	8.7	6.7	12.4	7.0	19.8	5.9
Total	129.6	100.0	176.2	100.0	338.4	100.0

Source: *1976 Savings and Loan Fact Book.*

Investment Policies

Savings and loan associations face a maturity problem in trying to match their savings accounts with their lending and investing policies. They borrow short-term and lend long-term. For example, withdrawals usually are honored upon request even though technically associations have the right to require at least 30 days notice prior to withdrawal. Savings certificates have average maturities of only a few years.

On the other hand, mortgage loans of 25 to 30 years are common. Thus, sources of funds often are relatively short-term and volatile, whereas the use of funds in the form of mortgage loans is long-term. As a result, liquidity problems arise during periods of disintermediation.

Table 11-4 shows that mortgage loans account for over 80 percent of the total assets of savings and loan associations and are approximately equal to the savings balance liabilities.

Table 11-4 Assets of Savings and Loan Associations
(In Billions of Dollars)

	1965		1970		1975	
	Amount	Percent	Amount	Percent	Amount	Percent
Mortgage Loans*	110.3	85.1	150.3	85.3	278.7	82.3
Cash and investment securities	12.1	9.3	16.5	9.4	30.9	9.1
Real estate owned	1.1	.9	.8	.4	1.6	.5
FHLB stock	1.2	.9	1.6	.9	2.6	.8
Other assets	4.9	3.8	7.0	4.0	24.6	7.3
Total	129.6	100.0	176.2	100.0	338.4	100.0
Type of Property						
1- to 4-family homes	94.2	85.4	125.0	83.1	225.3	80.8
Multifamily	8.1	7.3	13.8	9.2	25.4	9.1
Other properties	8.0	7.3	11.5	7.7	28.0	10.1
Type of Loan						
Conventional	98.8	89.6	131.6	87.6	248.1	89.0
FHA and VA	11.5	10.4	18.7	12.4	30.6	11.0

Source: *1976 Savings and Loan Fact Book.*

Over 80 percent of outstanding loans are of the 1- to 4-family home type. The other mortgage loans are approximately equally distributed among multifamily and commercial and other mortgage loans. Approximately 89 percent of the mortgage loans made by savings and loan associations are conventional loans.

Liquidity is of particular concern to savings and loan associations. In 1950 liquidity requirements were written into the Federal Home Loan Bank Act. The Federal Home Loan Bank Board also controls liquidity requirements in terms of liquidity ratios (savings deposits and short-term borrowings relative to liquid assets) and by specifying which assets qualify as liquid assets. The Board can vary the liquidity ratio between 4 percent and 10 percent. These relatively low liquidity ratios, along with the short-term liabilities versus long-term assets operating positions, indicate why savings and loan associations are heavily affected by changes in savings flows.

MUTUAL SAVINGS BANKS

Mutual savings banks, the oldest type of savings institution in the United States, provide an important real estate credit source in the Northeast. The approximately 500 banks are concentrated in New York, New Jersey, and the New England states. Safety of principal is stressed in conjunction with the thrift savings of bank members. From the beginning, mutual savings banks stressed investment in real estate mortgages.

Structure and Operation

As their name implies, mutual savings banks were organized for the mutual benefit of depositors and are owned by their depositors. Depositors are entitled to all earnings after provisions are made to insure adequate reserves. All mutual savings banks are state-chartered and thus are regulated by their respective states. Mutual savings banks are managed by boards of trustees.

While mutual savings banks are primarily concentrated in the Middle Atlantic and New England states, they have had an important role in the national mortgage market since 1950. At the end of 1975, mutual savings banks held approximately $77 billion in mortgages. Roughly $27 billion were mortgages on out-of-state properties; that is, mortgage holdings in non-savings bank states.[5]

Regulation and Control

Mutual savings banks are regulated by the states within which they operate. Legal restrictions have generally prevented geographical extension of the industry. These restrictions are tempered, however, by the fact that laws in several major states permit mutual savings banks to acquire mortgages outside their state boundaries.

The deposits in almost all mutual savings banks are insured. In 1975, 69 percent of mutual savings banks were insured by the Federal Deposit Insurance Corporation (in contrast with FSLIC insurance for savings and loan associations). The remaining banks, except for one, were insured by state funds such as the Mutual Savings Central Fund of Massachusetts.[6]

Importance of Savings Flows

The primary source of funds for mutual savings banks is savings deposits. Table 11-5 shows that deposits account for 90 percent of total

---

[5]*1976 National Fact Book of Mutual Savings Banking* (New York: National Association of Mutual Savings Banks, 1976), pp. 50 and 53.

[6]*Ibid.*, p. 11.

liabilities. Thus, like savings and loan associations, mutual savings banks are affected tremendously by changes in savings flows as reflected in periods of intermediation and disintermediation.

Mutual savings banks have not relied very heavily on borrowings to meet liquidity needs. The credit facilities of the Federal Home Loan Bank System are, of course, available to member banks. Furthermore, the states of New York and Massachusetts provide state-based liquidity facilities for their mutual savings banks in an attempt to cushion the impact of changes in savings flows.

Table 11-5 Liabilities of Mutual Savings Banks
(In Billions of Dollars)

	1965		1970		1975	
	Amount	Percent	Amount	Percent	Amount	Percent
Deposits	52.4	90.0	71.6	90.6	109.9	90.8
Other liabilities	1.1	1.9	1.7	2.2	2.8	2.3
General reserve accounts	4.7	8.1	5.7	7.2	8.4	6.9
Total	58.2	100.0	79.0	100.0	121.1	100.0

Source: *1976 National Fact Book of Mutual Savings Banking.*

Investment Policies

Mortgage loans continue to represent the major investment objective of mutual savings banks. According to Table 11-6, mortgage loans accounted for about 64 percent of the industry's assets in 1975. However, this represents a decline from the 1965 level. During the same period mutual savings banks have been increasing their investments in corporate bonds.

The dominant form of mortgage loan is in 1- to 4-family homes. In contrast with savings and loan associations, mutual savings banks have a relatively larger percentage of their mortgage loan portfolios invested in multifamily mortgages. Mutual savings banks have made much heavier commitments in their mortgage portfolios to FHA and VA mortgage loans than have savings and loan associations. But, as can be seen in Table 11-6, conventional loans have been growing in importance since the mid-1960s.

Liquidity and safety of principal are major objectives of mutual savings banks. Legal restrictions require managements to follow conservative lending and investment policies. Regulations identify the types of qualified investments as well as the minimum levels of quality acceptable for such investments. Certain investments also are restricted in amount relative to total assets or deposits. Even so, mutual savings banks have suffered in recent years from liquidity problems associated with periodic deposit outflows. This is caused, in part, because mutual savings banks hold approximately 5 percent to 6 percent of their total assets in cash or in securities maturing within one year.[7]

Table 11-6 Assets of Mutual Savings Banks
(In Billions of Dollars)

	1965		1970		1975	
	Amount	Percent	Amount	Percent	Amount	Percent
Mortgage loans*	44.4	76.3	57.8	73.1	77.2	63.7
Other loans	.9	1.5	2.2	2.8	4.0	3.3
U.S. gov't, state, & municipal secs.	5.8	10.0	3.3	4.2	6 3	5.2
Corporate & other bonds	3.7	6.4	10.4	13.2	23.6	19.5
Corporate stocks	1.4	2.4	2.5	3.2	4.3	3.6
Cash & other assets	2.0	3.4	2.8	3.5	5.7	4.7
Total	58.2	100.0	79.0	100.0	121.1	100.0
Type of Property						
1- to 4-family homes	30.1	67.8	37.5	64.9	46.0	59.6
Multifamily	10.0	22.5	12.4	21.4	17.8	23.0
Other properties	4.3	9.7	7.9	13.7	13.4	17.4
Type of Loan						
Conventional & other	19.2	43.2	29.7	51.4	50.4	65.3
FHA-insured	13.8	31.1	16.1	27.9	14.4	18.6
VA-guaranteed	11.4	25.7	12.0	20.7	12.4	16.1

Source: *1976 National Fact Book of Mutual Savings Banking.*

COMMERCIAL BANKS

Banking in the United States can be traced back to the colonial period. Considerable uncertainty and instability characterized banking, however, until the Federal Reserve Act of 1913 created a central banking system. Commercial banks have differed traditionally from thrift institutions in that they are permitted to provide "checking deposit" facilities.

As was noted earlier, commercial banks are the second largest institutional supplier of mortgage credit. This is sometimes overlooked though because commercial banks are also substantially committed to numerous other types of loans.

---

[7]*Ibid.,* p. 25.

Structure and Operation

All commercial banks are stock companies and are operated for the benefit of their stockholders. Commercial banks are either state-chartered or federally-chartered. Banks receiving federal charters are known as national banks and must become members of the Federal Reserve System. These banks receive their charters from, and are supervised by, the Comptroller of the Currency. State-chartered banks are under the supervision of state agencies. State banks also have the option of joining the Federal Reserve System.

There are over 14,000 commercial banks in the United States. While less than 6,000 banks are members of the Federal Reserve System, these banks control over three fourths of all commercial bank assets.

Regulation and Control

Member banks, all national banks, and state banks that have joined, are under the regulation and control of the Federal Reserve System. Control is exercised over member bank reserves and the cost of borrowing from the Fed. The maximum amount of interest that can be paid on time and savings deposits also is controlled. The significance of Federal Reserve System activities will be explored in greater detail in Chapter 12.

Insurance for deposits held in commercial banks dates back to the Steagall Amendment to the Glass Act of 1933. In 1935 a permanent deposit insurance plan established the Federal Deposit Insurance Corporation. Membership in the FDIC, with a current maximum insurance of $40,000 per account, is required of all national banks and state bank members of the Federal Reserve System. FDIC membership is also available to state banks who are not members of the Federal Reserve System. Approximately 98 percent of all commercial banks are insured by the FDIC.

Importance of Savings Flows

Commercial banks derive less than one half of their funds from time and savings deposits according to Table 11-7. However, when combined with demand deposits, total deposits account for over 80 percent of total liabilities. This is similar to the deposits to total liabilities ratios for savings and loan associations and mutual savings banks. The major difference, of course, is that demand or checking deposits are less stable than savings deposits. Thus, commercial banks must provide for greater liquidity cushions in the form of cash and short-term U.S. government securities. Liquidity problems associated with disintermediation affect commercial banks as well as thrift institutions.

Table 11-7 Liabilities of Commercial Banks
(In Billions of Dollars)

	1965		1970		1975	
	Amount	Percent	Amount	Percent	Amount	Percent
Demand deposits	184.8	42.4	247.9	43.0	323.6	33.5
Time & savings deposits	200.4	46.0	233.1	40.5	462.9	48.0
Other liabilities	15.4	3.6	52.2	9.1	109.6	11.3
Capital accounts	34.9	8.0	43.0	7.4	69.1	7.2
Total	435.5	100.0	576.2	100.0	965.2	100.0

Source: *Federal Reserve Bulletin* (Selected Issues).

Investment Policies

Investment by commercial banks in real estate loans account for only about 14 percent of total assets in 1975 (see Table 11-8). This is due, in part, to a need to provide for some balance between short-term liabilities and longer-term asset maturities. Commercial banks, in contrast with savings and loan associations and mutual savings banks, have more varied loan and investment objectives. The importance of securities investments and other loans is shown in Table 11-8.

Table 11-8 Assets of Commercial Banks
(In Billions of Dollars)

	1965		1970		1975	
	Amount	Percent	Amount	Percent	Amount	Percent
Cash & bank bals.	61.9	14.2	93.6	16.2	133.6	13.8
Securities investments	115.4	26.5	147.9	25.7	229.6	23.8
Real estate loans*	49.7	11.4	73.3	12.7	134.8	14.0
Other loans	197.2	45.3	240.0	41.7	411.7	42.7
Other assets	11.3	2.6	21.4	3.7	55.5	5.7
Total	435.5	100.0	576.2	100.0	965.2	100.0
Type of Property						
1- to 4-family homes	30.4	61.2	42.3	57.7	76.5	56.7
Multifamily	1.9	3.8	3.3	4.5	5.9	4.4
Other properties	17.4	35.0	27.7	37.8	52.4	38.9
Type of Loan						
Conventional & other	39.3	79.1	62.8	85.7	125.7	93.2
FHA-insured	7.7	15.5	7.9	10.8	6.0	4.5
VA-guaranteed	2.7	5.4	2.6	3.5	3.1	2.3

Source: *Federal Reserve Bulletin* (Selected Issues).

Even though real estate loans are a relatively small portion of total assets, the $134.8 billion of outstanding mortgages ranks only behind the mortgage holdings of savings and loan associations. While mortgages on 1- to 4-family homes account for over one-half of commercial bank mortgage portfolios, loans on commercial property are very important. Commercial banks also engage primarily in conventional mortgage loans.

LIFE INSURANCE COMPANIES

Life insurance companies are another major institutional supplier of funds to the primary mortgage market. At the same time it is important to recognize that life insurance companies were not organized primarily to finance mortgage needs. Thus, mortgage investments are in direct competition with other investment opportunities for the funds flowing into life insurance companies.

Savings flows that are important to thrift institutions and commercial banks are not of direct concern to life insurance companies. Rather than having to worry about periods of intermediation and disintermediation, the investment policies of life insurance companies are largely dependent upon the inflow of premiums paid by policy holders.

Structure and Operation

Life insurance companies may be organized as either mutual companies or as stock companies. Over 90 percent of the approximately 1,800 life insurance companies are stock companies owned by shareholders. However, mutual life insurance companies control 64 percent of the industry's total assets.[8]

Regulation and Control

Life insurance companies are regulated by the states within which they are chartered and by states in which they do business. State regulations focus primarily on the investment policies of life insurance companies. Of interest is the fact that a number of states require life insurance companies, in order to conduct business in their states, to invest a certain percentage of assets or reserves within the state. Limitations and standards often are placed on real estate and mortgage loan investments.

---

[8]*Life Insurance Fact Book 1976* (New York: Institute of Life Insurance, 1976), pp. 64 and 87.

Investment Policies

Table 11-9 shows that the primary source of funds (liabilities) for life insurance companies is from policy reserves. These reserves comprise over 80 percent of the industry's total liabilities.

Table 11-9 Liabilities of Life Insurance Companies
(In Billions of Dollars)

	1965 Amount	1965 Percent	1970 Amount	1970 Percent	1975 Amount	1975 Percent
Policy reserves	127.6	80.3	167.6	80.8	235.1	81.3
Paid-in and contributed surplus	10.0	6.3	12.4	6.0	15.7	5.4
Other obligations and funds	19.9	12.5	25.6	12.4	36.4	12.6
Capital (stock companies)	1.4	.9	1.7	.8	1.9	.7
Total	158.9	100.0	207.3	100.0	289.3	100.0

Source: *Life Insurance Fact Book 1976.*

Life insurance companies hold a variety of different types of assets. According to Table 11-10, the two dominant asset holdings are in the form of corporate bonds and mortgages. Mortgages account for over 30 percent of total assets. In addition, life insurance companies place approximately 3 percent of their assets in other forms of real estate investments.

Table 11-10 Assets of Life Insurance Companies

	1965 Amount	1965 Percent	1970 Amount	1970 Percent	1975 Amount	1975 Percent
Government securities	11.9	7.5	11.1	5.3	15.2	5.2
Corporate bonds	58.2	36.7	73.1	35.3	105.8	36.6
Corporate stocks	9.1	5.7	15.4	7.4	28.1	9.7
Mortgages*	60.0	37.8	74.4	35.9	89.2	30.8
Real estate	4.7	3.0	6.3	3.0	9.6	3.3
Other assets	15.0	9.3	27.0	13.1	41.7	14.4
Total	158.9	100.0	207.3	100.0	289.3	100.0
Type of Property						
1- to 4-family homes	29.9	49.8	26.7	35.9	17.6	19.7
Multifamily	8.4	14.0	16.0	21.5	19.6	22.0
Other properties	21.7	36.2	31.7	42.6	52.0	58.3
Type of Loan						
Conventional	41.2	68.7	57.0	76.6	76.8	86.1
FHA-insured	12.5	20.8	12.0	16.1	8.5	9.5
VA-guaranteed	6.3	10.5	5.4	7.3	3.9	4.4

Source: *Life Insurance Fact Book 1976* and *Federal Reserve Bulletin* (Selected Issues).

Since the mid-1960s, life insurance companies have reduced the significance of 1- to 4-family home loans in terms of their mortgage portfolios. Recent activity has stressed multifamily and commercial property mortgages with non-residential mortgages now comprising approximately 58 percent of mortgage portfolios.

ADDITIONAL SOURCES OF MORTGAGE FUNDS

The primary mortgage market is dominated by savings and loan associations, mutual savings banks, commercial banks, and life insurance companies. The long-run, since 1950, importance of these institutions as suppliers of mortgage funds is depicted in Figure 11-3, page 178, in the form of a ratio of mortgage loans to total assets.

Mortgage funds also are sometimes supplied to the primary mortgage market by mortgage companies, pension funds, credit unions, real estate investment trusts, and individuals. While their dollar amount of mortgage funds raised in recent years has been relatively small, they make a very important contribution to the primary mortgage market — particularly during periods of disintermediation as was previously shown in Figure 11-2.

Mortgage Banking Companies

Mortgage banking companies, while not major suppliers of mortgage funds, perform a very necessary "merchandising" or facilitating function in financing real estate. They are private corporations that depend heavily on short-term bank borrowing in order to finance their merchandising function. Mortgage companies frequently originate or negotiate residential mortgages. But, rather than hold the mortgages, mortgage companies resell the mortgages to institutions. They often continue to service the mortgage loans for the institutional owners by collecting the interest and principal payments. Mortgage banking companies will be discussed in detail in Chapter 13.

Pension Funds

Table 11-2 indicated that private, noninsured pension funds have been positive suppliers of funds to the mortgage market since 1973. At the same time, state and local retirement funds have not been very active suppliers of mortgage funds. In 1965 mortgage loans represented approximately 5 percent of the total assets of noninsured private pension plans. However, this ratio has been somewhat lower during the early 1970s. Mortgages relative to total assets were at about

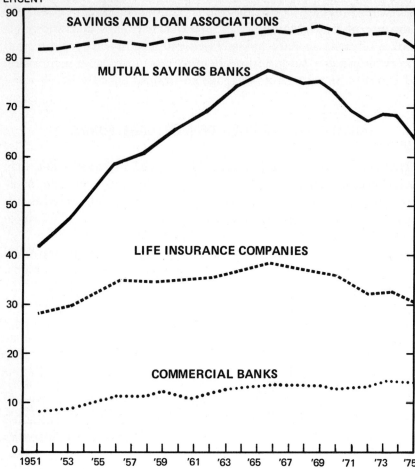

PERCENT

SAVINGS AND LOAN ASSOCIATIONS

MUTUAL SAVINGS BANKS

LIFE INSURANCE COMPANIES

COMMERCIAL BANKS

1951 '53 '55 '57 '59 '61 '63 '65 '67 '69 '71 '73 '75

Source: *1976 National Fact Book of Mutual Savings Banking,* p. 27.

Figure 11-3 Ratio of Mortgage Loans to Total Assets, Main Types of Financial Institutions, 1951–1975

the 11 percent level for state and local government retirement funds in 1965. Ratios though have been generally lower in recent years.[9]

The primary source of funds for noninsured or trusteed private pension funds is in the form of contributions from employers and employees. These funds are supplemented by investment income. State and local government retirement plans receive their sources of funds from government and employee contributions plus investment income.

---

[9]Herbert E. Dougall and Jack E. Gaumnitz, *Capital Markets and Institutions* (3d ed.; Englewood Cliffs, N.J.: Prentice-Hall, Inc., 1975), Chapter VI.

A significant portion of the liabilities of pension funds thus represent long-term commitments or obligations to employees. Consequently, pension plan investments also are predominantly long-term in nature. Noninsured private pension funds have a major portion of their assets committed to corporate common stocks and bonds. State and local government retirement funds also are heavily committed to investments in corporate common stocks and bonds.

Credit Unions

Credit unions, both federal and state, represent a third type of thrift institution. They supply, according to Table 11-2, less than $1 billion annually to the primary mortgage market. Thus, their impact on real estate financing has been substantially less than that of mutual savings banks and savings and loan associations. The Federal Credit Union Act of 1934 and subsequent amendments, while not directly prohibiting real estate mortgage loans, created an effective barrier by imposing relatively short loan maturity limits. However, now that this loan maturity barrier is in the process of legislative removal, credit unions should become a more important supplier of real estate mortgage funds in future years.

Real Estate Investment Trusts

Some form of real estate investment trusts (referred to as REITs) can be traced back to the 19th century. In 1960 the Real Estate Investment Trust Act provided for separation of investment from management responsibilities and problems — much like the operation of mutual funds. Thus, small investors were provided with a means for participating in both large and diversified real estate investments. Real growth developed during the 1969–70 tight money period and REIT assets reached $21 billion by the end of 1974 before declining to about $19 billion by yearend 1975.

If REITs meet certain qualifications, they are exempt from corporate income taxes. One requirement is that they pay out at least 90 percent of their taxable income to investors. Under the Tax Reform Act of 1976, the payout requirement will rise to 95 percent after 1979. Thus, retained earnings do not represent a major source of funds. The major source of funds for REITs has been in the form of term loans and lines of credit from commercial banks. Shareholders' equity, primarily in the form of new stock issues, has been the second largest source of funds. Commercial paper was also a significant source of funds during the early 1970s.[10]

---

[10]*REIT Fact Book 1976* (Washington: National Association of Real Estate Investment Trusts, 1976).

REITs must derive annually at least 90 percent of their gross income from certain passive sources and at least 75 percent must come from real estate sources. The Tax Reform Act of 1976 provides for the 90 percent gross income requirement to increase to 95 percent after 1979.

The Assets of REITs are largely in the form of mortgage loans with property ownership usually representing less than 20 percent of assets. Construction loans are the largest type of mortgage loans made by real estate investment trusts. In the early 1970s over 40 percent of total assets were held in the form of first mortgage construction loans. This, coupled with the fact that over one half of REIT funds were derived from bank loan and commercial paper sources, resulted in the development of substantial REIT problems.[11]

In Table 11-2 it can be seen that REITs were substantial suppliers of mortgage funds during the 1971–73 period. However, beginning in 1974 the role of REITs in the primary mortgage market changed dramatically. Rising interest rates during 1973 and 1974 and the ensuing recession created havoc for the REIT industry. Not only were there substantial defaults by builders on loans, but REITs were further squeezed because they were forced to pay very high short-term interest rates on their borrowings while they were "locked-in" to rates previously committed to builders. REIT stock prices dropped dramatically, a number failed, and many of the surviving REITs are still trying to work out of their problems. The future role of REITs as suppliers of mortgage funds will depend on their ability to solve their existing problems and their ability to control against the recurrence of similar problems.

Individuals

Individuals represent sources of funds in both the primary and secondary mortgage markets. Table 11-2 indicated that an "individuals and others" category has provided significant primary mortgage funds in recent years. However, because this is a "catch-all" category, it is difficult to isolate the role of individuals. Possibly a better indication of the role in the mortgage markets of individuals is that at the end of 1975 "individuals" (including small amounts by some U.S. agencies) held approximately $71 billion in outstanding mortgage debt. About one third of this mortgage debt was in the form of 1- to 4-family home mortgages.[12]

---

[11]*Ibid.*
[12]*Federal Reserve Bulletin* (August, 1976), p. A42.

Individuals provide funds for both first and second mortgage loans. In contrast with institutional lenders, individuals seldom make first mortgage loans for longer than ten years.

QUESTIONS FOR REVIEW

1. What are "savings" and why are they important to the U.S. financial system?
2. Briefly describe the differences between money and capital markets.
3. A substantial portion of funds available for investment purposes are directed into mortgages annually. Who are the major suppliers of these mortgage funds?
4. Briefly describe the terms: (a) intermediation and (b) disintermediation.
5. What are the primary differences between primary and secondary markets for residential mortgages?
6. Briefly describe and compare savings and loan associations, mutual savings banks, and commercial banks in terms of: (a) structure and operation, (b) regulation and control, (c) significance of savings flows, and (d) investment policies.
7. What is the role of life insurance companies as suppliers of mortgage and real estate investment funds?
8. There are a number of noninstitutional sources of mortgage funds. Briefly identify these suppliers of funds to the primary mortgage market.

PROBLEMS

1. An understanding of the flow of funds into mortgages is important to the development of an overall recognition of the importance of real estate financing. Assume that you have been asked to diagram the sources of funds supplied for mortgages. In your diagram indicate the relative importance of institutions and other suppliers of mortgage funds.

2. You are considering the purchase of commercial property that is appraised at $300,000 and are investigating the possibility of financing for the property. What type of institution is likely to be a potential financing source?

3. Assume that you are seeking FHA financing on a new home. Based on the fact that different institutions specialize in different types of loans, what type of institution would specialize in FHA financing?

Factors Affecting Sources of Funds

An effective financial system begins with a medium for exchanging goods and services. We often refer to this medium of exchange as *money*. Money also serves as a standard of value by providing a convenient method for comparing prices or values. Money is important to the savings-investment process since it, or money substitutes such as savings accounts and government and corporate securities, permits the storing of value. Additionally, since debts are generally expressed in terms of money, money is used as the basis for handling future promises to pay (i.e., it is a standard of deferred payment).

In addition to a medium of exchange, an effective financial system needs a monetary system for creating, controlling, and transferring money. The system also must contain institutions and facilities for channeling savings into investment. Finally, because of the long-term characteristics of many investments, an effective financial system must have markets designed to facilitate the buying and selling of securities and other claims to wealth.

The U.S. economy is based on the existence of an effective financial system. Rather than allowing economic activity to be decided solely by chance or the "free" market, efforts are made to guide or steer the economy. This is done primarily through monetary and fiscal policy. *Monetary policy* involves efforts to "manage" the economy by controlling the supply and cost of money and the availability of credit. The Federal Reserve System establishes monetary policy. Efforts to "manage" the economy also are carried out by *fiscal policy* through government spending, taxation of individuals and institutions, and public debt management. Fiscal policy is established by the executive and legislative branches of government.

ECONOMIC GOALS OR OBJECTIVES

Monetary and fiscal policy attempts to guide the economy in terms of several economic objectives or goals. Some of the objectives can be traced to the Employment Act of 1946 which include sustainable economic growth, stable prices, and full employment. *Economic growth* is frequently measured in terms of the gross national product or the total output of goods and services over a stated time period. Real sustainable economic growth is associated with rising standards of living, and is important because too rapid growth often leads to inflation and recessions. On the other hand, too slow growth leads to underutilization of economic resources.

Real sustainable economic growth is associated with stable prices or a stable price level. Economic growth due to rising prices or inflation does not result in higher living standards. Thus, the objective of *stable prices* is consistent with the maintaining of purchasing power.

Another major objective focuses on achieving full employment. Although difficult to define, *full employment* is generally reached when a 3 to 5 percent unemployment rate exists for the labor force.

We would like to achieve simultaneously the goals of sustainable economic growth, full employment, and stable prices. Recent history indicates, however, the difficulties associated with trying to achieve these multiple objectives through monetary and fiscal policy actions. Economic growth has not been sustained. This is reflected in the business cycles characteristic of the U.S. economy in recent years. Purchasing power has declined as reflected in rising prices in the form of inflation, while at the same time unemployment rates have fluctuated between 4 to 9 percent in recent years. Thus, while it may be possible to "manage" the economy to achieve all three objectives at the same time, it is apparent that the task is not an easy one.

A fourth objective of monetary and fiscal policy is concerned with achieving a *long-run balance in international payments*. Inflows and outflows of gold and currencies occur because of foreign trade, investments and loans, foreign aid, and military expenditures. International bankruptcy is possible unless a long-run balance of payments is achieved. Monetary policy attempts to balance this objective in conjunction with the objectives of economic growth, stable prices, and full employment.

THE FEDERAL RESERVE SYSTEM

The Federal Reserve System was established with the passage of the Federal Reserve Act in 1913. Twelve Federal Reserve districts, each with individual regional problems, were established. A Federal Reserve Bank was formed in each district through the purchase of stock by commercial banks operating within each district. These subscribing banks are known as "member banks" and technically "own" the Federal Reserve Banks. In actual practice, the Federal Reserve System is the central bank in the United States and monetary policy decisions are made and carried out by the Board of Governors of the Federal Reserve System. Monetary policy is implemented, or carried out, through the use of both general and selective controls.

General Controls

General controls are used to regulate and control the level and changes in the supply of money and the availability of credit. The regulation of the money supply in conjunction with the demand for money by governments, businesses, and individuals leads to an indirect regulation of interest rates. Regulation of money supply and credit impacts initially on short-term interest rates. The impact of general controls is slower in terms of long-term interest rates.

Reserve Requirements. The Federal Reserve System's most powerful general control is the ability to establish reserve requirements against member bank deposits. The commercial banking system in the United States is referred to as a *fractional reserve system* because banks are not permitted to lend 100 percent of their deposits. Congress establishes a range for reserve requirements on demand deposits or checking accounts and a range for time deposits or savings accounts. The Board of Governors has the authority to specify and change the legal reserve requirements within the established range.

Changes in reserve requirements impact member banks in two basic ways. First, when reserve requirements against existing deposits are changed, excess reserves are created or destroyed. Assuming that member banks are holding the correct amount of required reserves, an increase in required reserves (say from 10 percent to 20 percent) leads to a contraction in bank credit and generally a reduction in the money supply. A reduction in reserve requirements generally results in an expansion in bank credit and money supply. Second, under a fractional reserve system the amount of deposits that can be supported by a given volume of reserves is affected by reserve requirement changes. The commercial banking system has the capability of expanding and contracting deposit credit. For example, given a 20 percent reserve requirement, $10,000 of new reserves injected into the banking system could expand and thus support $50,000 in new deposits. A lowering of the reserve requirement to 10 percent in the above example would allow the expansion and support of $100,000 in new deposits.

A number of different definitions of money supply exist. In the narrowest sense *money supply* is defined as demand deposits in commercial banks plus currency and coin held by the public. Technically, foreign demand deposits at Federal Reserve Banks also are included. This traditional definition is referred to as the money stock or M_1. A somewhat broader definition of the money supply, M_2, includes, in addition to the M_1 components, time and savings deposits held by the public. Excluded are negotiable certificates of deposit in amounts of $100,000 or more. M_3 is a third measure of the money supply that adds to the M_2 definition the shares and savings certificates at savings and loan associations and deposits at mutual savings banks.

The Federal Reserve System can directly affect member bank reserves by altering requirements against demand and time deposits and thus can directly affect the M_1 and M_2 definitions of the money supply. While a large number of commercial banks do not belong to the Federal Reserve System, member bank deposits represent some 75 percent of total commercial bank deposits. This gives the Federal Reserve reasonably good control. At the same time, the Federal Reserve lacks control over deposits and shares in savings and loan associations and mutual savings banks.

The Discount Rate. The Federal Reserve System also provides a source for loans to member banks. The interest rate charged by Federal Reserve Banks to member banks can be altered and thus constitutes a second general tool, or control, for administering credit policy. Member banks can borrow against either their own notes generally secured by government obligations or by rediscounting notes and other debt instruments contained in their own portfolios. Thus, the *discount rate* represents the cost of borrowing to member banks.

In some instances member banks borrow from Federal Reserve Banks in order to meet reserve requirements rather than borrowing from other commercial banks or by selling short-term securities from their portfolios. Reserves that qualify to meet legal reserve requirements include vault cash and deposits held in their district Federal Reserve Bank. When the discount rate is increased, banks may be more inclined to meet reserve requirements by borrowing short-term funds known as *federal funds* from other commercial banks with excess reserves. This could result in higher federal funds interest rates. On the other hand, member banks also might sell some of their short-term government securities in order to meet reserve requirements. This greater supply would tend to lower short-term government security prices and thus raise their interest rates.

Changes in the discount rate also convey psychological implications. It is thought by many that discount rate changes are used by the

Federal Reserve System to signal the intended direction of future credit policy.

Open-Market Operations. The Federal Reserve System's most important general credit tool is its open-market operations. Through the Open Market Committee, policy is established in terms of the Federal Reserve's buying and selling of government securities. In essence, the Federal Reserve System possesses a massive portfolio of U.S. government securities to which securities may be added or from which securities may be sold. By selling securities in the open market, the Federal Reserve System moves to constrain credit expansion and money supply growth. When the purchasers pay for the securities with checks drawn on their demand deposits at member banks, the member bank reserves are reduced. Credit expansion capabilities thus are constrained.

If a large amount of government securities are sold, member bank reserves may fall below the legal reserve requirements. This could cause a contraction in bank credit and a reduction in money supply. Just as the commercial banking system can create a multiple credit expansion given an increase in new reserves, a reduction in reserves below the required level can cause a multiple impact in terms of credit contraction and reduction in the money supply. In addition, the selling of government securities by the Federal Reserve increases the supply, which causes prices to fall and interest rates to rise. Open-market operations are concerned primarily with the buying and selling of short-term government securities. The buying of securities by the Federal Reserve generally leads to credit expansion.

Moral Suasion. Moral suasion is considered by some to be an additional tool of monetary policy. It is sometimes referred to as "jawbone" policy in that Federal Reserve statements and comments are used to let commercial banks know how they are supposed to behave in light of Federal Reserve objectives.

Selective Credit Controls

In some instances it is desirable to regulate particular uses of money or credit. The Federal Reserve accomplishes this through the use of selective credit controls. Selective credit controls are designed to operate directly on the availability of credit in contrast with the general controls, which operate on commercial bank reserves. In the past the Federal Reserve has possessed the power to regulate consumer credit, real estate credit, and stock and bond market credit. At present, the Federal Reserve regulates only securities market credit by setting margin requirements. This power was established under the Securities Exchange Act of 1934.

Margin requirements represent the minimum down payment that is required to purchase securities. Margin purchases are permitted primarily on stocks and bonds listed on national exchanges. *Regulation T* is the most common example of margin requirements in that it is designed to regulate broker-dealer loans to customers. Loans against securities by commercial banks and other lenders also are regulated. Margin requirements are used to stimulate or constrain investor interest and speculation. During recessions and periods of depressed stock prices, margin requirements are lowered — often to levels of down payments in the 50–60 percent range. These requirements are often raised during periods of excessive security speculation.

From time to time Congress has provided the Federal Reserve with other selective credit controls. For example, in 1941 the Federal Reserve established specific "curbs" on the use of credit to finance the purchase of automobiles and other consumer durable goods. The objective was to avoid excessive upward pressure on prices because of the prevailing situation of increased purchasing power and consumer durable goods shortages.

The passage of the Production Act of 1950 permitted regulation of real estate financing. *Regulation X* was established and administered by the Federal Reserve System. The principal amount of real estate loans was regulated on the basis of maximum loan amounts and repayment time periods. Minimum periodic payments also were set. Restrictions on consumer durable goods and real estate credit were removed in 1952. However, the Board of Governors currently has the authority to regulate disclosure of credit terms under the Truth in Lending Act of 1968.

Other Controls

The Federal Reserve System also has the authority to set interest rate ceilings on member bank time and savings deposits. These rates are established under *Regulation Q*. Interest rate ceilings are set after consultation with the Federal Deposit Insurance Corporation and the Federal Home Loan Bank Board. Interest rate ceilings for nonmember, insured banks are regulated by the Federal Deposit Insurance Corporation while the Federal Home Loan Bank Board regulates dividend rates on member and other savings and loan associations.

Regulation Q can be used by the Federal Reserve's Board of Governors to influence economic activity. In the last chapter intermediation was defined as the process of accumulating savings in financial institutions which would, in turn, lend or invest these savings. Disintermediation occurs when savings are withdrawn or new savings are not accumulated in financial institutions. Investors bypass financial institutions and invest directly when other debt instruments and securities offer higher yields or returns. Thus, when interest rates on competitive investments (government and corporate securities) are rising above time and savings deposit celings, banks will find it difficult to compete for time money and bank credit will be constrained. An increase in Regulation Q rates relative to interest rates on competing investments would lead to expansion of bank credit.

FISCAL POLICY

Fiscal policy is concerned with government spending and how that spending is financed. Federal government expenditures are so large that they dwarf other U.S. institution and government expenditures. Federal government taxation provides the basis for meeting these expenditures. The combination of expenditures and tax receipts produces the federal budget. When expenditures exceed receipts we have a *deficit budget*. Tax receipts larger than expenditures result in a *surplus budget*. Deficit budgets act as a stimulus to the economy while surplus budgets tend to constrain the economy.

A deficit budget results in a national debt that must be financed by the United States Treasury by issuing and selling government securities. Deficit budgets have had a cumulative effect in recent years with the result being a substantial increase in the amount of outstanding federal debt.

Debt Management

Debt management involves the financing of outstanding federal debt and new debt arising from deficit budgets. The method of financing deficits influences the impact of deficits on the economy. The U.S. Treasury can finance deficits in three basic ways. Government securities can be sold to: (1) the nonbank public, (2) commercial banks, and (3) Federal Reserve Banks. When individuals, businesses, and nonbank financial institutions purchase government securities from the Treasury, bank reserves are not affected but there might be added upward pressure on interest rates. This is because the Treasury must compete against the private sector for the available supply of funds. If the Treasury sells government securities directly to commercial banks, bank reserves decrease and thus the ability of banks to expand credit is constrained. This is a form of competition between the public and private sectors of the economy in terms of bank reserves.

The least initial impact of debt management on interest rates occurs when the Treasury sells government securities directly to Federal Reserve Banks. The Treasury thus is not in direct competition with the private sector for available funds or bank reserves. In fact, bank reserves are actually increased when the Treasury deposits the funds from the sale of the government securities in commercial banks. This allows for possible further bank credit expansion.

U.S. Government Obligations

The federal government issues both marketable securities and non-marketable obligations. *Nonmarketable* issues can be redeemed only by turning them in to the Treasury, and are primarily in the form of savings bonds. Series E (sold at a discount) and Series H (pay a specified interest rate) bonds are available for sale to the public. A more important role in the financing of the national debt is played by *marketable securities* which may be bought and sold through financial institutions and intermediaries. A secondary market exists for marketable government securities. In addition to marketable and nonmarketable issues, some obligations are designed for specific ownership by government agencies.

Marketable securities are distinguished primarily on the basis of their maturity periods at time of issuance. *Treasury bills* are short-term securities with maturities ranging from 91 days up to one year. In contrast with other marketable government issues, Treasury bills are sold at a discount and mature at par. *Treasury notes* have maturities greater than one year but with a maximum of seven years. *Treasury bonds* generally have maturities in excess of five years and may exceed 20 years. Both Treasury notes and bonds are issued at specified interest rates.

Commercial banks are the largest holders of Treasury bills. These government issues provide both liquidity and safety of principal. Businesses and individuals seeking liquidity and safety also are investors in Treasury bills. Savings and time deposits are in direct competition with Treasury bills for the savings dollar. Treasury notes also are largely held by commercial banks. However, Treasury notes also compete against financial institutions for the savings of individuals and others. Life insurance companies and pension funds are heavy investors in Treasury bonds.

The ability of commercial banks, savings and loan associations, and mutual savings banks in performing the intermediation function of channeling savings into real estate mortgages is dependent on being able to compete effectively for the savings dollar. Since liquidity and safety of principal also are provided by Treasury bills and notes, time and savings accounts must be able to compete on a yield or return basis in order to avoid problems of disintermediation. However, as was seen in the last chapter, periods of disintermediation have occurred frequently in recent years. This was due, at least in part, to the fact that as Treasury and other security yields rose, commercial banks and thrift institutions found it difficult to compete effectively because of Regulation Q and other interest rate ceilings on time and savings accounts and shares in savings and loan associations.

THE MACRO ECONOMIC ENVIRONMENT

Ideally, monetary and fiscal policy should be combined so as to achieve the economic objectives of real sustainable economic growth, stable prices, and full employment. Emphasis on achieving these goals should be conducted in light of also maintaining a long-run balance in international payments. In actual practice, however, results pertaining to the simultaneous achievement of these goals have been less than desirable. In many instances, rather than working together, monetary and fiscal policy seem to have been in conflict with one another. Insight into monetary and fiscal policy activities can be better understood in terms of trends and changes in the macro economic goals.

Monetary and Fiscal Policy in the 1960s

The United States was in a mild recession during the last half of 1960. Thus, in early 1961 the private sector was characterized by excess capacity and unemployment approached the 7 percent level. Prices were reasonably stable as measured by low levels of inflation. At the same time, there was increased concern over our continued deficits in international payments and the meeting of these deficits with gold and dollar payments. Thus, beginning with the Kennedy Administration, a concerted effort was made to seek real sustainable economic growth, full employment, and a sustainable balance in international payments while maintaining reasonable price stability.

In order to achieve these objectives, the Federal Reserve undertook an expansionary monetary policy that lasted until mid-1965. Growth in the money supply and availability of bank credit relative to demand helped to hold interest rates down. At the same time, fiscal policy also was directed at stimulating the economy. For example, attempts were made to stimulate investment expenditures in the private sector in 1962 by enacting an investment tax credit (designed to reduce tax liabilities when making capital expenditures) and by liberalizing depreciation guidelines (permitting the use of accelerated depreciation methods and shorter depreciation lives). In addition, the Revenue Act of 1964 provided for the reduction in personal and corporate income taxes. Real GNP growth, declining unemployment rates, and relatively stable prices prevailed during this period.

However, inflationary pressures became pronounced beginning in mid-1965. Along with expansionary monetary policy and stimulative fiscal policy came rapid escalation of the Vietnam war. Increased military expenditures led to even larger deficit budgets. The private sector began operating at very high capacity levels, demand for funds rose, and labor shortages developed. This, in turn, led to price increases. Monetary policy became restrictive during the first half of 1966. Slowing of money supply growth along with continued demand for money pressures led to a "credit crunch" and rapidly rising interest rates. There was little restraint on the part of fiscal policy during this period.

The economy was on the verge of a recession at the beginning of 1967 and the Federal Reserve subsequently moved to rapid expansion of the money supply during 1967 and 1968. This, coupled with continued stimulative fiscal policy, resulted in even higher inflation rates.

In 1969 the Federal Reserve moved to a monetary policy of restraint. This, along with a small surplus budget for fiscal 1969, contributed to the mild recession of 1969–70. Interest rates peaked at high levels during 1969 and disintermediation became a major problem. However, strong inflationary pressures persisted and prices continued to rise during the recession.

Recent Developments in Macro Economic Goals

Two major economic downturns have occurred since the latter part of the 1960s. First was the rather mild recession during 1969–70 as was just discussed. The second more recent recessionary period began during the fourth quarter of 1973 and lasted until the second quarter of 1975. Figure 12-1, page 192, shows gross national product in current dollars and in "real" or 1972 dollars. The difference between the two measures since 1972 reflects inflation. The real product measure shows the severity of the most recent recession. It is apparent that the objective of real sustainable economic growth has not been achieved in recent years.

Figure 12-2, page 193, illustrates the severity of inflation during this decade. Wholesale prices expanded rapidly during 1973 and 1974 and even consumer prices reached double-digit levels of inflation during 1974. Of some consolation is the fact that the inflation rate for wholesale prices slowed sharply during 1975. However, the goal of stable prices certainly has not been achieved. At the same time, Figure 12-3 on page 194 illustrates the high unemployment rates that have prevailed. One segment of economic theory holds that a trade-off relationship exists between price increase or inflation and unemployment levels. Figures 12-2 and 12-3 seem to indicate that the high unemployment rates of 1975 and since seem to be associated with some slowing in the rate of inflation.

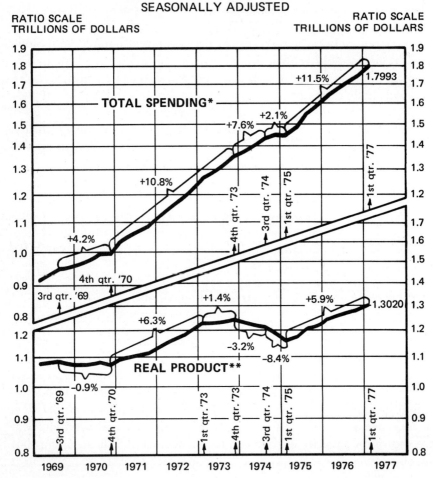

DEMAND AND PRODUCTION
QUARTERLY TOTALS AT ANNUAL RATES
SEASONALLY ADJUSTED

RATIO SCALE
TRILLIONS OF DOLLARS

RATIO SCALE
TRILLIONS OF DOLLARS

Source: U.S. Department of Commerce.
* GNP in current dollars.
** GNP in 1972 dollars.
Percentages are annual rates of change for periods indicated.
Latest data plotted: 1st quarter

Figure
12-1 Demand and Production, 1969–1977

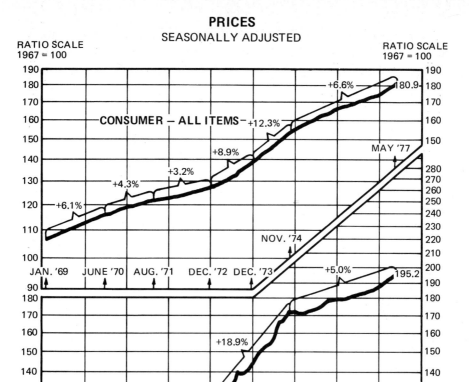

PRICES
SEASONALLY ADJUSTED

Source: U.S. Department of Commerce.
Percentages are annual rates of change for periods indicated.
Latest Data Plotted: May

Figure
12-2 Prices, 1969–1977

Furthermore, although not depicted graphically, the United States has continued to operate with deficits in international payments and has not moved toward a more balanced position.

Recent Monetary and Fiscal Policy Actions

While it is obvious that monetary and fiscal policy have had difficulty in achieving the macro economic objectives, it is still important

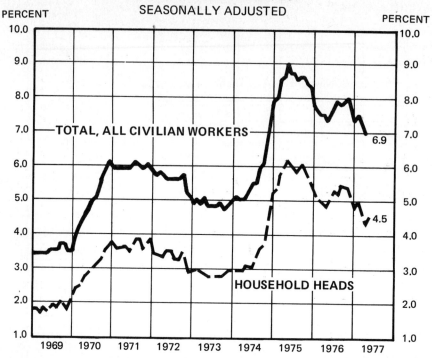

UNEMPLOYMENT RATES*
SEASONALLY ADJUSTED

**Figure
12-3** Unemployment Rates, 1969–1977
(Percentage of Civilian Labor Force in Group)

to have an understanding of their efforts. The Federal Reserve entered into a period of monetary expansion beginning in 1970 and continuing until mid-1973. Figure 12-4, page 195, depicts growth rates in money stock which is the M_1 measure of the money supply. It can be seen that the rate of growth in money stock slowed markedly during 1969 when the Federal Reserve moved to a policy of restraint prior to the 1969–70 recession. A slowing down in money supply growth also began during 1973 with even greater restraint being conducted during 1974. This, of course, led to the most recent recession.

Fiscal policy attempted a new approach to management of the economy with particular emphasis on controlling inflation. A price freeze was ordered in mid-1971 and was followed by institution of wage and price controls. A combination of mandatory and voluntary controls was maintained until early 1974. Inflation was not controlled

194

MONEY STOCK AND MONETARY BASE
MONTHLY AVERAGES OF DAILY FIGURES
SEASONALLY ADJUSTED

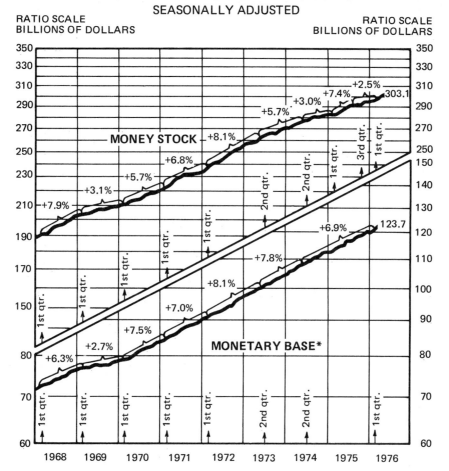

Source: Federal Reserve Bank of St. Louis.

*Uses of the monetary base are member bank reserves and currency held by the public and nonmember banks. Adjustments are made for reserve requirement changes and shifts in deposits among classes of banks. Data are computed by this Bank.

Percentages are annual rates of change for periods indicated.

Latest data plotted: May

Figure
12-4   Money Stock and Monetary Base

and the conclusion was that wage and price controls were a failure. Involvement in the Vietnam war ended in 1973. However, the oil embargo crisis contributed to economic pressures and fiscal policy continued to be characterized by large deficit budgets.

Real Estate Financing Implications

The ability to finance real estate investments is dependent upon the cost and availability of funds. Interest rate levels are determined by inflation expectations and the relative supply and demand for money. As we have seen, the Federal Reserve, by operating directly on the money supply, can influence interest rates and the availability of credit. The sensitivity of short-term interest rates in recent years is shown in Figure 12-5 below. The peaking of these interest rates is

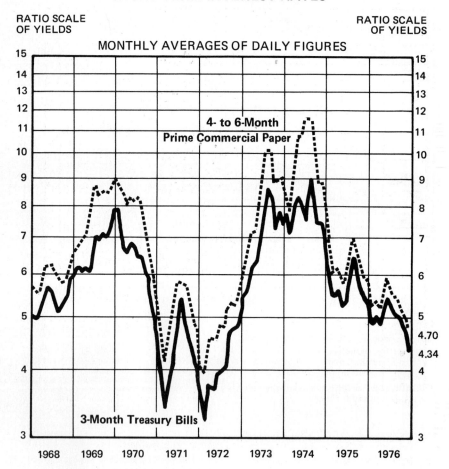

SHORT-TERM INTEREST RATES

RATIO SCALE
OF YIELDS

RATIO SCALE
OF YIELDS

MONTHLY AVERAGES OF DAILY FIGURES

4- to 6-Month
Prime Commercial Paper

3-Month Treasury Bills

4.70

4.34

1968 1969 1970 1971 1972 1973 1974 1975 1976

Source: Federal Reserve Bank of St. Louis.
Latest data plotted: December

**Figure
12-5**   Short-Term Interest Rates

generally consistent with the peaking of the economy in 1969 and 1973 and the subsequent downturns in 1970 and 1974. *Prime commercial paper*, depicted in Figure 12-5, represents short-term unsecured notes of major corporations having strong credit ratings.

Long-term interest rates, while not as volatile as short-term interest rates, also exhibited peaks during the recession years of 1969 and 1974 as can be seen in Figure 12-6 below. Inflation expectations have

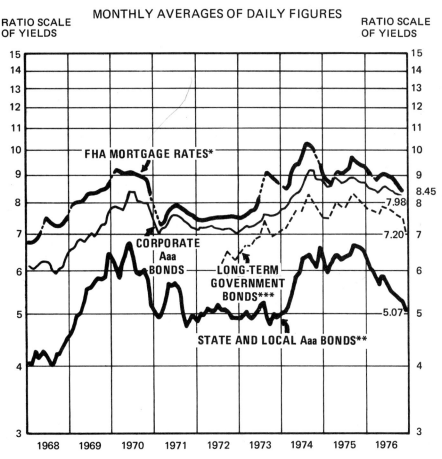

LONG-TERM INTEREST RATES
MONTHLY AVERAGES OF DAILY FIGURES

Source: Federal Reserve Bank of St. Louis.
*   FHA 30-year mortgages. Dashed lines indicate data not available.
** Monthly averages of Thursday figures.
*** Average of yields on coupon issues due or callable in ten years or more, excluding issues with Federal estate tax privileges. Yields are computed by this Bank.
    Latest data plotted: FHA-November; Others-December

**Figure
12-6**   Long-Term Interest Rates

contributed to long-term interest rates remaining at relatively high levels. This is shown in terms of highly quality corporate bonds, long-term federal government bonds, and state and local government bonds. FHA mortgage rates which peaked above the 9 percent level in early 1970 fell less than 2 percentage points before climbing above 10 percent in 1974.

The implications of interest rate levels and changes on real estate financing are many. Commercial banks, savings and loan associations, and mutual savings banks must compete against alternative investments for the savings dollars. When these institutions cannot compete effectively, for example because of interest rate ceilings on shares and time and savings deposits, disintermediation occurs. Consequently,

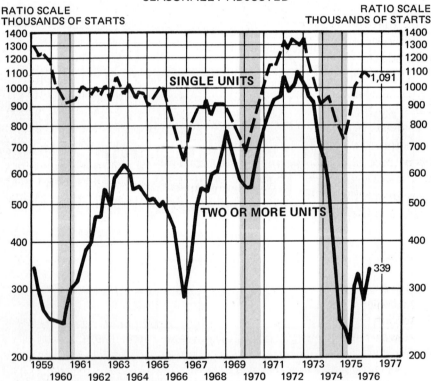

NEW PRIVATELY OWNED HOUSING UNITS
QUARTERLY TOTALS AT ANNUAL RATES
SEASONALLY ADJUSTED

Source: U.S. Department of Commerce.

The first two shaded areas represent periods of business recessions as defined by the National Bureau of Economic Research. The last shaded area is tentative and has been defined by the FRB of St. Louis.

Latest data plotted: 2nd quarter preliminary.

Figure
12-7 New Privately Owned Housing Units Started

fewer funds are available for the mortgage market from these institutions. And, as we saw in Chapter 11, the consequences are particularly significant because direct investment in real estate mortgages is generally inconsistent with individual saver objectives. Alternative investments include corporate stocks and bonds and federal and state and local government bonds. At least until recently these bond and stock investments offered greater liquidity because of better developed secondary markets. However, the liquidity disadvantages associated with direct investment in mortgages are being reduced as the secondary market for real estate mortgages continues to develop.

Factors Influencing Housing Cycles

In the past new housing expenditures have moved with changes in economic activity.[1] Existing evidence also suggests a link between housing starts and interest rates. More specifically, a recent study found that the demand for new housing starts is significantly affected by interest rates and rent levels, while interest rates and labor costs influence the supply of housing starts.[2]

The historical relationship between housing starts and business cycles in the economy is shown in Figure 12-7, page 198. Housing starts, both single and multiple units, peaked prior to the 1969 and 1973 peaks in the economy. Housing also traditionally begins recovering before the economy starts recovering from a recession. In the most recent recession, however, housing starts have been much slower in their recovery. This is probably due to the rapid escalation in housing costs in recent years, some tightness in the availability of mortgage funds, and the continued high mortgage interest rate levels.

QUESTIONS FOR REVIEW

1. Briefly outline the general economic goals and objectives developed for the United States.
2. Identify and explain the Federal Reserve's general economic controls. How do these differ from selective controls?
3. The commercial banking system is sometimes referred to as a fractional reserve system. Define and describe what this means. How does an increase in the reserve requirement by the Federal Reserve impact on the commercial banking system?

---

[1] This relationship is described in detail in Neil A. Stevens, "Housing: A Cyclical Industry on the Upswing," *Review*, Federal Reserve Bank of St. Louis (August, 1976), pp. 15–20.

[2] Francisco Arcelus and Allan H. Meltzer, "The Markets for Housing and Housing Services," *Journal of Money, Credit and Banking* (February, 1973), pp. 78–99.

4. There are a number of different definitions of money supply. Which are best controlled by the Federal Reserve?
5. How do the federal budget and debt management combine to control or administer fiscal policy?
6. There are a number of U.S. government securities or obligations. First, explain the difference between marketable and nonmarketable issues. Second, list and describe the different types of marketable securities.
7. Briefly trace the development of monetary and fiscal policy during the 1960s.

PROBLEMS

1. Assume that the Federal Reserve purchases $1,000,000 in U.S. government securities from a commercial bank. If the reserve requirement is 15 percent, what is the total amount of deposits that can be created in the commercial banking system?

2. The macro economic environment impacts heavily on real estate finance. Indicate and describe the degree of success in recent years (be as current as possible) in achieving the economic goals set for our country.

3. Housing starts traditionally have begun recovering prior to the economy's recovery from an economic recession. What has been the most recent experience in terms of housing starts? Be as current as possible in your answer.

Mortgage Banking and Secondary Mortgage Market Developments

A financial system, to be effective, must provide markets and procedures for handling and transferring claims to wealth. The *mortgage market*, broadly defined, involves three types of transactions or activities. As we have seen in the two previous chapters, the *primary mortgage market* involves the creation or origination of new mortgages. Savings are channeled into financial institutions which, in turn, perform the investment function by originating and holding mortgages. The holding of a mortgage, represents one form of a claim to wealth.

In some instances, financial institutions and other financial intermediaries are involved in the process of origination of new mortgages but without the intention of holding mortgage claims to wealth. In essence, these originators act as middlemen or agents in distributing mortgages to other investors. This *facilitating function* represents the second major activity or transaction in the mortgage market. Mortgage banking firms perform this facilitating or intermediary function.

The third segment of the mortgage market involves secondary market activities. The *secondary mortgage market* provides liquidity through improved marketability of mortgage claims to wealth. Mortgage bankers often sell their originated mortgages directly to institutions operating in the secondary mortgage market. And, just as stocks and bonds are traded in secondary markets, mortgage claims to wealth can be bought and sold in the secondary mortgage market.

NEED FOR A SECONDARY MORTGAGE MARKET

The origination of mortgages generally results in long-term claims to wealth. Since mortgage loans usually involve substantial dollar amounts, borrowers need long time periods over which to repay loan principal and interest obligations. Originators establish the terms of mortgage loans in the primary mortgage market. As we have previously seen, lender-originators such as commercial banks, mutual savings banks, and savings and loan associations often intend to hold the mortgage loans they originate until the loans mature. Returns on these claims to wealth are received in the form of interest payments. However, economic conditions influenced by monetary and fiscal policy actions often result in periods of disintermediation for these financial institutions. Severe disintermediation frequently produces liquidity pressures or cash needs that may require the liquidation of some mortgage holdings.

From time to time other holders of mortgages such as pension funds, life insurance companies and even individuals may find it necessary to meet liquidity needs. In other instances it might be desirable for institutions or individuals to sell some of their existing mortgage claims to wealth and purchase other mortgages or securities in order to meet their portfolio investment objectives. Thus, there is a need for a mechanism for facilitating the marketing of mortgage claims to wealth. In an effective financial system, markets need to be established to provide for the ready buying and selling of mortgages at reasonable prices and costs. Improved marketability of mortgage claims to wealth will result in greater liquidity for the holders of mortgages. Mortgage *marketability* thus relates to the time required to buy or sell mortgages as well as the cost involved in marketing secondary mortgage market transactions.

However, while the need for a well-functioning national secondary mortgage market is apparent, its early development was erratic. Lack of loan standardization practices and procedures undoubtably contributed to the slow development of a national market. Historically, loan originators often employed different loan application standards and requirements across the United States. Compounding these differences has been the importance of geographical areas, within which the pledged properties are located, in traditionally assessing the quality of mortgage loans. Of course, as further loan standardization practices and procedures take place, the national secondary mortgage market will become more efficient.

MORTGAGE BANKING

The facilitating function between the primary and secondary mortgage markets often is performed by mortgage banking firms. According to the 1946 Constitution of the Mortgage Bankers Association of

America, a *mortgage banker* is: "Any person, firm, or corporation . . . engaged in the business of lending money on the security of improved real estate in the United States and who publicly offers such securities, or certificates, bonds, or debentures based thereon, for sale as a dealer therein, or who is an investor in real estate securities, or is the recognized agent of an insurance company or other direct purchaser of first mortgage real estate securities for investment only."

In actual practice, a distinction sometimes is made between mortgage brokers and mortgage bankers. *Mortgage brokers* perform the loan origination function by bringing together lenders and borrowers in real estate loan transactions, which results in a mortgage placement fee for successful loan originations. Mortgage brokers specialize in commercial real estate properties and they seldom finance loans with their own capital. The role of a mortgage broker usually is terminated when the loan is placed. That is, mortgage brokers generally do not service loans after they have been delivered to the investor or lender.

Mortgage bankers also originate new real estate loans. They perform a significant role in residential real estate financings. While mortgage bankers sometimes finance or invest in the loans they originate, their more important role is as middlemen or agents in the distribution of mortgages to other investors. Mortgage bankers often perform a loan servicing function by collecting payments and inspecting real estate properties used as collateral for the loan they originated. Thus, mortgage bankers traditionally performed mortgage loan *origination*, *servicing*, and *placement* functions.

Mortgage Banker Operations

Traditional mortgage banking operations in an intermediary capacity can be illustrated with an example. Assume that a builder seeks the assistance of a mortgage banker in obtaining financing for a major real estate project. Two kinds of financing actually are needed: (1) a short-term construction or building loan, and (2) a long-term property mortgage loan. In practice, the two kinds of financing go hand-in-hand. A mortgage banker must be able to show that long-term mortgage funds can be obtained before short-term construction loans are acquired. The short-term building loan to cover construction activities is either supplied from the mortgage banker's own funds or is obtained through a short-term loan from a commercial bank. Security for the loan includes the underlying property plus the general credit of the builder and mortgage banker.

In order to obtain funds for a builder, the mortgage banker first secures the availability of long-term mortgage funds by obtaining an *advance* or *forward commitment* from the permanent investor which often is an insurance company or mutual savings bank. The permanent investor makes or enters into a firm commitment to purchase mortgage loans which will be placed on the property. This is done in advance of construction. The mortgage banker agrees to deliver the mortgages at some future date on the homes that are to be constructed on the property by the builder.

A *take-out letter* represents the agreement for the advance commitment and covers the delivery date, amount of loans, and fees connected with the long-term mortgages. The take-out letter aids the mortgage banker in the attempt to obtain the necessary construction loan funds. However, in certain instances the mortgage banker is unable to obtain an immediate advance commitment. This frequently occurs during periods of high or rising interest rates and brings about the need for a *standby commitment*. In this situation, the commercial banker enters into a firm or standby commitment to purchase the mortgage if the mortgage banker cannot find a permanent investor by a specified date. The commercial banker pays a *forfeiture price* or discount price in the event that a permanent investor cannot be found during the stated time period.

Under certain conditions mortgage bankers find it desirable to "warehouse" mortgages. *Mortgage warehousing* is an interim loan made by a commercial bank designed to cover the time period between when the mortgage banker closes the mortgage loan and the mortgage is accepted by the permanent investor. The most prevalent type of warehousing occurs when a time lapse develops between when the mortgage banker closes or originates the loan and when the loan is, in turn, delivered to the permanent investor. During this interim period, the amount of the mortgage is lent by the commercial bank to the mortgage banker.

Recent Trends and Developments

Earlier in this century mortgage banking grew out of the need by life insurance companies and mutual savings banks located in the northeast to invest in out-of-state mortgages. The assets of these institutions expanded rapidly and their officers sought additional opportunities for investments offering relatively high but safe yields. Mortgage bankers provided necessary assistance in facilitating the making of these out-of-state loans.

Mortgage banking also grew because mortgage bankers performed a necessary role in the development of *mortgage loan participations*. Briefly, in situations when local financial institutions could not meet the total amount requested for a loan, mortgage bankers sought to arrange participation in the mortgage loan by additional lenders.

The role of mortgage banking during the 1970s is depicted in Tables 13-1 and 13-2. Table 13-1 shows that the dollar amount of loans closed by mortgage bankers increased sharply as the economy moved out of the 1969–70 recession and continued at high levels until the 1974 economic downturn. First mortgage loan volume has remained above the $20 billion annual level since 1972. Throughout the first half of the 1970s first mortgage loans have accounted for at least two thirds of the total dollar amount of loans closed by mortgage bankers. The significance of first mortgage loans relative to total loans closed declined steadily from the end of the 1960s until 1974 when the dollar amount of construction loans closed dropped more rapidly during the economic downturn.

Table 13-1 Mortgage Banking Activity
(Loans Closed in Millions of Dollars)

Type of Loan	1970	1971	1972	1973	1974	1975
First mortgage loans*	$12,967	$17,956	$21,200	$20,968	$20,073	$20,265
Construction loans	3,963	5,532	7,765	8,503	5,588	3,274
Land development loans	154	382	824	937	553	306
Other loans	162	131	296	582	334	325
Total loans closed	$17,246	$24,001	$30,085	$30,991	$26,548	$24,170
Percent Breakdown						
First mortgage loans	100.0%	100.0%	100.0%	100.0%	100.0%	100.0%
Single-family (FHA/VA)	62.3	62.9	52.2	40.9	48.7	58.2
Single-family (conventional)	3.1	3.3	10.5	19.5	17.3	16.1
Multifamily	16.1	15.9	16.8	15.8	12.2	7.8
Nonresidential	18.5	17.9	20.5	23.8	21.8	17.9

Source: Mortgage Bankers Association of America.

Examination of the breakdown of first mortgage loans closed by mortgage bankers also indicates interesting recent developments. Mortgage bankers traditionally specialized in originating FHA-insured mortgage loans. Before the formation of the Federal Housing Administration (FHA) in 1934, the lack of standards for qualifying borrowers and collateral created substantial risks for investors lending funds on real estate mortgages. With the development of a standardized system for estimating property values and borrower credit capabilities, mortgage banking activity flourished. Emphasis on VA-guaranteed mortgage loans also developed rapidly after the passage by Congress of the Serviceman's Readjustment Act (commonly known as the GI Bill of

Rights) in 1944. Table 13-1 indicates that at the beginning of the 1970s FHA/VA loans comprised over 60 percent of the dollar amount of first mortgage loans closed by mortgage bankers.

Beginning in 1972, however, mortgage bankers have been closing relatively greater amounts of conventional first mortgage loans. Competition between mortgage bankers and permanent mortgage lenders has heightened during the 1970s. Many institutional mortgage lenders have opened their own regional offices and are willing to compete in terms of the cost of servicing fees. Further development of the secondary mortgage market, and the resulting liquidity advantages, have added to the competitive pressures on mortgage bankers.

However, mortgage bankers remain a significant factor in the origination of residential mortgage loans as Table 13-2 illustrates. Mortgage bankers originated approximately 20 percent of total institutional residential mortgage loan originations during the first half of the 1970s. Commercial banks originate approximately the same percentage amounts, while savings and loan associations consistently originate over 40 percent of the residential mortgage loans closed annually by institutions. The remaining loan closings, less than 20 percent, are made by mutual savings banks, life insurance companies, and federal credit agencies. In summary, mortgage bankers rank second, along with commercial banks, in terms of annual residential mortgage loan closings. Only savings and loan associations have consistently higher dollar amounts of closings.

Table 13-2 further points out that mortgage bankers continue to close in excess of 60 percent of both VA-guaranteed and FHA-insured

Table 13-2 Mortgage Banking Residential Loan Organizations As a Percentage of Six Institutional Mortgage Loan Organizations†

Type of Property and Type of Loan	1970	1971	1972	1973	1974	1975
Total residential	24.9%	22.2%	18.8%	17.2%	20.1%	18.7%
Single-family*	24.2	21.0	17.5	15.8	20.0	19.2
Multifamily	28.1	29.5	26.7	25.9	21.2	15.2
Single-Family Breakdown						
FHA	67.9%	68.3%	68.7%	70.2%	78.0%	73.6%
VA	70.6	62.6	61.4	63.2	74.8	70.6
Conventional	1.7	1.5	3.8	6.1	6.5	5.2

Source: Mortgage Bankers Association of America.

†Based on residential mortgage originations by mortgage bankers, savings and loan associations, commercial banks, mutual savings banks, life insurance companies, and federal credit agencies.

single-family residential mortgage loans. At the same time, mortgage bankers continue to service over 80 percent of the first mortgage loans that they originate. Thus, mortgage bankers continue to perform a dominant facilitating or intermediary role in the overall mortgage market.

DEVELOPMENT OF THE SECONDARY MORTGAGE MARKET

Secondary securities markets are well developed for stocks and bonds. For example, organized stock exchanges such as the New York Stock Exchange date back to the last century. A secondary mortgage market lacks such a history. While undoubtedly some buying, selling, or exchanging of mortgages between financial institutions was carried out on a local level, little regional and virtually no national secondary mortgage activity occurred prior to the 1930s. Thrift institutions such as commercial banks and savings and loan associations frequently faced problems of liquidity. These were compounded by the lack of marketability of mortgage loans.

Prior to the 1930s, only commercial banks that were members of the Federal Reserve System possessed a source that they could turn toward in order to temper liquidity pressures. As we saw in Chapter 12, member banks can borrow at the prevailing discount rate from Federal Reserve Banks. One way member banks can do this is by rediscounting notes or other debt instruments contained in their own portfolios. This ability to borrow against certain outstanding loans helped temper the lack of an active secondary mortgage market.

Savings and loan associations were not as fortunate. Although Congressional hearings as early as 1919 considered the establishment of a central credit system for the purpose of aiding mortgage lending institutions, formal action was not taken until the financial crisis of the 1930s. As we saw in Chapter 11, savings and loan associations were "loosely" regulated until the passage of the Federal Home Loan Bank Act of 1932. One important purpose of the creation of the Federal Home Loan Bank System was to provide credit in the form of advances to member mortgage lending institutions. Member institutions are permitted to borrow against their savings balances. This has helped, at least since the 1930s, to temper liquidity pressures associated with the lack of marketability for mortgage loans.

However, the need for a well-developed national secondary mortgage market remains. The overall mortgage market continues to be highly volatile. An improved secondary mortgage market is expected to help reduce overall volatility. A number of legislative efforts have taken place to stimulate and encourage the continued development of an efficient secondary mortgage market. Major federal laws affecting the development of the secondary market are listed in Table 13-3 and provide the basis for further discussion in this section.

Table 13-3 Major Federal Developments Affecting the Secondary Mortgage Market

Date	Federal Provisions and Developments
1934	*National Housing Act* Created the Federal Housing Administration. Also provided for the establishment of privately-owned mortgage institutions to operate a national secondary mortgage market.
1938	*Federal National Mortgage Association* (creation of) The Reconstruction Finance Corporation provided capital for the establishment of the Federal National Mortgage Association which was to operate as a government-sponsored secondary mortgage market.
1950	*Federal National Mortgage Association* (transference of) Provision was made to move the FNMA from under the Reconstruction Finance Corporation to the Housing and Home Finance Agency which was created in 1942 to coordinate federal home financing activities.
1954	*Federal National Mortgage Association Charter Act* The FNMA was rechartered as a federal agency with some corporate structural characteristics. It continued as an agency of the Housing and Home Finance Agency but was to become privately-owned.
1968	*Housing and Urban Development Act* The FNMA was reorganized as a separate, privately-owned corporation. At the same time, the Government National Mortgage Association was created as a wholly-owned government corporation under the direction of the Department of Housing and Urban Development.
1970	*Emergency Home Finance Act* Created the Federal Home Loan Mortgage Corporation for purposes of providing a secondary mortgage market for savings and loan association members of the Federal Home Loan Bank System. Also permitted FNMA to purchase and sell conventional mortgages.

Federal Developments During the 1930s and 1940s

The Federal Housing Administration was established with the passage of the National Housing Act of 1934. The Act also provided for the establishment of privately-owned mortgage institutions to operate a national secondary mortgage market.

The Reconstruction Finance Corporation purchased some mortgages on urban commercial properties, while avoiding residential mortgages, during 1935. By 1938, it was apparent that a national secondary mortgage market was not developing. Consequently, legislation was enacted in 1938 which created the Federal National Mortgage Association (FNMA). The objective was to develop a government-sponsored secondary market for residential mortgages.

More specifically, the FNMA which is commonly referred to as "Fannie Mae" was designed to provide a secondary market for Federal Housing Administration (FHA) insured mortgages. FHA-insured loans originated under the National Housing Act of 1934 when the Federal Housing Administration was created. It was anticipated that the development of FHA insurance of residential real estate loans would facilitate the establishment of a secondary market. However, a secondary market did not develop on a national level.

The Reconstruction Finance Corporation provided $10 million in capital to the FNMA when it was established in 1938. Additional funds could be raised by the FNMA by issuing its own notes when additional funds were needed. The FNMA had power to purchase FHA-insured mortgages from qualified sellers which, in turn, helped replenish available funds for making more FHA mortgage loans. In actual practice, however, the Federal National Mortgage Association purchased relatively few mortgages during most of the 1940s. It was 1948 before the FNMA's mortgage holdings began to increase substantially. This dramatic increase in holdings coincided with the broadening of the FNMA's operations in 1948 to allow purchase of Veterans Administration guaranteed loans.

Changes During the 1950s and 1960s

In 1950 the Federal National Mortgage Association was transferred from the jurisdiction of the Reconstruction Finance Corporation to the Housing and Home Finance Agency which was created in 1942 to coordinate federal home financing activities.

In 1954 FNMA was rechartered as a federal agency (it was previously a wholly-owned government corporation) under the Federal National Mortgage Association Charter Act. The FNMA continued as an agency of the Housing and Home Finance Agency but was to become privately-owned and have corporate structural characteristics. In other words, FNMA was to move from government ownership to private ownership. This was to be accomplished in the following fashion. First, preferred stock was to be issued to the U.S. Treasury so that the capital, surplus, and earnings of the old FNMA could be used for working capital.

Second, lenders doing business with FNMA were expected to become common stockholders of the secondary market facility. Lenders were required to invest 3 percent of the dollar amount of the loans they sold to FNMA in capital contributions that were then exchanged for common stock. This was changed to a stock purchase requirement of between 1 and 2 percent under the Housing Act of 1957. Further reductions in stock purchase requirements for sellers of mortgages to FNMA were made during the recessionary period of 1958.

The Charter Act of 1954 made three additional provisions relating to: (1) secondary market operations, (2) special assistance functions, and (3) management and liquidation functions. FNMA's secondary market operations were limited to FHA-insured (stemming from the 1938 National Housing Act) and VA-guaranteed (stemming from the 1944 Serviceman's Readjustment Act) mortgage loans. Under the 1954 Charter Act, insured or guaranteed loans could be purchased at par or discount prices depending upon prevailing economic and geographic conditions. The FNMA also was given discretion as to whether or not to accept submitted mortgages. That is, the FNMA could set its own mortgage acceptability standards. This flexibility permitted the FNMA to set profit objectives consistent with a movement toward private ownership.

The special assistance function provided the President with the power to authorize the FNMA to support special types of housing programs through advance commitments and purchases of mortgages. Special types of housing problems include urban renewal projects. FNMA assistance also has been used to stimulate the construction industry during recessionary periods. Another form of special assistance includes the purchase of mortgages on properties reconstructed after natural disasters.

The management and liquidation function provided in the 1954 Charter Act required that FNMA manage and liquidate its portfolio of mortgages acquired prior to November, 1954. Many of the mortgages owned by the FNMA prior to the 1954 Act did not meet new quality standards and were purchased during periods when the FNMA operated without profit objectives.

In 1965 FNMA became a subsidiary of the Department of Housing and Urban Development which replaced the Housing and Home Finance Agency. FNMA continued to operate in a quasi-public capacity, characterized by profit motives while maintaining U.S. Treasury support, until 1968.

Housing and Urban Development Act of 1968

The Federal National Mortgage Association was reorganized as a privately-owned corporation under the Housing and Urban Development Act of 1968. All stock owned by the U.S. Treasury was redeemed and replaced by the sale of common stock to the general public. The secondary mortgage operations remained with the new Fannie Mae. FNMA thus is a private corporation dealing in mortgage loan claims to wealth. The FNMA raises money by selling securities backed by its pool of mortgages. However, since this private corporation still has a public purpose, the U.S. Treasury still has the authority to purchase Fannie Mae obligations.

The special assistance and management and liquidation functions provided for under the 1954 Charter Act were reassigned to a new organization under the Housing and Urban Development Act of 1968. This new organization, the Government National Mortgage Association (GNMA), was created as a wholly-owned government corporation under the direction of the Department of Housing and Urban Development. As might be expected, it soon became known as "Ginnie Mae."

Fannie Mae and Ginnie Mae were designed to work together even though one is privately-owned and the other government-owned. FNMA raises funds to purchase mortgages by selling its common stock and by issuing mortgage-backed bonds and other debt instruments. Ginnie Mae, in turn, guarantees mortgage-backed bonds issued by FNMA. FNMA provides support for GNMA through its ability to purchase securities issued by GNMA.

Emergency Home Finance Act of 1970

FNMA's role in the secondary market was expanded with the passage of the Emergency Home Finance Act of 1970. After many years of exclusion, the FNMA was permitted to purchase conventional mortgages in addition to FHA-insured and VA-guaranteed mortgages. However, FNMA did not begin actual purchase of conventional mortgage loans until February, 1972. FNMA also was permitted to deal in mortgage loans issued to finance the construction and modernization of hospitals.

The Emergency Home Finance Act of 1970 also created the Federal Home Loan Mortgage Corporation (FHLMC) for purposes of providing a secondary mortgage market for savings and loan association members of the Federal Home Loan Bank System. The FHLMC, logically nicknamed "Freddie Mac," was permitted to purchase conventional, FHA-insured, and VA-guaranteed mortgages. Since savings and loan associations deal heavily in conventional mortgages, this is the area where the FHLMC was expected to be very active.

Recent Trends and Developments

Three major institutions or organizations have evolved as the secondary mortgage market developed over time. First was the evolution of FNMA which now is a privately-owned but government-authorized corporation, FNMA, although created in 1938, first developed as a secondary market institution in 1954. In 1968, GNMA was created as a government-owned and government-operated secondary market institution. Then, in 1970, the FHLMC was formed as a secondary market subsidiary of the Federal Home Loan Bank. With FNMA operating by itself through most of the 1950s and 1960s, the secondary mortgage market was slow to develop.

Secondary mortgage operations changed with involvement by all three secondary market institutions during the 1970s. Recent trends in mortgage debt held by FNMA, GNMA, and FHLMC are depicted in Table 13-4. Mortgage debt held by the three secondary market institutions more than doubled over the 1970–1975 period. This growth in mortgage debt holdings is due largely to activity by Fannie Mae and Freddie Mac as is shown in their secondary mortgage market activities depicted in Table 13-5. Both organizations have been relatively heavy

Table 13-4 Mortgage Debt Held by Secondary Market Institutions (Millions of Dollars)

Secondary Market Institution	1970	1971	1972	1973	1974	1975
FNMA	$15,502	$17,791	$19,791	$24,175	$29,578	$31,824
GNMA	5,222	5,321	5,111	4,045	4,849	7,242
FHLMC	325	968	1,788	2,604	4,586	4,987
Total	$21,409	$24,080	$26,690	$30,824	$39,013	$44,054

Sources: FNMA, GNMA, and FHLMC.

Table 13-5 FNMA and FHLMC Secondary Mortgage Market Activity (Millions of Dollars)

Year	FNMA Purchases	FNMA Sales	FHLMC Purchases	FHLMC Sales
1970	$5,078	—	$ 325	—
1971	3,574	336	778	113
1972	3,699	211	1,297	407
1973	6,127	71	1,334	409
1974	6,953	5	2,190	53
1975	4,263	1	1,713	1,021

Sources: FNMA and FHLMC.

purchasers of mortgages. However, policies pertaining to the selling of mortgages differed. FNMA, rather than engaging in buying and selling secondary mortgage functions, has been operating more as a lender adding to its permanent loan portfolio.

Our attention now turns to the operating characteristics of Fannie Mae. The operations of GNMA and the FHLMC will be examined in the next chapter along with other government real estate finance programs and activities. However, we should not lose sight of the fact that many of the FNMA, GNMA, and FHLMC secondary mortgage market activities are interrelated.

FEDERAL NATIONAL MORTGAGE ASSOCIATION

The development of the Federal National Mortgage Association was described in the last section. In the way of a brief review, FNMA, a government-sponsored corporation, was created as a government-owned organization in 1938. It became semi-privately-owned in 1954 and completely privately-owned in 1968.

Structure and Organization

FNMA still remains government-sponsored and is tied to the federal government in a number of ways. Fannie Mae is controlled by 15 directors. Ten members of the board are elected by FNMA's stockholders; and five members are appointed by the President. The Secretary of Housing and Urban Development also has regulatory authority over FNMA in a number of areas. For example, the Secretary can set FNMA size of debt and debt to capital ratio limits. FNMA also may be required to allocate a portion of its loan purchases for mortgages issued in conjunction with certain national housing programs.

FNMA's basic function is to provide a secondary market for residential mortgage claims to wealth by purchasing, servicing, and selling loans. FNMA is permitted to deal in conventional (since 1970), FHA-insured, and VA-guaranteed mortgage loans. FNMA traditionally has worked with mortgage bankers although it may deal with virtually any organization in performing its secondary mortgage market functions.

Table 13-6, page 214, indicates that as of yearend 1975, 93 percent of FNMA's total assets were in the form of FHA/VA mortgage loans or claims to wealth. These assets are financed almost exclusively with debt. The financing is primarily in the form of long-term debt since FNMA's mortgage holdings also are largely long-term commitments. Only about 3 percent of the assets are financed with stockholder equity

**Table
13-6** FNMA Statement of Condition
(Millions of Dollars)

	December 31, 1975	
	Amount	Percent
Cash and U.S. government securities	$ 318.7	1.0%
FHA/VA mortgages	29,396.8	93.0%
Conventional mortgages	2,519.1	8.0
Loan loss allowances and unamortized discounts	(1,120.5)	(3.5)
Other assets	482.1	1.5
Total assets	$31,596.2	100.0%
Short-term debt	$ 7,642.7	24.2%
Long-term debt	23,092.8	73.1
Common stock	298.7	.9
Paid-in-surplus	122.7	.4
Retained earnings	439.3	1.4
	$31,596.2	100.0%

Source: FNMA Annual Report.

indicating that FNMA is highly leveraged. FNMA raises new equity capital by: (1) selling common stock to the public, and (2) having institutions selling mortgages to FNMA subscribe to common stock on the basis of the value of the mortgages sold. The number of shares of common stock outstanding increased from approximately 42 million shares at the end of 1970 to approximately 48 million shares at the end of 1975.

It is apparent that FNMA depends heavily on its ability to sell debt obligations in order to purchase mortgages. Short-term debt often is in the form of discount notes (i.e., notes sold at a price below par value). Most financing comes from the issuing of debentures (secured by FNMA's general credit), mortgage-backed bonds, and debentures convertible into common stock.

Auction Market Operations

Prior to 1968 FNMA's procedure for carrying out its secondary market activities was based on setting in advance prices it would pay for the purchase of qualified mortgages. However, this was not felt to be a particularly efficient method for conducting a secondary mortgage market. Thus, in 1968 a *Free Market System Auction* was established and continues today.

The auction system operates as follows. FNMA announces, usually biweekly, the amount of funds it is willing to spend to purchase residential mortgages. Potential mortgage sellers may make either a competitive offering or a noncompetitive offering. In a *competitive offering*, the prospective seller specifies the yield to be paid to FNMA. Then, after examining all competitive bids or offerings, FNMA decides which bids to accept by working downward from the highest bid or offering.

Noncompetitive offerings or bids do not specify a yield. Rather, yields on noncompetitive bids are established as the weighted average yield calculated for the competitive bids accepted by FNMA.

Both types of bids or offerings are made by phone. FNMA announces an offering date with a notice such as the ones shown in Figures 13-1 below and 13-2, page 219. Bids or offers are received on the offering date. The next day FNMA announces the offers which were accepted, the range of yields on offers accepted, and the weighted average yield for the accepted offers. Figures 13-1 and 13-2 show the results of the previous day's auctions in addition to announcing the next offering date. As can be seen, separate FNMA auctions are held for FHA/VA mortgages and conventional mortgages. FNMA also limits the maximum amount a mortgage bidder can sell in a given auction. These limits are stated in Figures 13-1 and 13-2.

FNMA notifies successful bidders in writing the amount of acceptable mortgages that will be purchased. Successful bidders must

---

FEDERAL NATIONAL MORTGAGE ASSOCIATION

NOTICE   FNMA No. FMS-FHA/VA 14-77

July 12, 1977

TO: ALL FNMA FHA/VA SELLERS

SUBJECT: FREE MARKET SYSTEM/CONVERTIBLE STANDBY-
           FHA/VA

                NOTICE OF CURRENT FNMA COMMITMENT
                INFORMATION AND PROJECT REQUIREMENTS

The Federal National Mortgage Association announces that the next Free Market System (FMS) Auction for commitments to purchase eligible FHA/VA home loans will be as follows:

           Date of Auction: July 25, 1977
           Hours of Auction: 9 a.m. to 3 p.m., Washington, D.C. time
           Telephone Number: (202) 293-7500

Figure
13-1   Federal National Mortgage Association FHA/VA Mortgage Auction
           Notice (Continued)

The Offer(s) of a Seller for this Auction may not exceed the applicable maximums set forth below:

Funds Availabe:	NO LIMIT ESTABLISHED
Competitive Seller's Maximum Amount Per Offer:	$3,000,000
Competitive Seller's Maximum No. of Offers:	5
Seller's Non-competitive Maximum:	$ 250,000

This Auction will be conducted under the general rules which have been established for FMS Auctions as stated in the FNMA Selling Contract, and Section 203 of the FNMA Selling Agreement (Supplement) thereto.

Results of the FMS-FHA/VA Auction of July 11, 1977   (*In Millions)

Type of Contract	Total Offers Eligible*	Total Offers Accepted*	Accepted Yield Range	Weighted Average Yield/ Price of Accepted Offers
4-months	130.5	77.3	8.706–8.734	8.720/98.45

Home Loan Convertible Standby Commitments may be obtained in accordance with Section 204 of the FNMA Selling Agreement (Supplement).

— The current yield required is   9.350 , effective 1:00 p.m., 5/3/77

— The previous yield required was   9.250 .

— Convertible Standby Commitments issued:
   a) For the two-week period ending 7/11/77: $13,000,000
   b) Year to date volume is: $937,785,000

In accordance with Section 207 of the FNMA Selling Agreement Supplement, the current price differentials applicable to the purchase price of Graduated Payment Mortgages insured pursuant to Section 245 of the National Housing Act and delivered under outstanding FHA/VA Free Market System/Convertible Standby commitment contracts are as follows:

Plan Number	Price Adjustment
I	−0.10%
II	−0.20%
III	−0.30%
IV	−0.20%
V	−0.30%

Project Mortgage Requirements

The current Project Mortgage Requirements are as follows for mortgages insured under Sections 220, 221(d)(3), 221(d)(4), 223(e), 233, and 236 of the National Housing Act:

Figure
13-1   Federal National Mortgage Association FHA/VA Mortgage Auction Notice (Continued)

Immediate Purchase Yield required is 9.500 . This yield converts to a price of:

Standby Yield required is 10.250 This yield converts to a price of:

78.75	7% mortgages	73.71	7% mortgages
85.01	7 3/4% mortgages	79.63	7 3/4% mortgages
87.12	8% mortgages	81.63	8% mortgages
89.24	8 1/4% mortgages	83.63	8 1/4% mortgages
91.38	8 1/2% mortgages	85.65	8 1/2% mortgages
93.52	8 3/4% mortgages	87.68	8 3/4% mortgages
95.67	9% mortgages	89.71	9% mortgages
100.00	9 1/2% mortgages	93.81	9 1/2% mortgages

With regard to mortgages insured under Sections 207, 213, 213(j), 223(f), 231, 232, 232(i), 234(d), 241, 242, and Titles X and XI, or insured under any of the foregoing sections or titles pursuant to Section 223(d), FNMA will deduct 1.50 from both the Immediate Purchase and Standby Commitment prices listed above.

NOTE: SINCE THE ABOVE PRICES ARE BASED ON A 40 YEAR MORTGAGE WITH AN AVERAGE LIFE OF 20 YEARS, ADJUST-MENTS IN PRICE WILL BE MADE FOR MORTGAGES HAVING A DIFFERENT MORTGAGE TERM AND AVERAGE LIFE.

Financing Charge

The required percentage of financing charge in construction loans as re-ferred to in Section 308.05(b) of the FNMA Selling Agreement Supplement is:

2.10	7% mortgages	.84	8 1/2% mortgages
1.68	7 1/2% mortgages	.63	8 3/4% mortgages
1.47	7 3/4% mortgages	.42	9% mortgages
1.26	8% mortgages	.00	9 1/2% mortgages
1.05	8 1/4% mortgages		

/s/Regional Vice President

Figure
13-1   Federal National Mortgage Association FHA/VA Mortgage Auction Notice (Concluded)

purchase a specified amount of FNMA common stock when the bid is accepted and again when the mortgages are delivered to FNMA. FNMA will enter into agreements to hold committed funds for a specified time period for a commitment fee usually between ¼ percent and 1 percent. Tables 13-7, page 219 and 13-8, page 220, show the results of FNMA FHA/VA and conventional auctions for commitments to pur-chase home mortgages conducted on June 27, 1977.

Sellers of home mortgages are permitted to continue to service mortgages sold to FNMA. A 3/8 percent fee is paid by FNMA to have this loan servicing function performed by mortgage sellers.

FEDERAL NATIONAL MORTGAGE ASSOCIATION

NOTICE   FNMA No. FMS-CHM 14-77
                                                July 12, 1977

TO: ALL FNMA CONVENTIONAL SELLERS

SUBJECT: FREE MARKET SYSTEM/CONVERTIBLE STANDBY-
             CONVENTIONAL
             NOTICE OF CURRENT FNMA COMMITMENT
             INFORMATION

The Federal National Association announces that the next Free Market System (FMS) Auction for commitments to purchase eligible Conventional home loans will be as follows:

    Date of Auction: July 25, 1977
    Hours of Auction: 9 a.m. to 3 p.m., Washington, D.C. time
    Telephone Number: (202) 293-7500

The Offer(s) of a Seller for this Auction may not exceed the applicable maximums set forth below:

Funds Available: NO LIMIT ESTABLISHED
Competitive Seller's Maximum Amount
    Per Offer: $3,000,000
Competitive Seller's Maximum No. of
    Offers: 5
Seller's Non-competitive Maximum: $ 250,000

This Auction will be conducted under the general rules which have been established for FMS Auctions as stated in the FNMA Selling Contract, and Section 402 of the FNMA Conventional Selling Contract Supplement thereto.

Results of the FMS-CHM Auction of July 1, 1977 (*In Millions)

Type of Contract	Total Offers Eligible*	Total Offers Accepted*	Accepted Yield Range	Weighted Average Yield of Accepted Offers
4-months	163.9	101.6	9.054–9.144	9.084

Figure
13-2   Federal National Mortgage Association Conventional Mortgage
            Auction Notice (Continued)

Home Loan Convertible Standby Commitments may be obtained in accordance with Section 403 of the FNMA Conventional Selling Contract Supplement.

— The current yield required is __9,500__ , effective 1:00 p.m., 5/3/77
— The previous yield required was __9.400__ .
— Convertible Standby Commitments issued:
    a) For the two-week period ending 7/11/77: $7,660,000
    b) Year to date volume is: $367,970,000

/s/Regional Vice President

Figure
13-2 Federal National Mortgage Association Conventional Mortgage Auction Notice (Concluded)

Table
13-7 Federal National Mortgage Association Conventional Mortgage Auction Results

Results of Competitive Offerings Under the
Free Market System — Conventional
Auction of 06–27–77

	No.	Amount (000)	HOME LOAN
Offers Received:	215	$ 160,554	CONVERTIBLE STANDBY YIELD REQUIRED IS: 9.500
Less (−) Ineligible	0	0	
Eligible Offers Rec'd	215	$ 160,554	
% of (Eligible Offers Received / Offers Received)		100.00%	

Offers Accepted:		
Competitive	97	$ 91,219
Non-Competitive	65	14,235
Total	162	$ 105,454
% of (Total Accepted / Eligible Offers Rec'd.)		65.68%

Weighted Average Yield:	9.106
Range of Accepted Offers:	9.062–9.323

	No.	Amount (000)
Acceptance by Regions:		
Southeastern (Atlanta)	27	$ 12,753
Midwestern (Chicago)	18	$ 11,792
Southwestern (Dallas)	40	$ 13,403
Western (Los Angeles)	53	$ 50,006
Northeastern (Phila.)	24	$ 17,500
Total:	162	$ 105,454

Table 13-8 Federal National Mortgage Association FHA/VA Mortgage Auction Results

Federal National Mortgage Association   Date

RESULTS OF COMPETITIVE OFFERINGS UNDER THE
FREE MARKET SYSTEM — FHA/VA AUCTION   06-27-77

	No.	Amount (000)
OFFERS RECEIVED:	147	$ 90,823
Less(−) Ineligible	-0-	-0-
ELIGIBLE OFFERS REC'D	147	$ 90,823
% of (Eligible Offers Received) / Offers Rec'd		100.00 %

OFFERS ACCEPTED:	No.	Amount
Competitive	27	$ 31,750
Non-Competitive	84	17,968
TOTAL	111	$ 49,718
% of (Total Accepted) / Eligible Offers Rec'd		54.74 %

WEIGHTED AVERAGE YIELD: 8.725
PRICE (08.500%): 98.41
RANGE OF ACCEPTED OFFERS: 8.698-8.800

ACCEPTANCE BY REGIONS:	No.	Amount (000)
Southeastern (Atlanta)	18	$ 3,639
Midwestern (Chicago)	33	$ 23,013
Southwestern (Dallas)	22	$ 11,279
Western (Los Angeles)	27	$ 9,387
Northeastern (Phila.)	11	$ 2,400
TOTAL:	111	$ 49,718

Home Loan Convertible Standby Yield required is 9.350
This yield converts to a price of:

84.14	7.00% mortgages		94.18	8.50% mortgages
89.13	7.75% mortgages		95.88	8.75% mortgages
90.80	8.00% mortgages		97.59	9.00% mortgages
92.49	8.25% mortgages		100.00	9.50% mortgages

Project Immediate Purchase Yield required is 9.500
This yield converts to a price of:

78.75	7.00% mortgages		91.38	8.50% mortgages
85.01	7.75% mortgages		93.52	8.75% mortgages
87.12	8.00% mortgages		95.67	9.00% mortgages
89.24	8.25% mortgages		100.00	9.50% mortgages

Project Standby Yield required is 10.250
This yield converts to a price of:

73.71	7.00% mortgages		85.65	8.50% mortgages
79.63	7.75% mortgages		87.68	8.75% mortgages
81.63	8.00% mortgages		89.71	9.00% mortgages
83.63	8.25% mortgages		93.81	9.50% mortgages

INVOLVEMENT BY SAVINGS AND LOAN ASSOCIATIONS

Savings and loan associations, in addition to the FNMA, FHLMC, and GNMA secondary market institutions, are active participants in the secondary mortgage market.

Their secondary mortgage market activity consists of 90 percent participations. Generally a loan participation offer is made by telephone by a mortgage banker on behalf of the loan originator. The description of the offer is usually limited to the aggregate principal amount, the net yield to the purchasing association, the types of mortgages, and the location of the properties. The offer may be accepted orally or by a letter of commitment. A participation certificate or participation agreement is furnished by the seller.

In addition, what should happen, but has not happened in the past, is that the notes on the secured properties should be endorsed. The notes should be endorsed by the seller for the assignee and the seller in their respective undivided interests therein. In this way, there is an endorsement and a delivery which may be necessary to complete the action.

QUESTIONS FOR REVIEW

1. Explain what is meant by the statement that "the overall mortgage market involves three types of transactions or activities."
2. Why is there a need for a secondary mortgage market?
3. Mortgage banking operations often involve a number of activities. Explain what is meant by: (a) an advance or forward commitment, (b) a take-out letter, (c) a standby commitment, and (d) mortgage warehousing.
4. A number of major federal government developments and actions have affected the secondary mortgage market. Indicate and briefly describe these major laws and actions.
5. What do the nicknames Fannie Mae, Ginnie Mae, and Freddie Mac stand for? What are their relationships with the secondary mortgage market?
6. The Federal National Mortgage Association was initially created in 1938. How does its structure and organization differ today from when it was created?
7. Explain how FNMA's auction market system operates in terms of the secondary mortgage market. In your explanation differentiate between competitive offerings or bids and noncompetitive offerings or bids.

PROBLEMS

1. Mortgage banking plays an important role in the overall mortgage market as was depicted in Tables 13-1 and 13-2 in the chapter. Examination of the two tables indicates several major trends or changes that have occurred during the first half of the

1970s. Identify these major changes. Are they really trends or are they due at least in part to changes in economic conditions. Use more recent data where possible to help answer this problem.

2. Table 13-7 and 13-8 in the chapter show results for FHA/VA and Conventional mortgage auctions conducted in June 1977. The *Federal Reserve Bulletin* also contains summary results for FNMA mortgage auctions. Identify recent trends in FNMA auction rates and compare them with developments in other interest rates.

Government Real Estate Finance Programs and Activities

Chapter 14

The federal government impacts on real estate finance in a number of different ways. We saw in Chapter 12 that monetary and fiscal policy affect the availability and cost of funds for financing real estate projects. This included the activities of the U.S. Treasury and the Federal Reserve System. Regulation and control of institutions supplying real estate funds by the Federal Reserve, the Federal Home Loan Bank Board, and state regulatory bodies represents additional forms of government involvement.

The government also has made substantial contributions by providing insurance of thrift institution deposits and through insuring mortgage loans. Deposit insurance is provided by the Federal Deposit Insurance Corporation and the Federal Savings and Loan Insurance Corporation. And, as we saw earlier, Federal Housing Administration insurance and Veteran Administration guarantees have been important to the development of real estate financing.

Other government activities will be explored in this chapter, namely, the secondary mortgage market roles of GNMA and the FHLMC. Attention then will shift to the government's role in farm loans and public housing.

FEDERAL HOME LOAN MORTGAGE CORPORATION

The passage of the Emergency Home Finance Act of 1970 resulted in the creation of the Federal Home Loan Mortgage Corporation. FHLMC is a federally chartered, nonprofit institution operating in the secondary mortgage market under the control of the Federal Home Loan Bank System.

Structure and Organization

The FHLMC was initially funded in 1970 through a stock subscription of $100 million purchased by the 12 regional Federal Home Loan Banks. The Federal Home Loan Bank Board directs the mortgage activities of the FHLMC.

In prior chapters the seriousness of the 1969–1970 recessionary period was noted. High interest rates and "tight money" led to substantial amounts of disintermediation. Savings and loan associations were hit particularly hard. As a result, the FHLMC's primary objective as a secondary mortgage market institution was to assist savings and loan associations (and to a lesser extent other lending institutions) to acquire funds for making additional mortgage loans. This was to be accomplished by having the FHLMC purchase mortgage claims to wealth already owned by the lending institutions. Like FNMA, the FHLMC is permitted to deal in conventional, FHA-insured, and VA-guaranteed loans.

Table 14-1, page 225, indicates that as of yearend 1975, over 80 percent of the FHLMC's total assets were in mortgage loans. However, in contrast with FNMA's mortgage holdings, the FHLMC was heavily committed to "participation in" or "wholly owned" conventional mortgages. These assets, as was the case with FNMA, are financed almost totally with debt. In fact 95 percent of the assets shown in Table 14-1 were financed by issuing bonds or through advances or borrowings from the Federal Home Loan Banks. Capital accounts for less than 3 percent of funds available to meet financing needs. The FHLMC also actively sells mortgages from its portfolio.

Operations

The FHLMC originally was designed to do for conventional mortgages what FNMA was doing in the secondary market for FHA and VA mortgages. However, Freddie Mac purchased a larger volume of FHA/VA mortgages during its early operating years. This policy was attributed to the fact that greater loan standardization existed for FHA and VA mortgages. It was 1973 before FHLMC began purchasing greater dollar amounts of conventional loans relative to FHA/VA loans. The FHLMC has been actively involved in developing standardized procedures and documents for making conventional loans. These efforts by FHLMC are consistent with the objectives of assisting savings and loan associations which deal largely in origination of conventional mortgages.

The Federal Home Loan Mortgage Corporation does not utilize an auction market system to carry out its operations as is the case with

Table 14-1 FHLMC Statement of Condition
(Millions of Dollars)

| | December 31, 1975 | |
	Amount	Percent
Cash and investments	$ 978 8	16.6%
FHA-insured and VA-guaranteed loans	1,877.2	31.8
Participation in conventional loans	843.7	14.3
Conventional loans	2,241.8	38.0
Loan loss reserves and unamortized discounts	(101.2)	(1.7)
Other assets	58.4	1.0
Total assets	$5,898.7	100.0%
Bonds and advances	$5,609.2	95.1
Accrued interest	121.3	2.0
Other liabilities	15.6	.3
Capital reserve for management fee and guarantees	10.8	.2
Capital stock	100.0	1.7
Retained earnings	41.8	.7
	$5,898.7	100.0%

Source: *1976 Savings and Loan Fact Book.*

FNMA. Also in contrast with FNMA, the FHLMC can deal only with certain types of organizations. These are savings and loan associations, commercial banks, and mutual savings banks. A qualified institution desiring to sell some of its mortgages to the FHLMC does so by making an offer on the intermediate purchase contract shown in Figure 14-1, page 226, or by entering into a forward commitment purchase contract shown in Figure 14-2, page 227.

A selling price is stated by the selling institution as a percentage of the aggregate balance of the mortgages being offered for sale. Periodically, Freddie Mac publishes the yield it is willing to accept. These acceptable yields are usually set commensurate with prevailing long-term interest rates. Thus, during periods of rising interest rates, existing mortgages may have to be sold to the FHLMC (or other institutions) at substantial discounts from the principal balances due. FHLMC commitments to purchase mortgages are issued at specific interest rates (such as 8.75 percent on a single-family 80 percent conventional loan) or at a discount (such as a quote of 98, or rather the willingness to pay a purchase price amounting to 98 percent of the balance of an FHA/VA loan). Commitment fees vary depending on the type of mortgage. The FHLMC requires delivery of the loans committed for. This differs with FNMA's loan commitment policy.

IMMEDIATE PURCHASE CONTRACT
CONVENTIONAL HOME MORTGAGES

Sale: The undersigned Seller agrees to sell to the Federal Home Loan Mortgage Corporation ("The Mortgage Corporation" or "FHLMC") Conventional Home Mortgages in whole or in part, on the terms stated below, and in accordance with the Purchase Documents as defined in the Sellers' Guide Conventional Mortgages as in effect on the date of this offer, all of which are fully incorporated herein by reference.

Servicing: The undersigned Seller hereby agrees to service all mortgages sold hereunder, in accordance with the Purchase Documents as in effect on the date of this offer, all of which are fully incorporated herein by reference.

Contract Commitment Period: 2 months from FHLMC Date of Acceptance.

Aggregate Principal Amount of
FHLMC Commitment: $_____
(MULTIPLES OF $1,000)

Net Yield Offered by Seller:_____percent
(TO 3 DECIMAL PLACES)

SELLER

Seller's FHLMC Seller/
Servicer No.:_____

ADDRESS

Date of Offer:_____, 19____   By_____(Seal)
AUTHORIZED REPRESENTATIVE

_____
(TYPE NAME AND TITLE)

Nonmember fee, if applicable, will be deducted from amount due Seller on Funding Date.

Offer Accepted by   **Federal Home Loan Mortgage Corporation**
The Mortgage Corporation

Date of Acceptance:_____   By_____(Seal)
VICE PRESIDENT

Purchase Contract No.:_____

Required Delivery Date:_____   or ☐ Offer Declined by The Mortgage Corporation

Date of Declination:_____

Figure
14-1   FHLMC Mortgage Purchase Contract

TheMortgage Corporation

Federal Home Loan Mortgage Corporation

CONVENTIONAL HOME MORTGAGE PROGRAM
FORWARD COMMITMENT PURCHASE CONTRACT

Sale: The undersigned Seller hereby offers to sell to the Federal Home Loan Mortgage Corporation ("The Mortgage Corporation" or "FHLMC") Home Mortgages and/or undivided interest in Home Mortgages, on the terms stated below, in accordance with the Purchase Documents as defined in the Sellers' Guide Conventional Mortgages as in effect on the date of this offer and the Invitation number 1003 dated March 1, 1977, all of which are fully incorporated herein by reference.

Servicing: The undersigned Seller hereby agrees to service all mortgages sold hereunder, in accordance with the Purchase Documents as in effect on the date of this offer, all of which are fully incorporated herein by reference.

Commitment Period: Six Months

Aggregate Principal Amount (Amount of Commitment): $_____
(MULTIPLE OF $1,000)

Net Yield Offered for Conventional Home Mortgages:

_____percent
(TO 3 DECIMAL PLACES)

Enclosed Commitment Fee: (Non-Refundable) $_____

Seller's FHLMC Seller/
Servicer No.: _____

_____
SELLER

_____
ADDRESS

Date of Offer:_____, 19____

By_____(Seal)
AUTHORIZED REPRESENTATIVE

_____
(TYPE NAME AND TITLE)

Nonmember fee, if applicable, will be deducted from amount due Seller on Funding Date.

Offer Hereby Accepted by
The Mortgage Corporation

Federal Home Loan Mortgage Corporation

Date of Acceptance: _____

By_____(Seal)
VICE PRESIDENT

Purchase Contract No.: _____

Contract Expiration Date:_____

or ☐ Offer Declined by The Mortgage Corporation

Date of Declination:_____

Delivery Option must be
exercised not later than:_____

**Figure
14-2** Forward Commitment Purchase Contract

GOVERNMENT NATIONAL MORTGAGE ASSOCIATION

The Government National Mortgage Association was created as a result of the passage of the Housing and Urban Development Act in 1968. GNMA is a wholly-owned government corporation and operates under the direction of the Department of Housing and Urban Development.

Structure and Organization

GNMA with its establishment in 1968 inherited certain responsibilities that were previously under the domain of the old FNMA (that is, prior to FNMA becoming completely privately owned in 1968). Ginnie Mae was given responsibility for managing remaining FNMA mortgages that had been acquired prior to November, 1954. These mortgages were to be liquidated under the "management and liquidation function" responsibilities. Table 14-2 shows that by yearend 1975 only $358 million in these early FNMA mortgage loans remained to be liquidated.

The second responsibility, known as the "special assistance function," has expanded rapidly and now dominates GNMA's operating activities. GNMA is involved in assisting the financing of urban renewal and experimental housing projects. It also assists in tempering the impact of changes in interest rates on existing mortgage values. Table 14-2 shows that GNMA added over $2 billion in mortgages under various special assistance programs.

Table 14-2 GNMA Mortgage Holdings by Function
(Millions of Dollars)

Yearend	Special Assistance Function	Management and Liquidation Function	Total Loan Portfolio
1965	$1,340	$ 953	$2,293
1966	1,470	1,269	2,739
1967	1,742	1,668	3,410
1968	2,303	1,970	4,273
1969	2,937	1,928	4,865
1970	3,401	1,821	5,222
1971	3,648	1,673	5,321
1972	3,824	1,287	5,111
1973	3,576	469	4,045
1974	4,440	409	4,849
1975	6,884	358	7,242

Source: Government National Mortgage Association.

GNMA and FNMA Tandem Programs

One part of the special assistance function involves GNMA's role in reducing the impact of interest rate risk on mortgage lenders. Interest rate risk occurs because interest rates fluctuate over time. Since bonds and mortgages carry fixed coupon or specified interest rates, bond and mortgage values must change to reflect yields comparable to then prevailing market interest rates. In essence, there is an inverse relationship between interest rate changes and mortgage prices or values. For example, an 8 percent $20,000 mortgage will fall in value (i.e., be discounted) if current mortgage rates rise to 9 percent. The size of discount will be sufficient to make the 8 percent mortgage provide a 9 percent yield.

Rising market interest rates cause existing mortgages to sell at discounts. GNMA absorbs some of this discount under its *Tandem Programs*, so named because Fannie Mae and Ginnie Mae work jointly on mortgage loan purchases. These programs are particularly valuable during periods of high interest rates when existing mortgages sell at deep discounts. First, a commitment to purchase a mortgage at a specified price is made by GNMA to the potential mortgage seller. Then, after GNMA acquires the mortgage, it is sold to FNMA at the existing or prevailing market value. Discounts between the price paid to the mortgage seller and the price received from FNMA are absorbed by GNMA. In the way of an illustration, assume that Ginnie Mae agrees or commits to pay a seller $1 million for a mortgage on a housing project. In the meantime, after the purchase commitment has been made, interest rates rise and the mortgage drops in value to, say, $950,000. The mortgage then is sold to FNMA for $950,000 and GNMA absorbs the $50,000 difference or discount.

In the case of high risk mortgages such as those originated under Section 236, GNMA and FNMA share in any mortgage value discounts that may develop. By working together, GNMA has more funds available for financing special assistance projects.

A variation of the Tandem Program was developed in 1974 for handling conventional mortgages. Both FNMA and FHLMC can participate. A commitment is made, as an agent for Ginnie Mae, to buy from a private lender conventional mortgages that carry below-market interest rates. The commitment is made only if the lender agrees to pass the below-market rate on to the borrower. The resulting discounted mortgages are delivered to FNMA or FHLMC after the loans are closed. The discount is absorbed by GNMA. For example, assume that the going interest rate is 9 percent on conventional mortgage loans. A mortgage with a $1 million par value would immediately sell at a discount, say $950,000, if the mortgage were issued with an 8 percent below-market interest rate. FNMA or FHLMC would pay the $950,000 upon delivery of the mortgage and GNMA would pay the discount differential of $50,000 to the lender originating the mortgage loan.

Mortgage-Backed Security Program

GNMA also issues guarantees of FHA, VA, and Farmers Home Administration mortgages. Its so-called *mortgage-backed securities program*, supported by the credit and borrowing power of the U.S. government, guarantees timely payment of interest and principal to the mortgage holders. A sample of the GNMA guaranteed mortgage-backed certificate is shown in Figure 14-3, pages 232–33.

The GNMA guarantee permits mortgage originators and dealers to pledge a pool of their existing mortgage loans as collateral underlying a securities issue. Repayment of the mortgages in the pool provides funds to pay off the securities issue. Securities pools are used in lieu of direct sale of the underlying mortgages. In order to pool mortgages together, certain homogeneous requirements must be met in terms of types of properties and interest rates.

There are two basic types of mortgage-backed securities. The *bond-type security* is long-term, pays interest semiannually, and provides for payments of principal at specified redemption dates. The *pass-through security* provides for monthly interest and principal payments on the underlying mortgages. Table 14-3 shows the importance of GNMA's mortgage-backed security program during the first half of the 1970s. The bond-type security, not sold since 1971, can be issued only by the federal secondary mortgage market institutions. Pass-through securities are much more prevalent. However, it also is important to recognize that the GNMA is selective in that more applications are received than are guaranteed.

Table 14-3   FNMA Mortgage-Backed Security Transactions (Millions of Dollars)

Year	Pass-Through Securities		Bonds Sold
	Applications Received	Securities Issued	
1970	$ 1,126	$ 452	$1,315
1971	4,374	2,702	300
1972	3,854	2,662	. . .
1973	5,529	3,249	. . .
1974	6,203	4,784	. . .
1975	10,449	7,366	. . .

Source: Government National Mortgage Association.

The Futures Market

A futures market in GNMA pass-through securities was initiated in October, 1975. Trading activity takes place on the Chicago Board of Trade Exchange. In brief, a *futures market* allows the setting of delivery prices at some specified future date. Futures markets for agricultural commodities have existed for many decades. In theory, those who wish to avoid fluctuations in commodity prices can use the futures market to set in advance the price they will have to pay for the commodity when it is delivered at a future date. Likewise, participants in the GNMA futures market should be able to protect their loan commitments from the impact of the interest rate fluctuations. That is, they can "lock-in" at the current rate of return even though the delivery or consummation date may be sometime in the future.

The GNMA futures market involves trading in $100,000 units (principal amount) of GNMA pass-through securities. These securities usually bear an 8 percent coupon or interest rate. The securities are *modified pass-throughs* which provide payments to investors in the form of monthly principal installments and a fixed rate of interest on the remaining unpaid mortgage balances. These payments must be made whether or not they are collected by the issuer. In contrast, a *straight pass-through* security would make monthly principal and interest payments to investors from payments actually collected on the pooled mortgages underlying the security.

GNMA futures contracts can be written with delivery dates at the end of any calendar quarter and may be issued with maturities as long as 1 to 2 years. Contract prices are stated in terms of whole points and 32ds of a point. GNMA also provides for a 15-day, interest-free period to cover servicing delays. Thus, an 8 percent GNMA futures contract yields 8 percent when it sells at a price of 99–21 which means 99 and 21–32ds or 99.65625.

The use of hedging strategies has been suggested as a way to avoid interest rate risk. *Hedging* occurs when one makes a future commitment based on the current cash or spot market conditions and simultaneously takes an equal and opposite position in the futures market. Both long or short hedges can be used.[1] A *long hedge* might be used by a builder. Assume, for example, that a builder contracts with a mortgage banker in June to deliver mortgages to yield 8 percent in December. If mortgage rates fall between the commitment period and the delivery period, the builder stands to suffer a loss since the mortgages

---

[1]For a comprehensive treatment of hedging, see Paul L. Kasriel, "Hedging Interest Rate Fluctuations," *Business Conditions*, Federal Reserve Bank of Chicago (April, 1976), pp. 3–10.

MORTGAGE BACKED CERTIFICATE
GUARANTEED BY
GOVERNMENT NATIONAL
MORTGAGE ASSOCIATION

000000SF

DATE OF ISSUE
SINGLE FAMILY MORTGAGE POOL NO.
SERIES _____ INTEREST RATE _____%
INITIAL PAYMENT DATE
ORIGINAL PRINCIPAL AMT. $
ORIGINAL AGGREGATE AMOUNT OF POOL $
MATURITY DATE

THE ISSUER, NAMED BELOW, PROMISES
TO PAY TO THE ORDER OF:

ISSUER

EXCEPT AS HEREINAFTER UNDERTAKEN, THIS CERTIFICATE DOES NOT CONSTITUTE A LIABILITY OF NOR EVIDENCE ANY RECOURSE AGAINST THE ISSUER, SINCE IT IS BASED ON AND BACKED BY THE AGGREGATE DEBT OF THE MORTGAGES INSURED OR GUARANTEED AND BY THE GOVERNMENT NATIONAL MORTGAGE ASSOCIATION GUARANTY. PAYMENTS MAY BE MADE TO THE GOVERNMENT NATIONAL MORTGAGE ASSOCIATION IN THE EVENT OF ANY FAILURE OF TIMELY PAYMENT, AS PROVIDED FOR IN THE GUARANTY APPENDED HERETO.

IT IS CERTIFIED THAT THIS CERTIFICATE IS LEGAL AND REGULAR IN ALL RESPECTS, AND IS DULY AND VALIDLY ISSUED PURSUANT TO TITLE III OF THE NATIONAL HOUSING ACT, AND THAT NO RULE, REGULATION OR LAW HAS BEEN VIOLATED BY ITS ISSUANCE, AND NO CONTRACT OR OTHER AGREEMENT OF EITHER THE GOVERNMENT NATIONAL MORTGAGE ASSOCIATION OR THE ISSUER, OR OF BOTH, ADVERSELY AFFECTS THE RIGHTS AND POSITION OF THE HOLDER AS SET FORTH IN THIS CERTIFICATE.

HEREINAFTER CALLED THE HOLDER) THE SUM OF $ _____ IN PRINCIPAL AMOUNT, TOGETHER WITH INTEREST THEREON AND ON PORTIONS THEREOF OUTSTANDING FROM TIME TO TIME AT THE FIXED RATE SET FORTH HEREON, SUCH PAYMENTS TO BE IN MONTHLY INSTALLMENTS, ADJUSTABLE AS SET FORTH BELOW. ALL MONTHLY INSTALLMENTS SHALL BE FOR APPLICATION FIRST, TO INTEREST AT SUCH FIXED RATE AND THEN IN REDUCTION OF PRINCIPAL BALANCE THEN OUTSTANDING, AND SHALL CONTINUE UNTIL PAYMENT IN FULL OF THE PRINCIPAL AMOUNT, AND OF ALL INTEREST ACCRUING THEREON.

FURTHER, THE ISSUER CERTIFIES: THAT THIS CERTIFICATE, AND EACH OF THE LIKE SECURITIES COMPOSING THE ENTIRE ISSUE OF WHICH IT IS A PART, IS PROPORTIONATELY BASED ON AND BACKED BY ALL THE MORTGAGES POOLED UNDER THE MORTGAGE POOL SET FORTH HEREIN. ALL SUCH MORTGAGES BEING INSURED UNDER THE NATIONAL HOUSING ACT OR TITLE V OF THE HOUSING ACT OF 1949, OR INSURED OR GUARANTEED UNDER THE SERVICEMEN'S READJUSTMENT ACT OF 1944 OR CHAPTER 37 OF TITLE 38, UNITED STATES CODE; AND THAT WITH RESPECT TO THIS CERTIFICATE, THE BASE AND BACKING IS IN THE PROPORTION THAT THE PRINCIPAL AMOUNT SET FORTH BEARS TO THE TOTAL OF SUCH POOL, SUCH TOTAL BEING EQUAL TO THE AGGREGATE OF THE PRINCIPAL AMOUNTS OF LIKE SECURITIES COMPOSING THE ENTIRE ISSUE OF WHICH THIS CERTICATE IS A PART, AND BEING EQUAL TO THE AGGREGATE OF THE PRINCIPAL AMOUNTS OUTSTANDING ON THE MORTGAGES COMPOSING SUCH POOL, AND THAT THE HOLDER IS THE OWNER OF AN UNDIVIDED BENEFICIAL INTEREST IN THE POOL IN THE FOREGOING PROPORTION.

EACH OF THE MONTHLY INSTALLMENTS SHALL BE SUBJECT TO ADJUSTMENT TO REFLECT ANY REPAYMENTS OR OTHER EARLY OR SCHEDULED RECOVERIES OF PRINCIPAL HAD FROM TIME TO TIME, UNDER OR CONSISTENT WITH THE PROVISIONS OF THE MORTGAGES COMPOSING THE POOL, HOWEVER, THE ISSUER SHALL REMIT, AS HEREINAFTER CALLED FOR, AMOUNTS IN WHICH SUCH AN ADJUSTMENT IS MADE. DUE MONTHLY, BELOW, MONTHLY PAYMENTS OF NOT LESS THAN THE AMOUNTS OF PRINCIPAL COMING DUE MONTHLY, TOGETHER WITH ANY APPORTIONED PREPAYMENTS OR OTHER EARLY RECOVERIES OF PRINCIPAL AND BACKING.

THE ISSUER SHALL REMIT TO THE HOLDER ALL SUCH MONTHLY PAYMENTS REQUIRED UNDER THIS CERTIFICATE BY THE FIFTEENTH (15TH) DAY OF EACH CALENDAR MONTH, SUCH MONTHLY REMITTANCES SHALL COMMENCE BEFORE THE FORTY-FIFTH (45TH) DAY FOLLOWING THE DATE OF ISSUE OF THIS CERTIFICATE, AND SHALL CONTINUE UNTIL PAYMENT IN FULL OF ALL AMOUNTS OWING UNDER THIS CERTIFICATE. ALL REMITTANCES SHALL BE BY CHECK TO THE REGISTERED HOLDER, AND FINAL PAYMENT SHALL BE MADE ONLY UPON SURRENDER OF THIS CERTIFICATE.

THIS CERTIFICATE IS FREELY AND FULLY TRANSFERABLE AND ASSIGNABLE, BUT ONLY UPON THE BOOKS OF THE ISSUER, AS TO THE ISSUER AND GOVERNMENT NATIONAL MORTGAGE ASSOCIATION. REISSUES AND DENOMINATIONAL EXCHANGES SHALL BE MADE ON REQUEST AND PRESENTATION OF THIS CERTIFICATE AT THE OFFICE OF GOVERNMENT NATIONAL MORTGAGE ASSOCIATION OR THEIR CO-TRANSFER AGENT IN NEW YORK.

GUARANTY: THE UNDERSIGNED, PURSUANT TO SECTION 306(G) OF THE NATIONAL HOUSING ACT, HEREBY GUARANTEES THE TIMELY PAYMENT OF THE PRINCIPAL AND INTEREST SET FORTH IN THE ABOVE INSTRUMENT, SUBJECT ONLY TO THE TERMS AND CONDITIONS THEREOF. THE FULL FAITH AND CREDIT OF THE UNITED STATES IS PLEDGED TO THE PAYMENT OF ALL AMOUNTS WHICH MAY BE REQUIRED TO BE PAID UNDER THIS GUARANTY.

GOVERNMENT NATIONAL MORTGAGE ASSOCIATION

ATTEST: _____ ACTING SECRETARY

_____ PRESIDENT

SPECIMEN

**Figure
14-3**   GNMA Guaranteed Mortgage-Backed Certificate (Continued)

ASSIGNMENT

I AM THE OWNER, OR THE DULY AUTHORIZED REPRESENTATIVE OF THE OWNER, OF THE WITHIN MORTGAGE BACKED CERTIFICATE AND FOR VALUE RECEIVED HEREBY ASSIGN THE SAME TO

_____
(ASSIGNEE)

AND AUTHORIZE THE TRANSFER THEREOF ON THE BOOKS OF THE ISSUER.

_____
(SIGNATURE OF ASSIGNOR)

PERSONALLY APPEARED BEFORE ME THE ABOVE NAMED PERSON, WHOSE IDENTITY IS WELL KNOWN OR PROVED TO ME, AND SIGNED THE ABOVE ASSIGNMENT, ACKNOWLEDGING IT TO BE HIS FREE ACT AND DEED. WITNESS MY HAND, OFFICIAL DESIGNATION, AND SEAL.

_____   _____
(SIGNATURE OF WITNESSING OFFICER)   (OFFICIAL DESIGNATION)

SEAL   DATED AT_____   _____, 19____.

ASSIGNMENT

I AM THE OWNER, OR THE DULY AUTHORIZED REPRESENTATIVE OF THE OWNER, OF THE WITHIN MORTGAGE BACKED CERTIFICATE AND FOR VALUE RECEIVED HEREBY ASSIGN THE SAME TO

_____
(ASSIGNEE)

AND AUTHORIZE THE TRANSFER THEREOF ON THE BOOKS OF THE ISSUER.

_____
(SIGNATURE OF ASSIGNOR)

PERSONALLY APPEARED BEFORE ME THE ABOVE NAMED PERSON, WHOSE IDENTITY IS WELL KNOWN OR PROVED TO ME, AND SIGNED THE ABOVE ASSIGNMENT, ACKNOWLEDGING IT TO BE HIS FREE ACT AND DEED. WITNESS MY HAND, OFFICIAL DESIGNATION, AND SEAL.

_____   _____
(SIGNATURE OF WITNESSING OFFICER)   (OFFICIAL DESIGNATION)

SEAL   DATED AT_____   _____, 19____.

SPECIMEN

INSTRUCTIONS

TO ASSIGN THIS MORTGAGE BACKED CERTIFICATE, THE OWNER, OR HIS DULY AUTHORIZED REPRESENTATIVE, SHALL APPEAR BEFORE AN OFFICER AUTHORIZED TO WITNESS ASSIGNMENTS, ESTABLISH HIS IDENTITY TO THE SATISFACTION OF SUCH OFFICER, AND IN HIS PRESENCE EXECUTE THE ASSIGNMENT, USING ONE OF THE ABOVE FORMS. THE WITNESSING OFFICER MUST THEN AFFIX HIS SIGNATURE, OFFICIAL DESIGNATION, AND SEAL, IF ANY, AND ADD THE PLACE AND DATE OF EXECUTION. OFFICERS AUTHORIZED TO WITNESS ASSIGNMENTS INCLUDE EXECUTIVE OFFICERS OF BANKS AND TRUST COMPANIES IN-CORPORATED IN THE UNITED STATES OR ITS ORGANIZED TERRITORIES, AND THEIR BRANCHES, DOMESTIC AND FOREIGN. IF ADDITIONAL ASSIGNMENTS ARE REQUIRED, A FORM SIMILAR TO THE ABOVE MAY BE WRITTEN OR TYPED HEREON. FULL INFORMATION REGARDING ASSIGNMENTS MAY BE OBTAINED FROM GOVERNMENT NATIONAL MORTGAGE ASSOCIATION.

— IMPORTANT —

THE PRESENT PRINCIPAL BALANCE OF THIS MORTGAGE BACKED CERTIFICATE IS NOT NECES-SARILY THE ORIGINAL PRINCIPAL AMOUNT SHOWN ON ITS FACE. THE PRESENT PRINCIPAL BALANCE OF THE CERTIFICATE MAY BE ASCERTAINED FROM THE ISSUER NAMED THEREON OR A DEALER IN SUCH SECURITIES.

Figure 14-3 GNMA Guaranteed Mortgage-Backed Certificate (Concluded)

will be discounted at delivery to yield the contracted-for 8 percent. However, had the builder purchased GNMA futures contracts in June to yield 8 percent, the contracts would have risen in value (as mortgage rates declined) and this gain in the futures market could have been used to offset the builder's loss in the cash market.

On the other hand, the mortgage banker in the above example would suffer if mortgage rates had risen between the June commitment date and the December delivery date. In essence, the mortgage banker would be lending at below-market interest rates if, say, existing market mortgage rates were 9 percent in December.

A *short hedge* would be used to protect against rising mortgage interest rates. The mortgage banker, when entering into the commitment with the builder in June to purchase the mortgages yielding 8 percent in December, should sell a comparable dollar amount of GNMA contracts with an 8 percent yield in June. Thus, if mortgage rates rise between June and December, the futures market gain (due to a drop in the value of the GNMA contract) will offset the "opportunity loss" in the cash market caused by the mortgage banker lending at below-market mortgage rates.

FARM CREDIT SYSTEM

The passage of the Federal Farm Loan Act of 1916 led to the establishment of the cooperative Farm Credit System. Rural homeowners, farmers, ranchers, and owners of businesses with farm-related activities have always required unique real estate financing arrangements because of crop uncertainties associated with climate conditions and supply and demand factors. The cooperative Farm Credit System was designed to assist in meeting these unique financing requirements.

The Farm Credit System is comprised of 12 autonomous Farm Credit Districts. Each district supplies one member to the Federal Farm Credit Board with a thirteenth member being appointed by the Secretary of Agriculture. The Board, in turn, appoints an administrative head of its supervisory agency located in Washington, D.C., and referred to as the Farm Credit Administration. The Farm Credit System is known as a cooperative system since it is owned by the farmers, ranchers, and business cooperatives that have business transactions with it.

Federal Land Banks and Associations

Twelve Federal Land Banks, one in each of the Farm Credit Districts, were established in 1917. Congress sought to provide low-cost, long-term mortgage loans tailored to meet the needs of rural homeowners, farmers, ranchers, and certain farm-related businesses. In addition to rural home mortgage loans, mortgage loans are available for agricultural land and farms, farm machinery and equipment, livestock, and so forth.

Federal Land Bank loans are issued on the average for 20 years and generally provide for regular repayment of principal and interest. In certain instances the loans may be specially tailored because of unique problems. Many of the loans are written with *variable interest rate* provisions. That is, loan interest rates can be adjusted to reflect the then prevailing market mortgage interest rates.

The Federal Land Banks are owned by over 500 Federal Land Bank Associations operating within the 12 districts. Table 14-4 shows the 1975 capital positions for the Federal Land Banks and Associations. The Federal Land Banks depend heavily on debt capital to finance the mortgage loans they make. Capital stock held by the Associations accounted for less than 6 percent of the 1975 total capital structure of the Federal Land Banks. Federal Land Banks meet most of their loan demands by issuing Consolidated Federal Land Bank Bonds (secured by all 12 Banks) and discount notes for purchase by the general public. In addition, Farm Credit Investment Bonds are sold to Bank borrowers. Associations are owned, in turn, by their borrower-members.

Table 14-4 Capital Positions of Federal Land Banks and Associations (Millions of Dollars)

	December 31, 1975	
	Amount	Percent
Federal Land Banks		
Bonds outstanding	$14,800	90.4%
Capital invested by associations	950	5.8
Accumulated savings	625	3.8
Total capital	$16,375	100.0%
Net Worth of Associations		
Capital invested by members	$ 941	
Accumulated savings	157	
Total association net worth	$ 1,098	

Source: Farm Credit Administration.

In order to borrow funds from a Federal Land Bank, one must be a member of a Federal Land Bank Association in that district. The procedure for obtaining a mortgage loan is as follows. First, the member must submit a loan application to the Association for approval. An approved loan, if endorsed by the district bank, becomes guaranteed by the Association. Each borrower must purchase stock from the Association equal to 5 percent of the loan. This provides some protection for the Association in the event there is a default on the loan. The District Bank also is protected in the event of a default because it holds reserves of the Association's stock amounting to 5 percent of the Association's approved loans.

At the end of 1975, according to the Farm Credit Administration, over 467,000 Federal Land Bank and Association loans were outstanding. The amount of the loans exceeded $16 billion.

Other Farm Credit System Organizations

The Agricultural Credit Act of 1923 established 12 Federal Intermediate Credit Banks with one being located in each of the Farm Credit Districts. Since the Federal Land Banks were designed to provide long-term farm-related mortgage funds, a need for short-term and intermediate-term funds remained. The Federal Intermediate Credit Banks were designed to provide these shorter-term funds needed to finance agricultural-related production and distribution efforts.

The organizational structure of the Federal Intermediate Credit Banks is similar to that for Federal Land Banks. Capital stock issued by the Credit Banks is owned by more than 400 Production Credit Associations. Borrower-members, in turn, own the Associations. The organization of local cooperative Production Credit Associations by farmers and ranchers was authorized with the passage of the Farm Credit Act of 1933. Production Credit Associations make loans to farmer and rancher members to finance their operations. These loans may be for as long as 7 years and are generally secured by collateral in the form of equipment, crops, and livestock. Borrowers become members of the Credit Association since they must purchase stock in the Association equal to 5 percent of the amount of their loans.

Table 14-5, page 237, indicates that Production Credit Associations finance most of their loans through equity capital generated from the purchase of stock by members and through the accumulation of savings over time. On the other hand, Federal Intermediate Credit Banks rely heavily on debt funds to finance their lending operations. Bonds and notes are sold to the general public as well as to members of the Production Credit Associations. The Federal Intermediate Credit Banks possess certain secondary market characteristics since they often provide funds to financial institutions by purchasing their farm-related loans on a discount basis.

According to Farm Credit Administration data, the Production Credit Associations had over 330,000 member loans outstanding at the end of 1975. The amount of these loans approached $11 billion.

The Farm Credit System also is aided by 13 Banks for Cooperatives. Each Farm Credit District has one of these "banks" designed to make seasonal and short-term loans to eligible cooperatives. The 13th bank is located in Denver, Colorado, and operates as a central bank for cooperatives and sometimes participates when large loans are requested. Assistance is made available to a variety of farm-related business cooperatives.

In 1946 the Farmers Home Administration was established to provide a source of funds for farmers and ranchers when other lending sources were not available. The Farmers Home Administration also is actively involved in making and insuring rural housing loans. A family unable to obtain mortgage funds from private sources, and where the real estate property is located in a town of 10,000 (in special cases 20,000) or fewer persons, may be able to qualify for a Farmers Home Administration mortgage loan.

**Table
14-5**   Capital Position of Federal Intermediate Credit Banks and Production
Credit Associations
(Millions of Dollars)

	December 31, 1975	
	Amount	Percent
Federal Intermediate Credit Banks		
Consolidated bonds outstanding	$9,200	93.3%
Capital invested by users	456	4.6
Accumulated savings	206	2.1
Total capital	$9,862	100.0%
Net Worth of Production Credit Associations		
Capital stock invested by members	$1,158	
Equity reserves	16	
Capital invested by FICB's	1	
Accumulated savings	607	
Total net worth	$1,782	

Source: Farm Credit Administration.

HOUSING AND URBAN DEVELOPMENT (HUD)

As we saw in the last chapter, the Federal Housing Administration was created under the National Housing Act of 1934. In 1947 the FHA was moved under the Housing and Home Finance Agency. The Department of Housing and Urban Development (HUD) was created in 1965 to extend the programs and activities of the Housing and Home Finance Agency. At the same time, the FHA was made part of HUD.

HUD's Role in Housing and Mortgage Markets

Prior to the late 1960s, federal agency involvement in the housing and mortgage markets was of two basic types. One area involved the insuring of mortgage loans by the Federal Housing Administration along with the Veterans Administration's loan guaranteeing efforts. The second area focused on public housing programs. For example, the Housing Acts of 1954 and 1961 provided aid and assistance for urban renewal efforts.

The passage of the Housing and Urban Development Act of 1968 increased federal involvement in the housing and mortgage financing markets. First, as we saw in the last chapter, the Act of 1968 authorized the creation of the Government National Mortgage Association and placed GNMA under the direction of HUD. Thus, the Department of Housing and Urban Development now has administrative responsibilities over both the FHA and GNMA.

Second, the 1968 Act created two new subsidy programs designed to assist qualified families in rental housing and home ownership efforts. Section 235 was designed so that the government would pay a portion of the monthly interest on a home buyer's mortgage. Under Section 236, the government would pay a rent subsidy to the owner of an apartment. The intention is to keep monthly rental payments down to low levels. These subsidy programs were designed, of course, to assist low and moderate income families in obtaining adequate housing.

The development of the Section 235 interest subsidy and Section 236 rent subsidy programs during the 1970s is shown in Table 14-6. A substantial number of units were started under these programs during 1970, 1971, and 1972. However, in 1972 a number of program abuses were identified. Included were questionable construction activities and the falsifying of credit reports. These and other subsidy programs were suspended in January, 1973. Management was improved and certain program modifications were instituted before the programs were reinstated in 1975. The slow recovery in the interest and rent subsidy programs was due, in part, to the continuing recession during 1975.

Other HUD Activities

Besides the interest and rental subsidy programs cited above, the Department of Housing and Urban Development is involved in a number of other urban renewal, rehabilitation, and public housing projects and programs. For example, HUD provides funds for slum clearance and neighborhood renewal efforts. In addition, loans and

grants are made available to owners and tenants interested in rehabili-
tating their properties located in urban areas.

Public housing programs prior to the mid-1960s often focused on
the construction of new public housing units and projects. But beginning in 1965 HUD was authorized to provide financial assistance to
local housing authorities to aid them in developing *turnkey* programs.
In essence, the turnkey program is designed to make use of private
industry efforts in the planning, construction financing, and construction phases of public housing project developments. One form of the
turnkey program involves the acquisition of new, privately built housing or existing housing. The local housing authority also usually assumes operating responsibility for the turnkey project established for
the benefit of low income tenants.

**Table
14-6**   Units Started Under HUD Interest and Rent Subsidy Programs

Year	Section 235 Interest Subsidy	Section 236 Rent Subsidy	Total
1970	116,073	105,160	221,233
1971	133,222	107,604	240,826
1972	82,807	80,688	163,495
1973	26,402	44,775	74,177
1974	3,222	20,502*	23,724
1975	454	14,284*	14,738

Source: Department of Housing and Urban Development.
*Commitments issued before program suspension.

Passage of the Demonstration Cities and Metropolitan Development Act of 1966 established the "demonstration cities" or "model
cities" program. Under this program, loans and grants are made available for prototype projects to be planned and developed in certain
cities. An example might be the renovation and redevelopment of a
blighted downtown area by employing unique construction and mass
transportation systems.

IN 1968 the New Communities Act authorized HUD to support the
development of new preplanned communities. Such communities are
to reflect balanced housing, industrial, commercial, and recreational
facilities.

Real Estate Foreclosures

The Federal Home Loan Bank Board compiles annual real estate
foreclosure data. Table 14-7 shows the number of foreclosures and the
foreclosure rate per 1,000 mortgaged structures. Foreclosures

increased throughout the first half of the 1970s. It is frequently contended that at least some of the increase in foreclosures can be traced to the problems associated with HUD's subsidy programs. As a result, a large number of foreclosures occurred in several major cities.

STATE REAL ESTATE ASSISTANCE AGENCIES

State governments have become increasingly involved in the housing and mortgage markets in recent years. State housing agencies had been formed in 40 states by the end of 1975. These agencies attempt to improve the quality of housing and can assist local communities into attracting business and industry. A number of states provide their own real estate mortgage insurance programs to assist in special community real estate projects. Other state agencies assist in the development of industrial parks so that communities can attract new industry.

State agencies finance their real estate assistance efforts through the issuance of bonds. And, to the extent that the interest paid on these bonds is exempt from federal income taxes, the federal government is providing a form of subsidy for these state agency activities.

Table 14-7 Real Estate Foreclosures

Year	Number of Foreclosures	Rate per 1,000 Mortgaged Structures
Nonfarm		
1950	21,537	2.17
1955	28,529	1.94
1960	51,353	2.71
1965	116,664	4.93
1966	117,473	4.81
1967	110,541	4.38
1968	90,941	3.47
Total		
1967	134,203	5.72
1968	110,404	4.63
1969	95,856	3.97
1970	101,070	4.13
1971	116,704	4.62
1972	132,335	5.07
1973	135,803	5.12
1974	140,496	5.21
1975*	147,470	5.41

Source: Federal Home Loan Bank Board.
*Preliminary.

QUESTIONS FOR REVIEW

1. Indicate a number of different ways in which the federal government impacts on real estate finance.
2. Describe briefly how the Federal Home Loan Mortgage Corporation was created and how it operates as a secondary mortgage market institution.
3. The Government National Mortgage Association was created in 1968 and was given certain responsibilities that had been under the domain of the old FNMA in the past. What are these responsibilities? Give some indication as to how they have been carried out.
4. Explain what is meant by: (a) GNMA and FNMA Tandem Programs, (b) GNMA's mortgage-backed securities program, and (c) the "futures" market for GNMA pass-through securities.
5. What is the purpose of the Farm Credit System? Within the System, what are the roles of Federal Land Banks and Associations? What other types of organizations are important to the effectiveness of the Farm Credit System?
6. The Housing and Urban Development Act of 1968 created two new housing subsidy programs which frequently are referred to as Section 235 and Section 236 programs. Briefly describe these programs and indicate their success.
7. What is a state real estate assistance agency?

PROBLEMS

1. In its Tandem Program efforts, GNMA operates to reduce the impact of interest rate risk on mortgage lenders. As we saw in this chapter, interest rate risk exists because interest rates fluctuate over time. For example, an existing 8 percent $20,000 mortgage will fall in value (be discounted) if comparable market interest rates rise to 9 percent. If the mortgage is for 20 years, what will be its discounted value? (Hint: Use the concepts learned in Chapter 3.)

2. Assume that a builder agrees to deliver to a mortgage banker $99,656.25 in mortgages that carry an 8 percent coupon rate. The agreement takes place in June with the delivery date set for December. The market mortgage rate in June was 8 percent. How can the builder "hedge" against the possibility that mortgage rates might drop from 8 percent to, 7.5 percent by December? How would the builder feel about a rise in mortgage rates to 8.5 percent by December?

Loan Application, Loan Analysis, and Loan Closings

The subject matter of loan applications, loan analysis, and loan closings can be broken down into two broad categories: (1) residential real estate, and (2) income producing real estate. As will be pointed out later in the chapter, there are different problems involved with each category, depending upon the type of property involved.

RESIDENTIAL LOANS

The residential or home loan can be utilized where property is sold with new financing or where an existing mortgage is assumed.

New Financing

Regardless of whether the loan is to be FHA, VA, conventional or conventional with mortgage insurance, the loan begins with a loan application. The application form shown in Figure 15-1, pages 244-45, is a standard Federal Home Loan Mortgage Corporation, Federal National Mortgage Association form. It can, however, be used by the institution for a straight conventional mortgage or a conventional mortgage insured by a private mortgage insurance company by simply checking the proper box.

Analysis of the Loan Application

Each loan application is considered on a "case by case" basis. The security of the mortgage rests not only on the value of the property but also upon the borrower's ability and willingness to meet obligations. To this end the Federal Home Loan Mortgage Corporation has created guidelines in reviewing the creditworthiness of borrowers. In general, lenders follow these guidelines regardless of the type of residential mortgage involved. The guidelines, monthly housing expense-to-income ratio and monthly debt payments-to-income ratio, are discussed in the following paragraphs.

Monthly Housing Expense-to-Income Ratio. Normally, monthly housing expense (first and second mortgage payments, less escrows, impounds for taxes, insurance premiums, leasehold payments) and other expenses required to be paid under the mortgage must not exceed approximately 25 percent of the borrower's "stable monthly income." *Stable monthly income* is gross monthly income from primary base earnings plus recognizable secondary income. Secondary income of the borrower, such as bonuses, commission, overtime, or part-time employment is only recognized in stable monthly income if such items of secondary income are typical for the occupation.

The FHLMC strongly suggests that items such as age, education, training, technical skills, occupation, and past employment be taken into account on a case-by-case basis in determining stable monthly income. If the income of the applicant-borrower is from self-employment, then the lender must examine both the previous year's profit and loss statements and the tax returns to verify the income.

Monthly Debt Payments-to-Income Ratio. The FHLMC normally requires that monthly housing expense plus all other monthly payments on all installment debts having reversionary terms of more than seven months not exceed approximately 33 1/3 percent of the borrower's stable monthly income. Alimony and/or child support payments are considered long-term monthly obligations unless there is evidence of a court-approved reduction or termination.

For example, assume that the stable monthly income is $1,500. The home loan payment is $300 and the debt payments amount to $150, or a total of $450. Assuming no other problems, then in all probability the loan will be made. However, if the loan payment is $300 and debt payments are $300, then there is a strong chance the loan will be denied.

Without being specific the FHLMC guidelines state that higher percentages may be appropriate with respect to lower income borrowers, "depending on conditions prevalent in the area in which the mortgaged property is located and a review of the borrower's recent ratio of monthly housing expense and total debt payments to income." (The "conditions" are not spelled out in the guidelines.)

Also, FHLMC declares higher ratios may be offset by a demonstrated ability of the borrower to accumulate wealth and by histories of good debt service. Such ratios may also be offset by larger down

RESIDENTIAL LOAN APPLICATION

MORTGAGE APPLIED FOR	Type	Amount	Interest Rate	No. of Months	Monthly Payment Principal & Interest	Escrow/Impounds (to be collected monthly)
	☐Conv. ☐FHA ☐VA	$	%		$	☐Taxes ☐Hazard Ins. ☐MI ☐

Prepayment Option   In accordance with Regulatory Agencies

SUBJECT PROPERTY

Property Street Address	City	County	State	Zip	No. Units

Legal Description (Attach description if necessary)	Year Built	Property is: ☐Fee ☐Leasehold ☐Condo ☐PUD ☐DeMinimis PUD

Purpose of Loan: ☐Purchase ☐Construction-Perm. ☐Construction ☐Refinance ☐Other (Explain)				

Complete this line if Construction-Perm. or Construction Loan	Lot Value Data	Original Cost	Present Value (a)	Cost of Imps. (b)	Total (a+b)	ENTER TOTAL AS PURCHASE PRICE IN DETAILS OF PURCHASE
	Year Acquired ____	$	$	$	$	☐

Complete this line if a Refinance Loan	Purpose of Refinance	Describe Improvement [ ] made [ ] to be made
Year Acquired	Original Cost	Amt. Existing Liens		Cost: $

Title Will Vest in What Names?	How Will Title Be Held? (Tenancy)

Note Will Be Signed By?	Source of Down Payment and Settlement Charges?

BORROWER / CO-BORROWER*

BORROWER				CO-BORROWER*			
Name	Age	Sex**	School Yrs	Name	Age	Sex**	School Yrs
Present Address No. Years ____		☐Own	☐Rent	Present Address No. Years ____		☐Own	☐Rent
Street				Street			
City/State/Zip				City/State/Zip			
Former address if less than 2 years at present address				Former address if less than 2 years at present address			
Street				Street			
City/State/Zip				City/State/Zip			
Years at former address		☐Own	☐Rent	Years at former address		☐Own	☐Rent

Marital Status	☐Married Yrs. ____ ☐Unmarried ☐Separated	(Check One)** ☐American Indian ☐Negro/Black ☐Oriental ☐Spanish American ☐Other Minority ☐White (Non-minority)	Marital Status	☐Married Yrs. ____ ☐Unmarried ☐Separated	(Check One)** ☐American Indian ☐Negro/Black ☐Oriental ☐Spanish American ☐Other Minority ☐White (Non-minority)
Dependents other than Co-Borrower			Dependents other than listed by Borrower		
Number	Ages		Number	Ages	

Name and Address of Employer	Years employed in this line of work or profession? ____ years Years on this job ____ ☐Self Employed***	Name and Address of Employer	Years employed in this line of work or profession? ____ years Years on this job ____ ☐Self Employed***
Position/Title	Type of Business	Position/Title	Type of Business

GROSS MONTHLY INCOME / MONTHLY HOUSING EXPENSE / DETAILS OF PURCHASE

Item	Borrower	Co-Borrower	Total	Rent	PREVIOUS	PROPOSED		
Base Income	$	$	$	First Mortgage (P&I)		$	a. Purchase Price	$
Overtime				Other Financing (P&I)			b. Total Closing Costs	
Bonuses				Hazard Insurance			c. Pre Paid Escrows	
Commissions				Taxes (Real Estate)			d. Total (a + b + c)	$
Dividends/Interest				Assessments			e. Amt. This Mortgage	( )
Net Rental Income				Mortgage Insurance			f. Other Financing	( )
Other (SEE SCHEDULE BELOW)				Homeowner Assn. Dues			g. Present Equity in Lot	( )
				Total Monthly Pmt	$	$	h. Amt. of Deposit	( )
				Utilities			i. Closing costs paid by Seller	( )
Total	$	$	$	Total	$	$	j. Cash required for closing	$

DESCRIBE OTHER INCOME

☐ B—Borrower C—Co-Borrower   NOTE: ALIMONY/CHILD SUPPORT PAYMENTS NEED NOT BE LISTED UNLESS THEIR CONSIDERATION IS DESIRED

	Monthly Amt.
	$

IF EMPLOYED IN CURRENT POSITION FOR LESS THAN TWO YEARS COMPLETE THE FOLLOWING

B/C	Previous Employer/School	City/State	Type of Business	Position/Title	Dates From/To	Monthly Salary
						$

QUESTIONS APPLY TO BOTH BORROWERS

If Yes, explain on attached sheet

	Borrower Yes or No	Co-Borrower Yes or No		Borrower Yes or No	Co-Borrower Yes or No
Have you any outstanding judgments, ever taken bankruptcy, had property foreclosed upon, or given deed in lieu thereof?			Do you have health and accident insurance?		
Co-Maker or endorser on any notes?			Do you have major medical coverage?		
Defendant/Participant in a Law Suit?			Do you intend to occupy property?		
Obligated for child support/alimony payments?			Will this property be your primary residence?		
Any portion of the down payment borrowed?			Have you previously owned a home?		
			Value of previously owned home	$	$

*Complete this section and all other co-borrower questions about spouse if the spouse will be jointly obligated with the borrower on the loan or if the borrower is relying on the spouse's income or on community property in obtaining the loan.
**This information is requested only for statistical purposes in accordance with the intent of fair housing law. Furnishing this information is voluntary, but borrowers are urged to do so. No lending decision will be made on the basis of this information or on whether or not it is furnished.
***FHLMC requires self employed to furnish signed copies of one or more most recent Federal Tax Returns or audited Profit and Loss Statements. FNMA requires business credit report, signed Federal Income Tax returns for last two years, and, if available, audited P/L plus balance sheet for same period.

Figure 15-1 Residential Loan Application (Continued)

This Statement and any applicable supporting schedules may be completed jointly by both married and unmarried co-borrowers if their assets and liabilities are sufficiently joined so that the Statement can be meaningfully and fairly presented on a combined basis; otherwise separate Statements and Schedules are required (FHLMC 65A/FNMA 1003A). If the co-borrower section was completed about spouse, complete this statement and supporting schedules about spouse also.

☐ Completed Jointly   ☐ Not Completed Jointly

ASSETS		LIABILITIES AND PLEDGED ASSETS		
Description	Cash or Market Value	Owed To (Name, Address and Account Number)	Mo. Pmt. and Mos. left to pay	Unpaid Balance
Cash Toward Purchase held by		*Indicate by (*) which will be satisfied upon sale or upon refinancing of subject property.		
		Installment Debt (include "revolving" charge accounts) $ Pmt./Mos.		$
Checking and Savings Accounts (Indicate names of Institutions/Acct. Nos.)			/	
			/	
			/	
Stocks and Bonds (No./description)			/	
Life Insurance Net Cash Value			/	
Face Amount ($)		Automobile Loan		
SUBTOTAL LIQUID ASSETS			/	
Real Estate Owned (Enter Total Market Value from Real Estate Schedule)		Real Estate Loans (Itemize and Identify Lender)		
Vested Interest in Retirement Fund				
Net Worth of Business Owned (ATTACH FINANCIAL STATEMENT)				
Auto (Make and Year)		Other Debt Including Stock Pledges (Itemize)		
			/	
Furniture and Personal Property		Alimony and Child Support Payments		
Other Assets (Itemize)			/	
		TOTAL MONTHLY PAYMENTS	$	
TOTAL ASSETS	A. $	NET WORTH (A.−B.) $	TOTAL LIABILITIES	B. $

SCHEDULE OF REAL ESTATE OWNED (If Additional Properties Owned Attach Separate Schedule)

Address of Property (Indicate S if Sold, PS if Pending Sale or R if Rental being held for income)	Type of Property	Present Market Value	Amount of Mortgages & Liens	Gross Rental Income	Mortgage Payments	Taxes, Ins. Maintenance and Misc.	Net Rental Income
TOTALS →							

LIST PREVIOUS CREDIT REFERENCES

B—Borrower C—Co-Borrower	Owed To (Name and Address)	Account Number	Purpose	Highest Balance	Date Paid
				$	

AGREEMENT: The undersigned hereby applies for the loan described herein to be secured by a first mortgage or trust deed on the property described herein and represents that no part of said premises will be used for any purpose forbidden by law or restriction and that all statements made in this application are true and made for the purpose of obtaining the loan. Verification may be obtained from any source named herein. The original or a copy of this application will be retained by the lender even if the loan is not granted.

I fully understand that it is a federal crime punishable by fine or imprisonment or both to knowingly make any false statements concerning any of the above facts, as applicable under the provisions of Title 18, United States Code, Section 1014.

Signature (Borrower) _____ Date _____ Signature (Co-Borrower) _____ Date _____

Home Phone _____ Business Phone _____ Home Phone _____ Business Phone _____

The Federal Equal Credit Opportunity Act prohibits creditors from discriminating against credit applicants on the basis of sex or marital status. The Federal Agency which administers compliance with this law concerning this federal savings and loan association is Federal Home Loan Bank Board, Washington, D.C.

Additionally the Federal Fair Housing Act also prohibits discrimination on the basis of race, color, religion, sex or national origin.

BORROWER	CO-BORROWER
Social Security # _____	Social Security # _____
Employee or Badge # _____	Employee or Badge # _____

Applicant's Attorney   Real Estate Agent or Builder

Name _____ Tel. No. _____   Name _____ Tel. No. _____

Address _____   Address _____

Name Present Owner _____ Occupant _____

Property now Mortgaged to _____

If vacant, key at _____ Tel. No. _____

Annual Real Estate Taxes $ _____ BRANCH _____

It is understood and agreed there are no conditions under which this application fee of $ _____ will be refunded in whole or in part.

Figure 15-1   Residential Loan Application (Concluded)

payments and net worth to substitute enough to repay the loan regardless of debt-to-income ratios.

Credit Report

Regardless of the type of mortgage a borrower is seeking, a credit report will be required by the lender. Specifically, if the lender is thinking of doing business with the FHLMC, the FHLMC requires a credit report if the loan-to-value ratio exceeds 90% of the lower of the purchase price or appraisal value of the property securing the loan.

Furthermore, if the property is located within a standard metropolitan statistical area, the report must verify current employment, salary, and all debts listed on the credit application including terms, balances, and ratings; and list all other debts discovered and all legal information, such as suits, judgments, foreclosures, garnishments, bankruptcies, and divorce actions. In the case of a change in employment within the past two years, the report must also contain information as to the borrower's previous employment, location, and salary.

Borrower's Credit Reputation

In addition to the above information, a lender will look at the borrower's credit reputation, considering such things as:

1. Bankruptcy. If the borrower has been bankrupt, the lender will try to verify that at the moment the borrower evidences sufficient creditworthiness.
2. Job Tenure/Change of Residence. Three or more changes in occupation by the borrower within the previous five years, or four or more changes of residence within the previous six years, must be satisfactorily explained.
3. Slow Payments on Credit Report. If the borrower has a recent history of slow payments on a previous mortgage or mortgages, the FHLMC requires a detailed written explanation.

Furthermore, slow payment of other debts, constituting a pattern which appears to indicate slow payment on debts related to basic needs while prompt payments were made on debts related to less important needs of the borrower and borrower's family, must also be satisfactorily explained.

Verification of Employment

At the time an application for a loan is made the applicant will be asked to sign an "Employment Verification Authorization" such as that shown in Figure 15-2, page 247.

Having been granted permission, the lender will then send a form to the applicant's employer. The form will request information regarding the employee such as job tenure and salary.

EMPLOYMENT VERIFICATION AUTHORIZATION

(Please type or print)

Gentlemen:

Please furnish Suffolk County Federal Savings and Loan Association the requested information on the enclosed form.

Signature: ....

Re :

TO:

Figure
15-2   Verification of Employment

Deposit Verification

As a general rule, if the loan-to-value ratio is 80 percent or more, the lending institution will want to verify the down payment. Put another way, if the down payment is going to be 20 percent or less, the lender will demand verification. Consequently, the applicant will give the proposed lender consent to obtain the information. The lender then uses the form or a modification of the form shown in Figure 15-3, page 248, to obtain this information.

Non-Discrimination

The Equal Credit Opportunity Act, 15 USC 1691, prohibits discrimination against credit applicants on the basis of sex and marital status. Furthermore, an amendment to the act (beginning March 23, 1977) extends this to race, color, religion, national origin, age, whether all or part of the applicant's income is derived from any public assistance program, or if the applicant has in good faith exercised any right under the Consumer Credit Protection Act. The lender must provide the notice of the agency administering the Act either on the application or some other separate sheet of paper. In addition, the notice must provide the name of the lender's supervising agency. This is done on the application form shown in Figure 15-1.

Sellers' Discounts

Sellers' discounts are not difficult to understand. Most of the time, though not always, they apply to FHA and VA loans. There are two basic reasons for this: (1) legally a buyer cannot pay discounts on FHA and VA loans — the discounts, if any, must be paid by the seller; and (2) there are interest rate ceilings imposed on both FHA and VA loans. Although it should be remembered that these interest rate ceilings change from time to time.

VETERANS ADMINISTRATION
AND
U. S. DEPARTMENT OF HOUSING AND URBAN DEVELOPMENT
FEDERAL HOUSING ADMINISTRATION

REQUEST FOR VERIFICATION OF DEPOSIT

INSTRUCTIONS: LENDER – Complete Items 1 thru 7. Have applicant complete Items 8 and 9. Forward directly to bank or other depository named in Item 1.
ADDRESSEE – Please complete Items 10 thru 13. Return directly to Lender named in Item 2.

PART I – REQUEST

1. TO (Name and Address of Bank or other Depository)	2. FROM (Name and address of lender)		
3. SIGNATURE OF LENDER	4. TITLE	5. DATE	6. FHA OR VA NUMBER

7. STATEMENT OF APPLICANT

A. NAME AND ADDRESS OF APPLICANT	B. TYPE OF ACCOUNT	BALANCE	ACCOUNT NUMBER
	CHECKING	$	
	SAVINGS	$	

I have applied for a mortgage loan and stated that I maintain account(s) with the bank or depository named in Item 1. My signature below authorizes that bank or other depository to furnish the lender named in Item 2 the information set forth below in Part II. Your response is solely a matter of courtesy for which no responsibility is attached to your institution or any of your officers.

8. SIGNATURE OF APPLICANT	9. DATE

PART II – VERIFICATION

10A. DOES APPLICANT HAVE ANY OUTSTANDING LOANS?			CURRENT STATUS OF ACCOUNTS		
☐ YES ☐ NO (If "Yes," enter total in Item 10B)				CHECKING	SAVINGS
10B. TYPE OF LOAN	MONTHLY PAYMENT	PRESENT BALANCE	11A. IS ACCOUNT LESS THAN TWO MONTHS OLD? (If "Yes," give date opened in Item 11B)	☐ YES ☐ NO	☐ YES ☐ NO
SECURED	$	$			
UNSECURED	$	$	11B. DATE ACCOUNT OPENED		
10C. PAYMENT EXPERIENCE			11C. CURRENT BALANCE		
☐ FAVORABLE ☐ UNFAVORABLE (If unfavorable, explain in Remarks)			11D. IS ACCOUNT OTHER THAN INDIVIDUAL, E.G., JOINT OR TRUST? (If "Yes," explain in remarks)	☐ YES ☐ NO	☐ YES ☐ NO

12. REMARKS

The above information is provided in strict confidence in response to your request.

13A. SIGNATURE OF OFFICIAL OF BANK OR OTHER DEPOSITORY	13B. TITLE	13C. DATE

THE INFORMATION ON THIS FORM IS CONFIDENTIAL. IT IS TO BE TRANSMITTED DIRECTLY, WITHOUT PASSING THROUGH THE HANDS OF THE APPLICANT OR ANY OTHER PARTY.

**Figure
15-3**   Request for Verification of Deposit

It should also be remembered that institutions are not compelled to make either FHA or VA loans. Consequently, a lending institution has alternatives. For example, suppose the institution has the opportunity to make a conventional mortgage at 9½ percent or an FHA mortgage with the rate frozen at 8 percent. Obviously, not being compelled to make the FHA loan, the institution would make the loan at 9½ percent. However, with seller's discounts available to the institution, the interest rates between the two types of loans can be equated. The discount, expressed in "points" (actually one point is equal to 1 percent), is the amount deducted from the face value of the loan to increase the effective yield.

For example, assume an FHA mortgage is to be $25,000. The institution determines that two "points" are necessary for the FHA loan to equate to the market yield on a conventional loan. What this means is that at the closing the seller will receive the down payment made by the purchaser plus $25,000 minus $500 ($25,000 × .02 = $500), or $24,500. The purchaser signs a note and mortgage (or deed of trust) agreeing to pay the institution $25,000 plus interest. The yield is greater because the institution only put out $24,500 but will receive from the purchaser $25,000 plus interest. Put another way, the institution is receiving $500 plus interest which it never loaned out.

One question remains. Why would a seller insist on an FHA or VA loan knowing that the face value of the loan would not be received? The answer is that it frequently broadens the market for the seller. Furthermore, the seller may attempt to compensate for the loss by increasing the price of the home. If the seller is a builder, corners may sometimes be cut to make up the difference in the discount, thereby reducing construction costs.

FARMERS HOME ADMINISTRATION LOANS

The Farmers Home Administration is a rural credit agency of the U.S. Department of Agriculture. The extent of the lending activities of the FmHA is greater than its name implies. In addition to farm ownership loans available to qualified persons who receive a substantial share of their income from farming, other loans are available.

Home Ownership Loans

The FmHA provides loans for homes in rural areas. By definition, *rural areas* include open country and places with populations of 10,000 or less that are rural in character and not closely associated with urban areas. Loans may also be in towns with populations between 10,000 and 20,000 that are outside standard metropolitan statistical areas *if* the Secretary of Agriculture and the Secretary of HUD find there is a serious lack of mortgage credit.

While applications from eligible veterans are given preference, both veterans and non-veterans must be able to meet the same basic requirements. The home ownership loans are designed for low and moderate income families who:

1. Are unable to obtain a loan from commercial lenders on terms and conditions they can reasonably be expected to meet.
2. Have sufficient income to make house payments, insurance premiums, taxes, maintenance, and other debts and necessary living expenses. Persons with inadequate repayment ability may obtain co-signers.
3. Possess the character, ability, and experience to meet loan obligations.
4. Are without decent, safe, and sanitary housing.

FmHA Loan Terms

FmHA loans may be made for up to 100 percent of the FmHA appraised value of the site and the new home if construction site inspections were made by FmHA, VA, or HUD. Homes over one year old are also eligible for 100 percent loans. The maximum repayment period for both new and older homes is 33 years.

Although the payment period can be made for 33 years, the FmHA mortgage (or deed of trust) provides for borrower refinancing. When the financial position of the family is such that the loan can be refinanced through a commercial lender, the loan contract provides that this shall be done.

FmHA Rural Rental Housing

Loans are obtainable from the FmHA to construct rural rental housing. This housing is limited to persons with low or moderate incomes and for persons 62 or older.

In addition to actual construction costs, funds can be used to:

1. Buy and improve the land on which the buildings are to be constructed.
2. Provide streets and water and waste disposal.
3. Supply appropriate recreation and service facilities.
4. Install laundry facilities and equipment.
5. Landscape the property.

The maximum repayment period for the rental housing program is 50 years. However, when the financial position of the borrower reaches the point where the loan can be repaid or refinanced through a commercial lender, the borrower must do so.

The borrower may be either a non-profit organization or an organization for profit. In both cases, the maximum loan is $750,000 per project. More than one project may be built if the need for housing is clearly shown. All applicants are required to provide initial operating capital equal to at least two percent of the cost of the project.

Loans to non-profit organizations can be up to 100 percent of the appraisal value or the development costs, whichever is less. All other applicants are limited to not more than 95% of appraised value or development cost, whichever is less.

Construction or interim financing must be obtained through local lenders when available. When such funds are unavailable, the FmHA will provide interim financing.

Rural Housing Repair Loans

If an applicant is located in a rural area, the FmHA will make loans for repairs provided the applicant:

1. Has an urgent need for repairs.
2. Has sufficient money — including welfare payments — to repay the loan.
3. Has so little income that the applicant is unable to qualify for an FmHA loan to build or buy a new home.

THE PROPERTY AS SECURITY

So far the discussion has centered about the individual as a credit risk; however, it is the real property which is the basis of the loan. Consequently, prior to approving the loan, a lending institution will require an appraisal of the property. If a VA or FHA loan is to be made, the VA or FHA is requested to make the appraisal. If the loan is to be a conventional loan, the institution makes its own appraisal.

The appraisal of real property requires specialized knowledge and skill. Because of its complexity, only the basics can be discussed here. Essentially, the appraiser uses three approaches to value and attempts to correlate the three approaches into the final estimate of value.

The Cost Approach

Generally with this approach the replacement cost of the building minus depreciation plus the value of the land equals the estimated value of the property.

Cost is generally obtained by multiplying the cost of replacement per square foot times the number of square feet, which equals the replacement cost.

The depreciation estimated by the appraiser can consist of three possible types:

1. *Physical deterioration*. This is the decay and natural wear and tear on a building. For example, the shingles on a home may be rotted.
2. *Functional obsolescence*. This is an impairment of desirability and usefulness brought about by changes in design or in the arts. For

example, bathroom fixtures may be outdated. The homeowner has little or no control over this.

3. *Economic obsolescense*. This is the impairment of desirability or useful life of the property arising from economic forces. Here again, an owner has no control as it is an external factor causing a loss of value. For example, a flight pattern from a nearby airport may be changed, causing a loss of value due to a shift in demand for property in that particular neighborhood.

The Market Data Approach

This approach is sometimes called the "sales-comparison approach," which involves a comparison of sales prices that have been obtained for like properties. Because similar properties are not usually sold on the same date and because "similar" properties are not exactly similar, adjustments have to be made. These adjustments include such things as time, number of square feet in the building, number of baths, types of construction, garage, and even the number of stories.

The Income Approach

The rationale for the income approach is simply that value is equal to the present worth of future income. Consequently, the income is "capitalized" to give the property value. Thus, if the income from a piece of real property were $12,000 and the capitalization rate were, say, 10 percent, then:

$$\text{Value} = \frac{\text{annual net income}}{\text{capitalization rate}}$$

$$\text{or} \quad \text{Value} = \frac{12,000}{.10}$$

$$= \$120,000.$$

However, in residential properties a "gross rent multiplier" is used. In essence, the appraiser again goes to the "market." Here, the appraiser finds the sales prices of similar homes and their gross monthly rents. For example, a $40,000 home rents for $350 per month. The $350 is divided into $40,000 to obtain the gross rent multiplier. Thus, $\frac{40,000}{\$350}$ = 114 (rounded off). In practice, five or six similar homes and their sales prices and rentals are obtained and a gross rent multiplier is obtained, averaging say, 118. Then an estimate of rent is made on the house under appraisement, say $400 per month, and this is multiplied by the multiplier to obtain the estimate of value (118 × 400 = $47,200).

The form shown in Figure 15-4, page 253, is an FHA appraisal form. The application of the FHA appraisal is made at the same time

FHA UNDERWRITING REPORT

1. FHA MORTGAGEE NO.

2. FHA CASE ▲ NO.

3. NEIGHBORHOOD CODE

| ▲1.□ Core City | 2.□ Other City | 4.□ Sub-urban | ▲1.□ Model City | 2.□ Peri. of MC | 4.□ | ▲1.□ Rural | Code Enf. □ URA | Code Bligh- ted | ▲1.□ | 2.□ | 4.□ |

MORTGAGE TO BE INSURED UNDER

3

□ SEC. 203(b) □ SEC.

4. ▲ PROPERTY ADDRESS

LEGAL-LOT   BLK.   TR./SUBD.

5. MORTGAGEE

6. **ESTIMATE OF VALUE AND CLOSING COSTS**

VALUE OF PROPERTY $

Closing Costs . . . . $
TOTAL (For Mortgage Insurance Purposes) . . $

8. APPROVED FOR COMMITMENT

7. MONTHLY EXPENSE ESTIMATE

Fire Ins. . . . . $
Taxes . . . . . $
Main. & Repairs $
Heat & Utilities $

9. COMMITMENT

Issued 19
Expires 19

10. COMMITMENT TERMS MAX. MORT. AMT. $ _____ NO. MOS. _____ MAX. INTEREST _____ %

11. □ EXISTING □ PROPOSED

12. ▲ EXISTING HOUSE 4.□ Name of Occupant (or person to call if unoccupied)   Tel. No.   Key Encl. □ (If unfurnished)

Mon. & Yr. Completed ▲ □ Never Occup. □ Vacant   Occupied by □ Owner □ Tenant at $ ____ Per Mo. □ Furn. □ Unfurn

13. ▲ PROPOSED 1.□ SUBSTAN. REHAB. 2.□ UNDER CONSTR. 3.□ Builder's Name & Address Including ZIP Code   Tel. No.   Model Identification

Plans: □ First Subm. Prob. Repeat Cases □ Yes □ No   □ Prev. Proc. as FHA Case No.

14. DESCRIPTION

▲1.□ Wood siding	▲ ____ Stories	▲ ____ Bedrooms	□ Store Rm	Mineral Rights Reserved	▲ Type of Heating
▲1.□ Detached	2.□ Wood shingle	7.□ Split Foyer	____ Liv. room	□ Util. Rm	□ No □ Yes (Explain)	
2.□ Semi-det.	3.□ Asb. shingle	8.□ Bi-Level	____ Din. room	▲1.□ Garage	Util- ities: Public Comm. Individual	▲1.□ Cent. Air Cond.
3.□ Row	4.□ Fiber board	9.□ Split Level	____ Kitchen	9.□ Carport	Water ▲1.□ 2.□ 3.□	2.□ Wall Air Cond.
▲1.□ Frame	5.□ Brick or stone	▲1.□ Full Basement	____ No. rms.	□ No cars	Gas □ □ □	Type of Paving (Str.)
2.□ Masonry	6.□ Stuc. or c.blk.	2.__% Basement	▲ ____ Baths	▲1.□ Built-in	Elect. □ □ □	□ None
3.□ Concrete	7.□ Aluminum	3.□ Slab on Gr.	▲ ____ ½ Baths	2.□ Attached	▲1.□ Underground Wiring	□ Curb & Gutter
Factory Fabricated	8.□ Asph. siding	4.□ Crawl Space		3.□ Detached	Sanitary: Sept. Cess tank Pool	□ Sidewalk
▲1.□ Yes 2.□ No	9.□	▲ ____ Living Units	____ % Non-res.		Sewer ▲1.□ 2.□ 3.□ 4.□	□ Storm Sewer

EXTRA FEATURES
▲1.□ Fireplace 2.□ Rec. Room 4.□ Sw. Pool ▲1.□ Enclosed Porch 2.□ Breezeway 4.□ Fence
▲1.□ Extra Fire Pl. 2.□ Expand Attic 4.□ Fin. Attic ▲1.□ Open Porch 2.□ 4.□

15 SPEC. ASSESS. Prepayable $ _____ Non-Prepay. $ _____
Int.___% Ann. Pay. $ _____ Unpd.Bal. $ _____ Rem.Term ___ Yrs.

16. ▲ LOT ____ X ____ 1.□ Irr. 2.□ Acres ____ Sq.Ft.

17. GENERAL LOCATION:

18. ANN. R.EST. TAXES $

19. ANN. FIRE INS $

20. ▲ SALE PRICE $ $ Mo.   Yr.

21. EQUIPMENT IN VALUE: ▲1.□ Range or Counter cook unit & oven 2.□ Refrig. 4.□ Dishwasher
▲1.□ Auto. washer 2.□ Dryer 4.□ ▲1.□ Garb. Disp. 2.□ Vent. fan 4.□ Carpet

22. ▲ LOC. CODE
23. BASIC CASE
24. SUB FILE NO.
25. REM. LIFE □ ECON. □ PHYS. YRS.
26. CONDITION AS APPRAISED ▲1 □ Excellent 2.□ Good 3.□ Fair 4.□ Poor
27. NEIGHBORHOOD DATA
Pres. Land Use
Anticip. Land Use
Owner Occp. Appeal
Demand for Amenity Inc. Prop.
___ % Blt. up ___ % own. ___ % Ten. ___ % Vac.
Age Typ. Bldg. ____ to ____
Typ. Mo. Rent $ ____ to $ ____
▲ Price Range $ ____ to $ ____
28. ▲ Location □ Acceptable □ Reject □ 223e
Property □ Acceptable □ Reject
29. IMPROVED ▲ LIVING AREA ____ Sq. Ft.

30. COST DATA: 2800-3 for   □ Integ.
2014-d   □ 2014
Cost @ $ ____ Per Sq.Ft. = $

31. BLDG. DESC/VARS.   —   +
Fdns. ____ Frpl. ____
Ext. Wall
Shtg.
Sub. Fl. ____ Fin. Fl.
Rfg. ____ Int. Wall
Plg.
Htg. ____ Insul.

Equip.
Total Variations $

Net variations - - - - - - - $
Basic cost - - - - - - - - $
Main Bldg. (Subtotal) - - - $
Gar./Carport - - - - - - - $
Porches/Terraces - - - - - $
Walks/Drives - - - - - - - $
Ldsp./Pltg./Fin. Gr. - - - $
Other on-site imp. - - - - $
On-site imp. unadj. (Total) $
2511 Comb. ____ % X wkmp. ___ % = ___ %
On-site imp. adj. - - - - - $
Arch. services - - - - - - $
Water/sewer tap charges - $
EST. REPL. COST IMP. - $

32. REPL. COST   Review
▲ Repl. cost imp. $
▲ Mkt.Price Eq.site $
Misc.Allow Costs $
Mktg. Expense - - $
▲ Repl.Cost - - - - $

33. COST OF REPAIRS/IMPROVEMENTS
Prop. $ Req. $

34. COMPARABLE PROPERTIES	Sq.Ft. Imp.Area	Sto-ries	Rms.	Bed Rms.	Bath	Const.	Gar.	Yr. /cond.	Price	Date	S L	Date Inspec.	+/=	Variations
SUBJECT PROPERTY														
(1)														
(2)														
(3)														

35. CAP. INCOME: Mon. Rent $ ____ — Excess exp. $ ____ = $ ____ X Rent multiplier of ____ = CAP. INCOME $

36. APPRAISAL SUMMARY: Capitalized Income $ ____ Cost $ ____ Market ▲ $
VALUE: Val. (Excl. Cl. Costs) $ ____ Closing Costs $ ____ Total ▲ $

37. LEASE: ANN. GRD. RENT $ ____ CAP. AT ____ % = ▲ $ ____ Val. of Leased Fee. Val. of Leasehold Est. $

38. (1) Remarks (2) Spec. Cond. (3) Rej. Reasons (4) Neigh. Charac. (5) Land excl. From Val. (6) Items Excl. From Repl. Cost.

39. INSPECTIONS: □ Repair
□ Proposed Construction
□ Mortgagee's Certificate
□ Appr. Arch. Proc.   Date
□ Reject
Review

□ Commit. Staff Val.   □ Other
□ Reject
Review   Date

WARNING: All persons by signing this report certify that they have no interest present or future, in the property, application or mortgage.

Figure 15-4 FHA Underwriting Report

the loan application is made. It should be noted that VA and conventional mortgage appraisals are done on what amounts to a variation of this form. A copy of the FHLMC/FNMA Residential Appraisal Report form, along with guidelines for completing the form, is shown in Appendix G.

The Real Estate Settlement Procedures Act

The Real Estate Settlement Procedures Act (RESPA) was first passed by Congress in 1974 and amended in 1975. The result was chaos — within six months its provisions were suspended.

In June 1976 the Act was amended in its current form. The Act must be complied with by all federally regulated lenders. It covers all federally related mortgages secured by single-family dwellings, condominiums, and cooperatives occupied by one-to-four families.

Exempt from the Act are properties in excess of 25 acres, construction loans, and loans on vacant lots.

The lender is required to furnish the borrower a copy of a HUD approved information booklet at the time application is made for the loan or within three days. This booklet entitled, *Settlement Procedures Special Information Booklet*, specifies the main procedures cited by the Act and lists unfair practices prohibited under the Act.

Furthermore, the lender must furnish a "good faith" estimate of settlement costs to the loan applicant within three days of the written loan application. The standard "good faith" estimate is shown in Figure 15-5 on page 256.

The third requirement under the Act is to furnish the borrower a standard form to be used in all regulated settlements (or closings). If the borrower requests it, the settlement costs, to the extent known, must be made available to the borrower 24 hours before settlement. This settlement form is shown in Figure 15-6, pages 258–59.

The following excerpts from the HUD information booklet discuss each specific settlement service as shown on Section L of the Uniform Settlement Statement form.

700. SALES/BROKER'S COMMISSION. — This is the total dollar amount of sales commission, usually paid by the seller. Fees are usually a percentage of the selling price of the house, and are intended to compensate brokers or salesmen for their services. Custom and/or the negotiated agreement between the seller and the broker determine the amount of the commission.

701–702. Division of Commission. — If several brokers or salesmen work together to sell the house, the commission may be split among them. If they are paid from funds collected for settlement, this is shown on lines 701–702.

703. Commission Paid at Settlement. — Sometimes the broker will retain the earnest money deposit to apply towards his commission. In this case, line 703 will show only the remainder of the commission which will be paid at settlement.

800. ITEMS PAYABLE IN CONNECTION WITH LOAN. — These are the fees which lenders charge to process, approve and make the mortgage loan.

801. Loan Origination. — This fee covers the lender's administrative costs in processing the loan. Often expressed as a percentage of the loan, the fee will vary among lenders and from locality to locality. Generally the buyer pays the fee unless another arrangement has been made with the seller and written into the sales contract.

802. Loan Discount. — Often called "points," a loan discount is a one-time charge used to adjust the yield on the loan to what market conditions demand. It is used to offset constraints placed on the yield by state or federal regulations. Each "point" is equal to one percent of the mortgage amount. For example, if a lender charges four points on a $30,000 loan this amounts to a charge of $1,200.

803. Appraisal Fee. — This charge, which may vary significantly from transaction to transaction, pays for a statement of property value for the lender, made by an independent appraiser or by a member of the lender's staff. The lender needs to know if the value of the property is sufficient to secure the loan if you fail to repay the loan according to the provision of your mortgage contract, and the lender must foreclose and take title to the house. The appraiser inspects the house and the neighborhood, and considers sales prices of comparable houses and other factors in determining the value. The appraisal report may contain photos and other information of value to you. It will provide the factual data upon which the appraiser based the appraised value. Ask the lender for a copy of the appraisal report or review the original.

The appraisal fee may be paid by either the buyer or the seller, as agreed in the sales contract. In some cases this fee is included in the Mortgage Insurance Application Fee. See line 806.

804. Credit Report Fee. — This fee covers the cost of the credit report, which shows how you have handled other credit transactions. The lender uses this report in conjunction with information you submitted with the application regarding your income, outstanding bills, and employment, to determine whether you are an acceptable credit risk and to help determine how much money to lend you.

805. Lender's Inspection Fee. — This charge covers inspections, often of newly constructed housing, made by personnel of the lending institution or an outside inspector. (Pest or other inspections made by companies other than the lender are discussed in connection with line 1302.)

ESTIMATED CLOSING COSTS

The following are estimates of the amount of costs for certain services which Borrowers are likely to purchase in connection with the settlement on the purchase of real property.

These estimated amounts reflect charges experienced in the locality, but may be substantially different from the actual costs you will incur.

This is not a loan commitment.

ESTIMATED CLOSING COSTS BASED ON A LOAN AMOUNT OF $ _____ .
RATE _____ TERM _____ RATIO _____

NO. ON
UNIFORM
SETTLEMENT
STATEMENT

801	LOAN ORIGINATION FEE	_____	**APPROXIMATE LOAN PAYMENT**
804	CREDIT REPORT	_____	P&I = _____
805	INSPECTION (APPRAISAL) FEE	_____	TAX = _____
806	PRIVATE MTG. INS.	_____	INS = _____
	APPLICATION REVIEW FEE		MTG
807	ASSUMPTION FEE	_____	INS = _____
808	COMMITMENT FEE _____ %	_____	TOTAL = _____
901	INTEREST ____ days	_____	
902	PRIVATE MTG. INS. PREMIUM	_____	
903	MORTGAGEES HAZARD INSURANCE PREMIUM*	_____	**APPROXIMATE SETTLEMENT AMOUNT:**
1001	INSURANCE RESERVE	_____	
1002	PRIVATE MTG. INS. RESERVE **	_____	A. PURCHASE PRICE _____
1102	ABSTRACT OR TITLE SEARCH	_____	B. REPAIRS AND
1103	TITLE EXAMINATION	_____	IMPROVEMENTS _____
1107	ATTORNEYS CERTIFICATE OF TITLE	_____	C. TOTAL CLOSING COSTS _____
1108	TITLE INSURANCE-LENDER'S COVERAGE	_____	D. PREPAID ESCROWS _____
			E. TOTAL _____
1111	TAX SERVICE	_____	F. AMT. THIS LOAN _____
1201	RECORDING FEES	_____	G. OTHER FINANCING _____
1203	DOCUMENTARY FEE	_____	H. DEPOSIT TO DATE _____
1301	SURVEY	_____	I. CLOSING COSTS
____	TAX CERTIFICATE	_____	PAID BY SELLER _____
____	FHA INSURANCE RESERVE	_____	J. CASH REQUIRED
____	OTHER	_____	FOR CLOSING _____

* Hazard insurance is required. You may purchase insurance from any person or organization you choose.
** Mortgage insurance, if required, is paid from the interest charged.

An attorneys certificate of title will be provided to the lender at an estimated cost of $ _____ ,

by (name) _____

(address) _____ (phone) _____ .
This provider has a business relationship with Midland Federal Savings.

THIS FORM DOES NOT COVER ALL ITEMS YOU WILL BE REQUIRED TO PAY IN CASH AT SETTLEMENT, FOR EXAMPLE, DEPOSIT IN ESCROW FOR REAL ESTATE TAXES. YOU MAY WISH TO INQUIRE AS TO THE AMOUNT OF SUCH OTHER ITEMS.

Date: _____

_____   _____
BORROWER   LOAN COUNSELOR

_____
BORROWER

**Figure
15-5** Estimated Closing Costs

806. Mortgage Insurance Application Fee. — This fee covers processing the application for private mortgage insurance which may be required on certain loans. It may cover both the appraisal and application fee.

807. Assumption Fee. — This fee is charged for processing papers for cases in which the buyer takes over payments on the prior loan of the seller.

900. ITEMS REQUIRED BY LENDER TO BE PAID IN ADVANCE. — You may be required to prepay certain items, such as interest, mortgage insurance premium and hazard insurance premium, at the time of settlement.

901. Interest. — Lenders usually require that borrowers pay at settlement the interest that accrues on the mortgage from the date of settlement to the beginning of the period covered by the first monthly payment. For example, suppose your settlement takes place on April 16, and your first regular monthly payment will be due June 1, to cover interest charges for the month of May. On the settlement date, the lender will collect interest for the period from April 16 to May 1. If you borrowed $30,000 at 9% interest, the interest item would be $112.50. This amount will be entered on line 901.

902. Mortgage Insurance Premium. — Mortgage insurance protects the lender from loss due to payment default by the home owner. The lender may require you to pay your first premium in advance, on the day of settlement. The premium may cover a specific number of months or a year in advance.

903. Hazard Insurance Premium. — This premium prepayment is for insurance protection for you and the lender against loss due to fire, windstorm, and natural hazards. This coverage may be included in a Homeowners Policy which insures against additional risks which may include personal liability and theft. Lenders often require payment of the first year's premium at settlement.

1000. RESERVES DEPOSITED WITH LENDERS. — Reserves (sometimes called "escrow" or "impound" accounts) are funds held in an account by the lender to assure future payment for such recurring items as real estate taxes and hazard insurance.

You will probably have to pay an initial amount for each of these items to start the reserve account at the time of settlement. A portion of your regular monthly payments will be added to the reserve account. RESPA places limitations on the amount of reserve funds which may be required by the lender.

1001. Hazard Insurance. — The lender determines the amount of money that must be placed in the reserve in order to pay the next insurance premium when due.

1002. Mortgage Insurance. — The lender may require that part of the total annual premium be placed in the reserve account at settlement. The portion to be received in reserve may be negotiable.

A. U.S. DEPARTMENT OF HOUSING AND URBAN DEVELOPMENT	B. TYPE OF LOAN		
	1. ☐ FHA 2. ☐ FMHA 3. ☐ CONV. UNINS.		
	4. ☐ VA 5. ☐ CONV. INS.		
DISCLOSURE/SETTLEMENT STATEMENT	6. FILE NUMBER 7. LOAN NUMBER		
If the Truth-in-Lending Act applies to this transaction, a Truth-in-Lending statement is attached as page 3 of this form.	8. MORTG. INS. CASE NO.		

C. NOTE: This form is furnished to you prior to settlement to give you information about your settlement costs, and again after settlement to show the actual costs you have paid. The present copy of the form is:

☐ ADVANCE DISCLOSURE OF COSTS. Some items are estimated, and are marked "(e)." Some amounts may change if the settlement is held on a date other than the date estimated below. The preparer of this form is not responsible for errors or changes in amounts furnished by others.

☐ STATEMENT OF ACTUAL COSTS. Amounts paid to and by the settlement agent are shown. Items marked "(p.o.c.)" were paid outside the closing; they are shown here for informational purposes and are not included in totals.

D. NAME OF BORROWER	E. SELLER	F. LENDER	

G. PROPERTY LOCATION	H. SETTLEMENT AGENT	I. DATES	
		LOAN COMMITMENT	ADVANCE DISCLOSURE
	PLACE OF SETTLEMENT	SETTLEMENT	DATE OF PRORATIONS IF DIFFERENT FROM SETTLEMENT

J. SUMMARY OF BORROWER'S TRANSACTION		K. SUMMARY OF SELLER'S TRANSACTION	
100. GROSS AMOUNT DUE FROM BORROWER:		**400. GROSS AMOUNT DUE TO SELLER:**	
101. Contract sales price		401. Contract sales price	
102. Personal property		402. Personal property	
103. Settlement charges to borrower *(from line 1400, Section L)*		403.	
		404.	
104.			
105.		Adjustments for items paid by seller in advance:	
		405. City/town taxes to	
Adjustments for items paid by seller in advance:		406. County taxes to	
		407. Assessments to	
106. City/town taxes to		408. to	
107. County taxes to		409. to	
108. Assessments to		410. to	
109. to		411. to	
110. to			
111. to		**420. GROSS AMOUNT DUE TO SELLER**	
112. to		*NOTE: The following 500 and 600 series section are not required to be completed when this form is used for advance disclosure of settlement costs prior to settlement.*	
120. GROSS AMOUNT DUE FROM BORROWER:			
200. AMOUNTS PAID BY OR IN BEHALF OF BORROWER:		**500. REDUCTIONS IN AMOUNT DUE TO SELLER:**	
		501. Payoff of first mortgage loan	
201. Deposit or earnest money		502. Payoff of second mortgage loan	
202. Principal amount of new loan(s)		503. Settlement charges to seller *(from line 1400, Section L)*	
203. Existing loan(s) taken subject to		504. Existing loan(s) taken subject to	
204.		505.	
205.		506.	
		507.	
Credits to borrower for items unpaid by seller:		508.	
		509.	
206. City/town taxes to			
207. County taxes to		Credits to borrower for items unpaid by seller:	
208. Assessments to			
209. to		510. City/town taxes to	
210. to		511. County taxes to	
211. to		512. Assessments to	
212. to		513. to	
220. TOTAL AMOUNTS PAID BY OR IN BEHALF OF BORROWER		514. to	
300. CASH AT SETTLEMENT REQUIRED FROM OR PAYABLE TO BORROWER:		515. to	
		520. TOTAL REDUCTIONS IN AMOUNT DUE TO SELLER	
301. Gross amount due from borrower *(from line 120)*		**600. CASH TO SELLER FROM SETTLEMENT:**	
302. Less amounts paid by or in behalf of borrower *(from line 220)*		601. Gross amount due to seller *(from line 420)*	
		602. Less total reductions in amount due to seller *(from line 520)*	
303. CASH ☐ REQUIRED FROM OR ☐ PAYABLE TO BORROWER:		603. **CASH TO SELLER FROM SETTLEMENT**	

HUD-1A (6-75) AS & AS (1323)

LENDER'S COPY

Figure 15-6 Disclosure/Settlement Statement (Continued)

L. SETTLEMENT CHARGES		PAID FROM BORROWER'S FUNDS	PAID FROM SELLER'S FUNDS
700.	SALES/BROKER'S COMMISSION based on price $ @ %		
701.	Total commission paid by seller Division of commission as follows:		
702.	$ to		
703.	$ to		
704.			
800.	ITEMS PAYABLE IN CONNECTION WITH LOAN.		
801.	Loan Origination fee %		
802.	Loan Discount %		
803.	Appraisal Fee to		
804.	Credit Report to		
805.	Lender's inspection fee		
806.	Mortgage Insurance application fee to		
807.	Assumption/refinancing fee		
808.			
809.			
810.			
811.			
900.	ITEMS REQUIRED BY LENDER TO BE PAID IN ADVANCE.		
901.	Interest from to @ $ /day		
902.	Mortgage insurance premium for mo.		
903.	Hazard insurance premium for yrs. to		
904.	yrs. to		
905.			
1000.	RESERVES DEPOSITED WITH LENDER FOR:		
1001.	Hazard insurance mo. @ $ /mo.		
1002.	Mortgage insurance mo. @ $ /mo.		
1003.	City property taxes mo. @ $ /mo.		
1004.	County property taxes mo. @ $ /mo.		
1005.	Annual assessments mo. @ $ /mo.		
1006.	mo. @ $ /mo.		
1007.	mo. @ $ /mo.		
1008.	mo. @ $ /mo.		
1100.	TITLE CHARGES:		
1101.	Settlement or closing fee to		
1102.	Abstract or title search to		
1103.	Title examination to		
1104.	Title insurance binder to		
1105.	Document preparation to		
1106.	Notary fees to		
1107.	Attorney's Fees to		
	(includes above items No.:)		
1108.	Title insurance to		
	(includes above items No.:)		
1109.	Lender's coverage $		
1110.	Owner's coverage $		
1111.			
1112.			
1113.			
1200.	GOVERNMENT RECORDING AND TRANSFER CHARGES		
1201.	Recording fees: Deed $; Mortgage $ Releases $		
1202.	City/county tax/stamps: Deed $; Mortgage $		
1203.	State tax/stamps: Deed $; Mortage $		
1204.			
1300.	ADDITIONAL SETTLEMENT CHARGES		
1301.	Survey to		
1302.	Pest inspection to		
1303.			
1304.			
1305.			
1400.	TOTAL SETTLEMENT CHARGES (entered on lines 103 and 503, Sections J and K)		

The Undersigned Acknowledges Receipt of This Disclosure Settlement Statement and Agrees to the Correctness Thereof.

_____   _____
Buyer or Agent   Seller or Agent

NOTE: Under certain circumstances the borrower and seller may be permitted to waive the 12-day period which must normally occur between advance disclosure and settlement. In the event such a waiver is made, copies of the statements of waiver, executed as provided in the regulations of the Department of Housing and Urban Development, shall be attached to and made a part of this form when the form is used as a settlement statement.

HUD-1B (6-75) AS & AS (1323)

LENDER'S COPY

Figure
15-6 Disclosure/Settlement Statement (Concluded)

1003–1004. City/County Property Taxes. — The lender may require a regular monthly payment to the reserve account for property taxes.

1005. Annual Assessments. — The reserve item covers assessments that may be imposed by subdivisions or municipalities for special improvements (such as sidewalks, sewers or paving) or fees (such as homeowners association fees).

1100. TITLE CHARGES. — Title charges may cover a variety of services performed by the lender or others for handling and supervising the settlement transaction and services related thereto. The specific charges discussed in connection with lines 1101 through 1109 are those most frequently incurred at settlement. Due to the great diversity in practice from area to area, your particular settlement may not include all these items or may include others not listed.

1101. Settlement or Closing Fee. — This fee is paid to the settlement agent. Responsibility for payment of this fee should be negotiated between the seller and buyer, at the time the sales contract is signed.

1102–1104. Abstract or Title Search, Title Examination, Title Insurance Binder. — These charges cover the costs of the search and examination of records of previous ownership, transfers, etc., to determine whether the seller can convey clear title to the property, and to disclose any matters on record that could adversely affect the buyer or the lender. Examples of title problems are unpaid mortgages, judgment or tax liens, conveyances of mineral rights, leases, and power line easements or road right-of-ways that could limit use and enjoyment of the real estate. In some areas, a title insurance binder is called a commitment to insure.

1105. Document Preparation. — There may be a separate document fee that covers preparation of final legal papers, such as a mortgage, deed of trust, note, or deed. You should check to see that these services, if charged for, are not also covered under some other service fees; ask the settlement agent.

1106. Notary Fee. — This fee is charged for the cost of having a licensed person affix his or her name and seal to various documents authenticiating the execution of these documents by the parties.

1107. Attorney's Fees. — You may be required to pay for legal services provided to the lender in connection with the settlement, such as examination of the title binder or sales contract. Occasionally this fee can be shared with the seller, if so stipulated in the sales contract. If a lawyer's involvement is required by the lender, the fee will appear on this part of the form. The buyer and seller may each retain an attorney to check the various documents and to represent them at all stages of the transaction including settlement. Where this service is not required and is paid for outside of closing, the person conducting settlement is not obligated to record the fee on the settlement form.

1108. Title Insurance. — The total cost of owner's and lender's title insurance is shown here. The borrower may pay all, a part or none of this cost depending on the terms of the sales contract or local custom.

1109. Lender's Title Insurance. — A one-time premium may be charged at settlement for a lender's title policy which protects the lender against loss due to problems or defects in connection with the title. The insurance is usually written for the amount of the mortgage loan and covers losses due to defects or problems not identified by title search and examination. In most areas this is customarily paid by the borrower unless the seller agrees in the sales contract to pay part or all of it.

1110. Owner's Title Insurance. — This charge is for owner's title insurance protection and protects you against losses due to title defects. In some areas it is customary for the seller to provide the buyer with an owner's policy and for the seller to pay for this policy. In other areas, if the buyer desires an owner's policy he must pay for it.

1200. GOVERNMENT RECORDING AND TRANSFER CHARGES. — These fees may be paid either by borrower or seller, depending upon your contract when you buy the house or accept the loan commitment. The borrower usually pays the fees for legally recording the new deed and mortgage (item 1201). These fees, collected when property changes hands or when a mortgage loan is made, may be quite large and are set by state and/or local governments. City, county and/or state tax stamps may have to be purchased as well (item 1201 and 1203).

1300. ADDITIONAL SETTLEMENT CHARGES

1301. Survey. — The lender or the title insurance company may require that a surveyor conduct a property survey to determine the exact location of the house and the lot line, as well as easements and rights of way. This is a protection to the buyer as well. Usually the buyer pays the surveyor's fees, but sometimes this may be handled by the seller.

1302. Pest and Other Inspections. — This fee is to cover inspections for termite or other pest infestation of the house. This may be important if the sales contract included a promise by the seller to transfer the property free from pests or pest-caused damage. Be sure that the inspection shows that the property complies with the sales contract before you complete the settlement. If it does not you may wish to require a bond or other financial assurance that the work will be completed. This fee can be paid either by the borrower or seller depending upon the terms of the sales contract. Lenders vary in their requirements as to such an inspection.

Fees for other inspections, such as the structural soundness, are entered on line 1303.

1400. TOTAL SETTLEMENT CHARGES. — All the fees in the borrower's column entitled "Paid from Borrower's Funds at Settlement" are totaled here and transferred to line 103 of Section J, "Settlement charges to borrower" in the *Summary of Borrower's Transaction* on page 1 of the Uniform Settlement Statement. All the settlement fees paid by the seller are transferred to line 502 of Section

K, *Summary of Seller's Transaction* on page 1 of the Uniform Settlement Statement.

Truth in Lending

Lenders are required to furnish a truth-in-lending statement to borrowers at the time the loan is made. This statement must disclose the annual percentage rate or effective interest rate which will be paid on the loan.

The effective rate is usually higher than the contract rate. The reason for this is that the effective rate includes not only the interest to be paid on the loan but discounts, origination fees, financing charges and any other charges that might have been made to obtain the loan.

In addition, the truth-in-lending statement must disclose any additional charges to the borrower for prepayment of the mortgage.

Assuming the Existing Mortgage

Recent action has been taken by financial institutions to include a "non-assumption" clause in their conventional mortgages or deeds of trust; however, FHA and VA mortgages can still be assumed. For example, A has an existing mortgage of $25,000. The sales price is $35,000. A agrees to sell to B who gives A $10,000 in cash and agrees to assume A's $25,000 mortgage.

The initial agreement whereby B agrees to assume the mortgage will appear in the Contract for Sale of Real Property (or Binder in some states). The second place where it appears is in the deed from A to B written substantially as follows:

> The conveyance hereunder is subject to a certain mortgage executed by A as mortgagor to Personal Savings and Loan Association as mortgagee, which mortgage is dated April 2, 19____ and was recorded April 3, 19____ in the Office of the Clerk of the County of _____ in liber 1348 of mortgages page 87 on which mortgage there is now due $25,000 with interest thereon at the rate of 7¾ percent per annum and that the grantor hereby assumes and covenants to pay such mortgage debt and interest as part of the consideration of this conveyance.

Assumption Statement. In the case above, A has informed B that the amount to be assumed is $25,000. The question is, how does B know it amounts to $25,000 and not, say, $30,000? The person who knows is the lender, in this case the Personal Savings and Loan Association. If a real estate broker is handling the transaction one of three things will be requested from the lender, depending on the state. In some cases the Mortgagor's Information Letter will be requested. Essentially, this is a letter from the lender stating the amount due on the loan as of the date of closing. In some states the lender will sign and deliver a Mortgagee's Certificate of Reduction as shown in Figure 15-7.

Mortgagee's Certificate of Reduction

The undersigned, the owner and holder of the following mortgage and of the note (or bond) secured thereby:

Mortgage dated the 2nd day of April, 19____ made by A to the Personal Savings and Loan Association in the principal sum of $37,000 and recorded in the Office of the Clerk of the County of _____ in Liber 1348 of Mortgages page 87 and covering premises situated in the City of _____, County of _____, in consideration of the sum of One Dollar, the receipt whereof is hereby acknowledged, Does

Hereby certify that there is now due and owing upon said note or bond and mortgage the principal sum of Twenty-five thousand and 00/100 ($25,000) Dollars, with interest thereon at the rate of 7¾ percent per annum from the 15th day of March 19____ and that said mortgage is now a lien on premises covered thereby only to the extent of said last mentioned principal sum and interest.

Dated the 1st day of April, 19____.

In the presence of:

J. D. DeFoe

/s/ Albert King
Vice-President
Personal Savings and Loan Assn.

(Acknowledgement)

Figure
15-7 Mortgagee's Certificate of Reduction

In most states the broker or seller will request what is termed either an "assumption statement" or a "statement for assumption of loan." An example of the statement for assumption of loan is shown in Figure 15-8 on page 264.

Loan Assumption and Transfer Fees. As explained previously, the Contract for the Sale of Real Property will call for B to assume A's mortgage. The contract will also contain a statement regarding loan assumption or, as they are sometimes called, transfer fees. Typically, the buyer pays the fee, although sometimes it is paid by the seller. The contract will state: "The purchaser agrees to pay the assumption fee," or there may be a limitation in the contract, namely, "the purchaser

EAST LAKE SAVINGS

STATEMENT FOR ASSUMPTION OF LOAN

(Figures effective through..)

To: RE: .... Loan ....
                                 .... Rate ....

The following amounts must be paid before the assumption can be completed:

.... $.........................

....

Due Tax Reserve ....
Due Insurance Reserve.. ....

     TOTAL AMOUNT THAT MUST BE PAID BEFORE LOAN CAN BE ASSUMED .... $_____

Balances:

....

....

     Principal Balance............................... $...........................
         Tax Reserve .... $ ....
         Insurance Reserve.......... ....
         Total Reserves................................ $...........................

The monthly payment is:
     Principal and Interest................ $ ....
     Payment to Tax Reserve ....
     Payment to Insurance Reserve.......... ....
         Total Monthly Payment.......... $ _____

    Payments are due the 1st of each month and become delinquent after the 10th. Following the assumption of this loan, the next monthly payment will be due ....

    According to our records, taxes for the year.............were paid in the amount of $..

Insurance Information: (1)   (2)

	(1)	(2)
Company	....	....
Agent	....	....
Amount	.... Dwg.	.... Dwg.
	.... HHG	.... HHG
Structure	....	....
Type	....	....
Term	....	....
Expires	....	....
Premium	....	....

TO ASSIST US IN CHANGING OUR RECORDS, WILL YOU PLEASE COMPLETE THE FOLLOWING:

1. *Have present owners and purchasers sign enclosed assumption form.*
2. *Have present owners and their insurance agent execute enclosed insurance assignments.*
3. *Send us the above forms together with your check for any amounts due.*
4. *Record the Warranty Deed without delay. If there is an abstract, it should be certified and returned to us promptly.*

CUSTOMER SERVICE DEPARTMENT

Date:...   By ....

Figure 15-8   Statement for Assumption of Loan

agrees to pay the assumption fee up to $100, the balance being paid by the seller."

What then is the *assumption fee*? It is a fee charged by the lending institution, as they put it, to "change their records and otherwise process the records for the new debtor." Although the suggested amount for both FHA and VA is about $35, some institutions charge an assumption fee as a percentage of the sale price.

Tax Stamps

Whether property is sold by having the buyer assume the mortgage or with new financing, tax stamps are affixed to the deed. The underlying purpose of this is to give both the assessors and appraisers an idea of the value of the property. The rates are nominal. The methods of computing the tax vary from state to state. In some states it is based on the purchase price. In others, it is based on so many cents per thousand dollars of taxable consideration, which is the sales price minus existing loans and encumbrances.

Release from Liability

When a VA loan is assumed, the veteran seller can be released from liability in the note. For example, assume the veteran's home is sold and the mortgage to be assumed is $22,000. Under the normal assumption, the seller is still liable in the note. However, when the seller has a VA-guaranteed loan, a release can be obtained from a liability — $22,000 in this case — from the lender.

COMMERCIAL REAL ESTATE LOANS

In the area of relatively small loans, both the borrower's financial status and the property are carefully scrutinized. With larger loans most of the emphasis is placed on the property itself. The main question from the viewpoint of the lender is whether or not the property itself will support the loan. Consequently, most lenders in this situation will require a feasibility study, or as it is sometimes called, an economic feasibility study. For the most part, these studies are prepared by professional consultants. In general, the format is the same, but with varying emphasis, depending on the purpose of the study. For example, a developer might want to build a condominium with 300 units to sell at $65,000 per unit. The lender might want to know whether the area chosen for the proposed project can absorb 300 units and, more important, can it absorb 300 units at $65,000 per unit? The feasibility study might conclude that the area can absorb 300 units priced perhaps at $37,000, but not at $65,000.

In general, then, a study might cover the following minimum topics:

1. How many people live in the area? What is the population trend? What is the average family size? (In general, condominium units sell to families of small size.) What is the size breakdown of the population? This is very relevant in trying to forecast the demand for rental units. People below the age of 30 and over the age of 65 are more likely to rent apartment units than in the over 30 to 65 age group.
2. What is the income of the population in the area?
3. What sort of employment is in the area? Is it a "one industry town, or is it well balanced? Is employment fairly stable?
4. What sort of transportation is available?
5. What is the real estate market in terms of number of projects, dollar volume, average prices?
6. How many dwelling units or commercial units are being constructed? What is the nature of these units (i.e., single family, multi-family, or shopping centers, for example)?
7. How is land being used within the area? What are the planned areas? What is the average market value by type of use?
8. What sort of zoning regulations and land-use restrictions are there?
9. What are current rents in the area of the proposed project?
10. What are current vacancy rates in similar projects?
11. What are current interest rates? Is the project feasible, given current rates?
12. Is the area growing? What is the rate of land absorption by type of use? What is the direction of growth?
13. What is the competition?

The preceding list is by no means complete. A real estate professional will go into much more detail, for more detail will be demanded by a financial institution before the loan is granted.

PRO FORMA FINANCIAL PROJECTIONS

In addition to a feasibility study, lenders are interested in pro forma financial projections. Both are analyzed by lenders and must certainly be as realistic as possible.

For example, if a project totaling $1 million has land costs of $200,000 and improvement costs of $800,000, with a proposed 30-year loan at 9.8 percent, the pro forma financial projections would be as follows:

Capital Costs:

Building construction costs (includes non-construction items such as legal, architectural, engineering)	$ 800,000
Land	200,000
Total	$1,000,000

Estimated Income and Expenses:

Rents		$ 200,000
Less 5% for vacancy		10,000
Expected gross income		$ 190,000

Operating Expenses:

Real estate taxes	$15,000	
Fuel and energy	25,000	
Maintenance	15,000	
Management	15,000	
Insurance	3,000	
Miscellaneous	17,000	
Total		90,000
Net operating income		$ 100,000

Economic Value and Mortgage:

Net operating income	$ 100,000
Project economic value capitalized at 10%	1,000,000
Assume a 75% loan-to-value ratio; loan is	750,000

Debt Service and Cash Flow:

Net operating income	$ 100,000
Less debt service on $750,000 at 10.352%[1] constant (9.8% for 30 years)	77,640
Cash flow before taxes	$ 22,360

Equity and Yield:

Total costs	$1,000,000
Mortgage	750,000
Cash down payment	$ 250,000

$$\text{Yield on cash paid down} = \frac{\text{cash flow}}{\text{cash down}} = \frac{\$ 22,360}{\$250,000} = 8.94\%.$$

Analyzing the Financial Projections

The starting point for analyzing the figures in the financial projections is the effective gross income. The *effective gross income* is simply the projected rental income minus the vacancy costs. From the preceding figures:

Effective gross income	$190,000
Less operating expenses including taxes	90,000
Net income	$100,000

Now assume a 10 percent decrease in the effective gross income ($190,000 − $19,000 = $171,000). Then:

---

[1]The 10.352% is multiplied times the $750,000, which then equals $77,640.

Effective gross income	$171,000
Less operating expenses and taxes	90,000
Net income	$ 81,000

You can see by this example that a 10 percent decrease in effective gross income results in a 19 percent reduction in net income, or $100,000 − $81,000 = $19,000 ÷ $100,000 = 19% drop.

The seriousness of a miscalculation of effective gross income is readily seen when comparing it with a miscalculation in operating expenses. For example, if a 10 percent error in operating expenses occurs, then:

Effective gross income	$190,000
Less operating expenses and taxes now of	99,000
Net income	$ 91,000 (instead of $100,000)

Thus, while net income is reduced from $100,000 to $91,000 because of an error of 10 percent in the operating expenses, the percentage change in net income amounts to $100,000 − $91,000 = $9,000 ÷ $100,000 = 9% drop.

Margin and Break-Even

Margin can best be thought of as a cushion. It is the difference between 100 percent occupancy and the point at which either operating expenses and debt service must be met out of pocket or the property is threatened by foreclosure. In simple formula form, it is total charges to the investor (debt service and expenses) ÷ gross potential income = breakeven point. This subtracted from 100 percent = margin (allowable vacancy before the need for out-of-pocket payments).

For example, looking at the preceding problem:

Potential gross before vacancy	$200,000
Less operating expenses	90,000
Potential net	$110,000
Less debt service (interest plus principal)	77,640
	$ 32,360

Assume:	Debt service	$ 77,640
	Operating expenses	$ 90,000
	Total charges	$167,640

Thus: $\dfrac{\$167,640}{\$200,000}$ = 83.8% break-even point

Then: 100% − 83.8% = 16.2% margin (allowable vacancy or rental decrease before out-of-pocket funds are necessary).

LOAN CLOSING STATEMENT

Borrower...Date.............................
Seller..Agent...................................
Address of Property...

The following costs are based on information available at this time. This association is not a party to the sale of the property and figures related to sale are included hereon only as an accomodation.

Loan Charges	Loan Fee..	$_____	
	Attorney's Opinion................................		
	Credit Report......................................		
	Documentary Fee..................................		
	Appraisal Fee......................................		
	....		
Recording	Release—Deed of Trust........................		
	Warranty Deed....................................		
	Deed of Trust......................................		
Abstracting	Abstracting To Date.............................		
	Release—Deed of Trust........................		
	Warranty Deed....................................		
	Deed of Trust......................................		
	....		
	Abstract Certificate.............................		
Title Insurance	Owner's Policy....................................		
	Mortgagee's Policy..............................		
Survey.............................			
Taxes	Tax Certificate....................................		
	(General Taxes 19..........................)		
	Tax Reserve to 1st Payment (.............)		
	Special Assessments............................		
Insurance	$.........Expires.........Prem..............		
	Additional..		
	Insurance Reserve to 1st Payment (.......)		
Encumbrances	....		
	....		
.............Interest on $.................. to 1st Payment (.................)			
Total............		$	

Loan Amount $_____

Total Costs _____

Net Proceeds $_____

Approved and Copy Received

_____   _____

_____   _____

Figure
15-9 Loan Closing Statement

The concept of margin is important where second mortgages, or "gap" financing, is to be used in financing a sale. The payments on the second mortgage must be met, and the payments become a part of the debt service. In this case, the margin, or cushion, can disappear rapidly. For example, in the case preceding assume that the builder-developer decides to use a second mortgage to finance the loan. The debt service on the second mortgage is $17,000 per year. Then:

Potential gross	$200,000
Less operating expenses	90,000
	$110,000
Potential tax	$110,000
Less debt service	77,640
Cash flow before taxes	$32,360

Then assume:

Debt service on first mortgage	$ 77,640
Debt service on second mortgage	17,000
Operating expenses	90,000
	$184,640

Thus, $\dfrac{\$184,640}{\$200,000}$ = 92.3% break-even. Then, 100% − 92.3% = 7.7% margin (allowable vacancy).

Thus, with the addition of a second mortgage to the debt service of $17,000 per annum, a vacancy rate over 7.7% means out-of-pocket payments.

THE LOAN CLOSING STATEMENT

The Loan Closing Statement is not a seller's or buyer's closing statement; it is simply a statement by a financial institution or title insurance company concerning the disbursement of borrowed funds. For example, assume a loan of $200,000 (the sales price may have been $300,000 or whatever) has a loan fee of one percent. For purposes of simplification assume no other disbursements by the institution; then the net proceeds to the borrower would be $200,000 − $2,000 = $198,000.

A form commonly used for the loan closing statement is shown in Figure 15-9, page 269.

QUESTIONS FOR REVIEW

1. How does the Federal Home Loan Mortgage Corporation define stable monthly income?

2. What are the three items that lenders examine closely in terms of a borrower's credit reputation?
3. The Equal Credit Opportunity Act as amended beginning March 23, 1977, prohibits discrimination against credit applicants. What sort of discrimination does the Act prohibit?
4. Explain what is meant by sellers' discount points. Include the reasons why they exist.
5. How does the Farmers Home Administration define rural areas?
6. What is included in the lender's assumption statement? Why is it necessary?
7. Explain the concept of margin and break-even in commercial real estate lending. How is it useful?

PROBLEMS

1. A request is made for a residential mortgage loan. The potential borrower has a gross monthly income from primary base earnings of $1,000, and a secondary income, which is typical for the borrower's occupation, of $200 per month. Payments on the home mortgage loan are expected to be $300 per month. The borrower has additional installment loan commitments of $200 per month. Is the loan likely to be granted? What would be the situation if the installment loan commitments were $100 per month. Finally, would the loan be granted if the monthly housing expenses were $350 and there were no additional installment loan commitments?

2. A prospective home buyer wants an FHA-insured mortgage loan for $35,000. If the conventional loan rate is higher that the FHA rate, then "points" will be used to equate the two rates. Assume the equating rate is 3 points. How much will the seller receive?

3. Assume that you consider building a commercial real estate project. Land acquisition costs will be $300,000 with building construction costs estimated at $900,000. Rental income is expected to be $300,000 if fully occupied. Operating expenses are estimated at $120,000. A $1,000,000 mortgage loan is available on the project. The loan will be 30 years at 9 percent interest. What flexibility, in terms of allowable vacancy or rental declines, is available?

Mortgage Foreclosures, Foreclosure Sales, and Redemption

Chapter 16

In order for the mortgagee to foreclose, the mortgagor must first default. Basically a *default* occurs when the borrower has failed to fulfill one or a number of the contractual obligations agreed to in the original instrument. As pointed out in Chapter 2, this may mean failure to pay on the principal, interest, or insurance. It can also mean failure to keep the premises in good repair, failure to furnish an estoppel certificate, or any of the other mortgage covenants previously discussed.

Once default occurs, the acceleration clause in the mortgage and note provides that the entire balance of the indebtedness is due and payable. Foreclosure then becomes the next step.

FORECLOSURE AND REDEMPTION

Historically the English law simply held that there was no need for foreclosure. The courts enforced the strict written terms of the mortgage. Debts had to be paid if the borrower wished to retain rights in the land; failure to pay debts resulted in the termination of land rights.

About the middle of the 19th century, there developed a right of a borrower to redeem the land at a future date. This right was known as the *equity of redemption*. This concept worked a hardship on the borrower's creditor because the creditor might never receive the money owed. Consequently, a time limit was placed on the equity of redemption by a decree of foreclosure issued by a court. By virtue of the decree of foreclosure, the right to redeem was cut off unless the debt was paid by the time named in the decree. Today the time limit for re-deeming the property is set by statute in the various states.

The Foreclosure Process

While the methods of foreclosure may vary from state to state, the meaning of *foreclosure*, "to shut out, exclude, or bar," is still the same in all states. The actions beginning and ending the foreclosure process are discussed in the following paragraphs.

Commencing the Action. The summons and the complaint begin the foreclosure action. A copy of the summons and a copy of the complaint are served on the mortgagor and on any of the lienors deter-mined from the title search. If the mortgagor has a defense against the foreclosure, the mortgagor answers the complaint, thus raising an issue that is triable by jury. In some states a "master in chancery" hears the matter without a jury. In the event that the mortgagor de-faults (fails to answer the summons and complaint), the foreclosure proceeds to its conclusion.

At the time of the filing of the summons and the complaint, a *lis pendens* (notice of pendency of action) is filed with the clerk of the county in which the property is located. The *lis pendens* is a warning to anyone concerned with, or about to be concerned with, the mortgaged property that there is an action pending on it.

Completing the Action. If a default is made by the mortgagor, the mortgagee is entitled to a judgment which is filed with the court. This judgment directs that the property be sold at public auction, either by a referee appointed by the court or by the sheriff, or in states using a deed of trust by the public trustee. Notice of the sale is given to all defendants, and it is published in such newspapers as the judge or statute directs for the number of times required by law. At the sale bids are made on the property. If the mortgagee does not think the bids are high enough, the mortgagee may also bid on the property.

If there is a surplus of monies resulting from the sale, the other defendants in the foreclosure divide it according to the outcome of a surplus money action which establishes their priorities. If there is a deficiency, the mortgagee obtains a judgment for the deficiency on the note or bond against the mortgagor and seeks to collect that amount. In some states, Oregon and California, for example, it is not possible to obtain a deficiency judgment on a purchase money mortgage. Defi-ciency judgments have also been abolished in Nebraska and South Dakota.

Types of Foreclosure

Basically, there are four methods of foreclosure; some states use one or a combination of several. The methods are: (1) strict foreclosure, (2) foreclosure by sale in a judicial process, (3) foreclosure by exercise of power of sale, and (4) foreclosure by entry and possession.

Strict Foreclosure.[1] The procedure in a strict foreclosure is the same as that outlined in the preceding discussion on the foreclosure process. If there has been a default, the court determines if the mortgagee has a right to foreclose. In the absence of a valid defense a judgment is entered setting out the amount due. Generally the judgment will specify that the borrower has from two to six months within which to redeem by paying the amount due. Further, the judicial decree states that if the borrower fails to pay, then all persons claiming under this action shall be forever barred and foreclosed. The mortgagee becomes the sole owner of the property and there is no sale.

Because of the lack of sale and the value of the property not being taken into account, the courts regard the strict foreclosure as a harsh remedy.

Foreclosure by Sale in a Judicial Process.[2] The procedure used here is identical with that of a strict foreclosure *except* that in the judicial sale the land is sold at public auction. The theory behind this process is that the property may bring more than the indebtedness. If so, this excess is turned over to the borrower.

One of the basic steps taken by the mortgagee in pursuing this foreclosure action is to have a title search or abstract of title prepared. The *abstract of title* is a brief history of the particular property with which the action is concerned. The reason for having the abstract prepared is that presumably the mortgagee has the first lien on the property; in addition, it is necessary to bring in all other parties in interest, who generally are lienors junior to the mortgagee's lien. There may be a good possibility of the foreclosure cutting off the rights of the other lienors, and consequently they must have notice of this action. Otherwise, they will be deprived of their day in court. This violates the 14th Amendment of the Constitution; namely, a deprivation of property without due process. Furthermore, if any surplus monies result from a

---

[1]In theory the strict foreclosure can be used in many states; however, it is used only in Vermont and Connecticut.

[2]In Arizona, California, Florida, Idaho, Illinois, Iowa, Kansas, Montana, New Jersey, New Mexico, North Dakota, Oklahoma, and Oregon a foreclosure suit is the *only* method of foreclosing on a mortgage.

foreclosure sale, the junior lienors then have the requisite notice to commence a surplus money proceeding in order to establish their rights to the surplus monies.

Foreclosure by Exercise of Power of Sale. This method of foreclosure constitutes a foreclosure without recourse to the courts. Here the mortgage instrument provides for the remedy in case of default. The instrument spells out what shall be considered a default and confers power on the mortgagee (or public trustee in case of a trust deed) to sell the property after public notice at public auction.

Power of sale is the customary method in 21 states. All formalities and requirements must be meticulously observed; otherwise, the sale may be set aside by the courts.

Foreclosure by Entry and Possession. In four states (Maine, Massachusetts, New Hampshire, and Rhode Island) the mortgagee may foreclose by taking peaceful possession of the mortgaged premises and by remaining in possession for a specified time. The entry is made in the presence of witnesses and a certificate of that fact is filed. The mortgagor has a period in which to redeem the property. If the mortgagor does not redeem the property, the mortgagee receives good title to the premises. In a real sense this procedure comes fairly close to being a strict foreclosure.[3]

Other Aspects of Foreclosure

In addition to the preceding types of foreclosure methods, there are various other actions that may be taken in relation to a foreclosure.

Deficiency Judgments. The idea behind the deficiency judgment is quite simple. For example, suppose A owes a lender $20,000 on a mortgage. If the foreclosure sale of the property only brings $19,000, then A still owes the lender $1,000. Depending on the state, the lender either obtains a personal judgment against A at the time of the sale or the lender obtains a judgment for $1,000 after the sale.

The deficiency judgment came under attack during the depression of the 1930s. Many states passed legislation providing that the deficiency judgment be limited between the mortgage debt and the "fair market value." The fair market value is determined by qualified

---

[3]Foreclosure in Maine is quite unique. It is called foreclosure by advertisement and the property concerned is described and a statement made that the conditions of the mortgage were broken. Foreclosure is made by serving an attached copy of this notice on the borrower and recording the service. The mortgagor has one year within which to redeem, the period dating from the first publication.

appraisers. Thus, in the preceding example, if the fair market value was $20,000, then there was no deficiency judgment. In addition, some states outlawed the deficiency judgment (Nebraska and South Dakota) completely. Further, California, North Carolina, and Montana outlawed deficiency judgments on purchase money mortgages. For all practical purposes, the deficiency judgment has been abandoned in practice.

Deed in Lieu of Foreclosure. Because the cost of foreclosure is high, arrangements frequently are made between the lender and the borrower whereby the borrower gives the lender a deed to the property. Often a small amount is paid to the borrower in exchange for the deed. In such cases the lender exercises great care in the transaction because the courts will, upon proper legal action by the borrower, examine the transaction for fraud or undue influence on the part of the lender. Where a deed is given in lieu of foreclosure it is generally a quitclaim deed.

The Soldiers' and Sailors' Relief Act. With the advent of the draft immediately prior to World War II, it became apparent even to Congress that many draftees would suffer financial hardship. Consequently, in 1940 Congress passed the Soldiers' and Sailors' Relief Act. Among the things the act provided for were (1) a moritorium on foreclosure proceedings against members of the armed services, and (2) reduced mortgage payments against a mortgagor in the military.

In order for these provisions to apply, the default had to occur after induction into the service. Furthermore, service members were not entitled to this sort of lenience if they were career military personnel.

Foreclosure and Junior Lienors. As was previously pointed out, one of the reasons why interest rates on second mortgages are normally higher than on first mortgages is because the risk is greater. The foreclosure proceeding is the proof of the high risk pudding.

In the event of foreclosure there is either (1) a surplus over the amount owed to the first mortgagee, or (2) no surplus. If there happens to be a surplus, then after the indebtedness and costs are paid to the senior lienor the surplus is distributed according to the priority rights of the junior lienors. (Junior lienors, may, in addition to second mortgagees, consist of mechanics lienors, judgment creditors, and so forth.)

What happens if the surplus is insufficient to entirely satisfy the junior lienor? For example, suppose the property is sold for $15,000 and the first mortgage is $10,000. There is also a second mortgage of $8,000. The first mortgagee is paid $10,000, and the $5,000 is paid to the second mortgagee who may then sue the mortgagor for the $3,000 owed on the note that was signed in conjunction with the second mortgage.

Suppose there is no surplus. In this case the second mortgagee or any other junior lienors may sue on their claims, obtain a judgment, and hope to satisfy their debts out of the mortgagor's other assets, if any.

Sometimes junior lienors will pay off senior lienors and foreclose themselves, hoping again to recoup their funds.

Appointment of a Receiver. In Chapter 2 it was pointed out that many mortgages provide for the appointment of a receiver in the event of foreclosure. The purpose of the receiver is to protect the property from the time of the commencement of the foreclosure to its conclusion. For example, borrowers will frequently abandon the property once the foreclosure proceeding begins. In this case, the receiver will rent the property and apply this rent to the reduction of the mortgage debt. Often, too, there is a business involved in the foreclosure proceeding. In this case the receiver will run the business during the foreclosure process. The receiver's function is to keep a disgruntled mortgagor from running the business into the ground or from committing waste.

A Word About Land Contracts. As previously pointed out, the Land Contract, Installment Land Contract or Contract for Deed, as it is sometimes called, contains a forfeiture clause. Briefly, this provides that if the purchaser under a contract fails to make a payment, the seller who has retained title is entitled to possession. In addition to possession, the contract provides that the seller is entitled to all funds previously paid by the buyer.

Some states by statute prohibit a forfeiture, California for example. In other states, the courts will prevent a forfeiture, at a point. But at what point is often unclear. For example, suppose a parcel of property is sold under a $20,000 land contract and $500 is paid when the default occurs. Probably the courts will permit the seller to regain possession of the property and keep the $500. But suppose the buyer has paid $19,500 and then defaults. Obviously it would be unfair to permit the seller to keep the $19,500 and regain possession of a piece of property presumably worth $20,000 when only $500 is owed on it.

Some states have a so-called "period of grace" statute that requires the seller to give notice to a defaulting buyer. The statute then provides time in which to cure the default by performing the defaulted condition. Iowa and Minnesota provide a grace period of 30 days, North Dakota one year, and in Arizona the time depends on the buyer's equity. In Ohio the seller must foreclose on the contract if the buyer has an equity of 40 percent.

Consequently, in addition to cases where forfeitures are prohibited by statute the seller must foreclose on the contract. Basically, the procedure is the same as in the mortgage foreclosure.

A Word About Tax Liens. Even though a first mortgage is senior to other recorded liens, the real property tax takes precedence. Consequently, in the event of foreclosure the real property taxes are generally paid by the lender and added to the amount due in the foreclosure proceeding.

ALTERNATIVES TO FORECLOSURE

In many instances it is possible to work out an arrangement with the mortgagee if the mortgagor cannot meet the payments on a loan. Examples of such arrangements are the extension agreement, the consolidation and extension agreement, and the spreading agreement.

Extending the Mortgage

The situation may arise when a mortgage payment is soon to come due and the mortgagor cannot make the payment. If the payment is not made, the mortgage will either be foreclosed or remain open. In the latter case the mortgagee has the right to foreclose at any time. The mortgagee may, however, be willing to extend the time in which the mortgagor must pay off the mortgage indebtedness. This is done by means of an extension agreement.

The *extension agreement* is a device employed to extend the due date of the mortgage, and in some cases to modify the original bond or note and mortgage. This modification may take the form of a different interest rate, a different method of amortization, or both.

The instrument recites the parties, the old mortgage, and the amount presently due and payable. It also states that the mortgagor covenants to pay a certain rate of interest, which may or may not be the same rate as that called for by the original mortgage. If the mortgagor cannot make the payments due, this rate will probably be higher than the rate called for in the mortgage instrument itself. All of the covenants of the original mortgage instrument (the covenant to pay taxes, the warrant of title, etc.) are contained in the extension agreement. This instrument should also contain substantially the following clause:

> (The mortgagor) is now the owner and holder of the premises upon which said mortgage is a valid lien for the amount above

specified, with interest at the rate above set forth, and there are no defenses or offsets to said mortgage, or the debt which it secures.

This clause will prevent the mortgagor from later asserting any defenses that might have been valid prior to the date of the extension agreement.

A question arises concerning the position of the original signer of the bond or note in the event that the property is sold. The signer's liability depends upon what happens to property values. Before the signing of the extension agreement, the original mortgagor on the bond or note can demand that the mortgage be foreclosed. If property values are high, the mortgagor will know that a foreclosure will not result in a deficiency judgment. However, after an extension agreement is executed, the original mortgagor, or maker of the note, is not liable for any value that the property might lose after the signing of the extension agreement because the mortgagor is no longer a surety. For example, *A* obtains a mortgage from *B* in the amount of $15,000 on a parcel of property valued at $20,000. *A* sells the property to *X*, who takes it subject to the mortgage. Later the time for payment becomes due and the mortgage is open. The property has risen in value to $30,000. *A* can demand that *B* foreclose on the mortgage. *B* does not foreclose, but gives *X* an extension. Thus, *B* cannot foreclose. Later the value of the property declines to $10,000 and *X* defaults. *B* cannot collect the difference between $10,000 and $15,000 from *A* under the original note or bond signed by *A*.

Consolidation and Extension

A mortgagee, either by having made a first and second mortgage on a single piece of property or by having purchased two mortgages on one piece of property, may desire to create a single mortgage. This may be done by means of a *consolidation and extension agreement*. This arrangement would relieve the mortgagor of the burden of high amortization payments because the length of time for payment is usually extended, meaning that the monthly payments decline.

The instrument converts both of the mortgages into a single mortgage which becomes a first mortgage. It describes the property and recites the interest and payments to be made, and also the date when the final payment shall become due. The due date is included because, generally speaking, second mortgages have a due date prior to that of first mortgages; by this means the monies due under the previously existing mortgages become due and payable at the same time.

The form shown in Figure 16-1, pages 280–82, is a standard FNMA, FHLMC consolidation/extension agreement. It can be used as either a

CONSOLIDATION/EXTENSION AGREEMENT

THIS AGREEMENT is made this .... day of
................, 19 .... between ....
.... (herein "Borrower") and ....
....................., a corporation organized and existing under the laws of
........, whose address is ....
.... (herein "Lender").

WHEREAS, Lender is the holder of a mortgage made by ....
.... as Mortgagor, to ....
....
as Mortgagee, in the principal sum of ....
.... Dollars (U.S. $ ....), dated ....,
19...., and recorded in the Office of ....
of the County of ....,
State of New York, in Liber ...., of Section ....
of Mortgages, page ...., which mortgage is a lien on the property located in
the County of ....
................................., State of New York (herein "Property"),
which has the address of ....
(Street)

....
(City)   (State and Zip Code)

[and is more particularly described in Schedule "A" attached hereto and made a
part hereof]*, and was given to secure a note dated ....,
19...., on which there is now due, without defense or offset of any kind, the principal sum of ....
....
Dollars (U.S. $ ....), with interest thereon.

[Whereas, Lender is also the holder of a mortgage made by ....
.... as Mortgagor, to
....
as Mortgagee, in the principal sum of ....
.... Dollars (U.S. $ ....),
dated ....,19....,
intended to be recorded herewith, which mortgage is also a lien on the Property,
and was given to secure a note dated ....,
19 ...., on which there is now due, without defense or offset of any kind, the
principal sum of ....
.... Dollars (U.S. $ ....), with interest thereon.]**

[Whereas, Lender, the holder of the aforesaid mortgages and notes secured
thereby, and Borrower, the owner of [the fee interest]** [a leasehold estate]** in
the Property, desire to consolidate the aforesaid notes and consolidate and coordinate the liens of the aforesaid mortgages and modify the terms therein in the following manner; and]**

---

 *Delete bracketed material if not necessary for recordation.
 **Delete bracketed material if not applicable.

Figure
16-1 Consolidation/Extension Agreement (Continued)

WHEREAS, Lender, the holder of the aforesaid mortgage(s) and note(s) secured thereby, and Borrower, the owner of *[the fee interest]*** *[a leasehold estate]*** in the Property, desire to extend and modify the terms of payment of the principal sum, with interest thereon, in the following manner;

Now, THEREFORE, in consideration of the mutual promises of the parties and other valuable consideration, the parties hereto mutually covenant and agree as follows:

[1. *The liens of the aforesaid mortgages be and the same are consolidated and coordinated so that together they will constitute in law but one first mortgage and a single lien on the Property, securing the principal sum of* . . . . *Dollars (U.S. $* . . . . *), with interest thereon.*]**

2. The time of payment of said principal sum evidenced by the aforesaid note(s) secured by the aforesaid mortgage(s) [, *as consolidated,*]** is hereby extended until the . . . . day of . . . . , 19. . . . , and Borrower promise(s) to pay . . . . , or order, said principal sum of . . . . Dollars (U.S. $ . . . .), with interest on the unpaid principal balance from the date of this agreement, until paid, at the rate of . . . . percent per annum. Principal and interest shall be payable at . . . . or such other place as Lender may designate, in consecutive monthly installments of . . . . Dollars (U.S. $. . . . .), on the . . . . day of each month beginning . . . . , 19. . . . Such monthly installments shall continue until the entire indebtedness evidenced by this Agreement is fully paid, except that any remaining indebtedness, if not sooner paid, shall be due and payable on . . . . , 19. . . .

3. Borrower shall pay to Lender a late charge of . . . . percent of any monthly installment not received by Lender within . . . . days after the installment is due.

4. Any prepayment privilege heretofore reserved or granted is hereby cancelled, and the following shall be the sole rights of prepayment of the aforesaid note(s): Borrower may repay the principal amount outstanding in whole or in part. Lender may require that any partial prepayments (i) be made on the date monthly installments are due and (ii) be in the amount of that part of one or more monthly installments which would be applicable to principal. Any partial prepayment shall be applied against the principal amount outstanding and shall not postpone the due date of any subsequent monthly installments or change the amount of such installments, unless Lender shall otherwise agree in writing. If within twelve months from the date of this Agreement, Borrower make(s) any prepayments with money lent to Borrower by a lender other than the Lender hereof, Borrower shall pay Lender . . . . percent of the amount by which the sum of prepayments made in such twelve month period exceeds twenty percent of the original principal amount of this Agreement.

5. Borrower covenants and warrants that Borrower is the owner of *[the fee interest]*** *[a leasehold estate]*** in the Property.

**Figure
16-1**   Consolidation/Extension Agreement (Continued)

6. Borrower hereby assumes all obligations of the obligor and mortgagor, respectively, under the aforesaid mortgage(s) and note(s), as herein modified, and covenants to perform and comply with all of the terms, provisions, conditions and covenants of the aforesaid mortgage(s) and note(s), as herein modified. Except as herein modified, the terms, provisions, covenants and conditions of the aforesaid mortgage(s) and note(s) are hereby ratified and confirmed, with the same force and effect as if herein incorporated and set forth in full. *[If there should be any ambiguity or conflict between the terms, provisions, conditions and covenants of the aforesaid mortgages or notes, the terms, provisions, conditions and covenants of the mortgage and note most recently executed by Borrower shall govern.[** *

7. No termination, alteration or amendment of this Agreement shall be effective unless in writing and signed by the party sought to be charged or bound thereby, and this Agreement shall be binding upon the heirs, executors, administrators, successors and assigns of the parties hereto.

IN WITNESS WHEREOF, this Agreement has been duly executed by the parties hereto the day and year first above written.

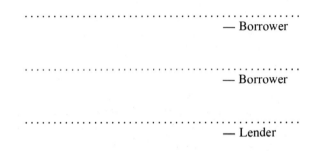

.... — Borrower

.... — Borrower

.... — Lender

**Delete bracketed material if not applicable.

(Acknowledgment)

Figure
16-1 Consolidation/Extension Agreement (Concluded)

consolidation agreement, an extension agreement, or both. It is designed to become a part of a mortgage to be sold to either FNMA or FHLMC.

Spreading Mortgages

The spreading agreement is used by a mortgagee to incorporate other lands owned by the mortgagor under the terms of an existing mortgage. The situation usually arises when the mortgagor requests an extension of a mortgage that is about to become an open mortgage or go into default. The mortgagee may feel that additional security is needed in order to extend the mortgage. If this is the case, the mortgagor will be asked to allow the mortgagee to cover with the existing mortgage additional lands owned by the mortgagor. This is done by means of the spreading agreement, which is acknowledged and recorded. In effect, it becomes a blanket mortgage.

The same form used for the consolidation and extension agreement may be quite readily adapted for the spreading agreement.

QUESTIONS FOR REVIEW

1. What type of circumstances may lead to foreclosure? Give examples.
2. What is the right of equity of redemption?
3. Name the four types of foreclosure processes.
4. What is the rationale behind the judicial sale of land as opposed to strict foreclosure? Or, vice versa, what is the legal limitation of a strict foreclosure?
5. What is the difference between foreclosure by a judicial sale and foreclosure by exercise of power of sale?
6. What is a deficiency judgment and what is its current status?
7. Explain the interpretations of the forfeiture clause in land contracts.
8. How is an extension agreement used? What are its usual provisions? How does it affect a seller of a home purchased subject to the existing mortgage?
9. Why might a lender request a spreading agreement?

PROBLEMS

1. Assume that foreclosure proceedings take place on a piece of property carrying a $30,000 first mortgage and a $10,000 second mortgage. If the property is sold for $35,000, what will happen to the claims of the first and second mortgagees?

2. Assume that two parcels of property are sold for $30,000 each under a land contract agreement. The purchaser of one parcel pays $1,000 per year for 2 years before defaulting on the land contract. The second purchaser pays $1,000 per year for 20 years before defaulting. What is likely to happen in these two situations?

Case

PINCKNEY STREET

In the summer of 1964, Charles Manning began searching for a small income-producing apartment building in which to invest. Mr. Manning had graduated that June from Harvard College, and he was working for a manaufacturing firm in Newton, Massachusetts. He had grown up in Boston and was attracted to the investment potential of the Back Bay-Beacon Hill area, which he considered the best residential section of downtown Boston. Many of his contemporaries were renting apartments or had purchased homes there, and he and his wife had attended many of their parties. He considered paying rent to someone else a waste of a capital building opportunity, since he was building up someone else's equity.

Mr. Manning wanted to gain experience in the real estate field, and build an equity base for future real estate investments. He hoped to increase his return by managing and operating his property on weekends and after normal working hours. Manning had only $10,000 of his own funds to invest, and he wanted to achieve maximum leverage for this equity. Although he had no real estate experience, he had a working knowledge of carpentry from three years of designing and building sets for Harvard's Hasty Pudding Show.

Beacon Hill Properties

Manning began to spend all his free evenings and weekends becoming familiar with the area. He obtained a copy of the U.S. Census

---

This case was prepared as the basis for class discussion rather than to illustrate either effective or ineffective handling of an administrative situation.

Copyright © 1968 by the President and Fellows of Harvard College. Reproduced by permission.

Tract, Boston, SMSA to check the demographic data on age breakdowns, education, employment, marital status, income, length of stay, and ethnic background of present Beacon Hill residents. Most were transient, and either single or young married couples. He checked maps for distances to the city's office, shopping, cultural, and entertainment centers, and found that Beacon Hill was close to all of these urban amenities.

He studied the real estate sections of newspapers for brokers' names and to get an idea of the types of offerings and range of prices available. He found that the Sunday papers had by far the largest real estate advertising sections. He answered some advertisements in order to meet real estate brokers, and learn about the available properties. He specifically attempted to visit those offices that did the most advertising (or that appeared to do the most business in the area). All were located around Charles Street, the major commercial street of Beacon Hill. He visited William Codman & Co., Wm. F. Otis, Inc., Street and Co., Hunneman and Co., and Chamberlain Real Estate. Normally, the brokers wanted to know the type of property in which he was interested, the amount of cash he had to invest, and whether he would live in the building.

Mr. Manning was quite disappointed in the offerings that were shown to him. Although the income and expense statements of one building on Myrtle Street had made it seem quite attractive the situation was very different when he actually visited the building. It was in a rundown state, and the apartments, occupied by groups of students, were in deplorable condition. The income statement of another property on Myrtle Street showed a 20% return on investment; however, this made no allowance for repairs, vacancies, or management expenses. When considered, these costs reduced the return to 3%. Rentals in another building seemed too high. When Mr. Manning spoke with one of the tenants, he found that the landlord had asked a rental of $180 per month for the apartment, but, when offered $150 per month, accepted on the condition that there be no rent the first two months and then $180 rent per month thereafter. This arrangement would enable the landlord to show a higher monthly income after the initial two months. Most properties sold for $80,000 and higher, and required an investment of more than $10,000. Mr. Manning expected to obtain a bank loan for part of the purchase price through a mortgage (a legal instrument by which property is hypothecated to secure the payment of a debt or obligation). But institutional lenders were prohibited by law from lending more than 60%–80% of the capitalized value of the property. Additional money might be raised by placing a second or junior mortgage on the property, but interest rates on this type of secondary financing were often 10%–15%, and the personal credit of the borrower was often required as additional collateral. However, sellers were often willing to take a purchase money mortgage as part of the purchase consideration of the property to ensure the sale. Nevertheless, having only $10,000 equity proved a major factor in limiting the buildings Mr. Manning might purchase.

Mr. Manning became discouraged. Although the real estate brokers were friendly, they never seemed to show him what he considered desirable properties. There rarely appeared to be an opportunity to create value by increasing rents or reducing expenses; if there were, the seller had already taken it into consideration in establishing his price. Mr. Manning soon learned that many of the brokers owned buildings themselves, and were thus, in a sense, competitors of their own customers. Few properties in the area were sold by the owners themselves. Usually they were listed with several brokers who competed to receive the 5% sales commission by selling the property to one of their customers. Since there was considerable investor interest in the area, and listings were rarely exclusive with one broker, the brokers had to act quickly on the desirable properties to make their commissions. Therefore, most of the brokers had a few favored customers to whom they gave the chance at purchasing the properties listed with the brokers. These customers usually had the necessary resources to act quickly to acquire the most desirable situations.

Factors Affecting Value

The same factors which caused Mr. Manning to want to purchase on Beacon Hill, had attracted many doctors, engineers, and businessmen also anxious to own real estate. As a result, the market values of most buildings on the Hill had doubled in the past ten years.

The area's location had considerable natural advantages. To the west was the Charles River; to the south was the Boston Public Gardens which led to Newbury Street, Boston's best shopping area; and to the east was the State House and Boston's financial district. The West End slums and the undesirable commercial activity of adjacent Scollay Square to the north, had restrained values in past years. This had been especially true of the northern slope of the Hill, which had become known as the "back slope" because of its many lower-rent rooming houses. Under Boston's urban redevelopment program, however, the West End slums were torn down and were to be replaced by Charles River Park, a luxury apartment house development. Scollay Square was to be replaced by a new Government Center. Construction had begun in both areas and the first buildings were already occupied.

As a result of this redevelopment, values all over Beacon Hill had increased, but most drastically on the back or north slope. Rentals there had increased approximately 30% as real estate operators began to buy and improve the properties; they now ranged from $150–$175 for one-bedroom apartments and $200–$250 for two-bedroom apartments. In spite of this, because most purchasers in this section were real estate operators who expected a high return on their investment, Mr. Manning felt there would be further growth, as investors who were accustomed to lower returns from properties on the lower section of the hill began to buy buildings on the north slope from these real estate operators.

The Massachusetts State Legislature had established the entire Beacon Hill area as an historic district, and set up a commission to preserve the character of the area. The approval of the commission had to be obtained for any changes to the exterior of a structure before the building department would issue a building permit. The commission would not permit the erection of any new buildings in the area. While this protected and enhanced the values of existing buildings, it provided a ceiling on land values, since land could not be reused for a different, more valuable purpose.

Mr. Manning knew that this activity and interest in the area, which had driven prices up and was proving a disadvantage in his attempts to buy a property, would turn into an advantage once he owned a building. He could expect a potential buyer of his property to use a conservative capitalization rate to determine value based upon his net income in appraising or capitalizing its value. Many investors in Beacon Hill appeared to be satisfied with an 8% net return, which meant that for every $1,000 net income, which remained after deducting all charges or costs from gross income, he could expect a buyer to pay $12,500. In an area of higher risk an investor might look for a 12.5% return, in which case $1,000 of income would be worth only $8,000.

All of these factors led Mr. Manning to believe that there was considerable safety in an investment in the area. There was little chance of depreciation for functional or economic causes. To obtain maximum capital appreciation, however, he would probably have to narrow his investment search to the "back slope" of Beacon Hill, where values had not risen as much as on the "lower slope." He also realized that he would have to purchase a building that would require considerable renovation. Otherwise, once the income had become established, the owner would ask a high selling price that would preclude much short-term growth in value. He had learned that he would have to act quickly if he did find an attractive opportunity. He would also have to check all figures given him carefully since few small buildings had audited financial statements and he could not rely solely on statements made by real estate brokers. Lastly, he knew that his $10,000 equity would limit him to acquiring a relatively small building.

Operating Expenses

Mr. Manning became familiar with some of the expenses involved in running property. Real estate taxes and mortgage carrying charges alone take up about two-thirds of income.

Real estate taxes are general property taxes based on the assessed value of a property. After calculating its expected revenues a city or locality will set a property tax rate which, when applied to the assessed value of the properties within its jurisdiction, will result in the additional revenues it needs for schools, roads, sewers, and police and fire protection. In 1950 property taxes on a national basis accounted for 52.1% of all local revenue. In Boston, the figure was much higher because the city had no other major source of revenue, such as a sales or income tax. To balance the rising costs of providing municipal services, Boston had to increase its assessments on existing properties and raise its overall tax rate. Technically, all properties in Boston were supposed to be assessed at full market value, but this was impractical; with the Boston tax rate in 1963 at $96 per $1,000 of assessment, if a $40,000 house were assessed at full value, the tax bill would be $3,840, an amount so large that few individuals would build homes in Boston.

Many cities assess on a percentage of value basis rather than full market price. For example, New York City has a rate of $45.20 per $1,000 of assessed valuation, and the city assesses property at approximately 80% of value. A $40,000 house would then, according to the New York City formula, pay a tax bill of $1,444.

Boston had no established percent of value formula for assessments. Mr. Manning had heard that the lowest percentage assessment to value ratios actually occurred in lower and middle income areas, where there were a great many registered voters, while in Beacon Hill, with a high number of absentee landlords and nonvoting transient tenants, the assessment to value ratio was much higher. This resulted in most landlords paying from 25% to 30% of the rental income in property taxes. Most communities around Boston assess income property so that the tax bill is from 15% to 20% of the property's income. Mr. Manning had also heard that if he purchased a property with a low valuation on which the taxes to income ratio was below that of similar properties, the assessors would very likely revalue his property upwards based upon purchase price. He had been shown a property on

Chestnut Street at a purchase price of $60,000 with a rent roll of $10,000. The return on his $10,000 investment was shown as $2,000, after an estimated real estate tax expense of $1,200, based on the present $12,000 assessment. Mr. Manning thought that with a change of ownership a revaluation of the building to $24,000 would be likely, which would reduce his return to $800.

The other major operating expense would be mortgage servicing costs. The amount of the mortgage, he had discovered, would determine the amount of equity required. The payment terms determined by the interest rate charged and the length of the mortgage would also affect the net income available for return on this equity. As an example, a $10,000 mortgage with interest charged on the unpaid balance at 6% for a term of 20 years, would result in an annual cost of 8.62%, while a mortgage of the same amount at the same interest rate for a term of 15 years would cost 10.16% annually. Thus, the terms of a mortgage, depending upon the particular lender's opinion of the property, would considerably affect the owner's cash return on his investment. Because of its stability Beacon Hill was considered a desirable area by most local mortgage bankers, and there was usually an ample supply of first mortgage funds available from savings banks all over greater Boston for loans in this area. Mortgage funds for Roxbury, on the other hand were scarce.

Often a buyer and seller could come to an agreement on a sale by the seller's taking back as secondary financing a purchase money second mortgage at the time of sale, thereby reducing the cash that the buyer would have to pay and increasing, if the interest rate were low, the buyer's return on investment. Therefore, to know the sales price of a property without knowing the terms of the sale could be misleading.

Most of the other operating expense could be estimated with reasonable accuracy based upon comparative local data. Mr. Manning learned that a rule-of-thumb figure of $100 to $125 per room per year was used with a one-bedroom apartment counting as 3 rooms and a two-bedroom apartment as 4 rooms. Included in this figure were heat, light, water, insurance and janitor service expenses. In addition, the management fees charged by real estate firms were usually 5%. Also, an expense figure of 10% was normally carried to allow for repairs and vacancies; this figure could vary considerably depending upon the quality and condition of the building, the rents charged and the services provided for these rents, and the particular market conditions and practices. As an example, in Harvard Square where rental demand was very high, many landlords did little repair work on older buildings. In new buildings, however, where the rents were higher and the competition more intense, the landlords had to keep the property in better repair. In Beacon Hill, the 10% figure was normally used as an estimate, and then adjusted to allow for special circumstances.

19 Pinckney Street

In December of 1964, Mr. Manning learned of a 4-unit apartment house on Beacon Hill that was for sale. A local broker with whom he was friendly had called to tell him that 19 Pinckney Street had just come on the market, and that if he acted quickly, he might be able to outbid several real estate brokers who were interested in the property. Mr. Manning knew that brokers always attempted to convey a sense of urgency, but since he was aware that desirable properties did sell quickly, he decided to investigate the property at once.

The property was located on the "back slope of the Hill" in an improving neighborhood. The removal of the slums that had abutted this section had resulted in some increase in property values. Mr. Manning expected still greater increases when the construction presently in progress on the former slum land was completed. The property was located in the middle of the block, and was set back 100 feet from the road, which would afford an opportunity for creating an attractive entranceway and garden. The property had been built in the mid-1800's, probably as a middle-income town house. After being used as a rooming house for 20 years it had been gutted by a fire in 1963. Only the structural shell remained. An architect had purchased the shell for $32,000, but the combination of the purchase price and the cost of renovation, already $12,000 with the work only half completed, had proved greater than he had expected, and had forced him to discontinue the renovation and place the property on the market. Mr. Manning felt that the architect's plans for renovation were in good taste and that thus far had been done well. Each of the first three floors was to have one two-bedroom apartment while the fourth floor would have a large one-bedroom apartment. For the first time, Mr. Manning felt that he had seen a property that met his investment criteria. The property had profit potential; it was aesthetically desirable, in the area he wanted, and, with an asking price of $45,500, was within his price range.

Mr. Manning was told that the $45,500 price was firm because considerable interest had already been shown in the property. A contractor to whom Mr. Manning was referred estimated that it would cost approximately $10,000 to complete the architect's plans, which would result in a total cost of $55,500.

Mr. Manning prepared an income and expense statement to see whether the net income of the property would justify its price (see

Exhibit 1). He figured that each of the three two-bedroom apartments could be rented at $225 per month, and the top floor one-bedroom apartment at $200 per month. This would total $10,500 annually. From this figure, he subtracted a 5% vacancy allowance, which would represent two apartments sitting vacant for slightly more than a month. There was the additional possibility that if he did not rent the apartments himself, he would have to pay a broker's commission, set by the Boston Real Estate Board at 5% of the apartment rental. The broker, licensed by the State, receives this commission for showing the property to prospective tenants, for bringing the tenants and landlord together, and helping to negotiate the contract between them.

Mr. Manning estimated real estate taxes at 25% of the net income, or $2,500. This represented a tax rate of $96 per $1,000 of assessment on an assessed value of $26,000, which was approximately 50% of market value, and $11,000 above the present $15,000 assessment. He obtained a quotation of $250 annual premium from his real estate broker's firm for a package insurance policy providing protection against fire, extended coverage perils, public liability, loss of rents, and boiler explosion. The tenants would pay the electric bills for their own apartments, but the landlord would pay the bill for the public areas. A janitor would keep the public halls clean, change the light bulbs, and take out the trash. There were several services around Beacon Hill that performed this function for an annual fee of $300. Mr. Manning had expected to do some of the repair work and all of the management work himself to increase his cash return, but his broker told him that since potential mortgage lenders or future purchasers would include these costs in their "setups," Mr. Manning would have to do so, too. Also, if he should leave the area, he would have to hire outside firms to perform these services.

His projections showed net before financing of $5,350, without any allowance for the work he would do himself. This provided a 9.7% cash return on investment based on a free and clear ownership of the property, that is, with no encumbrances or mortgages on it.

Mr. Manning was very pleased. He told his wife that he had found a building that would be just right with its skylights, beamed ceiling, and natural brick walls, the top floor apartment was just what they wanted to live in. They could live "rent free," while making money by doing their own managing and renting. They could take out the trash and clean the halls themselves. Mr. Manning felt that although outside management would be more experienced, it wouldn't have as much interest as he would in managing the property well. Rent from the other apartments would pay the other expenses, and he would gain real estate experience.

His wife said that while the apartment seemed very nice, she was not sure she liked the idea of living in a building they owned. She would get complaints while he was at work. Also, she thought there might be a problem in doing business with their neighbors if they got friendly with them. She doubted that they would be able to charge maximum rents or raise rents.

The real estate broker questioned his decision to act as his own general contractor because of his lack of experience and time. He said that it was difficult, particularly on a part-time basis, to coordinate several subcontractors who never showed up when they said they would. The work might take longer than Mr. Manning anticipated. Also, the Boston Building Department had a maze of rules and many inspectors; his renovation could be quite costly if he were forced to comply exactly with every regulation. Experienced contractors usually found ways of getting around these requirements. He would have to be careful however, to minimize changes and avoid extras once the job had been started, since most subcontractors would charge a premium for extras, because it would be too late to get competitive quotes on small amounts of work.

Mr. Manning replied that any remodeling job would involve changes in adapting to field conditions. To avoid the extra charges by subcontractors was one of the reasons he wanted to do the work himself. In giving him a firm bid, an outside contractor would carry a heavy contingency allowance. Certainly the contractor who gave him the $10,000 estimate to complete the renovation must have carried at least $1,000 for profit. Mr. Manning reasoned that he had at least that $1,000 to spend before his lesson in remodeling began to cost him money.

Mortgage Financing

Mr. Manning then went to see Mr. Smith, the mortgage officer of the savings bank who had recently given the original $40,000 loan on the building. Mr. Smith told him that the existing mortgage was on a constant payment basis, which meant that the payments, including amortization and interest, remained the same throughout the entire term of the loan, but that the portion applicable to interest became less as the balance of the mortgage loan decreased. Correspondingly, the portion applicable to amortization increased. This particular loan was for a term of 20 years with 6% interest paid on the outstanding balance, resulting in an annual cost of $3,448 or 8.62%. The mortgage payments with a payment of one-twelfth of the estimated real estate taxes were made to the bank monthly. The bank also kept two months' real estate taxes in escrow as additional security. The banker explained that the loan could be paid off at any time, but that if it were paid off during the first five years of the loan the bank would charge a prepayment penalty of 2% of the unpaid balance.

Mr. Manning explained his plans for finishing the work and gave Mr. Smith his projected income and expense statements for the property. (See Exhibit 1.) He asked whether the bank would increase its mortgage to $46,000. He explained that he might live in the building, manage it, and do some of the work himself, which would create more cash flow to serve the debt. The banker replied that he could not take this extra income into account in making his decision, since the bank always had to consider a loan in light of the costs the bank would incur if it had to foreclose and run the property itself. (A foreclosure occurs when property pledged as security for a loan is sold to pay the debt in the event of default in payment or terms.)

Mr. Smith noticed that Mr. Manning's rental figures were $1,200 higher than those originally submitted by the present owner. At that time the bank had valued the property at $50,000 and given an 80% mortgage, the maximum permitted by law. He asked whether Mr. Manning knew his total costs. Mr. Manning told him of the contractor's $10,000 bid. Mr. Smith told him that he should also consider carrying costs while the renovation work was going on. The bank might waive principal payments on the mortgage for six months during construction, but interest of $1,200 on the $40,000 must be paid, as well as real estate taxes of $750, assuming the $15,000 assessment would remain in effect until the renovation was complete. In addition, he still had to pay for six months' insurance at $125 and heat and electricity at $225. These costs totalled $2,300. There was also the two-month real estate tax escrow of $250, which was a cash outlay even though it would eventually be returned to him.

Mr. Manning could assume the architect's existing mortgage, thus eliminating the need for new documents and a new title search by the bank's lawyer. (Assumption for a mortgage occurs when, in purchasing a property, the buyer assumes liability for payment of an existing note secured by a mortgage on the property.) Mr. Smith doubted that the bank would be interested in increasing its loan at this time since it was not certain that Mr. Manning could get the increased rentals. However, Mr. Smith added that if the income level was increased when the building became rented and seasoned the bank might re-examine his request.

Mr. Manning next visited Mr. Harris, the mortgage loan officer at another local savings bank to find out whether his bank would be interested in a $46,000 mortgage. Mr. Manning showed him the income and expense projections, told him his costs, and explained his plans. Mr. Harris said that because of the 80% restriction, his bank would have to appraise the property at $57,500 to justify a $46,000 loan. Appraisals, he told Mr. Manning, could be made on the basis of replacement cost, capitalized income, or market value based on recent comparable sales. He said that his bank preferred the income approach as the most realistic. Taking a capitalization rate of 9% on the $5,350 projected net income, he arrived at an assessed value of $59,450. Mr. Harris considered it likely that based on this appraisal he could justify a $46,000 mortgage at 6% interest for 20 years. He believed that the $5,350 annual net income should be adequate to carry the $3,965 financing charge. He added that he was familiar with the area and considered Mr. Manning's projected figures realistic, although he would have to see the property to be certain of this.

He questioned Mr. Manning about his current personal income. Mr. Manning told him that his present salary was $10,000 per year. Mr. Harris said he would require credit references and certain other information about Mr. Manning since Mr. Manning would be signing the note personally as additional protection to the bank against loss. Mr. Manning asked why he would have to become personally liable since there was ample value in the property. He knew that his friends who had bought brownstones in New York had not assumed any personal liability. Mr. Smith said that this was the policy of virtually all savings banks in the Boston area for smaller buildings, especially when the loan to value ratio was as high as 80%. If Mr. Manning had confidence in the building, he should not worry. Each year the mortgage and his liability declined as a portion of the mortgage loan was amortized.

Mr. Manning asked whether there were other costs such as closing the mortgage, that he would have to assume. Mr. Harris replied that Mr. Manning would be responsible for legal and title expenses at closing, amounting to about $300, which would cover the cost of the bank's lawyer and his own attorney's fee. (The bank's lawyer is responsible for certifying to the bank that the owner has a valid fee simple ownership in the property, which means that the owner has the right to dispose of it, pledge it, or pass it on to his heirs as he sees fit. Also, he ascertains that there are no liens on the property senior to the bank's interest. The seniority of a lien depends on the date it was recorded at the County Registry of Deeds Office. When a lien is paid off a discharge is put on record. There are some liens that are a matter of record that a bank will accept as senior to its position. These include zoning or use regulations, building codes, party wall agreements, where two buildings share the same wall, or certain easements where one party has specific rights or privileges on the land of the other. The certification of title is often done through the issuance of an insurance policy written by a title insurance company at a one time cost paid by the borrower or purchaser.)

Legal Advice

Mr. Manning then consulted Mr. Guber, his family's attorney about the whole transaction. Mr. Manning was disturbed about the bank's requirement that he sign the mortgage note personally. His attorney told him that he did not want to minimize the risk, but that this was a customary bank practice in making small mortgage loans in Massachusetts, where banks were often more conservative than in other areas of the country.

Mr. Manning inquired about alternate methods for raising the extra $6,000. Mr. Guber believed that secondary financing could be obtained, but at an interest rate of 10% and only with a personal endorsement. The seller might take back a purchase money second mortgage, but again, Mr. Manning would probably have to sign the note personally and repay the entire loan over a 3- to 5-year period. In addition, if the demand for the property were as strong as Mr. Manning indicated, an all-cash offer might have a better chance of winning the property than one contingent upon a purchase money second mortgage.

Mr. Manning asked whether he would not be taking a big risk in making an offer for the property without having his financing secured. Mr. Guber explained that while he would have to submit a written offer for the property together with a deposit to be held by the real estate broker, he could make his offer contingent upon his being permitted to assume the seller's mortgage. This would give him some safety, while still permitting him to attempt to find a higher mortgage. If Mr. Manning's offer were accepted, a purchase and sales contract would be signed, based on a standard Boston Real Estate Board form. (See Exhibit 2.) Mr. Guber said that in case of forfeiture as a result of the buyer's failure to perform, the sales deposit, normally 5%–10% of the purchase price, would be kept by the seller as liquidated damages. Therefore, Mr. Manning's risk would be limited to about $2,500.

Also, if the seller could not deliver a quit-claim deed, relinquishing any interest he held in the property and giving a clear title to the buyer, the buyer would be entitled to a refund of his deposit.

Mr. Guber then asked Mr. Manning whether he had adequate funds to complete the project even with a $46,000 mortgage. The asking price for the property was $45,500; the remodeling cost $10,000; carrying costs during construction $2,300; closing costs $400; and escrow funds $250. These costs totalled $58,450. The $46,000 mortgage or mortgages and his $10,000 equity would still leave him $2,450 short. Mr. Manning replied that he planned to save money by acting as his own general contractor, and he hoped to remodel and rent the property in four rather than six months. A $46,000 first mortgage with an annual carrying charge of $3,965, although requiring a personal guarantee, would give him leverage, increasing his cash return on $10,000 from the 9.7% return based on all-cash basis to 13.9%. In addition, he would be amortizing a mortgage. The return would be even greater if he lived in the building and managed it himself.

The lawyer said that Mr. Manning's anlysis seemed reasonable, but it did not put a dollar value on Mr. Manning's time. He wondered whether this should be considered. Also, he wanted Mr. Manning to realize the seriousness of this time commitment since his full-time job was still his prime responsibility. Finally, he asked him to consider carefully the amount of the offer he was submitting and the risks involved.

Exhibit 1
PINCKNEY STREET

Income

1st floor	$225/month
2nd floor	225/month
3rd floor	225/month
4th floor	200/month
	$875 × 12 = $10,500
Allowance for Vacancies	500
	$10,000

Operating Expenses

Real Estate Taxes	$2,500
Heat	400
Electricity	100
Water	100
Insurance	250
Janitor	300
Repairs @ 5%	500
Management @ 5%	500
	$4,650
Net Before Financing (as if free and clear)	$5,350

Exhibit 2

PURCHASE AND SALE AGREEMENT

page 1

This   day of   19

1. PARTIES
(fill in)

hereinafter called the SELLER, agrees to SELL and

hereinafter called the BUYER or PURCHASER, agrees to BUY, upon the terms hereinafter set forth, the following described premises:

2. DESCRIPTION

(fill in and include title reference)

3. BUILDINGS, STRUCTURES, IMPROVEMENTS, FIXTURES

(fill in or delete)

Included in the sale as a part of said premises are the buildings, structures, and improvements now thereon, and the fixtures belonging to the SELLER and used in connection therewith including, if any, all venetian blinds, window shades, screens, screen doors, storm windows and doors, awnings, shutters, furnaces, heaters, heating equipment, stoves, ranges, oil and gas burners and fixtures appurtenant thereto, hot water heaters, plumbing and bathroom fixtures, electric and other lighting fixtures, mantels, outside television antennas, fences, gates, trees, shrubs, plants, and, if built in, air conditioning equipment, ventilators, garbage disposers, dishwashers, washing machines and driers, and but excluding

4. TITLE DEED
(fill in)
* *Include here by specific reference any restrictions, easements, rights and obligations in party walls not included in (b), leases, municipal and other liens, other encumbrances, and make provision to protect SELLER against BUYER'S breach of SELLER'S covenants in leases, where necessary.*

Said premises are to be conveyed by a good and sufficient deed running to the BUYER, or to the nominee designated by the BUYER by written notice to the SELLER at least seven days before the deed is to be delivered as herein provided, and said deed shall convey a good and clear record and marketable title thereto, free from encumbrances, except

(a) Provisions of existing building and zoning laws;

(b) Existing rights and obligations in party walls which are not the subject of written agrement;

(c) Such taxes for the then current year as are not due and payable on the date of the delivery of such deed;

(d) Any liens for municipal betterments assessed after the date of this agreement;

*(e)

5. PLANS

If said deed refers to a plan necessary to be recorded therewith the SELLER shall deliver such plan with the deed in form adequate for recording or registration.

6. REGISTERED TITLE

In addition to the foregoing, if the title to said premises is registered, said deed shall be in form sufficient to entitle the BUYER to a Certificate of Title of said premises, and the SELLER shall deliver with deed all instruments, if any, necessary to enable the BUYER to obtain such Certificate of Title.

7. **PURCHASE PRICE**
   (fill in); space is al-
   lowed to write out
   the amounts if de-
   sired
   (provide for pay-
   ment by certified or
   Bank's Check ac-
   ceptable to the
   SELLER, if re-
   quired)

The agreed purchase price for said premises is

                                                    dollars, of which

$ have been paid as a deposit this day and

$ are to be paid at the time of delivery of the deed in cash.

$
   _____

$ *TOTAL*

8. **TIME FOR**
   PERFORMANCE;
   DELIVERY OF
   DEED *(fill in)*

Such deed is to be delivered at   o'clock   M. on the
day of   19   , at the
Registry of Deeds, unless otherwise agreed upon in
writing. It is agreed that time is of the essence of this agreement.

9. **POSSESSION** and
   CONDITION of
   PREMISES.
   (attach list of excep-
   tions, if any)

Full possession of said premises free of all tenants and occupants, except as
herein provided, is to be delivered at the time of the delivery of the deed, said
premises to be then (a) in the same condition as they now are, reasonable use
and wear thereof excepted, and (b) not in violation of said building and zoning
laws, and (c) in compliance with the provisions of any instrument referred to in
clause 4 hereof.

10. **EXTENSION TO**
    PERFECT TITLE
    OR MAKE
    PREMISES
    CONFORM
    (Change period of
    time if desired.)

If the SELLER shall be unable to give title or to make conveyance, or to
deliver possession of the premises, all as herein stipulated, or if at the time of
the delivery of the deed the premises do not conform with the provisions
hereof, then any payments made under this agreement shall be refunded and
all other obligations of the parties hereto shall cease and this agreement shall
be void and without recourse to the parties hereto, unless the SELLER elects
to use reasonable efforts to remove any defects in title, or to deliver possession as provided herein, or to make the said premises conform to the provisions hereof, as the case may be, in which even the SELLER shall give written notice thereof to the BUYER at or before the time for performance
hereunder, and thereupon the time for performance hereof shall be extended
for a period of thirty   days.

11. **FAILURE TO**
    PERFECT TITLE
    OR MAKE
    PREMISES
    CONFORM,etc.

If at the expiration of the extended time the SELLER shall have failed so to
remove any defects in title, deliver posession, or make the premises conform,
as the case may be, all as herein agreed, or if at any time during the period of
this agreement or any extension thereof, the holder of a mortgage on said
premises shall refuse to permit the insurance proceeds, if any, to be used for
such purposes, then, at the BUYER'S option, any payments made under this
agreement shall be forthwith refunded and all other obligations of all parties
hereto shall cease and this agreement shall be void without recourse to the
parties hereto.

12. **BUYER'S**
    ELECTION TO
    ACCEPT TITLE

The BUYER shall have the election, at either the original or any extended
time for performance, to accept such title as the SELLER can deliver to the
said premises in their then condition and to pay therefor the purchase price
without deduction, in which case the SELLER shall convey such title, except
that in the event of such conveyance in accord with the provisions of this
clause, if the said premises shall have been damaged by fire or casualty insured
against, then the SELLER shall, unless the SELLER has previously restored
the premises to their former condition, either
   (a) pay over or assign to the BUYER, on delivery of the deed, all amounts
       recovered or recoverable on account of such insurance, less any

amounts reasonably expended by the SELLER for any partial restoration, or

(b) if a holder of a mortgage on said premises shall not permit the insurance proceeds or a part thereof to be used to restore the said premises to their former condition or to be so paid over or assigned, give to the BUYER a credit against the purchase price, on delivery of the deed, equal to said amounts so recovered or recoverable and retained by the holder of the said mortgage less any amounts reasonably expended by the SELLER for any partial restoration.

13. ACCEPTANCE OF DEED

The acceptance of a deed by the BUYER or his nominee as the case may be, shall be deemed to be a full performance and discharge of every agreement and obligation herein contained or expressed, except such as are, by the terms hereof, to be performed after the delivery of said deed.

14. USE OF PURCHASE MONEY TO CLEAR TITLE

To enable the SELLER to make conveyance as herein provided, the BUYER may, at the time of delivery of the deed, use the purchase money or any portion thereof to clear the title of any or all encumbrances or interests, provided that all instruments so procured are recorded simultaneously with the delivery of said deed.

15. INSURANCE
* Insert amount (list additional types of insurance and amounts as agreed)

Until the delivery of the deed, the SELLER shall maintain insurance on said premises as follows:

Type of Insurance	Amount of Coverage
(a) Fire	* $
(b) Extended coverage	*
(c)	

16. ASSIGNMENT OF INSURANCE
(delete entire clause if insurance is not to be assigned)

Unless otherwise notified in writing by the BUYER at least seven   days before the time for delivery of the deed, and unless prevented from doing so by the refusal of the insurance company(s) involved to issue the same, the SELLER shall assign such insurance and deliver binders therefor in proper form to the BUYER at the time for performance of this agreement. In the event of refusal by the insurance company(s) to issue the same, the SELLER shall give notice thereof to the buyer at least two   business days before the time for performance of this agreement.

17. ADJUSTMENTS
(list operating expenses, if any, or attach schedule)

Collected rents, mortgage interest, prepaid premiums on insurance if assigned as herein provided, water and sewer use charges, operating expenses (if any) according to the schedule attached hereto or set forth below, and taxes for the then current year, shall be appointed and fuel value shall be adjusted, as of the day of performance of this agreement   and the net amount thereof shall be added to or deducted from, as the case may be, the purchase price payable by the BUYER at the time of delivery of the deed. Uncollected rents for the current rental period shall be apportioned if and when collected by either party.

18. ADJUSTMENT OF UNASSESSED AND ABATED TAXES

If the amount of said taxes is not known at the time of the delivery of the deed, they shall be apportioned on the basis of the taxes assessed for the preceding year, with a reapportionment as soon as the new tax rate and valuation can be ascertained; and, if the taxes which are to be apportioned shall thereafter be reduced by abatement, the amount of such abatement, less the reasonable cost of obtaining the same, shall be apportioned between the parties, provided that neither party shall be obligated to institute or prosecute proceedings for an abatement unless herein otherwise agreed.

19. BROKER'S
COMMISSION
(fill in space)

A commission, according to the present schedule of commission rates recommended by the Greater Boston Real Estate Board, is to be paid by the SELLER to

the Broker(s) herein, but if the SELLER pursuant to the terms of clause 22 hereof retains the deposits made hereunder by the BUYER, said Broker(s) shall be entitled to receive from the SELLER an amount equal to one-half the amount so retained or an amount equal to the commission according to such schedule for this transaction, whichever is the lesser.

20. BROKER(S)
WARRANTY
(fill in name)

The Broker(s) named herein
warrant(s) that he (they) is (are) duly licensed as such by the Commonwealth of Massachusetts.

21. DEPOSIT
(fill in, or delete reference to broker(s) if SELLER holds deposit)

All deposits made hereunder shall be held by the broker(s)
                        as agent for the SELLER, subject to the terms of this agreement and shall be duly accounted for at the time for performance of this agreement.

22. BUYER'S
DEFAULT;
DAMAGES

If the BUYER shall fail to fulfill the BUYER'S agreements herein, all deposits made hereunder by the BUYER shall be retained by the SELLER as liquidated damages unless within thirty days after the time for performance of this agreement or any extension hereof, the SELLER otherwise notifies the BUYER in writing.

23. VETERANS
FINANCING
(fill in blank spaces or delete entire clause)

The BUYER, being a Veteran, intends to use his so-called Veterans Administration loan benefits to finance the purchase of said premises; it is understood and agreed that if on or before
                        a Certificate of Reasonable Value for not less than the purchase price shall not be issued by the Veterans Administration Loan Guaranty Division and if an accredited lending institution shall not approve and accept a mortgage loan of $, payable in   years at a rate of interest not to exceed   % per year, based upon the aforesaid Certificate of Reasonable Value, then all payments hereunder by the BUYER shall be forthwith refunded and all other obligations of all parties hereto shall cease and this agreement shall be void and without recourse to the parties hereto.

24. F.H.A.
FINANCING
(fill in blank spaces or delete Clauses 24 & 25)

The BUYER agrees to apply promptly for a U.S. Government Federal Housing Administration insured loan for not less than $, payable in   years at a rate of interest not to exceed   % per year, and if he shall not be able to obtain a firm commitment for such loan on or before   , then at the BUYER'S option, all payments hereunder by the BUYER shall be forthwith refunded and all other obligations of all parties hereto shall cease and this agreement shall be void and without recourse to the parties hereto.

25. F.H.A.
APPRAISAL
STATEMENT
(fill in amount or delete Clauses 25 & 24)

(the wording of this clause is required verbatim by F.H.A. Rules & Regulations)

It is expressly agreed that, notwithstanding any other provisions of this contract, the PURCHASER shall not be obligated to complete the purchase of the property described herein or to incur any penalty by forfeiture of earnest money deposits or otherwise, unless the SELLER has delivered to the PURCHASER a written statement issued by the Federal Housing Commissioner setting forth the appraised value of the property for mortgage insurance purposes of not less than $, which statement the SELLER hereby agrees to deliver to the purchaser promptly after such appraised value statement is made available to the SELLER. The PURCHASER shall, however, have the privilege and option of proceeding with the consummation of this contract without regard to the amount of the appraised valuation made by the Federal Housing Commissioner.

300

26. **SALE OF PERSONAL PROPERTY**
(fill in and attach list or delete entire clause)

The BUYER agrees to buy from the SELLER the articles of personal property enumerated on the attached list for the price of $
and the SELLER agrees to deliver to the BUYER upon delivery of the deed hereunder, a warranty bill of sale therefor on payment of said price. The provisions of this clause shall constitute an agreement separate and apart from the provisions herein contained with respect to the real estate, and any breach of the terms and conditions of this clause shall have no effect on the provisions of this agreement with respect to the real estate.

27. **RELEASE BY HUSBAND OR WIFE**

The SELLER'S spouse hereby agrees to join in said deed and to release and convey all statutory and other rights and interests in said premises.

28. **BROKER AS PARTY**

The broker(s) named herein, join(s) in this agreement and become(s) a party hereto, in so far as any provisions of this agreement expressly apply to him (them), and to any amendments or modifications of such provisions to which he (they) agree(s) in writing.

29. **LIABILITY OF TRUSTEE, SHAREHOLDER, BENEFICIARY, etc.**

If the SELLER or BUYER executes this agreement in a representative or fiduciary capacity, only the principal or the estate represented shall be bound and neither the SELLER or BUYER so executing, nor any shareholder or beneficiary of any trust, shall be personally liable for any obligation, express or implied, hereunder.

30. **CONSTRUCTION OF AGREEMENT**
* delete "triplicate" and substitute "quadruplicate" if required. (See "Instructions in General," 1.)

This instrument, executed in triplicate*   is to be construed as a Massachusetts contract, is to take effect as a sealed instrument, sets forth the entire contract between the parties, is binding upon and enures to the benefit of the parties hereto and their respective heirs, devises, executors, administrators, successors and assigns, and may be cancelled, modified or amended only by a written instrument executed by both the SELLER and the BUYER. If two or more persons are named herein as BUYER their obligations hereunder shall be joint and several. The captions and marginal notes are used only as a matter of convenience and are not to be considered a part of this agreement or to be used in determining the intent of the parties to it.

31. **ADDITIONAL PROVISIONS**

....
Husband or Wife of Seller   *SELLER*

....
Husband or Wife of Buyer   *BUYER*

....
Broker

SCHEDULE

Extension

Date...

The time for the performance of the foregoing agreement is extended until .... o'clock

...... M. on the .... day of .... 19......, time still being of the essence of this agreement as extended.

This extension, executed in triplicate, ... is intended to take effect as a sealed instrument.

....
Husband or Wife of Seller

....
SELLER

....
Husband or Wife of Buyer

....
BUYER

....
Broker

INSTRUCTIONS IN GENERAL
(These instructions are suggestions only; consult your ATTORNEY for particulars and details.)

1. Prepare agreement in quadruplicate if BUYER intends to apply for VA-guaranteed or FHA-insured loan; otherwise in triplicate.
2. Any lists or schedules to be attached should be properly incorporated by reference and initialed by all parties concerned.
3. This agreement, in its printed form, may not be suitable for use by trustees or other fiduciaries unless amended.
4. Each party should bring his agreement with him when passing title.

INSTRUCTIONS TO SELLER
After this agreement has been executed by all parties, arrange at once for drawing the deed and assigning insurance and obtaining binders if insurance is to be transferred.

Bring at the appointed time to the place designated for completing the transaction:

1. The deed signed by you and your spouse, properly acknowledged before a Notary, and if registered land, the owner's certificate of title.
2. A list of tenants and lessees, with a statement of amount of rents and the dates to which the rents are paid.
3. All leases on the premises and tenancy at will agreements; also all permits you have for use of the premises.
4. If Buyer has agreed to purchase insurance, all insurance policies (some or all of the policies may be in the custody of the holder of the mortgage on said premises, and if so, obtain certificates of such policies from your insurance agent in advance); receipted insurance bills or a statement from the insurance agent that premiums are paid in full; and assignments of SELLER'S insurance to BUYER and binders from your insurance agent in favor of the BUYER.
5. Receipted bills for taxes for the last two years and all bills for taxes for the current year, whether receipted or not.
6. Water bills for the period of one year next preceding the time of performance.
7. Receipt for your last payment of interest on the mortgage, the mortgage pass book and, if any reduction has been made in the principal of the mortgage, bring a statement from the holder thereof showing how much is due.
8. If an existing mortgage on said premises is to be discharged, be sure to have the mortgage note available for cancellation in addition to the discharge.
9. Guarantees for roof, sidewalls, plumbing, heating or other fixtures.
10. Documentary stamps (Federal and State).

INSTRUCTIONS TO BUYER
If you are giving a mortgage, your spouse must join in signing it and so should be present at time of passing title.

Bring at the appointed time to the place designated for completing the transaction:

1. A certified or Bank's Check (if acceptable to the SELLER) drawn payable to your order and one hundred dollars in cash, the total amount to equal the amount of payment to be made at time of passing title.
2. Sufficient additional cash to pay for apportionment of rents, taxes, water rates, insurance premiums, and other adjustments, attorney's bill, plot plans, and recording fees.

It is customary for the BUYER to pay for drawing any mortgage given by him and fees for recording his deed and purchase money mortgage.

He also pays for examination of title and for Tax Collector's report showing whether there are any municipal liens or unpaid taxes.

PURCHASE and SALE AGREEMENT

SELLER ....

BUYER ....

Property Address ....

Date of Agreement ....

Date for Delivery of Deed ....

FROM THE OFFICE OF

MEMBER
Greater Boston Real Estate Board

Copyright 1962 Greater Boston Real Estate Board

Revised 1-62

Real Estate Finance

QUESTIONS FOR DISCUSSION

1. What are the elements that affect the demand for a property and its selling price?
2. How did Mr. Manning attempt to find a property? What problems did he face?
3. What were the forms of financing available to him? What are the advantages and disadvantages of each?
4. Should Mr. Manning buy the property? What risks is he taking, personal and financial? How reliable are his income and expense figures?
5. What are the advantages and disadvantages of a real estate investment?

503 RUGBY ROAD

The 503 Rugby Road project started in 1961 when Mason Speed Sexton inherited a stucco house located on a 14,000 sq. ft. lot approximately one block from the main campus of the University of Virginia. Four years later he attended that institution as a freshman and immediately took over the management of the property. This was his first exposure to real estate management and to the benefits and problems of rental property.

Even before he took control, the house had been divided into individual rooms which were rented to students. There were 7 double bedrooms, 6 large single bedrooms, 2 kitchens, a large living room, and 5½ bathrooms. He spent two summers with a local handyman cleaning, painting, refurnishing and generally improving the property which had been long neglected. After this remodelling, he was able to raise the rents by percentages that varied from 25% to 100% and operate the property at a profit for the first time (See Exhibit 1). His experience enabled him to understand certain crucial factors. He realized that the location of the property as shown in Exhibit 2 made it possible to demand rents out of proportion to the space and the facilities provided. He also understood that the age of the current structure and the amount of upkeep and repairs required to maintain it were consuming the little profit there was. As the building continued to age and deteriorate, he thought that the situation would only get worse.

This case was prepared as a basis for class discussion rather than to illustrate either effective or ineffective handling of an administrative situation.

Copyright © 1972 by the President and Fellows of Harvard College. Reproduced by permission.

During the period of his management, he filled the house with undergraduate friends of his. As a precaution he required his tenants to sign a formal lease drawn by his lawyer and to get their parents' signature if they were under twenty-one. Among these friends were two architecture students who came to him three years later in the Spring of 1970 proposing to build an apartment house at 503 Rugby Road. Their original concept was to design an "architectural commune" under the supervision of one of their professors in their graduate program. The idea seemed logical to Mr. Sexton since many of the tenants had always been architecture students and since architect friends had managed the property for him after he had left Charlottesville to work in New York City.

Planning a New Building

In mid-1970, Mr. Sexton was planning to start the first year at the Harvard Business School. At that time he sought the advice of his mother on tearing down the old house and erecting an apartment building. In his opinion, her 20 years of real estate experience as a successful broker on Long Island combined with her interest in the property made her a source of sound judgment and invaluable aid. After the first set of plans had been submitted by five different groups of architecture students, he and his mother were able to visualize a feasible design which would provide the best use of the property. They had learned that under Charlottesville zoning laws for this location, which was zoned R-3, they were restricted to building one housing unit per thousand square feet of available land. This meant that they could put a maximum of 14 units, but these were unrestricted as to the size or number of rooms in each unit as long as the required setbacks from the property line and the 5-story height limitation were respected. At this point, he made the decision to try to optimize the value of the property with any project that might be built, since it was his only inheritance and he wanted to make the most of it both in terms of current cash flow and cash to be realized at the time of sale.

After choosing the design and architect which he liked best, Mr. Sexton spent many hours with his mother and the architect constantly revising the sketches and the floor plans until he was satisfied that he had met his maximum use criteria and had an esthetically pleasing and economically feasible set of plans. Among the decisions which were made at this time which determined the final shape of the project were (1) to use concrete decking planks and brick bearing walls as the primary means of construction because of their cost advantages over other building systems and their long durability and maintenance-free characteristics; (2) to build all bedrooms large enough and with enough closet space for at least two people; (3) to build all bathrooms, kitchens, and facilities to withstand maximum wear and tear while requiring the least possible amount of maintenance; (4) within the constraints above, to make the apartments as attractive, airy, convenient, luxurious as possible. The major goal of this early planning phase was to build something of lasting value that would require a minimum of time and expense to maintain.

In conjunction with the design phase, Mr. Sexton became concerned about property management and the marketing of his property. Since his mother was sixty-five, he decided to suggest that she retire, move to Charlottesville, and take over the management of the building. Due to the location of the property, he determined that his prime rental market was going to have to be the more affluent students which was a departure from his original concept of a luxury, high-rise for young marrieds. In order to make this proposal attractive to his mother, who was divorced, he promised her a "penthouse, designed to her specifications" and a comfortable management fee on which to live.

Concurrently, he surveyed the list of available contractors in Charlottesville who were willing and able to undertake this kind of job. To his great chagrin he discovered that only one man of those he found willing to talk had ever built a high-rise apartment house before and that project had been in Richmond, 90 miles away. The problem was that his project was to be one of the first high-rise apartment buildings in Charlottesville and most local contractors were hesitant even to bid on it. He explained his concept to the one general contractor with some experience and showed him his plans and sketches asking for an estimate of what he thought it would cost to build. Within a day the contractor produced the construction cost estimate of $300,000 and Mr. Sexton had estimated his total development costs. Next, based on his knowledge of the local rental market and some preliminary research he had conducted with the help of the general contractor, he projected the rents that he could get for each apartment, estimated his operating expenses and debt service, and derived his expected cash flow. On the basis of these very rough numbers he decided that the project was economically feasible and that he should go ahead with it. This was an important decision since up to this point he had invested a relatively small amount of time and money in the project. His architect friend had done the sketches and designs on speculation with the understanding that if and when the project was built he would receive either fair compensation for his work or a small share in the building.

Market Research

Before making any major dollar commitment to the project, Mr. Sexton wanted to do a more in-depth survey of the local rental housing market and, if possible, get a verbal commitment for permanent financing on the basis of the plans and numbers he had at that time. He spent two full days talking to the local real estate brokers to determine what the demand might be for luxury apartments and whether or not he could get the rents he was projecting. Reactions were mixed with most agreeing that such rents were too high for young families, professionals, and non-students in general — especially for the three-bedroom penthouse units. A visit to the Off-Grounds Housing Bureau was much more encouraging. There he learned that the off-grounds housing situation was critical. Students would pay almost anything for good, clean housing that is within walking distance of the University. The director informed him that in the last two years available apartments had been given out by lottery. More recently, they had done away with even that system as unworkable and the current situation was described as a "free-for-all" with local landlords responding with sharply increasing rents.

During this same trip to Charlottesville, Mr. Sexton got a break in the form of a tip from his contractor that a "Special Report" from the Housing Guidance council had recently been released and that he might get a copy from one of the largest builder-developers in central Virginia. He called the developer's office and a secretary told him that he could read the report while he was there, but that it couldn't leave the office. He therefore took a small tape recorder and recorded the parts he felt to be important to his project while he was in an empty conference room.

In general the report indicated that there was a strong market for rental property within walking distance of the university and that demand would remain strong through 1975 even without further expansion by the University of Virginia.

A major problem had arisen in getting information on apartment and rent comparables for the immediate neighborhood and the Charlottesville area in general. He was not able to identify comparable buildings or apartments. There were no high-rise apartments, no luxury apartments, and no three-bedroom apartments within easy walking distance of the University. Therefore, when he would compare a small two-bedroom unit with tiny kitchen, living room, and small bath which rented for $225 to $245 one block away to his projected rents, he had an unfavorable and distorted comparison. In addition, since he planned to rent to students who were willing and able to live two to a bedroom, he had to make rent comparisons on a per student basis.

The large rooms in the existing 85 year old, deterioriating structure have rented during the last 3 to 5 years for over $100 per bedroom with four or five people sharing the same bathroom and kitchenette. Occupancy levels have been virtually at the 100% level for the entire period of his ownership with long waiting lists for any available rooms. Many students seem to be quite willing and able to pay this price for housing that is conveniently located despite its run-down condition and lack of amenities. Bedrooms in the new structure would rent for an average of $120 per month and could easily accommodate 2 persons, resulting in a per-person cost of $60 per month.

Availability of Credit

Armed with his new market data, the "Special Report" excerpts, and a pro forma income and expense statement as shown in Exhibit 3, Mr. Sexton visited the Charlottesville Savings and Loan Association where, after presenting his proposal, he got a verbal commitment for $18,500 per unit or a $260,000 first mortgage at 8%. This was some $40,000 below the loan he was hoping for. He was told that the bank had never lent more than $16,500 per unit before and that they were stretching themselves even at that level. Other visits to the Shenandoah Life Insurance Company, the local savings banks, etc., produced similar results with the general feeling that this project was "too rich for our blood." In his opinion, this experience pointed up the problem of dealing with small town, local financial institutions. First, since this was a pioneering effort in the sense that it was to be the first high-rise in the town and since it was aimed at students, most lenders approached it cautiously and, in his opinion, with undue conservatism. Secondly, he believed that the size of the loan was, in some cases, "too heavy" for the institution, although that was never stated.

Seeking additional sources he sought out the most reputable mortgage broker in town. He couldn't spend any more time in Charlottesville and was not getting very encouraging results. The gentleman to whom he was referred turned out to be the executive vice-president of the commercial bank where he kept a house account. He was very helpful in suggesting sources of mortgage money and assured Mr. Sexton that for 2% of the loan he could secure financing quickly and easily. Unfortunately, he would have to get final bids on the project to determine the construction costs more exactly against which a commitment could be made. This, in turn, required that a complete set of working drawings and specifications by an architect certified in Virginia be procured. The architect that had done all the work up to this point was with a New York firm. In addition, a local engineer had to take test borings on the land to determine what kind of foundation would be needed. To proceed further would require a commitment of almost $15,000 in architect's, engineer's and landscape architect's fees. These would have to be paid whether the building was built or not. On the basis of Mr. Sexton's mother's credit, they would be able to delay payment of these bills until they got financing or the project was shelved.

Problems with the Planning Commission

In late August, 1970, a disturbing piece of news arrived which caused Mr. Sexton added expense and worry through the Fall. As of October 1, all plans for multi-family housing, office and industrial buildings had to be approved by a new City Planning Commission. His project was the first to seek approval and it was being treated somewhat as a test case. The young planning director was very "tough" in his meetings with Mr. Sexton and insisted that he didn't disturb a single tree or bush in putting up the building or he wouldn't receive his certificate of occupancy. In addition, Mr. Sexton had to present detailed landscaping plans and elevations of the building to get his project approved. He therefore hired a local landscape architect to do the plans and appear before the commission in his behalf at a cost of $1,500. The outcome of all this was that his plans were not only approved, but were "hailed" by the Planning Commission which asked if they could use the project as a model for future development in Charlottesville.

New Cost Estimates

Once the working drawings were completed, the general contractor sent out invitations to local subcontractors to bid on the property. By March 1971, when the bids were returned, the building market had taken a dramatic turn from what it had been a year earlier. The previous year, in addition to a still lethargic economy, the biggest developer in Charlottesville had gone bankrupt leaving debts of $17 million. The contractors, architects and other subcontractors who had worked for this developer were out of jobs and hungry for work. By the following year, however, the economy was heating up and construction in Charlottesville, especially in single-family homes and townhouses on the outskirts of the city, was booming. These reasons combined with the contractor's inexperience with high-rise construction and the fact that this was Mr. Sexton's first project made it difficult just to get people to bid on the project. When he got bids, his worst fears were realized. As can be seen in Exhibit 4, the original bids of $429,700 were approximately $125,000 over his original estimates.

Case 2 / 503 Rugby Road

There were a number of factors behind this huge difference which required a great deal of time and effort to discover and, in some cases, eliminate. Ultimately, this work paid off by reducing the original bids by almost $50,000 which was absolutely critical to keeping the project economically viable and saleable to investors. A major reason for the high construction costs was the fact that the test borings showed the need for reinforced spread footings which had to go down 40 feet for the foundation. This automatically cost $50,000 extra including the cost of the underground garage. To get around this problem, Mr. Sexton attempted to swap his piece of land for a similarly-sized, but less attractively located piece owned by the University. Unfortunately, the Board of Overseers was not interested in his proposal and he was stuck with the extra cost.

During this period, his general contractor, architects, and his mother were tremendous help in finding ways to save money and cut costs. For instance, he quickly discovered that he could save $9,400 on the masonry (see Exhibit 4) by changing from the 8'4" ceilings called for in the plans to 8 ft. ceilings and by using oversized instead of standard brick. This meant that precut, regulation 8 ft. wallboard could now be installed without the extra labor it would require to patch every piece and use extenders. It also meant a 10% saving on the cost of the cheaper bricks and correspondingly less mortar and labor. Some other ways in which he cut costs (see Exhibit 4) were to: (1) eliminate all the ceramic tile work; (2) take out all dishwashers and garbage disposal units making them optional on a rental basis; (3) change from the $2.50 electric switches called for in the specifications to ones costing $.69 and move the position of the boxes while using cheaper electrical cable; (4) make kitchens smaller by 1½ feet and switch to inferior-grade cabinets. Fortunately, he was not the only one in Charlottesville facing high building costs. A recent article in the local paper showed that at an average cost of $19.92 per square foot Charlottesville has among the highest building costs in the nation. Even at these cost levels, Mr. Sexton expected a return on his investment. The total development budget is shown in Exhibit 5.

Pro Forma Income Statement

A major reservation which he had to confront on the part of potential lenders was centered around his pro forma income statements. His sources of income are shown in Exhibit 6; a pro forma income statement is shown in Exhibit 5. Specifically, bankers believed that his operating expenses of $11,758 and management fee of $2,836 were too low since they totalled less than 25% of the net rent of $56,715. They wanted to see operating expenses, including real estate taxes, in the neighborhood of 34% of net rental income since their experience had shown that this is what it would cost them to run the building should there be a default on the mortgage. His case was further complicated by the fact that the owner/developer, his mother, was also the manager of the property. The question arose as to whether the management fee was an expense or part of profit. For this reason, the pro forma income statement was drawn up showing net income before and after the management fee. Exhibit 7 also shows net profit before a vacancy factor given the negligible vacancy rate of less than 1% for Charlottesville as a whole. If the income statement projects expenses at 34% of net income of $56,715 after taking out a 5% vacancy rate Mr. Sexton would be left with a very small cash flow and correspondingly poor return on investment as can be seen in Exhibit 8.

These calculations raised in the banker's mind questions about the economic feasibility of the entire project, especially if they assumed that rents were overstated by, for example, 10% and expenses were even higher than 34%. The project was disastrous. The return on investment using the net profit, without a vacancy allowance, of $11,866 with the same equity basis of $117,000 was projected to be a much more acceptable 10.14%. This was better than average for a project of this size according to studies done by the Institute of Real Estate Management.

Naturally, the primary source of the problems which arose in regard to rates of return, expense ratios, interest coverage, etc., was the high cost of construction which was projected at $27,071 per apartment unit. This created the need for a large mortgage with correspondingly high fixed interest and amortization charges which severely reduces the cash flow from the project. In spite of these adverse factors, there were a number of factors which Mr. Sexton believed made the project an attractive investment. These were the hedge against inflation and the tax shelter available.

Tax Shield and Discounted Cash Flow — Analysis of Return

Exhibit 9 was prepared by Mr. Sexton to illustrate potential investor return from the project. A large percentage of the after-tax net cash flow from the project was projected to come from the tax shield created by the large depreciation and interest deductions taken. The actual savings in tax that these "losses" would produce for an investor were treated as cash income, since the investor would save this cash amount in taxes. The amount of savings decline each year as both the interest payments and depreciation deduction are reduced. The other major element of return for the investor was the potential equity appreciation.

As part of his analysis Mr. Sexton analyzed the value of the tax shelter alone for a 50% bracket individual. He looked at just the available tax shield from the project alone and assumed that an investor would accept a 10% after-tax return on his investment, over a period of 8 years. He calculated that an investor would pay approximately $29,000 for the shelter.

Mr. Sexton hoped that the full amount of the shelter could be sold without paying out any of the cash flow from the project by raising the management fee paid to his mother to a level where any positive cash flow was eliminated. He had not yet consulted a tax specialist and knew that the viability of that kind of arrangement would depend upon the careful evaluation of a tax attorney guided by the pertinent I.R.S. regulations.

He had decided to use the D.C.F.-Analysis of Return format in the pro forma, because he believed it was the only method which would relate estimated value of a project with its cash flow or the dividend rate. He knew that real estate investors establish value and base their investment decisions on four sources of entrepreneurial reward: (1) possible appreciation (2) possible loan amortization (3) possible income tax savings and (4) possible cash flow or dividend. He believed that the method used in the analysis integrated these elements and told "The Rugby Road Story" in what he felt was the best way. The 22% after-tax projected return was, he thought, impressive and would awaken the interest of most investors.

Current Situation

By September 1971 when Mr. Sexton returned to the second year M.B.A. program, the project was in flux. He had not been able to obtain the permanent financing on acceptable terms. He had almost completely ceased to deal with his original mortgage broker due to repeated failures to live up to his promises and claims for securing the take-out. At this point his architects had become very helpful in arranging meetings with interested potential lender/investors. On his own, he had spoken to a number of REITs to which he sent proposals. These were still being evaluated and reviewed. Unfortunately, he had thus far had no favorable responses. Moreover, as time passed, it became less and less likely that the building could be completed before the original target date of January 1, 1973. This meant that he would miss the change in semesters at the University when a new influx of students would be looking for housing. Consequently, he would have a difficult time renting the property until the following September which would mean large additional carrying costs. He was left wondering about his next steps.

Exhibit 1
503 RUGBY ROAD
Income and Expense Statement for Present Use

Gross Rental Income (Note 1)	$12,000	
Allowance for Vacancies and Bad Debts	400	
Net Rental Income		$11,600
Operating Expenses:		
Real Estate Taxes	$ 1,521	
Water and Sewer	271	
Heat and Electricity	1,403	
Insurance	393	
Janitor	400	
Repairs	997	
Management Fee	600	
Total Operating Expenses		$ 5,585
Income from Operation		$ 6,015

Note 1: 13 rooms with 20 students paying $50 per room, per person, per month.

Exhibit 2

See page 314.

Exhibit 3
503 RUGBY ROAD
Preliminary Pro Forma Income and Expense Statement

Gross Rental Income	$58,920	
Vacancy Allowance (5% of gross rent)	2,946	
NET RENTAL INCOME		$55,974
Operating Expenses:		
Real Estate Taxes	6,035	
Water and Sewer	480	
Gas	2,400	
Insurance	893	
Janitor	750	
Reserve for General Repairs	900	
Electricity	300	
Management Fee (5% of net rent)	2,796	
TOTAL OPERATING EXPENSES		14,554
Income from Operations (Note 1)		$41,420

Note 1: Total development cost estimated at $388,000 including land at $65,000.

Exhibit 2
503 Rugby Road

Exhibit 2
373-146

- 10 -

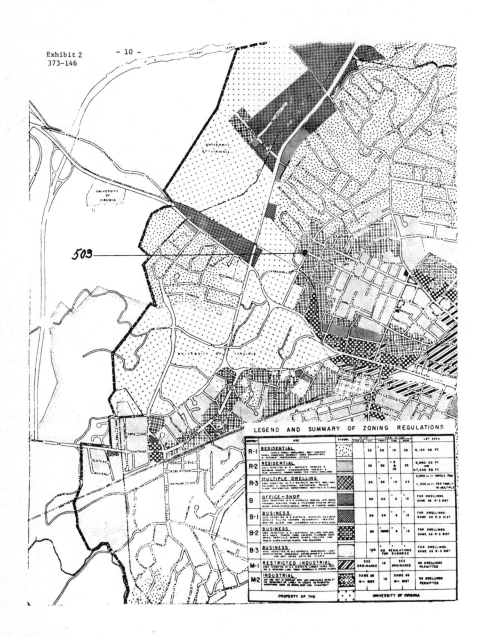

Exhibit 4
503 RUGBY ROAD
Projected Construction Cost

	Original	Revised	Differences
Reinf. & Steel	—0—	$ 1,350	+ $ 1,350
Concrete	$ 24,715	24,315	− 400
Masonry	78,355	68,955	− 9,400
Str. Stl.	10,036	9,686	− 350
St. Stairs	6,231	6,231	——
Ro. Carpentry	11,983	11,383	− 600
Ro. How.	500	500	——
Fin. Carp.	9,282	8,282	− 1,000
Fin. Hdw.	1,150	1,150	——
Drainage	1,066	1,066	——
Roofing	6,115	6,115	——
Door A. Met.	1,804	1,804	——
Bi Fold	1,040	1,040	——
Windows	555	555	——
	10,399	6,899	− 3,500
Drywall	10,480	9,920	− 500
Tile Work	219	——	− 219
Resil. Tile	1,700	1,700	——
Painting	5,000	3,334	1,666
SPFC	919	919	——
Kit. Cabs.	10,564	5,164	− 5,400
Appliance	7,700	5,672	− 2,028
Blinds & Shades	888	888	——
Carpets	8,616	8,616	——
Met. Shelving	905	905	——
Elevators	21,919	16,191	− 5,000
Plumbing	33,000	27,115	− 5,885
Tubs & Showers, Toilets & Basins	2,885	2,885	——
Termites	165	165	——
Precast Slabs	33,400	33,400	——
HTT. Vent. AC.	16,000	16,000	——
Elec.	21,485	16,085	5,400
Fireplace	850	425	− 425
Caulk	480	480	——
Earth	4,482	4,482	——
Site	1,500	1,500	——
Walks, Etc.	5,990	4,490	− 1,500
Lawns	3,000	——	3,000
Gen. Req.	33,200	33,200	——
Tools	1,500	1,500	
TOTAL	$390,498	$345,095	$44,403
Taxes	11,090	9,812	1,278
Overhead & Profit	28,112	24,157	3,955
Total	$429,700	$379,164	$49,636

Exhibit 5
503 RUGBY ROAD

Total Development Cost Budget*

Land at Market Value	$ 65,000	
Development and Construction Costs	379,000**	
Architectural	6,000	
Legal	2,500	
Interest on Construction Loan	14,500	
Builder's Risk Insurance	500	
Real Estate Taxes During Construction	500	
Total Development Costs		$468,000
Less assumed loan of 75%	$351,000	
Equity investment required		117,000***
Less Land..	65,000	
Cash Required		52,000

*Based on plans and specifications included in *Proposal.*
**See *Projected Construction Costs* for a detailed breakdown.
***This figure used in following D.C.F.-*Analysis of Return Exhibit.*

Exhibit 6
503 RUGBY ROAD

Sources of Income

	Original Rent Schedule		New Rent Schedule	
	Monthly	Annual	Monthly	Annual
1 penthouse apt. w/fireplace	$400	$ 4,800	$425	$ 5,100
1 penthouse apt.	$400	4,800	$400	4,800
1 2-bedroom apt. 1st floor	$250	3,000	$265	3,180
1 2-bedroom apt. w/2 baths, 1st floor	$275	3,300	$300	3,600
3 2-bedroom apts.	$275	9,900	$275	9,900
7 3-bedroom apts.	$360	30,240	$360	30,240
12 indoor covered parking spaces	$ 20	2,880	$ 20	2,880
Total Estimated Income		$58,920		$59,700

Exhibit 7
503 RUGBY ROAD
Pro Forma Income and Expense Statement

Gross Rental Income		$59,700
Vacancy Allowance (5% gross rent)		2,985
NET RENTAL INCOME		$56,715
Real Estate Taxes ($4.79/$100 assessor's value. $126,000 Assessment)	$6,035	
Water & Sewer	480	
Gas	2,400	
Insurance	893	
Janitor	750	
Reserve for general repairs	900	
Electricity	300	
TOTAL OPERATING EXPENSES		− $11,758
Management Fee (5% net rent)		− 2,836
Debt Servicing (9.47% constant. 75% financing. 8.25%–25 year. $351,000 total mortgage).		− 33,240
Net profit after Management Fee & Vacancy allowance		$ 8,881
Net Profit before Management Fee (Additional risk $2,836)		$11,717
Net Profit before any Vacancy Allowance and after Management Fee		$11,866

Exhibit 8
503 RUGBY ROAD
Cash Flow Analysis

	Income and cash flow	Expenses as a percentage of net rents
Gross rents	$59,700	
Less: 5% vacancy	2,985	
Net rental income	$56,715	100.0%
Total expenses	19,283	34.0%
Net cash flow — if free and clear of debt	37,432	64.0%
Debt service annually*	33,240	58.6%
Net cash flow after debt servicing	$ 4,192	7.4%

*Assumes 80% financing as in *setup*.

$$\frac{\text{Cash flow after debt service}}{\text{original equity}} = \frac{\$4,192}{\$117,000} = 3.58\% \text{ Return on Investment}$$

Exhibit 9
503 RUGBY ROAD

Discounted Cash Flow — Analysis of Return

Assumed Equity Investment of $117,000

A. Refinancing
Original mortgage amount (75%) $351,000
Balance owing at end of 10 years 285,537

Net proceeds from refinancing end of 10 years .... $ 65,463

B. (1) Sales Price
Assume we can sell property to yield an investor a cash re-
turn on his investment of 8%.
(2) Cash flow at end of 10 years
Present cash flow* .... $ 8,881
Compounded rent increases (7%/year)..... 47,553
Compounded expenses increases
(10%/year)** 16,053
Compounded net increase in cash flow $31,500
Present debt-servicing cost (9.47% con-
stant)*** 33,240
Estimated debt-servicing cost on refi-
nancing (7% interest, 8.58% constant,
25-year mortgage..................................... 30,116
Net cash flow increase from refinancing .... $ 3,124

Cash flow at end of 10 years $43,505

(3) Capitalized at 8% = $\dfrac{\$43,505}{8\%}$ = $543,812 sales price (equity)

(4) Cash proceeds from sale.. $543,812
Less: Brokerage commission (5%) 27,190

Net cash proceeds from sale $516,622

C. Capital gains tax payable on sale of property
(1) Original cost.. $468,000
Depreciation taken over 10 years****..................... 200,856

Tax basis (depreciated basis)................................... $267,144

(2) Sales price for tax purposes-net mortgage transferred (after adjustment for prepayment pen-
alty) $351,000
Net cash realized on sale 516,622

Total Sales Price $867,622

(3) Sales Price... 867,622
Depreciated basis 267,144

Net capital gain 600,478

---

*Taken from *Expected Cash Flow*.
**Assumes operating expenses *exclusive* of management fee increase at 10%/year.
***Taken from *Set-up*.
****Assumes 30 year average life and $403,000 value of building as depreciable base
($468,000 total project cost − $65,000 land cost).

318

Exhibit 9 (continued)

(4) Depreciation taken under double declining............ 200,856
Depreciation if straight line method used............. 134,332

Excess of accelerated over straight line .... $ 66,524
Property held for 120 months: 80% of excess is
   subject to recapture provisions under 1969 tax
   reform act.
Taxed as ordinary income (80% × $66,524) = $ 53,219
Tax payable on recaptured amount (assume 50%
   bracket) =   26,610

(5) Net capital gain 600,478
Less: Recaptured amount 53,219

Net capital gain $547,259
Capital gains tax at 35% × $547,259 =   191,541

D. Net-net proceeds at end of tenth year from refinancing, and sale net of capital gains tax and recapture provisions.
(1) Refinancing .... $ 66,207
(2) Sale of equity 516,622

   $582,829
(3) Less: Recapture tax 26,610
   Capital gains tax 191,541

Net proceeds from Sale and Refinancing
After tax at end of 10th year..................................... $364,678

Exhibit 9 (continued)
503 RUGBY ROAD

Discounted Cash Flow — Analysis of Return

E. Annual Cash Income — After Taxes — Assuming 50% tax rate.
(000s omitted)

					Y E A R S					
	1	2	3	4	5	6	7	8	9	10
Gross rents (+ 7%/year)*	56.7	60.7	64.9	69.5	74.3	79.5	85.1	91.0	97.4	104.2
Less: Expenses & Mgt. Fee (+ 10%/year)*	14.6	15.8	17.1	18.5	20.1	21.8	23.7	25.7	28.0	30.6
Free and Clear Return	42.1	44.9	47.8	51.0	54.2	57.7	61.4	65.3	69.4	73.6
Interest Expense @ 8-1/4	29.0	28.6	28.2	27.8	27.3	26.8	26.3	25.7	25.0	24.3
Depreciation Expense	26.9	25.1	23.4	21.8	20.4	19.0	17.7	16.6	15.5	14.4
Taxable Income (loss)	(13.8)	(8.8)	(3.8)	1.4	6.9	11.9	17.4	23.0	28.9	34.9
Tax @ 50**	(6.9)	(4.4)	(1.9)	.7	3.5	6.0	8.7	11.5	14.5	17.5
Cash Flow	8.9	11.7	14.6	17.8	21.0	24.5	28.2	32.1	36.2	40.4
Plus: Tax Benefit Above	6.9	4.4	1.9	(.7)	(3.5)	(6.0)	(8.7)	(11.5)	(14.5)	(17.5)
Net Cash Flow After Taxes	15.8	16.1	16.5	17.1	17.5	18.5	19.5	20.6	21.7	22.9

*Net rents and expenses figures taken from Exhibit 7
**Excludes excess income tax after first $25,000

Exhibit 9 (continued)

Discounted Cash Flow-Analysis of Return

F. Present Value of Cash Flows Discounted at 22%
    (000's omitted)

Payments Made at End of Year	From E-Cash Flow & Tax Shelter	×	Present Value of $1 Discounted at 22%	=	Present Value of Cash Flow
1...........................	$15.8		.820		12.96
2...........................	16.1		.672		10.82
3...........................	16.5		.551		9.09
4...........................	17.1		.451		7.71
5...........................	17.5		.370		6.48
6...........................	18.5		.303		5.61
7...........................	19.5		.249		4.86
8...........................	20.6		.204		4.20
9...........................	21.7		.167		3.62
10.........................	22.9		.137		3.14

Net proceeds from sale and refinancing (A.T.) at end of 10th year — from D above ....

	$364,678		.137		49.96
					118.45

Amount that an investor would have to invest today to get the above cash flows, assuming he was satisfied to receive an effective rate of return on his outstanding investment of 22% $118.45

Total equity investment required from first page............................ $117,000

APPENDIX

Charlottesville and Albermarle County are situated in central Virginia along the eastern slope of the Blue Ridge Mountains just 30 minutes away from the Skyline Drive. Charlottesville is 67 miles west of Richmond and 115 miles southwest of Washington, D.C. Albermarle county had an estimated population of 41,000 in 1970 while the city had a population of 39,000. This represented an increase of 30% over the 1960 levels and 50% over the 1950 levels. Census projections indicated that the populations would continue to grow at an average rate of 3% per year, and that growth was expected to come in spurts rather than as a single smooth trend. The average income per household for both the city and the county was $9,371 in 1970 with a total estimated purchasing power of $224,000,000.

Housing construction in the Charlottesville — Albermarle area had kept pace with the increase in population. The level of completed housing was 70 units in 1954, 690 in 1960 but only 532 in 1971. The level of construction was expected to rise dramatically to the level of 1000 per year for the years 1972 through 1975.

Manufacturers in many different industries provided a payroll in excess of $65 million. There were nine electronics firms in the immediate area including General Electric, Sperry Marine Systems, and Stromberg-Carlson. Morton's Frozen Foods employed 1500 people in a plant twelve miles to the west of the city. Three printing plants, the Allen Press, the Michie Press and the Lindsey Printing Company employing 400 persons in all were located in Albermarle County. Martin Marietta operated a quarry to the north of the city. Two concrete manufacturers served the growing needs of the construction industry. Two clothing and textile firms had plants within the county. An office equipment manufacturer, the Acme Visible Record Co., and a tire plant for Uniroyal completed the list of major industrial installations.

Although there were indications that General Electric would locate another plant in the Charlottesville — Albermarle area, the prospect of further industry growth was limited by the diminished pool of available labor and the opposition of many local groups to any activity which might damage the local environment.

Charlottesville had many government jobs. The city served as a regional center for the state and as the county seat for Albermarle County. The federal government had a substantial payroll here on the staff of the Army Judge Advocate General's school and the Army Foreign Service Technological Center. Federal employment in the area was not considered likely to grow. It took substantial pressure from the local congressional delegation to bring in the Army Foreign Service Technological Center and even this did not replace all the jobs which had been lost when HEW vacated the federal office building several months earlier.

Albermarle County was still an active agricultural area. There were extensive apple and peach orchards within the county. Many large farms were still operating specializing in cattle-breeding, dairy products or horse raising.

The single most important influence upon the future of the county and the city was the University of Virginia. This was a prominent educational institution with schools of law, medicine and graduate business which ranked high among American professional schools. The University attracted to this area a well-educated and affluent group of professionals. It was also an important source of employment for unskilled workers in the county and city. The university served as the center of the cultural and much of the social life in the area by sponsoring concerts, lectures and exhibits. The university was playing a crucial role in the future of the city because it was thought by many to be a sure source of growth. Enrollment stood at slightly more than 10,000 and was scheduled to grow to about 18,000 by the year 1980.

The city's rich historical background, its natural scenic beauty and the remarkable examples of Jeffersonian architecture made it an important tourist center, drawing over 400,000 people a year.

The city and county were relatively well-served in terms of transportation. Interstate 64 ran east-west through the city connecting it with Richmond and Norfolk to the east, Roanoke and ultimately St. Louis to the west. Dual-lane Route 29 connected with Washington D.C. Both the Chesapeake and Ohio and the Southern Railroads served the city which was still an important switching point for them. Charlottesville had a regional airport with daily scheduled flights to points as distant as New York and Atlanta.

Charlottesville and its surrounding area represented one of the fastest and most sustained small growth areas in the South. While many communities were dependent for their growth on a single source like commerce, recreation, politics, professionals, or education, Charlottesville was fortunate enough to have a strong base in many of these areas. This guaranteed to the community as a whole a more stable status than would fall to one without these advantages.

Appendixes

Appendix A

GLOSSARY OF SELECTED TERMS

Abstract of Title. A condensed history of recorded documents affecting title to a specific parcel of real estate.

Accelerated Depreciation. A method for writing-off the value of an asset over time such that larger deductions occur during the early years of the asset's economic life and lower deductions occur during later years.

Acceleration Clause. In the event of default by the borrower in terms of interest and/or principal, this clause in a mortgage instrument provides for the entire debt to be immediately due.

Amortization. The systematic repayment of a loan in which the principal amount is repaid in installments over the life of the loan.

Annuity. A series of payments or receipts of a fixed amount that will continue over a number of years.

Assets. Anything of economic value such as real and personal property.

Assignment. The transfer of contract rights associated with a mortgage or other instrument such as a bond or lease by an assignor to an assignee.

Assumption. A contractual arrangement whereby a purchaser of property takes over or assumes the obligations of an existing mortgage.

Balloon Payment. A final large payment that results at maturity when the periodic installment payments are not adequate to retire the principal amount of debt.

Bankruptcy. A legal procedure, carried out under the jurisdiction of courts of law, whereby a debtor's property is taken over for the benefit of the creditors.

Blanket Mortgage. A mortgage that is secured by the pledge of more than one parcel of property.

Book Value. The value of an asset remaining after accumulated depreciation has been deducted from the asset's original cost.

Capitalization Rate. A discount or interest rate used to find the present value of a series of future cash flows. This also is commonly referred to as the *discount rate.*

Chattel Mortgage. A mortgage on personal property such as equipment.

Collateral. Assets used as security for a loan.

Compound Interest. Interest paid on the original principal and on the accrued interest (i.e., interest on interest).

Construction Loan. Usually a short-term mortgage loan designed to finance construction of buildings on a property whereby periodic advances are made by the lender to the builder as the work progresses.

Conventional Mortgage. A mortgage loan without governmental backing in the form of Federal Housing Administration insurance or Veterans Administration guarantees.

Covenants. Detailed clauses in loan agreements that are designed to protect lenders.

Debt Service. The periodic payment of principal and interest required in the loan agreement.

Deed. A written instrument by which title to real property is transferred from one person to another person.

Default. The failure to fulfill a contractual obligation when it comes due such as the failure to make interest and/or principal payments.

Depreciation. The decline in the value over time of an asset as it is used or depreciates. This also refers to the writing-off the value of the asset over time.

Discount Points. Mortgages that are issued below market interest rates are discounted in terms of points, where 1 point equals 1 percent, in order to increase the effective yield. Points are subtracted from the face value of the loan.

Discount Rate. The interest rate used to find the present worth or value of a series of future cash flows. It is often called the *capitalization rate.*

Disintermediation. The process whereby savings are withdrawn from thrift institutions and commercial banks and are channeled into alternative investments.

Earnest Money. Money deposited by the purchaser to show evidence of good faith and intent to complete an agreement.

Economic Life. The useful life of a property.

Equity. The owner's interest or share of value in a property. This is determined as the difference between the current market value of the property and any outstanding loans or mortgage debt.

Escalator Clause. A clause in a loan instrument that permits the lender to raise or lower the rate of interest in a loan agreement on the basis of some schedule or index.

Escrow. Something of value such as real or personal property held by a third party until the performance of certain conditions or the happening of some act.

Federal Deposit Insurance Corporation (FDIC). This agency insures deposits and supervises member commercial banks.

Federal Home Loan Bank System. This system, which is headed by the Federal Home Loan Bank Board (FHLBB), supervises and regulates member savings and loan associations.

Federal Home Loan Mortgage Corporation (FHLMC). This agency provides a secondary market for the mortgages written by savings and loan associations that are members of the Federal Home Loan Bank System.

Federal Housing Administration (FHA). This agency provides mortgage loan insurance on homes that meet FHA requirements and standards.

FHA-Insured Mortgage. A mortgage loan that is insured by the Federal Housing Administration.

Federal National Mortgage Association (FNMA). This corporation purchases and sells mortgages in the secondary mortgage market. Although privately owned, the corporation is government regulated.

Federal Reserve System. This system, which is headed by the Federal Reserve Board, sets monetary policy and supervises and regulates member commercial banks.

Federal Savings and Loan Insurance Corporation (FSLIC). This agency insures deposits and supervises member savings and loan associations.

Fee Simple. A title to property without restrictions. This legal term indicates absolute ownership.

Foreclosure. Legal action to collect a debt against property secured by a mortgage.

Government National Mortgage Association (GNMA). A government-owned corporation that participates in the secondary mortgage market.

Housing and Urban Development, Department of (HUD). Created in 1965, HUD has a wide range of responsibilities including the regulation of the Federal Housing Administration and the Government National Mortgage Association.

Installment Land Contract. A contract used in the sale of property whereby the title is not conveyed until the installment payments are completed.

Internal Rate of Return (IRR). This is the actual compound rate of return on an investment and is found by determining the discount rate which equates the present value of future cash flows with the investment's cost.

Junior Mortgage. A mortgage that is subordinate to another mortgage. A similar relationship would hold in terms of a *junior lien.*

Leverage. The use of borrowed funds that have a fixed cost to purchase property.

Lien. A legal claim that is placed against property as security for payment of a debt.

Loan-To-Value Ratio. The percentage relationship between the amount of a mortgage loan and value of the property.

Mortgage. A pledge of property as security for the payment of a debt.

Mortgage Banker. A financial intermediary that originates mortgage loans and services mortgage loans.

Mortgage Broker. An agent that brings together buyers and sellers for real estate loans but does not service the mortgages.

Mortgagee. The lender of money secured by the mortgage.

Mortgagor. The borrower of the money secured by the mortgage.

Net Present Value (NPV) Method. This is a method for evaluating alternative investment proposals. The NPV is equal to the present value of future cash flows, discounted at a specified interest rate, minus the present value of the investment's cost.

Nominal Interest Rate. The stated interest rate in a contract.

Note. A written or signed instrument that acknowledges a debt and promises repayment.

Open-End Mortgage. A mortgage that can be increased by subsequent advances of principal after part of the original loan has been repaid.

Option. The right to purchase or lease property at a specific price for a designated time period.

Origination Fee. An amount charged by a financial institution for handling mortgage loan applications and the processing of the loan.

Package Mortgage. A mortgage secured by both real and personal property.

Partially Amortized Mortgage. A mortgage which will not be fully amortized at maturity and thus will require a *balloon payment* of the remaining principal at maturity.

Participation Mortgage. Several lenders have a share in a single mortgage.

Percentage Lease. A lease where the rental amount is stated as a percentage of business transacted on the leased property. This is usually a percentage of gross sales.

Personal Property. An item of value that is not real property or real estate.

Prepayment Clause. A mortgage clause that permits the payment of the mortgage principal, in part or in full, prior to the maturity date. This clause frequently provides for a penalty payment if the clause is exercised.

Principal. The amount of a loan or debt.

Property Tax. A tax levied against the owner of real and/or personal property based on the value of the owned property.

Purchase Money Mortgage. A mortgage given by the borrower to the seller as part of the purchase price of the real property.

Quit Claim Deed. A deed conveying the grantor's interest in real property without warranty in that the grantor is not responsible for failure to convey a clear title.

Real Estate. Land and its attachments. It also is referred to as *realty* or *real property*.

Real Estate Investment Trust (REIT). A trust authorized to invest in real estate that is managed and controlled by trustees and is exempt from federal corporate income taxes.

Real Property. Land and its attachments. It is used synonymously with *realty* and *real estate.*

Redemption. The right of the original owner of property to reclaim the property in the event of default by paying the loan principal and all related costs.

Release Clause. A provision that, upon payment of a specific amount of money, a stipulated lien will be removed from the property.

Replacement Cost. The current cost of replacing an existing property with a new property that has equivalent utility value.

Return on Assets or Investment (ROA or ROI). This is the income or yield on an investment expressed as a percentage of the total investment in assets.

Return on Equity (ROE). This is the income or yield on an investment expressed as a percentage of the owner's investment in assets. Since a portion of the investment in assets is frequently financed with debt, this use of *leverage* often causes ROE to differ from ROA.

Reversion Value. The value of property at some future date when the property reverts back to the owner in the case of a lease or to the grantor of the property.

Sale and Buyback. A financing arrangement whereby property is sold by a developer to an investor who in turn sells it back to the developer under a long-term sales arrangement. Title is retained by the investor.

Sale and Leaseback. A financing arrangement whereby a business sells real estate it owns and uses to an investor who in turn leases back the real estate to the business firm. This method of financing is usually on a long-term basis.

Second Mortgage. A mortgage that is subordinate to another mortgage (i.e., a first mortgage). This would be an example of a *junior mortgage.*

Secondary Mortgage Market. The market where previously issued mortgages are bought and sold amongst financial institutions and others. This differs from the primary mortgage market where new mortgage loans are originated between lender and borrower.

Security. Property used as collateral for a loan.

Servicing Fee. A fee charged by a financial intermediary to cover collection of mortgage payments, property inspection, payment of property taxes, and possible foreclosure expenses.

Simple Interest. Interest computed on the loan's remaining principal balance.

Straight-Line Depreciation. The writing-off the value of an asset in equal amounts over the life of the asset. This assumes a level decline in the value of the asset over time.

Subordination Clause. A clause in a mortgage or lease that places the holder in a secondary or subordinate position to the claims of another mortgagor.

Take-out Commitment. A loan commitment on the part of a lender to provide back-up support for construction financing until permanent financing is arranged.

Tandem Plan. A secondary mortgage market plan that combines GNMA guarantees with FNMA activities.

Term Mortgage. A mortgage that does not provide for amortization of principal over the life of the mortgage but rather requires payment of the total principal at maturity.

Trust Deed. A deed that conveys title to real estate to a third party trustee to be held for the benefit of a lender or beneficiary. This also is often referred to as a deed of trust.

Usury. Interest rates deemed to be excessive by state laws.

Variable Payment Mortgage. A mortgage that requires a constant payment of principal over the life of the mortgage (i.e., the mortgage is amortized in equal payments of principal).

Variable Rate Mortgage. A mortgage where the interest rate can be changed over time in relation to changes in a specified index.

VA-Guaranteed Mortgage. A mortgage where a portion of an eligible veteran's loan is guaranteed in terms of repayment to the lender by the Veterans Administration.

Warranty Deed. A deed under which the grantor guarantees title to the real property that is being sold. In the event of a bad title, the grantee has the right to sue the grantor for breach of warranty.

Wraparound Mortgage. A second or junior mortgage designed to encompass an existing mortgage. Payment on the existing mortgage is continued while a new larger (in dollar amount and often in terms of the interest rate) mortgage is given to the borrower. Thus, the new mortgage "wraps around" the original mortgage.

Appendix B

TABLES

Table 1 Compound Sum of $1

Year	1%	2%	3%	4%	5%	6%	7%	8%	9%	10%
1	1.010	1.020	1.030	1.040	1.050	1.060	1.070	1.080	1.090	1.100
2	1.020	1.040	1.061	1.082	1.102	1.124	1.145	1.166	1.186	1.210
3	1.030	1.061	1.093	1.125	1.158	1.191	1.225	1.260	1.295	1.331
4	1.041	1.082	1.126	1.170	1.216	1.262	1.311	1.360	1.412	1.464
5	1.051	1.104	1.159	1.217	1.276	1.338	1.403	1.469	1.539	1.611
6	1.062	1.126	1.194	1.265	1.340	1.419	1.501	1.587	1.677	1.772
7	1.072	1.149	1.230	1.316	1.407	1.504	1.606	1.714	1.828	1.949
8	1.083	1.172	1.267	1.369	1.477	1.594	1.718	1.851	1.993	2.144
9	1.094	1.195	1.305	1.423	1.551	1.689	1.838	1.999	2.172	2.358
10	1.105	1.219	1.344	1.480	1.629	1.791	1.967	2.159	2.367	2.594
11	1.116	1.243	1.384	1.539	1.710	1.898	2.105	2.332	2.580	2.853
12	1.127	1.268	1.426	1.601	1.796	2.012	2.252	2.518	2.813	3.138
13	1.138	1.294	1.469	1.665	1.886	2.133	2.410	2.720	3.066	3.452
14	1.149	1.319	1.513	1.732	1.980	2.261	2.579	2.937	3.342	3.797
15	1.161	1.346	1.558	1.801	2.079	2.397	2.759	3.172	3.642	4.177
16	1.173	1.373	1.605	1.873	2.183	2.540	2.952	3.426	3.970	4.595
17	1.184	1.400	1.653	1.948	2.292	2.693	3.159	3.700	4.328	5.054
18	1.196	1.428	1.702	2.026	2.407	2.854	3.380	3.996	4.717	5.560
19	1.208	1.457	1.754	2.107	2.527	3.026	3.617	4.316	5.142	6.116
20	1.220	1.486	1.806	2.191	2.653	3.207	3.870	4.661	5.604	6.728
25	1.282	1.641	2.094	2.666	3.386	4.292	5.427	6.848	8.623	10.835
30	1.348	1.811	2.427	3.243	4.322	5.743	7.612	10.063	13.268	17.449

(continued)

Table
1 Compound Sum of $1 (concluded)

Year	12%	14%	15%	16%	18%	20%	25%	30%
1	1.120	1.140	1.150	1.160	1.180	1.200	1.250	1.300
2	1.254	1.300	1.322	1.346	1.392	1.440	1.563	1.690
3	1.405	1.482	1.521	1.561	1.643	1.728	1.953	2.197
4	1.574	1.689	1.749	1.811	1.939	2.074	2.441	2.856
5	1.762	1.925	2.011	2.100	2.288	2.488	3.052	3.713
6	1.974	2.195	2.313	2.436	2.700	2.986	3.815	4.827
7	2.211	2.502	2.660	2.826	3.185	3.583	4.768	6.276
8	2.476	2.853	3.059	3.278	3.759	4.300	5.960	8.157
9	2.773	3.252	3.518	3.803	4.435	5.160	7.451	10.604
10	3.106	3.707	4.046	4.411	5.234	6.192	9.313	13.786
11	3.479	4.226	4.652	5.117	6.176	7.430	11.642	17.922
12	3.896	4.818	5.350	5.926	7.288	8.916	14.552	23.298
13	4.363	5.492	6.153	6.886	8.599	10.699	18.190	30.288
14	4.887	6.261	7.076	7.988	10.147	12.839	22.737	39.374
15	5.474	7.138	8.137	9.266	11.974	15.407	28.422	51.186
16	6.130	8.137	9.358	10.748	14.129	18.488	35.527	66.542
17	6.866	9.276	10.761	12.468	16.672	22.186	44.409	86.504
18	7.690	10.575	12.375	14.463	19.673	26.623	55.511	112.46
19	8.613	12.056	14.232	16.777	23.214	31.948	69.389	146.19
20	9.646	13.743	16.367	19.461	27.393	38.338	86.736	190.05
25	17.000	26.462	32.919	40.874	62.669	95.396	264.70	705.64
30	29.960	50.950	66.212	85.850	143.371	237.376	807.79	2620.00

Table 2 Present Worth of $1

Year	1%	2%	3%	4%	5%	6%	7%	8%	9%	10%
1	.990	.980	.971	.962	.952	.943	.935	.926	.917	.909
2	.980	.961	.943	.925	.907	.890	.873	.857	.842	.826
3	.971	.942	.915	.889	.864	.840	.816	.794	.772	.751
4	.961	.924	.889	.855	.823	.792	.763	.735	.708	.683
5	.951	.906	.863	.822	.784	.747	.713	.681	.650	.621
6	.942	.888	.838	.790	.746	.705	.666	.630	.596	.564
7	.933	.871	.813	.760	.711	.665	.623	.583	.547	.513
8	.923	.853	.789	.731	.677	.627	.582	.540	.502	.467
9	.914	.837	.766	.703	.645	.592	.544	.500	.460	.424
10	.905	.820	.744	.676	.614	.558	.508	.463	.422	.386
11	.896	.804	.722	.650	.585	.527	.475	.429	.388	.350
12	.887	.788	.701	.625	.557	.497	.444	.397	.356	.319
13	.879	.773	.681	.601	.530	.469	.415	.368	.326	.290
14	.870	.758	.661	.577	.505	.442	.388	.340	.299	.263
15	.861	.743	.642	.555	.481	.417	.362	.315	.275	.239
16	.853	.728	.623	.534	.458	.394	.339	.292	.252	.218
17	.844	.714	.605	.513	.436	.371	.317	.270	.231	.198
18	.836	.700	.587	.494	.416	.350	.296	.250	.212	.180
19	.828	.686	.570	.475	.396	.331	.276	.232	.194	.164
20	.820	.673	.554	.456	.377	.312	.258	.215	.178	.149
25	.780	.610	.478	.375	.295	.233	.184	.146	.116	.092
30	.742	.552	.412	.308	.231	.174	.131	.099	.075	.057

(continued)

Table
2 Present Worth of $1 (concluded)

Year	12%	14%	15%	16%	18%	20%	25%	30%
1	.893	.877	.870	.862	.847	.833	.800	.769
2	.797	.769	.756	.743	.718	.694	.640	.592
3	.712	.675	.658	.641	.609	.579	.512	.455
4	.636	.592	.572	.552	.516	.482	.410	.350
5	.567	.519	.497	.476	.437	.402	.320	.269
6	.507	.456	.432	.410	.370	.335	.262	.207
7	.452	.400	.376	.354	.314	.279	.210	.159
8	.404	.351	.327	.305	.266	.233	.168	.123
9	.361	.308	.284	.263	.226	.194	.134	.094
10	.322	.270	.247	.227	.191	.162	.107	.073
11	.287	.237	.215	.195	.162	.135	.086	.056
12	.257	.208	.187	.168	.137	.112	.069	.043
13	.229	.182	.163	.145	.116	.093	.055	.033
14	.205	.160	.141	.125	.099	.078	.044	.025
15	.183	.140	.123	.108	.084	.065	.035	.020
16	.163	.123	.107	.093	.071	.054	.028	.015
17	.146	.108	.093	.080	.060	.045	.023	.012
18	.130	.095	.081	.089	.051	.038	.018	.009
19	.116	.083	.070	.060	.043	.031	.014	.007
20	.104	.073	.061	.051	.037	.026	.012	.005
25	.059	.038	.030	.024	.016	.010	.004	.001
30	.033	.020	.015	.012	.007	.004	.001	.000

Table 3 Compound Sum of a $1 Annuity

Year	1%	2%	3%	4%	5%	6%
1	1.000	1.000	1.000	1.000	1.000	1.000
2	2.010	2.020	2.030	2.040	2.050	2.060
3	3.030	3.060	3.091	3.122	3.152	3.184
4	4.060	4.122	4.184	4.246	4.310	4.375
5	5.101	5.204	5.309	5.416	5.526	5.637
6	6.152	6.308	6.468	6.633	6.802	6.975
7	7.214	7.434	7.662	7.898	8.142	8.394
8	8.286	8.583	8.892	9.214	9.549	9.897
9	9.369	9.755	10.159	10.583	11.027	11.491
10	10.462	10.950	11.464	12.006	12.578	13.181
11	11.567	12.169	12.808	13.486	14.207	14.972
12	12.683	13.412	14.192	15.026	15.917	16.870
13	13.809	14.680	15.618	16.627	17.713	18.882
14	14.947	15.974	17.086	18.292	19.599	21.051
15	16.097	17.293	18.599	20.024	21.579	23.276
16	17.258	18.639	20.157	21.825	23.657	25.673
17	18.430	20.012	21.762	23.698	25.840	28.213
18	19.615	21.412	23.414	25.645	28.132	30.906
19	20.811	22.841	25.117	27.671	30.539	33.760
20	22.019	24.297	26.870	29.778	33.066	36.786
25	28.243	32.030	36.459	41.646	47.727	54.865
30	34.785	40.568	47.575	56.805	66.439	79.058

(continued)

Table 3 Compound Sum of a $1 Annuity (continued)

Year	7%	8%	9%	10%	12%	14%
1	1.000	1.000	1.000	1.000	1.000	1.000
2	2.070	2.080	2.090	2.100	2.120	2.140
3	3.215	3.246	3.278	3.310	3.374	3.440
4	4.440	4.506	4.573	4.641	4.770	4.921
5	5.751	5.867	5.985	6.105	6.353	6.610
6	7.153	7.336	7.523	7.716	8.115	8.536
7	8.654	8.923	9.200	9.487	10.089	10.730
8	10.260	10.637	11.028	11.436	12.300	13.233
9	11.978	12.488	13.021	13.579	14.776	16.085
10	13.816	14.487	15.193	15.937	17.549	19.337
11	15.784	16.645	17.560	18.531	20.655	23.044
12	17.888	18.977	20.141	21.384	24.133	27.271
13	20.141	21.495	22.953	24.523	28.029	32.089
14	22.550	24.215	26.019	27.975	32.393	37.581
15	25.129	27.152	29.361	31.772	37.280	43.842
16	27.888	30.324	33.003	35.950	42.753	50.980
17	30.840	33.750	36.974	40.545	48.884	59.118
18	33.999	37.450	41.301	45.599	55.750	68.394
19	37.379	41.466	46.018	51.159	63.440	78.969
20	40.995	45.762	51.160	57.275	72.052	91.025
25	63.249	73.106	84.701	98.347	133.334	181.871
30	94.461	113.283	136.308	164.494	241.333	356.787

(continued)

Table 3 Compound Sum of a $1 Annuity (concluded)

Year	16%	18%	20%	25%	30%
1	1.000	1.000	1.000	1.000	1.000
2	2.160	2.180	2.200	2.250	2.300
3	3.506	3.572	3.640	3.813	3.990
4	5.066	5.215	5.368	5.766	6.187
5	6.877	7.154	7.442	8.207	9.043
6	8.977	9.442	9.930	11.259	12.756
7	11.414	12.142	12.916	15.073	17.583
8	14.240	15.327	16.499	19.842	23.858
9	17.518	19.086	20.799	25.802	32.015
10	21.321	23.521	25.959	33.253	42.619
11	25.733	28.755	32.150	42.566	56.405
12	30.850	34.931	39.580	54.208	74.327
13	36.786	42.219	48.497	68.760	97.625
14	43.672	50.818	59.196	86.949	127.91
15	51.660	60.965	72.035	109.69	167.29
16	60.925	72.939	87.442	138.11	218.47
17	71.673	87.068	105.931	173.64	285.01
18	84.141	103.740	128.117	218.05	371.52
19	98.603	123.414	154.740	273.56	483.97
20	115.380	146.628	186.688	342.95	630.17
25	249.214	342.603	471.981	1054.80	2348.80
30	530.312	790.948	1181.882	3227.20	8730.00

Table 4 Present Worth of a $1 Annuity

Year	1%	2%	3%	4%	5%	6%
1	0.990	0.980	0.971	0.962	0.952	0.943
2	1.970	1.942	1.913	1.886	1.859	1.833
3	2.941	2.884	2.829	2.775	2.723	2.673
4	3.902	3.808	3.717	3.630	3.546	3.465
5	4.853	4.713	4.580	4.452	4.329	4.212
6	5.795	5.601	5.417	5.242	5.076	4.917
7	6.728	6.472	6.230	6.002	5.786	5.582
8	7.652	7.325	7.020	6.733	6.463	6.210
9	8.566	8.162	7.786	7.435	7.108	6.802
10	9.471	8.983	8.530	8.111	7.722	7.360
11	10.368	9.787	9.253	8.760	8.306	7.887
12	11.255	10.575	9.954	9.385	8.863	8.384
13	12.134	11.348	10.635	9.986	9.394	8.853
14	13.004	12.106	11.296	10.563	9.899	9.295
15	13.865	12.849	11.938	11.118	10.380	9.712
16	14.718	13.578	12.561	11.652	10.838	10.106
17	15.562	14.292	13.166	12.166	11.274	10.477
18	16.398	14.992	13.754	12.659	11.690	10.828
19	17.226	15.678	14.324	13.134	12.085	11.158
20	18.046	16.351	14.877	13.590	12.462	11.470
25	22.023	19.523	17.413	15.622	14.094	12.783
30	25.808	22.397	19.600	17.292	15.373	13.765

(continued)

4 Present Worth of a $1 Annuity (continued)

Year	7%	8%	9%	10%	12%	14%
1	0.935	0.926	0.917	0.909	0.893	0.877
2	1.808	1.783	1.759	1.736	1.690	1.647
3	2.624	2.577	2.531	2.487	2.402	2.322
4	3.387	3.312	3.240	3.170	3.037	2.914
5	4.100	3.993	3.890	3.791	3.605	3.433
6	4.766	4.623	4.486	4.355	4.111	3.889
7	5.389	5.206	5.033	4.868	4.564	4.288
8	5.971	5.747	5.535	5.335	4.968	4.639
9	6.515	6.247	5.995	5.759	5.328	4.946
10	7.024	6.710	6.418	6.145	5.650	5.216
11	7.499	7.139	6.805	6.495	5.938	5.453
12	7.943	7.536	7.161	6.814	6.194	5.660
13	8.358	7.904	7.487	7.103	6.424	5.842
14	8.745	8.244	7.786	7.367	6.628	6.002
15	9.108	8.559	8.060	7.606	6.811	6.142
16	9.447	8.851	8.312	7.824	6.974	6.265
17	9.763	9.122	8.544	8.022	7.120	5.373
18	10.059	9.372	8.756	8.201	7.250	6.467
19	10.336	9.604	8.950	8.365	7.366	6.550
20	10.594	9.818	9.128	8.514	7.469	6.623
25	11.654	10.675	9.823	9.077	7.843	6.873
30	12.409	11.258	10.274	9.427	8.055	7.003

(continued)

Table 4 Present Worth of a $1 Annuity (concluded)

Year	16%	18%	20%	25%	30%
1	0.862	0.847	0.833	.800	.769
2	1.605	1.566	1.528	1.440	1.361
3	2.246	2.174	2.106	1.952	1.816
4	2.798	2.690	2.589	2.362	2.166
5	3.274	3.127	2.991	2.689	2.436
6	3.685	3.498	3.326	2.951	2.643
7	4.039	3.812	3.605	3.161	2.802
8	4.344	4.078	3.837	3.329	2.925
9	4.607	4.303	4.031	3.463	3.019
10	4.833	4.494	4.193	3.571	3.092
11	5.029	4.656	4.327	3.656	3.147
12	5.197	4.793	4.439	3.725	3.190
13	5.342	4.910	4.533	3.780	3.223
14	5.468	5.008	4.611	3.824	3.249
15	5.575	5.092	4.675	3.859	3.268
16	5.669	5.162	4.730	3.887	3.283
17	5.749	4.222	4.775	3.910	3.295
18	5.818	5.273	4.812	3.928	3.304
19	5.877	5.316	4.844	3.942	3.311
20	5.929	5.353	4.870	3.954	3.316
25	6.097	5.467	4.948	3.985	3.329
30	6.177	5.517	4.979	3.995	3.332

Table
5 Monthly Payments Needed to Amortize a $1,000 Loan

Year	6.0%	6.5%	7.0%	7.5%	8.0%	8.5%	9.0%
1	86.08	86.31	86.54	86.77	86.99	87.22	87.45
2	44.33	44.55	44.78	45.00	45.23	45.46	45.69
3	30.43	30.65	30.88	31.11	31.34	31.57	31.80
4	23.49	23.72	23.95	24.18	24.41	24.65	24.89
5	19.34	19.57	19.80	20.04	20.28	20.52	20.76
6	16.58	16.81	17.05	17.29	17.53	17.78	18.03
7	14.61	14.85	15.09	15.34	15.59	15.84	16.09
8	13.14	13.39	13.63	13.88	14.14	14.39	14.65
9	12.01	12.26	12.51	12.76	13.02	13.28	13.54
10	11.10	11.36	11.61	11.87	12.13	12.40	12.67
11	10.37	10.62	10.88	11.15	11.42	11.69	11.96
12	9.76	10.02	10.28	10.55	10.82	11.10	11.38
13	9.25	9.51	9.78	10.05	10.33	10.61	10.90
14	8.81	9.08	9.35	9.63	9.91	10.20	10.49
15	8.44	8.71	8.99	9.27	9.56	9.85	10.14
16	8.12	8.39	8.67	8.96	9.25	9.55	9.85
17	7.83	8.11	8.40	8.69	8.98	9.28	9.59
18	7.58	7.87	8.16	8.45	8.75	9.05	9.36
19	7.36	7.65	7.94	8.24	8.55	8.85	9.17
20	7.16	7.46	7.75	8.06	8.36	8.68	9.00
25	6.44	6.75	7.07	7.39	7.72	8.05	8.39
30	6.00	6.32	6.65	6.99	7.34	7.69	8.05
35	5.70	6.04	6.39	6.74	7.10	7.47	7.84
40	5.50	5.85	6.21	6.58	6.95	7.33	7.71

(continued)

Table 5 Monthly Payments Needed to Amortize a $1,000 Loan (concluded)

Year	9.5%	10.0%	10.5%	11.0%	11.5%	12.0%
1	87.69	87.92	88.15	88.39	88.62	88.85
2	45.92	46.15	46.38	46.61	46.84	47.08
3	32.03	32.27	32.50	32.74	32.98	33.22
4	25.12	25.36	25.60	25.85	26.09	26.34
5	21.00	21.25	21.49	21.74	21.99	22.25
6	18.28	18.53	18.78	19.04	19.29	19.55
7	16.34	16.60	16.86	17.12	17.39	17.65
8	14.91	15.17	15.44	15.71	15.98	16.25
9	13.81	14.08	14.35	14.63	14.90	15.18
10	12.94	13.22	13.49	13.78	14.06	14.35
11	12.24	12.52	12.80	13.09	13.38	13.68
12	11.66	11.95	12.24	12.54	12.83	13.13
13	11.19	11.48	11.78	12.08	12.38	12.69
14	10.78	11.08	11.38	11.69	12.00	12.31
15	10.44	10.75	11.05	11.37	11.68	12.00
16	10.15	10.46	10.77	11.09	11.41	11.74
17	9.90	10.21	10.53	10.85	11.18	11.51
18	9.68	10.00	10.32	10.65	10.98	11.32
19	9.49	9.81	10.14	10.47	10.81	11.15
20	9.32	9.65	9.98	10.32	10.66	11.01
25	8.74	9.09	9.44	9.80	10.16	10.53
30	8.41	8.78	9.15	9.52	9.90	10.29
35	8.22	8.60	8.98	9.37	9.76	10.16
40	8.10	8.49	8.89	9.28	9.68	10.09

Note: This Table indicates the required monthly payment necessary to amortize each $1,000 in loans. Thus, to find the monthly payment on, say, a $20,000 25-year 9 percent loan, we take the monthly payment on a $1,000 25-year 9 percent loan which is $8.39 and then multiply it by a factor of 20. This, in turn, results in a monthly payment of $167.80 for the $20,000 loan.

Table 6 Annual Constant Percentages

Year	6%	7%	8%	9%	10%	11%	12%
1	103.30	103.84	104.39	104.95	105.50	106.07	106.63
2	53.19	53.73	54.28	54.82	55.37	55.93	56.49
3	36.51	37.06	37.61	38.16	38.72	39.29	39.86
4	28.19	28.74	29.30	29.86	30.44	31.02	31.60
5	23.20	23.76	24.33	24.91	25.50	26.09	26.69
6	19.89	20.46	21.04	21.63	22.23	22.84	23.46
7	17.53	18.11	18.70	19.31	19.92	20.55	21.18
8	15.77	16.36	16.96	17.58	18.21	18.85	19.50
9	14.41	15.01	15.62	16.25	16.89	17.55	18.22
10	13.32	13.93	14.56	15.20	15.86	16.53	17.22
11	12.44	13.06	13.70	14.35	15.02	15.71	16.41
12	11.71	12.34	12.99	13.66	14.34	15.04	15.76
13	11.10	11.74	12.40	13.08	13.77	14.49	15.22
14	10.58	11.23	11.90	12.59	13.30	14.03	14.78
15	10.13	10.79	11.47	12.17	12.90	13.64	14.40
16	9.74	10.41	11.10	11.81	12.55	13.31	14.09
17	9.40	10.08	10.78	11.51	12.25	13.03	13.81
18	9.10	9.79	10.50	11.24	12.00	12.78	13.58
19	8.83	9.53	10.25	11.00	11.78	12.57	13.38
20	8.60	9.30	10.04	10.80	11.58	12.39	13.21
25	7.73	8.48	9.26	10.07	10.90	11.76	12.64
30	7.20	7.98	8.81	9.66	10.53	11.43	12.34
35	6.84	7.67	8.52	9.41	10.32	11.24	12.19
40	6.60	7.46	8.34	9.26	10.19	11.14	12.10

Note: An annual constant percentage value is calculated by first taking the sum of 12 monthly payments and then expressing this sum as a percentage of the principal loan amount. In formula fashion this becomes:

Annual Constant = (12 × Monthly Payment × 100)/Principal Loan Amount.

The 100 factor is used to express the annual constant in percentage form. For example, the monthly payment on a $20,000 25-year 9 percent loan is $167.80 (calculated from Table 5 in the Appendix). The monthly payment times 1200 is $201,360. This figure divided by the $20,000 loan gives an annual constant value of 10.07 (see year 25 at 9 percent in the above table).

Table 7 Remaining Loan Balances
(Percentage of Original Loan Amount)

Age of Loan in Years	6% Rate Original Loan Length in Years					7% Rate Original Loan Length in Years				
	10	15	20	25	30	10	15	20	25	30
1	92.5%	95.8%	97.3%	98.2%	98.8%	92.8%	96.1%	97.6%	98.5%	99.0%
2	84.5	91.3	94.5	96.3	97.5	85.2	91.9	95.1	96.8	97.9
3	76.0	86.5	91.5	94.3	96.1	76.9	87.4	92.3	95.1	96.7
4	67.0	81.4	88.3	92.2	94.6	68.1	82.6	89.4	93.2	95.5
5	57.4	76.0	84.9	89.9	93.1	58.6	77.4	86.3	91.2	94.1
10	0.0	43.6	64.5	76.3	83.7	0.0	45.4	66.8	78.6	85.8
15		0.0	37.0	58.0	71.0		0.0	39.1	60.9	74.0
20			0.0	33.3	54.0			0.0	35.7	57.3
25				0.0	31.0				0.0	33.6
30					0.0					0.0

Years	8% Rate					9% Rate				
	10	15	20	25	30	10	15	20	25	30
1	93.2%	96.4%	97.9%	98.7%	99.2%	93.5%	96.7%	98.1%	98.9%	99.3%
2	85.8	92.5	95.6	97.3	98.3	86.5	93.1	96.1	97.7	98.6
3	77.8	88.3	93.1	95.7	97.3	78.7	89.1	93.8	96.3	97.8
4	69.2	83.7	90.4	94.1	96.2	70.3	84.8	91.4	94.9	96.9
5	59.8	78.8	87.5	92.3	95.1	61.0	80.1	88.7	93.3	95.9
10	0.0	47.1	68.9	80.8	87.7	0.0	48.9	71.0	82.7	89.4
15		0.0	41.2	63.6	76.8		0.0	43.3	66.2	79.3
20			0.0	38.1	60.5			0.0	40.4	63.5
25				0.0	36.2				0.0	38.8
30					0.0					0.0

Table
7 Remaining Loan Balances (concluded)

Age of Loan in Years	10% Rate Original Loan Length in Years					11% Rate Original Loan Length in Years				
	10	15	20	25	30	10	15	20	25	30
1	93,9%	97.0%	98.3%	99.1%	99.4%	94.2%	97.2%	98.5%	99.2%	99.5%
2	87.1	93.6	96.5	98.0	98.8	87.7	94.1	96.9	98.3	90.0
3	79.6	89.9	94.5	96.9	98.2	80.4	90.7	95.1	97.3	98.5
4	71.3	85.8	92.3	95.3	97.4	72.4	86.8	93.1	96.2	97.9
5	62.2	81.3	89.8	94.2	96.6	63.3	82.5	90.8	95.0	97.2
10	0.0	50.6	73.0	84.6	90.9	0.0	52.3	74.9	86.2	92.3
15		0.0	45.4	68.8	81.7		0.0	47.5	71.1	83.8
20			0.0	42.8	66.4			0.0	45.1	69.1
25				0.0	41.3				0.0	43.8
30					0.0					0.0

Years	12% Rate				
	10	15	20	25	30
1	94.5%	97.5%	98.7%	99.3%	99.6%
2	88.3	94.6	97.3	98.6	99.2
3	81.3	91.4	95.6	97.7	98.8
4	73.4	87.7	93.8	96.7	98.2
5	64.5	83.6	91.7	95.7	97.7
10	0.0	53.9	76.7	87.8	93.4
15		0.0	49.5	73.4	85.7
20			0.0	47.3	71.7
25				0.0	46.2
30					0.0

Note: This Table indicates the loan balance remaining on a previously made mortgage loan. For example, the remaining loan balance on a $20,000, 25-year, 9 percent loan that has been outstanding for 5 years can be found by first turning to the 9% rate. Then, begin by reading across at the 5 year "age of the loan" row until the 25-year original loan column is found. This indicates that 93.3 percent (or $18,660) of the $20,000 loan will still be outstanding.

MAJOR LEGISLATION AFFECTING REAL ESTATE FINANCE

Date	Legislation

1932 Federal Home Loan Bank Act

Established the Federal Home Loan Bank System in form similar to the Federal Reserve System. There is a Federal Home Loan Bank Board and 12 regional banks. This Act provided a central credit structure to assist institutions engaged in making home mortgage loans.

1933 Home Owners' Loan Act

Provided for the creation of a system of federal savings and loan associations. These federal associations were to be chartered and supervised by the Federal Home Loan Bank Board.

1934 National Housing Act

Created the Federal Housing Administration. Also provided for the establishment of privately-owned mortgage institutions to operate a national secondary mortgage market. Not only was the Federal Housing Administration established to insure home mortgages, but this Act also provided for the creation of the Federal Savings and Loan Insurance Corporation. The FSLIC provides insurance for savings accounts held at member associations.

1938 Federal National Mortgage Association (creation of)

The Reconstruction Finance Corporation provided capital for the establishment of the Federal National Mortgage Association which was to operate as a government-sponsored secondary mortgage market.

1944 Servicemen's Readjustment Act

Frequently referred to as the G.I. Bill of Rights. This Act established a program for the guarantee of mortgage loans made to veterans of the armed services. The Veterans Administration guarantees these home mortgage loans.

1949 Housing Act

Provided for national housing goals. Also aided municipalities to clear slum areas and provide public housing through federal grants. Rural areas also received financial assistance.

1950 Federal National Mortgage Association (transference of)

Provision was made to move the FNMA from under the Reconstruction Finance Corporation to the Housing and Home Finance Agency which was created in 1942 to coordinate federal home financing activities.

1950 Regulation X (real estate credit — not currently operational)

The Board of Governors of the Federal Reserve System, with concurrence of the Housing and Home Finance Administration, was authorized to regulate real estate credit. Maximum loan amounts, minimum down payments, and maximum repayment periods were set to restrain construction expansion and the related inflationary pressures during the Korean War. These restrictions were removed in 1952.

1954 Federal National Mortgage Association Charter Act

The FNMA was rechartered as a federal agency with some corporate structural characteristics. It continued as an agency of the Housing and Home Finance Agency but was to become privately-owned.

1961 Housing Act

Provided for further federal government involvement in housing. New programs included subsidized rental housing for low to moderate income families and FHA-insured loans for home repair and modernization for homes located in certain urban areas.

1968 Housing and Urban Development Act

Authorized further federal government participation in housing. Two new programs were created for home ownership (Section 235) and rental housing (Section 236) assistance in the form of subsidies whereby the federal government paid a portion of loan interest costs.

The FNMA was reorganized as a separate privately-owned corporation. At the same time, the Government National Mortgage Association was created as a wholly-owned government corporation under the direction of the Department of Housing and Urban Development.

1968 Truth in Lending Act (Regulation Z)

Established under the Consumer Credit Protection Act of 1968. The Board of Governors of the Federal Reserve System was given authority to regulate (Regulation Z) consumer credit costs in a way so as to make the cost statements more meaningful. Both the amount of finance charges and the effective annual percentage interest rate must be stated.

1970 Emergency Home Finance Act

Created the Federal Home Loan Mortgage Corporation for purposes of providing a secondary mortgage market for savings and loan association members of the Federal Home Loan Bank System. The secondary market was to be for FHA, VA, and conventional mortgages. The act also provided for the Federal National Mortgage Association to purchase and sell conventional mortgages.

1974 Equal Credit Opportunity Act

Prohibits discrimination in the decision to grant credit on the basis of sex or marital status.

1974 Real Estate Settlement Procedures Act

Provided a comprehensive set of guidelines to be used for handling loan closing costs and settlement practices and procedures.

1976 Equal Credit Opportunity Act Amendments

Broadened the scope of the Equal Credit Opportunity Act. Prohibits discrimination in the granting of credit on the basis of sex, marital status, race, color, religion, national origin, age, source of income, and the exercise of rights in good faith under the Consumer Protection Act of 1968.

1976 Real Estate Settlement Procedures Act Amendments

Made some of the requirements under the Real Estate Settlement Procedures Act less stringent. Lenders can provide good faith estimates of closing costs (instead of actual costs) and can tie disclosure timing to when loan applications are received (instead of at the closing date).

Appendix D

SOME SPECIAL FINANCING DEVICES

The financing devices described in this Appendix are included as examples only. An attorney should be consulted to handle the details of a transaction requiring the use of such a device.

Percentage Lease Clause

A clause such as the following may be inserted in a lease to make it a percentage lease with a minimum gross amount payable to the landlord:

> The Lessee shall, at (his or her) own expense, equip and operate the demised premises as a cheese and sausage shop and shall pay as rent 10 percent of the gross receipts from the operation of the said cheese and sausage shop to be paid on the fifth day of each and every month out of the gross receipts of the preceding month. The Lessee nevertheless agrees to pay a minimum rental of $400 per month regardless of the amount of gross receipts.

Note: In a shopping center, for example, if a builder-developer is able to obtain percentage leases (especially of one or more major chains) prior to construction, then lenders will readily finance the project.

The Wraparound Mortgage (All Inclusive Deed of Trust)

There is no special form for the wraparound mortgage. It is accomplished by insertion of a clause in an ordinary mortgage (deed of trust) form in the printed forms after the property description (its location simply being that there's more blank space there).

For example, Seller has a building worth $75,000 on which there is a 1964 mortgage of $30,000 with interest at 6%. Buyer arrives with $15,000 in cash. Substantially the clause may be written as follows:

> Buyer hereby assumes and promises to pay a certain mortgage executed by Seller to Ace-Hi Bank as mortgagee dated June 18, 1964, and recorded June 19, 1964, in the office of the Clerk of the County of , liber 149, page 69, of Mortgages on which there is now due the sum of $30,000 with interest thereon at the rate of 6 percent per annum and as further consideration for this mortgage, Buyer (mortgagor) agrees to pay an additional 3 percent per annum to Seller on the unpaid balance of the above mortgage (or deed of trust), this in addition to the conditions and terms as hereinafter set forth.

Thus, Buyer pays $15,000 cash and assumes a $30,000 first mortgage and gives Seller a second purchase money mortgage in the amount of $30,000 at, say, 9 percent interest for a total purchase price of $75,000. If the payments are paid annually, Seller receives $900 in the assumed $30,000 mortgage ($30,000 × .03), plus $2,700 on the second purchase money mortgage ($30,000 × .09), or $3,600 in interest.

Notes: (1) The deed from Seller to Buyer will contain an assumption clause. (2) Buyer should receive either a mortgagee's certificate of reduction or an assumption statement from Ace-Hi Bank so that Buyer will know that, in fact, $30,000 is due on the first mortgage (or deed of trust).

The Affidavit of Title

Almost all lending institutions insist that title be insured by a title company before approving a loan. It sometimes occurs that a title company may have some doubts as to the validity of the seller's title. For example, the seller may have a common name such as John Smith. The title Company may have found a judgment against a "John Smith." In this event our seller John Smith will be required to sign an Affidavit of Title indicating that he is not the John Smith with the Judgment against him.

If he signs the Affidavit of Title falsely, he is not only guilty of fraud, but may also be guilty of perjury. An Affidavit of Title is shown on page 351.

In many states a corporation cannot mortgage or place a deed of trust on a parcel of property until the Board of Directors passes a resolution to mortgage or place a deed of trust on the property. A certificate to Mortgage the property must be signed by the Corporate Secretary and recorded. A Certificate to Mortgage is shown on page 352.

Standard N.Y.B.T.U. Form 8051* 8-75-5M – Affidavit of Title

Affidavit of Title

State of New York }
County of } *ss.:*

Title No. ....

, being duly sworn, says:

*If owner is a corporation, fill in office held by deponent and name of corporation.

I reside at No.

I am the *

owner in fee simple of premises

and   the grantee   described in a certain deed of said premises recorded in the Register's Office of   County in (Liber) (Record Liber) (Reel)   of Conveyances, page   .

Said premises have been in $\frac{my}{its}$ possession since 19   ; that $\frac{my}{its}$ possession thereof has been peaceable and undisturbed, and the title thereto has never been disputed, questioned or rejected, nor insurance thereof refused, as far as I know. I know of no facts by reason of which said possession or title might be called in question, or by reason of which any claim to any part of said premises or any interest therein adverse to $\frac{me}{it}$ might be set up. There are no federal tax claims or liens assessed or filed against $\frac{me}{it}$. There are no judgments against $\frac{me}{it}$ unpaid or unsatisfied of record entered in any court of this state, or of the United States, and said premises are, as far as I know, free from all leases, mortgages, taxes, assessments, water charges, sewer rents and other liens and encumbrances, except

Said premises are now occupied by

No proceedings in bankruptcy have ever been instituted by or against $\frac{me}{it}$ in any court or before any officer of any state, or of the United States, nor $\frac{have\ I}{has\ it}$ at any time made an assignment for the benefit of creditors, nor an assignment, now in effect, of the rents of said premises or any part thereof.

*This paragraph to be omitted if owner is a corporation:

*I am a citizen of the United States, and am more than 18 years old. I am by occupation

     . I am married to   who is over the age of 18 years and is competent to convey or mortgage real estate. I was married to her on the day of   19   . I have never been married to any other person now living. I have not been known by any other name during the past ten years.

*This paragraph to be omitted if owner is not a corporation.

*That the charter of said corporation is in full force and effect and no proceeding is pending for its dissolution or annulment. That all license and franchise taxes due and payable by said corporation have been paid in full.

There are no actions pending affecting said premises. That no repairs, alterations or improvements have been made to said premises which have not been completed more than four months prior to the date hereof. There are no facts known to me relating to the title to said premises which have not been set forth in this affidavit.

This affidavit is made to induce

to accept a $\frac{of}{on}$ said premises, and to induce The Title Guarantee Company to issue its policy of title insurance numbered above covering said premises knowing that they will rely on the statements herein made.

Sworn to before me this

day of   , 19   _____

Consult Your Lawyer Before Signing This Instrument—This Instrument Should Be Used By Lawyers Only.

Standard N.Y.B.T.U. Form 8052 • 11-74-10M– Certificate of Directors' Resolution to Mortgage Corporate Property.

CONSULT YOUR LAWYER BEFORE SIGNING THIS INSTRUMENT—THIS INSTRUMENT SHOULD BE USED BY LAWYERS ONLY.

The undersigned, the secretary of

, a New York corporation,

DOES HEREBY CERTIFY:

1.   At a meeting of the board of directors of the above mentioned corporation, duly called and held this day at which a quorum was present and acted throughout, the board of directors unanimously adopted the following resolution, which has not been modified or rescinded:

RESOLVED, that the corporation execute and deliver to

or to any other person or corporation a mortgage covering the property owned by said corporation located at

such mortgage to be for the sum of $ to secure payment of a note of the corporation, bearing even date therewith, conditioned for the payment of said sum, with interest thereon,

that said note and mortgage be in such form and contain such interest rate or rates, time of payment, including installment payments, and such other terms, provisions, conditions, stipulations and agreements as the officer of the corporation executing the same may deem proper and advisable; and that the president or vice president or any other officer of the corporation be and each of them hereby is authorized to execute and deliver such note and mortgage and such other instruments as such officer may deem proper and advisable and to affix the seal of the corporation thereto.

2.   Neither the certificate of incorporation nor the by-laws contain any special requirement as to the number of directors required to pass such resolution.

3.   The certificate of incorporation of the corporation does not require any vote or consent of shareholders to authorize the making of such mortgage.

This certificate is made and delivered in order to induce the lender referred to in the foregoing resolution to make the loan and accept the mortgage referred to therein and to induce any title insurance company to issue a policy of title insurance insuring to such lender the validity and priority of such mortgage.

IN WITNESS WHEREOF, the undersigned has hereto affixed h   hand and the seal of the above mentioned corporation this   day of   , 19

(Corporate Seal)   ....

STATE OF NEW YORK

COUNTY OF   } ss.:

On the   day of   , 19   , before me came

to me known and known to me to be the individual described in and who executed the foregoing certificate and acknowledged to me that   he executed the same.

....
                                        Notary Public

Note: The mortgage should contain the following recital: "The execution of this mortgage has been duly authorized by the board of directors of the mortgagor."
See Section 911 of the Business Corporation Law.
Subdivision (e) of Section 715 of said law provides that the offices of president and secretary may not be held by the same person, except when that person owns all of the issued and outstanding stock of the corporation.

Appendix E

SUGGESTED READINGS BY SELECTED TOPICS

Apartment Building Financing

Smith, Charles C., and Harold A. Lubell. "New Look at Apartment House Financing," *Real Estate Review* (Spring, 1977), pp. 13–16.

Bankruptcy and Default

Rasmussen, Vaughn B., II. "Dealing with the Buyer of Property in Trouble," *Real Estate Review* (Winter, 1976), pp. 39–44.

Smith, Charles C., and Harold A. Lubell. "Lender Looks at Bankruptcy," *Real Estate Review* (Fall, 1976), pp. 7–11.

von Furstenberg, George M. "Default Risk on FHA-Insured Home Mortgages as a Function of the Terms of Financing, a Quantitative Analysis," *Journal of Finance* (June, 1969), pp. 455–65.

von Furstenberg, George M., and R. Jeffrey Green. "Home Mortgage Delinquencies: A Cohort Analysis," *Journal of Finance* (December, 1974), pp. 1545–48.

Condominiums

Clurman, David, and Edna L. Hebard. *Condominiums and Cooperatives*. New York: Wiley-Interscience, 1970.

Kozuch, James R., and Andrew G. Shank. "Management of Funds Is Key to Successful Condo Conversions," *Mortgage Banker* (November, 1974), pp. 5–12.

Levin, Michael R. "Financing the Commercial Condominium," *Real Estate Review* (Winter, 1975), pp. 71–77.

Weiss, Stephen J. "The Legal Corner: When Co-op. Shares and Condominiums Constitute Securities," *Real Estate Review* (Winter, 1976), pp. 15–17.

Construction Loans

Goldberg, Alfred M. "How HUD Handles Its Problem Construction Loans," *Real Estate Review* (Winter, 1976), pp. 45–48.

Hall, Cary H. "Successful Construction Loan Demands Expert Supervision, Careful Planning," *The Mortgage Banker* (October, 1976), pp. 92–98.

Roberts, Paul E. "Working out the Construction Mortgage Loan," *Real Estate Review* (Summer, 1975), pp. 50–57.

Schulkin, Peter A. "Construction Lending at Large Commercial Banks," *Real Estate Review* (Spring, 1971), pp. 54–60.

Tockarshewsky, J. B. "Reducing the Risks in Construction Lending," *Real Estate Review* (Spring, 1977), pp. 59–63.

Convertible Mortgages

Vitt, Lois A., and Joel H. Berstein. "Convertible Mortgages: New Financing Tool?" *Real Estate Review* (Spring, 1976), pp. 33–37.

Credit Availability

Meltzer, Allan H. "Credit Availability and Economic Decisions: Some Evidence from the Mortgage and Housing Markets," *Journal of Finance* (June, 1974), pp. 763–77.

Farm Real Estate Financing

Duncan, Marvin. "Farm Real Estate: Who Buys and How?" *Monthly Review*, Federal Reserve Bank of Kansas City (June, 1977), pp. 3–9.

Federal Home Loan Mortgage Corporation

Harrington, Philip N. "Freddie Mac: Big Man in Mortgages," *Real Estate Review* (Winter, 1974), pp. 102–4.

Federal Housing Administration

Cunningham, Robert P. "Requiem for FHA Is Premature," *The Appraisal Journal* (January, 1977), pp. 95–102.

Federal National Mortgage Association

Hunter, Oakley. "Fannie Mae Prepares for a New Role in Conventional Mortgage Markets," *Banking* (October, 1971), pp. 66–70.

Financing (General)

Smith, Charles C., and Harold A. Lubell. "Real Estate Financing: Handling Condemnation Awards and Insurance Proceeds," *Real Estate Review* (Winter, 1976), pp. 8–10.

Smith, Charles C., and Harold A. Lubell. "Real Estate Financing: Protecting the Lender," *Real Estate Review* (Summer, 1977), pp. 14–16.

Government National Mortgage Association

Connally, James J. "Historical Analysis of GNMA's Activity can Clarify Current Yields," *The Mortgage Banker* (May, 1977), pp. 83–93.

Housing Cycles

Board of Governors of the Federal Reserve System. *Ways to Moderate Fluctuations in Housing Construction*. Washington, D.C., 1972.

Cloos, George W., and William R. Sayre. "Bull Market in Homes," *Economic Perspectives*, Federal Reserve Bank of Chicago (July–August, 1977), pp. 7–16.

Stevens, Neil A. "Housing: A Cyclical Industry on the Upswing," *Review*, Federal Reserve Bank of St. Louis (August, 1976), pp. 15–20.

Housing Subsidies

Aaron, Henry J. *Shelter and Subsidies: Who Benefits from Federal Housing Policies?* Washington, D.C.: The Brookings Institution, 1972.

Brueggeman, William B. "Federal Housing Subsidies: Conceptual Issues and Benefit Patterns," *Journal of Economics and Business* (Winter, 1975), pp. 141–49.

Downs, Anthony. *Federal Housing Subsidies: How Are They Working?* Lexington, Mass.: Lexington Books, 1973.

Halperin, Jerome Y., and Michael J. Brenner. "Opportunities Under the New Section 8 Housing Program." *Real Estate Review* (Spring, 1976), pp. 67–75.

Investment Analysis

Dickerson, Frederick G. "A Technique for the Analysis of Owner-Financed Sales," *The Appraisal Journal* (January, 1976), pp. 55–62.

Pellat, P. G. K. "The Analysis of Real Estate Investments under Uncertainty," *Journal of Finance* (May, 1972), pp. 459–71.

Rams, Edwin M. "Investment Mechanics vs. Investment Analysis," *The Appraisal Journal* (January, 1974), pp. 62–65.

Roulac, Stephen E. "Life Cycle of a Real Estate Investment," *Real Estate Review* (Fall, 1974), pp. 113–17.

Whisler, William D. "Analyzing the Effects of Deviations from Forecasts in Real Estate Investment Analysis," *The Appraisal Journal* (January, 1977), pp. 35–48.

Wiley, Robert J. "Real Estate Investment Analysis: An Empirical Study," *The Appraisal Journal* (October, 1976), pp. 586–592.

Joint Ventures

Aronsohn, Alan J. B. "The Real Estate Limited Partnership and Other Joint Ventures," *Real Estate Review* (Spring, 1971), pp. 43–49.

Reiling, William S. "A Program for Joint Ventures," *The Mortgage Banker* (August, 1971), pp. 24, 36–42.

Leasing

Halper, Emanuel M. "What is a New Net Net Net Lease?" *Real Estate Review* (Winter, 1974), pp. 9–14.

Kempner, Paul S. "Investments in Single-Tenant Net Leased Properties," *Real Estate Review* (Summer, 1974), pp. 131–34.

Levy, Daniel S. "ABC's of Shopping Center Leases," *Real Estate Review* (Spring, 1971), pp. 12–16.

McMichael, Stanley L., and Paul T. O'Keefe. *Leases: Percentage, Short and Long Term.* Englewood Cliffs, N.J.: Prentice-Hall, Inc., 1974.

Starr, John O. "Lease Guarantee Insurance," *The Appraisal Journal* (April, 1972), pp. 175–87.

Legislation (General)

Duffy, Robert E., Jr. "The Real Estate Settlement Procedures Act of 1974," *Real Estate Review* (Winter, 1976), pp. 86–93.

McMullen, William H., Jr., "Truth in Selling: The Interstate Land Sales Full Disclosure Act of 1968," *Real Estate Review* (Spring, 1971), pp. 94–98.

Leverage

Clark, William Dennison. "Leverage: Magnificent Mover of Real Estate," *Real Estate Review* (Winter, 1972), pp. 8–13.

Limited Dividend Partnerships

Higginbottom, Elzie. "Fulfilling Nonprofit Housing Goals with Limited Dividend Partnerships," *The Mortgage Banker* (November, 1970), pp. 76–80.

Mortgage-Backed Securities

Kozuch, James R. "Study Analyzes Risks Facing Issuers of GNMA Mortgage-Backed-Securities," *The Mortgage Banker* (February, 1977), pp. 8–20.

"The GNMA Mortgage-Backed Security," a special issue of *The Mortgage Banker* (May, 1971).

Mortgage Futures Market

Kasriel, Paul L. "Hedging Interest Rate Fluctuations," *Business Conditions*, Federal Reserve Bank of Chicago (April, 1976), pp. 3–10.

Stevens, Neil A. "A Mortgage Futures Market: Its Development, Uses, Benefits and Costs," *Review*, Federal Reserve Bank of St. Louis (April, 1976), pp. 12–19.

Mortgage Interest Rate Ceilings

Peters, Helen F. "The Mortgage Market: A Place for Ceilings," *Business Review*, Federal Reserve Bank of Philadelphia (July–August, 1977), pp. 13–21.

Mortgage Prepayments

Kinkade, Maurice E. "Mortgage Prepayments and Their Effects on S & L's," *FHLBB Journal* (January, 1976), pp. 12–18.

Participations

Chesborough, Lawell D. "Do Participation Loans Pay Off?" *Real Estate Review* (Summer, 1974), pp. 95–100.

Dasso, Jerome J., William N. Kinnard, Jr., and Stephen D. Messner. "Lender Participation Financing: Applications of Sensitivity and Investment Analysis," *The Real Estate Appraiser* (July–August, 1971).

Opperman, John C. "Lender-Developer Participation," *The Mortgage Banker* (September, 1968), pp. 30–35, 38.

Rose, Cornelius C., Jr. "Equity Participations," *The Mortgage Banker* (June, 1968), pp. 44–47.

Pension Trusts

Haverkampf, Peter T. "The Pension Trusts Move into Real Estate — Slowly," *Real Estate Review* (Spring, 1974), pp. 126–29.

Rates of Return

Bleck, Erick K. "Real Estate Investments and Rates of Return," *The Appraisal Journal* (October, 1973), pp. 535–47.

Cooper, James R., and Stephan A. Pyhrr. "Forecasting the Rates of Return on an Apartment Investment: A Case Study," *The Appraisal Journal* (July, 1973), pp. 312–37.

Messner, Stephen D., and M. Chapman Findlay, III. "Real Estate Investment Analysis: IRR versus FMRR," *The Real Estate Appraiser* (July–August, 1975).

Raper, Charles F. "Internal Rate of Return — Handle with Care," *The Appraisal Journal* (July, 1976), pp. 405–411.

Strung, Joseph. "The Internal Rate of Return and the Reinvestment Presumptions," *The Appraisal Journal* (January, 1976), pp. 23–33.

Real Estate Franchises

Dowling, Raymond B., and Mary Alice Hines. "Here Come the Real Estate Franchises," *Real Estate Review* (Summer, 1977), pp. 48–52.

Real Estate Investment Trusts

Carrigan, Richard T., and Don M. Enders. "Don't Weep for the REITs: The New Valuation Rules Won't Hurt," *Real Estate Review* (Summer, 1977), pp. 65–71.

Hines, Mary Alice. "The REIT Shakeout in 1974," *Real Estate Review* (Winter, 1975), pp. 56–59.

Stevenson, Howard H. "What Went Wrong with the REITs?" *The Appraisal Journal* (April, 1977), pp. 249–260.

"The Real Estate and Mortgage Investment Trust," a special issue of *The Mortgage Banker* (September, 1970).

Wurtzebach, Charles H. "An Institutional Explanation of Poor REIT Performance," *The Appraisal Journal* (January, 1977), pp. 103–109.

Real Estate Law

Anderson, Ronald A., and Walter A. Kumpf. *Business Law*. Cincinnati, Ohio: South-Western Publishing Co., 1977, Part 11.

Fusilier, H. L. *Real Estate Law*. Boulder, Col.: Business Research Division, University of Colorado, 1977.

Kratovil, Robert. *Real Estate Law*. Englewood Cliffs, N.J.: Prentice-Hall, Inc., 1974.

Lusk, Harold F. *The Law of the Real Estate Business*. Homewood, Ill.: Richard D. Irwin, Inc., 1975.

Sales and Leasebacks

Haymes, Allan. "Real Estate Dealing: Survival of a Business With a Sale-Leaseback," *Real Estate Review* (Winter, 1976), pp. 12–14.

Sillcocks, H. Jackson. "Financial Sense in Real Estate Sales and Leasebacks," *Real Estate Review* (Spring, 1975), pp. 89–95.

Weil, S. Douglas, "Land Leasebacks Move Up Fast as Financing Technique," *Real Estate Review* (Winter, 1972), pp. 65–71.

Secondary Mortgage Market

Jones, Oliver. "Private Secondary Market Facilities," *The Journal of Finance* (May, 1968), pp. 359–66.

Wiggin, Charles E. "Doing Business in the Secondary Market," *Real Estate Review* (Summer, 1975), pp. 84–95.

Syndications

Fass, Peter N. "The Regulated World of the Real Estate Syndicates," *Real Estate Review* (Winter, 1972), pp. 52–56.

Mossburg, Lewis G., Jr. *Real Estate Syndicate Offerings, Law and Practice*. San Francisco: Real Estate Syndication Digest, 1974.

Parisse, Alan J. "How Not to Analyze a Syndication," *Real Estate Review* (Winter, 1974), pp. 89–96.

Tax Exempt Mortgage

Marvel, Josiah, and Peter A. Louis. "The Tax Exempt Mortgage: Solutions to High Interest Rates," *Real Estate Review* (Summer, 1977), pp. 44–47.

Williams, Marvin. "Financing Shopping Centers with Tax-Free Funds," *Real Estate Review* (Winter, 1976), pp. 67–71.

Variable Rate Mortgages

Brueggeman, William B., and Jerome B. Baesel. "The Mechanics of Variable Rate Mortgages and Implications for Home Ownership as an Inflation Hedge," *The Appraisal Journal* (April, 1976), pp. 236–46.

Candilis, Wray O. *Variable Rate Mortgage Plans.* Washington, D.C.: The American Bankers Association, 1971.

Epley, Donald R. "Variable Mortgage Plans and Their Unsolved Issues," *The Appraisal Journal* (April, 1977), pp. 242–248.

Lusht, Kenneth M. "A New Twist to the Variable Payment Mortgages," *Real Estate Review* (Summer, 1977), pp. 72–76.

Millar, James A., and Stanley R. Stansell. "A Comparison of the Characteristics of Fixed and Variable Rate Mortgages," *The Appraisal Journal* (January, 1976), pp. 63–68.

Tucker, Donald P. "The Variable-Rate Graduated-Payment Mortgage," *Real Estate Review* (Spring, 1975), pp. 71–80.

Wraparound Mortgages

Lieder, Arnold. "How to Wrap Around a Mortgage," *Real Estate Review* (Winter, 1975), pp. 29–34.

Appendix F

SOURCES OF CURRENT INFORMATION ON ECONOMIC, MONETARY, AND CAPITAL MARKET DEVELOPMENTS

There are a number of informational sources that are of value in understanding the prevailing economic and capital market conditions. Two monthly publications are the *National Economic Trends* and *Monetary Trends*, which are prepared by the Federal Reserve Bank of St. Louis. These publications are available by writing to the Federal Reserve Bank of St. Louis. They will provide the user with an update of the materials in Chapter 12 which draw heavily on materials supplied by the Federal Reserve Bank of St. Louis.

A third publication is prepared weekly by the Division of Research and Statistics, Board of Governors, Federal Reserve System. It is entitled *Capital Market Developments* and provides current information on recent developments in the debt and equity markets, as well as mortgage market information including mortgage commitments, changes in mortgage holdings, and the amount of mortgage debt outstanding. In addition, this publication contains information on recent housing permits and starts, average interest rates on home mortgages, and FNMA home mortgage commitments.

GUIDELINES
for Preparation of
FHLMC Form 70, Rev. 9/75 — FNMA Form 1004, Rev. 9/75

I. Lender's (Seller's) Section

All of the information requested in the section at the top of page one is to be furnished by the Seller prior to giving the form to the appraiser for a particular assignment. The property rights appraised are to be indicated by checking the appropriate box and the sale price of the subject property, loan charges to be paid by the seller of the property, and other sales concessions, are to be entered in the spaces provided.

Instructions to the appraiser will generally consist of directions to the property and the means of gaining access thereto.

II. Neighborhood Description and Analysis

Nothing in the form or the attachments thereto is intended to preclude the appraiser from considering the social and economic characteristics of the neighborhood to the extent that they presently, or are likely to, affect the value of the subject property. However, the appraiser is to report detrimental neighborhood conditions in factual, specific terms by giving the addresses of the affected properties and an exact description of the nature of the conditions involved in each case. For example: "There are junked and abandoned cars (or refrigerators, etc.) in the front (or rear) yards of the properties at (addresses);" or, "the houses at (addresses) are vacant (or boarded up, or vandalized as evidenced by broken windows, etc.);" or, "a lack of maintenance is evident in the neighborhood by uncut grass (or peeling paint, or fallen gutters and downspouts, etc.) at (addresses)." Furthermore, if the value trend in the neighborhood is declining as a result of detrimental conditions, statements to that effect must be supported by reporting actual property sales which demonstrate the trend. Such information may be provided in the comment section or in an addendum to the report.

Major considerations in this section of the form which may require further explanation and instruction are:

RESIDENTIAL APPRAISAL REPORT

File No. _____

To be completed by Lender

Borrower/Client	Census Tract _____ Map Reference _____
Property Address	
City	County _____ State _____ Zip Code _____
Legal Description	
Sale Price $ _____ Date of Sale _____ Property Rights Appraised ☐ Fee ☐ Leasehold ☐ DeMinimis PUD (FNMA only) ☐ Condo ☐ PUD	
Actual Real Estate Taxes $ _____ (yr) Loan charges to be paid by seller $ _____ Other sales concessions _____	
Lender _____ Lender's Address _____	
Occupant _____ Appraiser _____ Instructions to Appraiser _____	

NEIGHBORHOOD

				Good Avg. Fair Poor
Location	☐ Urban	☐ Suburban	☐ Rural	
Built Up	☐ Over 75%	☐ 25% to 75%	☐ Under 25%	Employment Stability ☐ ☐ ☐ ☐
Growth Rate ☐ Fully Dev.	☐ Rapid	☐ Steady	☐ Slow	Convenience to Employment ☐ ☐ ☐ ☐
Property Values	☐ Increasing	☐ Stable	☐ Declining	Convenience to Shopping ☐ ☐ ☐ ☐
Demand/Supply	☐ Shortage	☐ In Balance	☐ Over Supply	Convenience to Schools ☐ ☐ ☐ ☐
Marketing Time	☐ Under 3 Mos.	☐ 4–6 Mos.	☐ Over 6 Mos.	Quality of Schools ☐ ☐ ☐ ☐

Present Land Use ____% 1 Family ____% 2–4 Family ____% Apts. ____% Condo ____% Commercial   Recreational Facilities ☐ ☐ ☐ ☐
____% Industrial ____% Vacant ____%   Adequacy of Utilities ☐ ☐ ☐ ☐
Change in Present Land Use ☐ Not Likely ☐ Likely (*) ☐ Taking Place (*)   Property Compatibility ☐ ☐ ☐ ☐
(*) From _____ To _____   Protection from Detrimental Conditions ☐ ☐ ☐ ☐
Predominant Occupancy ☐ Owner ☐ Tenant ____% Vacant   Police and Fire Protection ☐ ☐ ☐ ☐
Single Family Price Range $ _____ to $ _____ Predominant Value $ _____   General Appearance of Properties ☐ ☐ ☐ ☐
Single Family Age _____ yrs to _____ yrs   Predominant Age _____ yrs   Appeal to Market ☐ ☐ ☐ ☐

Note: FHLMC/FNMA do not consider the racial composition of the neighborhood to be a relevant factor and it must not be considered in the appraisal.

Comments (including those factors adversely affecting marketability) _____

SITE

Dimensions _____ = _____ Sq. Ft. or Acres ☐ Corner Lot
Zoning classification _____ Present improvements ☐ do ☐ do not conform to zoning regulations
Highest and best use: ☐ Present use ☐ Other (specify) _____

	Public	Other (Describe)	OFF SITE IMPROVEMENTS	
Elec.	☐	_____	Street Access: ☐ Public ☐ Private	Topo _____
Gas	☐	_____	Surface _____	Size _____
Water	☐	_____	Maintenance: ☐ Public ☐ Private	Shape _____
San.Sewer	☐	_____	☐ Storm Sewer ☐ Curb/Gutter	View _____
	☐ Underground Elect. & Tel.		☐ Sidewalk ☐ Street Lights	Drainage _____

Is the property located in a HUD identified Flood Hazard Area? ☐ No ☐ Yes

Comments (favorable or unfavorable including any apparent adverse easements, encroachments or other adverse conditions) _____

IMPROVEMENTS

☐ Existing (approx. yr. blt.) 19___ No. Units ____ Type (det, duplex, semi/det, etc.) ____ Design (rambler, split level, etc.) ____ Exterior Walls _____
☐ Proposed ☐ Under Construction No. Stories ____

Roof Material _____	Gutters & Downspouts _____ ☐ None	Window (Type): _____	Insulation ☐ None ☐ Floor
		☐ Storm Sash ☐ Screens ☐ Combination	☐ Ceiling ☐ Roof ☐ Walls

BSMT

Foundation Walls _____	____% Basement ☐ Floor Drain	Finished Ceiling _____
	☐ Outside Entrance ☐ Sump Pump	Finished Walls _____
☐ Crawl Space	☐ Concrete Floor ____% Finished	Finished Floor _____
☐ Slab on Grade	Evidence of: ☐ Dampness ☐ Termites ☐ Settlement	

Comments _____

ROOM LIST

Room List	Foyer	Living	Dining	Kitchen	Den	Family Rm.	Rec. Rm.	Bedrooms	No. Baths	Laundry	Other
Basement											
1st Level											
2nd Level											

Total _____ Rooms _____ Bedrooms _____ Baths in finished area above grade.

INTERIOR FINISH & EQUIPMENT

Kitchen Equipment: ☐ Refrigerator ☐ Range/Oven ☐ Disposal ☐ Dishwasher ☐ Fan/Hood ☐ Compactor ☐ Washer ☐ Dryer ☐
HEAT: Type _____ Fuel _____ Cond. _____ AIR COND: ☐ Central ☐ Other _____ ☐ Adequate ☐ Inadequate

Floors	☐ Hardwood ☐ Carpet Over ☐ _____		Good Avg. Fair Poor
Walls	☐ Drywall ☐ Plaster	Quality of Construction (Materials & Finish)	☐ ☐ ☐ ☐
Trim/Finish	☐ Good ☐ Average ☐ Fair ☐ Poor	Condition of Improvements	☐ ☐ ☐ ☐
Bath Floor	☐ Ceramic	Rooms size and layout	☐ ☐ ☐ ☐
Bath Wainscot	☐ Ceramic ☐ _____	Closets and Storage	☐ ☐ ☐ ☐

Special Features (including fireplaces): _____

PROPERTY RATING

Plumbing—adequacy and condition ☐ ☐ ☐ ☐
Electrical—adequacy and condition ☐ ☐ ☐ ☐
Kitchen Cabinets—adequacy and condition ☐ ☐ ☐ ☐
ATTIC: ☐ Yes ☐ No ☐ Stairway ☐ Drop-stair ☐ Scuttle ☐ Floored   Compatibility to Neighborhood ☐ ☐ ☐ ☐
Finished (Describe) _____ ☐ Heated   Overall Livability ☐ ☐ ☐ ☐
CAR STORAGE: ☐ Garage ☐ Built-in ☐ Attached ☐ Detached ☐ Car Port   Appeal and Marketability ☐ ☐ ☐ ☐
No. Cars ____ ☐ Adequate ☐ Inadequate Condition _____   Effective Age ____ Yrs. Est. Remaining Economic Life _____ Yrs.

PORCHES, PATIOS, POOL, FENCES, etc. (describe) _____

COMMENTS (including functional or physical inadequacies, repairs needed, modernization, etc.) _____

FHLMC Form 70 Rev. 9/75   ATTACH DESCRIPTIVE PHOTOGRAPHS OF SUBJECT PROPERTY AND STREET SCENE   FNMA Form 1004 Rev. 9/75

Appendix G / FHLMC/FNMA Residential Appraisal Report Form and Guidelines   **363**

VALUATION SECTION

Purpose of Appraisal is to estimate Market Value as defined in Certification & Statement of Limiting Conditions (FHLMC Form 439/FNMA Form 1004B) If submitted for FNMA, the appraiser must attach (1) sketch or map showing location of subject, street names, distance from nearest intersection, and any detrimental conditions and (2) exterior building sketch of improvements showing dimensions.

COST APPROACH

Measurements		No. Stories		Sq. Ft.
x	x	=		
x	x	=		
x	x	=		
x	x	=		
x	x	=		
x	x	=		

Total Gross Living Area (List in Market Data Analysis below) _____

Comment on functional and economic obsolescence: _____

ESTIMATED REPRODUCTION COST — NEW — OF IMPROVEMENTS:

Dwelling _____ Sq. Ft. @ $ _____ = $ _____
_____ Sq. Ft. @ $ _____ = _____
Extras _____ = _____
_____ = _____
Porches, Patios, etc. _____ = _____
Garage/Car Port _____ Sq. Ft. @ $ _____ = _____
Site Improvements (driveway, landscaping, etc.) = _____
Total Estimated Cost New . . . . = $ _____

Less | Physical | Functional | Economic
Depreciation $ _____ | $ _____ | $ _____ = $ (_____)
Depreciated value of improvements . . . . = $ _____
ESTIMATED LAND VALUE . . . . = $ _____
(If leasehold, show only leasehold value)
INDICATED VALUE BY COST APPROACH . . . $ _____

MARKET DATA ANALYSIS

The undersigned has recited three recent sales of properties most similar and proximate to subject and has considered these in the market analysis. The description includes a dollar adjustment, reflecting market reaction to those items of significant variation between the subject and comparable properties. If a significant item in the comparable property is superior to, or more favorable than, the subject property, a minus (-) adjustment is made, thus reducing the indicated value of subject; if a significant item in the comparable is inferior to, or less favorable than, the subject property, a plus (+) adjustment is made, thus increasing the indicated value of the subject.

ITEM	Subject Property	COMPARABLE NO. 1		COMPARABLE NO. 2		COMPARABLE NO. 3	
Address							
Proximity to Subj.							
Sales Price	$	$		$		$	
Price/Living area	$	$		$		$	
Data Source							
Date of Sale and Time Adjustment	DESCRIPTION	DESCRIPTION	+(−)$ Adjustment	DESCRIPTION	+(−)$ Adjustment	DESCRIPTION	+(−)$ Adjustment
Location							
Site/View							
Design and Appeal							
Quality of Const.							
Age							
Condition							
Living Area Room Count and Total	Total / B-rms / Baths	Total / B-rms / Baths		Total / B-rms / Baths		Total / B-rms / Baths	
Gross Living Area	Sq.Ft.	Sq.Ft.		Sq.Ft.		Sq.Ft.	
Basement & Bsmt. Finished Rooms							
Functional Utility							
Air Conditioning							
Garage/Car Port							
Porches, Patio, Pools, etc.							
Other (e.g. fireplaces, kitchen equip., heating, remodeling)							
Sales or Financing Concessions							
Net Adj. (Total)		☐ Plus; ☐ Minus $		☐ Plus; ☐ Minus $		☐ Plus; ☐ Minus $	
Indicated Value of Subject		$		$		$	

Comments on Market Data _____

INDICATED VALUE BY MARKET DATA APPROACH . . . . $ _____
INDICATED VALUE BY INCOME APPROACH (If applicable) Economic Market Rent $ _____ /Mo. x Gross Rent Multiplier _____ = $ _____

This appraisal is made ☐ "as is" ☐ subject to the repairs, alterations, or conditions listed below ☐ completion per plans and specifications.

Comments and Conditions of Appraisal: _____

Final Reconciliation: _____

This appraisal is based upon the above requirements, the certification, contingent and limiting conditions, and Market Value definition that are stated in
☐ FHLMC Form 439 (Rev. 9/75)/FNMA Form 1004B filed with client _____ 19 _____ ☐ attached.
If submitted for FNMA, the report has been prepared in compliance with FNMA form instructions.
I ESTIMATE THE MARKET VALUE, AS DEFINED, OF SUBJECT PROPERTY AS OF _____ 19 _____ to be $ _____

Appraiser(s) _____ Review Appraiser (If applicable) _____
☐ Did ☐ Did Not Physically Inspect Property

1. *Present Land Use* — enter the estimated percentage of each type of property in the neighborhood. If the use is other than one of those indicated on the form, enter the percentage and state the type in the spaces provided. Use "0" where none of the listed uses are in evidence. The total of uses must equal 100%.

2. *Change in Present Land Use* — indicate by checking the appropriate box what your professional judgment indicates to be the trend of change in land uses in the neighborhood. Major factors to be considered in this category include present uses, market supply and demand, and zoning. If change is likely or is already taking place, state from what use and give the use to which the neighborhood is in transition. Elaborate further on such changes in the comment section or in a separate addendum.

3. *Predominant Occupancy* — indicate the predominant type of occupancy by checking the appropriate box or giving the estimated percentage of vacancy. It should be emphasized that this question refers to occupancy rather than to building types. For example, if the neighborhood consists of two family properties of which 90% are owner-occupied, then the owner box should be checked. If there is only a relatively small preponderance of owners over tenants (e.g. 60% owners vs. 40% tenants), then this situation should be reported in the comment section since the long term stability of the neighborhood could be adversely affected for single family residential purposes.

4. *Single Family Price Range* — enter the lowest and highest typical prevailing prices of single family residential properties in the neighborhood. However, isolated extremes at either end of the range should not be reported. Also, state the predominant price most frequently found.

5. *Single Family Age* — give the typical age range of single family properties in the neighborhood together with the predominant age. Do not report occasional extremes at either end of the range.

Neighborhood Rating Grid — as part of the neighborhood analysis, the appraiser is also to rate the various characteristics of the neighborhood in terms of good, average, fair or poor. These ratings are to be based on comparison by the appraiser of the subject neighborhood with comparison neighborhoods as to the present and probable future characteristic factors while recognizing the effect of these factors upon continued market appeal for residential purposes.

The quality ratings which the appraiser is being asked to provide are defined as follows:

Good — this rating is to be applied when the characteristics being considered are outstanding and superior to those found in competing neighborhoods.

Average — this indicates that the factors being rated are equal to the norm found to be acceptable in competing neighborhoods.

Fair — this rating is to be used where the factors concerned are below what is typical for comparable neighborhoods.

Poor — a rating of this nature is appropriate if the characteristics under consideration are either non-existent or in such small supply that single family residential values are, or may be, adversely affected.

In connection with these ratings, it should be noted that the appraiser must explain in the comment section the reasons for any ratings of "fair" or "poor." A separate addendum to the report should be used for this purpose if necessary.

Neighborhood Rating Factors — the following represent some of the considerations which should enter into rating the various aspects of the neighborhood. In this connection, the appraiser should remember that these ratings are based upon competitive locations and, therefore, should never rate a neighborhood in one price range against a non-competitive area. It should also be noted that different income and user groups may place more weight on some factors than others.

Employment Stability — consideration should be given to the number of employment opportunities and the variety and type of industries in the community. One-industry or cyclical industry areas would normally not be rated as favorably as those having a broader variety of employment with greater stability.

Convenience to Employment — the distance, both in terms of time and mileage, is to be considered here. This factor is particularly important in view of the increasing cost of gasoline.

The availability, cost, and convenience of public transportation is also to be considered as an alternative to customary means of private transportation.

Convenience to Shopping — rate the neighborhood in terms of distance, time, and required means of transportation, to shopping for daily necessities.

Convenience to Schools — consider the time and distance to schools. If bus transportation is required, travel time is a factor.

Quality of Schools — the reputation of neighborhood schools and/or the school system as a whole for quality education to the extent that it affects real estate value is to be considered here.

Recreational Facilities — consider the number, type, and quality of such facilities available in the neighborhood as compared to competing neighborhoods. The extent to which such facilities are expected by the market for properties in the subject's price range is also a consideration.

Adequacy of Utilities — rate the extent to which the utility systems (water, sewer, electricity, and gas, if the latter is available) serving the neighborhood are adequate to serve the residents' needs as compared to similar neighborhoods. Consideration of utilities includes public, private (community or subdivision) and individual.

Property Compatibility — factors to be considered in this category include the types of land uses prevalent in the neighborhood, lot sizes, price ranges, and building ages and styles.

Protection from Detrimental Conditions — the appraiser is to consider here the extent to which present, or probable future, land uses or environmental conditions presently, or are likely to, adversely affect single family residential property values in the neighborhood.

Police and Fire Protection — this rating covers the extent to which these services are adequate and equivalent to those provided for competing neighborhoods.

General Appearance of Properties — consider the extent to which properties in the subject neighborhood are receiving proper maintenance (both buildings and yards) to preserve property values.

Appeal to Market — this is essentially an overall summary rating of the extent to which all aspects of the property and the neighborhood will appeal to the market — i.e. an indication of the marketability of the subject property and the neighborhood.

Comments — in addition to the factors already mentioned, about which further explanation is to be given, this section should be used to elaborate upon any favorable or unfavorable aspects of the neighborhood which have not been adequately covered in the preceding analysis and which are likely to affect the long term stability of property values in the neighborhood. In summary, the basis for any deductions for economic obsolescence in the Cost Approach should be made evident in this section.

III. Site Description and Analysis

Detailed instructions are being given herein only for those items which may not be self-explanatory.

Zoning Classification — state the zoning category as designated by the local zoning code and the major permitted uses.

Highest and Best Use — this factor is critical and deserving of thorough analysis. Do not automatically check the box indicating the present use. If some other use would be more appropriate on the basis of zoning, market demand, and predominant land uses in the neighborhood, state the use specifically. Further explanation should then be provided in the comment section.

Electricity, Water, Sewer, etc. — "public" means governmentally supplied and regulated. It does not, therefore, include community systems sponsored, owned, or operated by the developer or a private company not subject to government regulation or financial assistance. If such systems are found, further explanation thereof must be given in the comment section or an addendum to the report.

Off-Site Improvements — if access to the subject property is by private street or other such right-of-way, describe the nature thereof and provision for maintenance in the comment section or attach an addendum giving details.

Topo, Size, Shape, etc. — provide a brief description of these features of the subject site and how they compare to other sites in the neighborhood. Elaborate under comments if additional information is needed to clarify an item.

Comments — this space is for further explanation of favorable and unfavorable factors which affect the value of the site. The appraiser should also describe any easements, encroachments, or other detrimental conditions.

IV. Description of Improvements

Detailed instructions are set forth herein only to the extent that the information desired in the form may need clarification.

Number of Units — this should be one unit in all cases since a different appraisal form is required for a greater number of units.

Number of Stories — this is the number of above-grade floors of finished living area and should be the same number used to calculate the gross living area in the Cost Approach.

Exterior Walls — specify the material used for the exterior wall covering, such as wood siding (e.g. — clapboard, board and batten, etc.), shingles, or brick. If the latter, specify whether veneer or solid masonry (either brick or brick on some form of masonry).

Roof Material — state the material used for roof covering — e.g. wood shingles or shakes, asphalt or asbestos shingles, tile, etc.

Gutters and Downspouts — specify the material used for both. If none are present, the appraiser should state the width of the roof overhang and note the site grading around the foundation walls together with any evidence of dampness in the basement.

Windows — list the type of windows — e.g. casement (wood or metal), sliding, double hung (wood or metal), etc.

Insulation — the appraiser should make every effort to determine and report the extent and adequacy of insulation since this is likely to have an increasing effect upon the value of the property due to the high cost of energy.

Foundation Walls — specify the material used — e.g. poured concrete, cinder or concrete block, etc.

Basement — calculate and enter the percentage of basement area in relation to first floor area and indicate the various features requested on the form to the extent present. Also, indicate the existence of any adverse conditions by checking the boxes provided. If the basement is partially finished, estimate and state the percentage of finished area to total area. Also, state the materials used for ceiling, wall, and floor finish.

Comments — the appraiser should here describe any physical deterioration or functional inadequacy found in the basic structure. Such conditions should then be reflected in the estimate of depreciation in the Cost Approach.

Room List — enter the number of each type of room on every level. For this purpose, baths are calculated as follows: three plumbing fixtures (wash bowl, toilet, tub or shower) constitute one bathroom, two fixtures are a half bathroom, one fixture (toilet only) is a quarter bathroom, and one fixture (wash bowl only) is a wash room and is listed under "other." The total count of rooms, bedrooms, and baths is to be reported for the finished area above grade only. These totals will then be used for the subject in the Market Data Analysis.

Interior Finish and Equipment:

1. *Floors* — this is intended to describe the floor finish in the major portion of the house. If hardwood, so indicate by checking the box provided for this purpose. If wall-to-wall carpeting, state the material over which the carpet is installed. If some other type of floor covering prevails, check the third box on the line and state the material. Floor covering in the kitchen or other areas such as the foyer may be described under special features.

2. *Trim/Finish* — this question refers to the sufficiency of this item as well as the quality of materials and workmanship. The definitions of good, average, fair, and poor to be applied in rating this item are the same as set forth in the section on Neighborhood Description.

3. *Bath Floor and Wainscot* — if other than ceramic, check the appropriate box and state the material.

4. *Special Features* — describe any features not mentioned previously in the report such as other floor finish, fireplaces (including location thereof), and built-ins (e.g. cabinets, bookcases, etc.)

Property Rating Grid — the property ratings indicate how the subject property compares to competing properties as to quality and soundness of construction, convenience of living, and appeal to the market. All of these factors have a major effect upon the marketability of any single family property. The rating factors of good, average, fair and poor are the same as previously defined in the instructions or the Neighborhood Description.

Quality of Construction — consideration is to be given to the quality of workmanship throughout and the quality and durability of materials used in all components of the building.

Condition of Improvements — the appraiser is to rate the condition of the building and is to take note of all apsects of physical depreciation and report these in the comment section.

Room Sizes and Layout — this item includes consideration of the adequacy of room sizes as well as proportions of the rooms and sufficient wall area to permit appropriate furniture groupings. The layout is to be rated as to the extent to which it facilitates the proper flow of traffic, privacy of sleeping areas, and easy access to all rooms without interfering with the intended use of other rooms. Stairways, halls, and doors must also have adequate width. A rating below average should be reflected by an estimate for functional obsolescence in the Cost Approach. Conversely, if a deduction is made for functional obsolescence, it should be supported by appropriate ratings in this item and "Overall liveability."

Closets and Storage — rate the adequacy and convenience of closets and general storage as compared to competing properties. This is an important item which can have a substantial effect on liveability and marketability and should, therefore, not be ignored by the appraiser.

Plumbing — Adequacy and Condition — considerations affecting this item include the number, style, and condition of plumbing fixtures; the materials used for piping and the condition thereof; and the proper operation of any on-site water or septic systems. In the event that the evaluation of adequacy and condition does not permit a single rating, the appraiser should give two ratings and explain or indicate which rating applies to each factor.

Electrical — Adequacy and Condition — this rating includes the adequacy of electrical service available within the building, the number and location of outlets and switches, the quality and condition of the wiring, and the adequacy and style of lighting fixtures. Split ratings are to be handled in the manner described above.

Kitchen Cabinets — rate the adequacy of the amount of kitchen storage space provided in relation to the likely number of occupants of the house. The style, quality, and condition of the cabinets are also factors in the rating to be given.

Compatibility to Neighborhood — this rating is to indicate the extent to which the size, age, price, architectural design, and construction of the subject property conform to the neighborhood.

Overall Liveability — this rating basically represents a composite of all of the above factors to the extent that they contribute to the sense of comfort and satisfaction likely to be experienced by an owner/occupant of the property.

Appeal and Marketability — consideration is to be given here to the overall appeal of the subject property to the market based on the above factors together with the architectural attractiveness of the property and, therefore, the demand which will probably be generated by the particular combination of these factors.

Effective Age — the appraiser is to report the estimated effective age of the subject property, as distinct from its chronological age, based on its utility and condition.

Remaining Economic Life — state here the estimated remaining number of years over which the improvements can still be expected to make a contribution to the value of the property.

Porches, Patios, Pools, Fences, etc. — describe all improvements which have not previously been mentioned and which will be included in the cost and market approaches.

Comments — the appraiser is to make specific, factual comments here on the reasons for any ratings of fair or poor. Furthermore, it is in this space that the appraiser must specifically describe all items of physical depreciation, whether curable or incurable, and provide an itemized listing of repairs needed to cure deferred maintenance together with the cost thereof.

If more space is required, a separate addendum sheet should be attached to the report. The appraiser should bear in mind at all times that the comments in this section will form the basis and support for the estimate of physical depreciation in the Cost Approach. If new construction, the appraiser is also to comment on whether the property is covered by the Home Owner's Warranty program.

V. Required Attachments to Form

Photos — attach to the report on a separate sheet, quality (sharp and clear) photos of the front and rear of the subject property as well as at least one street scene which includes the subject property. It is not necessary or even desirable to attach the photos in the margin at the bottom of page one of the form as indicated on the form.

Location map — submit, as an attachment to the report, a sketch or copy of a map showing the location of the subject property, its relation to major traffic arteries, distance to the nearest intersection, and the location of any favorable factors or detrimental conditions as previously reported in the neighborhood description.

Exterior Building Sketch — submit, as an attachment to the report, a perimeter plan of the building (not necessarily to scale) showing the exterior building lines with dimensions which must correspond to those used in the gross building area calculations set forth in the Cost Approach. In both cases, inches should be converted to *tenths of a foot*. Dimensions must be shown for every exterior wall. An interior layout would be helpful to the reviewer and may be provided in conjunction with the sketch but is optional.

VI. Cost Approach

Building Area Calculations — measurements must be exact and be the same as those shown in the exterior building sketch. The total gross building area thus calculated is to be entered on the line calling for "Total Gross Living Area." This is to include finished and habitable above-grade living area only. Finished basement or attic areas are to be calculated and shown separately for use in the cost estimate but are not to be included in the total gross living area.

Comment on Functional & Economic Obsolescence — use this space to fully describe the causes of these forms of obsolescence and support the estimate of the loss in value. No comment as to physical depreciation is needed here since it will already have been explained and estimated in the comment section of the building description.

Estimate of Reproduction Cost New — note that what is required here is reproduction cost — i.e. the cost of reproducing the subject structure using the same materials and workmanship as well as the same layout. It is, however, recognized that in some cases typically involving older buildings containing obsolete materials or unusual functional features, it will be difficult, if not impossible, to estimate reproduction cost new with any reasonable degree of accuracy. In such cases, therefore, replacement cost may be used but then this should be specifically stated along with a description of the materials and quality upon which the estimate of replacement cost is based as well as the functional deficiencies thereby eliminated.

Extras — these are to include such items as finished basement or attic areas and baths. Show square foot areas and cost factors.

Depreciation — this estimate is to reflect, and be supported by, the comments and calculations made previously on the form. In all instances, the depreciation estimate must be allocated to one of the three types shown on the form. A lump sum total estimate combining several forms of depreciation will not be acceptable.

Land Value — this will normally be estimated on the basis of comparison to sales of similar lots or, in the case of built-up neighborhoods, by extraction from sales of improved properties.

If the final value estimated by the appraiser is the value indicated by the Cost Approach, then the appraiser should also state on an attachment the source of data as to the cost factors and recite comparable land sales.

VII. Market Data Analysis and Approach to Value

It is expected that the appraiser will use comparables which have sold as recently as possible (usually no earlier than six months prior to the date of the appraisal), are located in the same neighborhood as the property being appraised and therefore subject to the same locational influences, and as similar as possible in size and physical features. If this is not possible, the appraiser shall attach an explanation as to the reasons for selecting comparables which do not meet the above criteria. Listings are not considered as indicative as actual sales but, in the absence of a sufficient number of truly comparable sales, no more than one listing may be used if accompanied by an explanation of the reason for the use of such listing and a complete analysis of the listing which shall include a supported estimate of the probable selling price.

Sales of properties with FHA or VA financing will not be acceptable unless an appropriate downward adjustment has been made to reflect the loan discount paid by the seller.

If the total adjustments for all factors exceed 25% of the sale price of the comparable, then the appraiser should reconsider whether the comparable is, in fact, truly comparable and should, therefore, be replaced by another, more indicative sale.

The appropriate descriptive information (or a rating as to good, fair, etc. as defined in the neighborhood description) is to be entered in the subject property column for each property characteristic set forth in the "Item" column. This is to assist the appraiser and the reviewer in relating the comparables to the subject property. In view of the brevity of the form, it is mandatory that the appraiser complete the analysis of all items.

It is felt that further explanation would be beneficial as to the following specific items in the market data analysis:

Address — identify location of subject property and all comparables with exact street number and name as well as the name of the town or city in which the property is located.

Proximity to Subject — give the distance of the comparable from the subject property in terms of blocks, fractions of a mile or miles as the case may be as well as the direction.

Sale Price — state the price for which the subject property and the comparables sold.

Price/Living Area — calculate the total sales price per square foot of gross above-grade building (living) area in order to provide this indicator of value.

Data Source — give the source from which the data pertaining to each comparable was obtained — e.g. deed records, recordation tax stamps, brokers, multiple listings, data bank, buyer or seller, etc.

Date of Sale and Time Adjustment — provide the month, day, and year of sale for the subject property and each comparable. Then proceed to make the appropriate adjustment indicated by the market for the time difference between the date of sale and the date of the appraisal. Of course, the comprables should be as current as possible in order to reduce the risk of error in making the adjustment.

Location — give an overall quality rating (e.g. good, average, etc.) for the subject and a comparison rating (e.g. superior, equal, inferior) for the comparables and make the adjustment indicated by the market for differences between the comparables and the subject property.

Site/View — an overall quality rating of good, average, fair or poor is to be given for the subject property and a comparison rating, as indicated under "location" above, should be provided for both site and view for each comparable. However, if an adjustment is being made for site features but not for view or vice-versa, enter the item in the box in lieu of the comparison rating so that the reviewer will know for what specific factor the adjustment was made. Factors to be considered by the appraiser under site include size, shape, topography, drainage, encroachments, easements or any detrimental site conditions.

Design and Appeal — this adjustment category considers such aspects of the property as appeal of exterior design, interior attractiveness and special features, and any other characteristics which would make the property attractive or unattractive to purchasers in general and otherwise enhance, or detract from, its marketability. The appraiser is to rate the subject property in accordance with the ratings given in the building description on page one of the form and is to give comparison ratings, as indicated for the preceding items above, for each of the comparables. The appropriate adjustments may then be made.

Quality of Construction — this item covers quality of materials and workmanship in all respects, including exterior walls, roof covering, framing (walls, floors, and roof), finish flooring, interior walls, trim, doors, hardware, plumbing and electrical systems, baths, kitchen, and mechanical equipment. The appraiser is to indicate an overall quality rating for the subject property commensurate with the rating shown on page one of the form and is to give comparison ratings, as indicated previously, for each of the comparables. The adjustments are to reflect the market's monetary reaction based on these comparisons.

Age — the appraiser is to report the effective age of the subject property as well as that of the comparables and make the necessary adjustments indicated by the market.

Condition — the appraiser's opinion of the condition of the subject property (whether good, average, fair or poor) is to be stated whereas for the comparables, comparison ratings of superior, equal, or inferior are to be reported and adjustments are to be made as indicated by the market.

Living Area, Room Count, and Total Living Area — the appraiser is to report the total room count (number of finished, above-grade rooms as indicated on page one of the form), the number of bedrooms and baths, and the total square foot living area (above grade — as obtained from the calculations in the Cost Approach) for the subject property and for each comparable. Adjustments which are reflective of the market are to be made for each item as indicated.

Basement and Basement Finished Rooms — the appraiser is to report basement improvements such as finished rooms, recreation room, etc. found in the subject property and the comparables. If there is no basement (slab or crawl space) or a partial basement, this should also be indicated. Appropriate adjustments are to be made to reflect differences between the comparables and the subject property.

Functional Utility — this item refers to room sizes and layout and, therefore, overall liveability. A rating should be given for the subject property which will summarize the ratings for these factors found on page one of the form. Comparison ratings such as those indicated previously are to be given for the comparables and appropriate adjustments made to represent the market's reaction to any differences.

Air Conditioning — the presence or absence of this feature and the type thereof (central, sleeve or window units) are to be noted for the subject property as well as the comparables and adjustments made accordingly.

Garage/Car Port — the appraiser is to report and make adjustments on the basis of whether the subject property and the comparables have garages or carports and, if so, the capacity in terms of the number of cars. This increase or decrease in value should not necessarily represent the cost of construction but should rather be based on the market's response.

Porches, Patio, Pools, etc. — the appraiser should indicate the presence or absence of these or similar exterior building or site improvements and make the necessary adjustments indicated by the market. Cost data may, at times, serve as a guide but are not necessarily indicative since improvements such as pools may not return their entire cost upon resale as added value.

Other — the items under this heading are to be reported for the subject property and the comparables whether or not adjustments are being made. The items shown are simply intended to illustrate some of the more common features which may be found and for which adjustments may be appropriate. Therefore, the appraiser should not feel constrained to consider only the physical features shown.

Sales or Financing Concessions — the monetary value of concessions such as builder or seller price discounts, financing charges or benefits (e.g. loan points which are included in the sale price, "buy-downs" of the mortgage interest rate by the builder), gifts of merchandise (e.g. "a free new car in the garage with every purchase") must be reported for the subject property and the comparables and the value adjusted accordingly. It is not acceptable for the appraiser to simply ignore these items and say that they have no effect upon value.

The two blank lines following the above item are for such other adjustments as the appraiser feels are appropriate under the circumstances of the particular appraisal assignment and are intended to provide the appraiser with sufficient flexibility to do a professional job.

Net Adjustments (Total) — report the net total of the adjustments made for all the above items and indicate whether, on balance, the total is plus or minus. If the total adjustments appear excessive in relation to the sale price, the appraiser would be well advised to re-examine the comparable for comparability.

Indicated Value of Subject — add or subtract the net total adjustments from the sale price at the top of each column to arrive at the value of the subject property indicated by each of the comparables. It is expected that the indicated values will not be identical for all comparables.

Comments on Market Data — reconcile the values indicated by the comparables as adjusted in the market data analysis above and explain the reasons for giving more weight to one comparable over the others.

Indicated Value by Market Data Approach — the estimated value resulting from reconciliation.

VIII. Indicated Value by the Income Approach

If the subject property is located in a neighborhood where rentals predominate and rental data is readily available together with sales, then this approach to value should be used prior to final reconciliation. If the final estimate of value is based upon the Income Approach, the supporting rental and sales data along with calculations of the indicated rent multipliers must be attached as an addendum to the report.

IX. Requirements of the Appraisal, Comments, and Final Reconciliation

Indicate by checking the appropriate box whether the subject property was appraised in "as is" condition or whether the appraisal is based on certain repairs, alterations, or other conditions in order to achieve the estimated value. Also, if the property being appraised is proposed or under construction, indicate that the valuation is subject to satisfactory completion in accordance with plans and specifications.

Comments and Conditions of Appraisal — this space is to be used to itemize in detail the required repairs or other conditions as indicated above together with the estimated cost thereof. Comments on any portion of the report are also appropriate in this section if further explanation is needed to support the property analysis or the value estimate. If the space provided is not sufficient, attach an addendum to the report.

Final Reconciliation — the appraiser is to explain in this space the relevance and validity of each approach to value and present justification for the value selected as the final value estimate. It should be emphasized that final reconciliation is not an averaging process.

X. Other Requirements for Completion of Form

The appraiser is to indicate, by checking the appropriate box, whether FNMA Form 1004B (Certification, Contingent and

Limiting Conditions, and Market Value Definition) have previously been filed with the client (Seller) and, if so, on what date. This procedure may be followed only if these items are applicable to the appraisal at hand and do not vary from the previous appraisal for which Form 1004B was submitted. The date of such filing must then be given in every instance. Otherwise, since it is recognized that a particular appraisal assignment may require different or additional limiting conditions, the appraiser may add these to Form 1004B and file it with the report. However, if there are no such changes, the appraiser may prefer, as a matter of practice, to file Form 1004B with the client in connection with each report. This, of course, will also be acceptable.

The appraiser is expected to be familiar with these instructions for proper completion of the appraisal report and, by signing the report, certifies that it is in compliance with the instructions.

The estimated market value is to be reported as of a specific date and in numbers which have been rounded off to the nearest one hundred dollars.

The space for the signature of a review appraiser has been provided only in recognition of the fact that some appraisals will be performed by multi-appraiser firms which require that the principal of the firm co-sign each report. Only in such instances will a review appraiser's signature be applicable. In this event, it should be indicated whether the review appraiser co-signing the report has personally inspected the property.

INDEX

A

abstract of title, 274
acceleration clause, 11; in mortgage, 23
accounting procedures, tract, 108
acknowledgment, of mortgage and deed of trust, 27
advance commitment, cost of, 91
affidavit, pre-construction, 101
Agricultural Credit Act of 1923, 236
annual constant, 58, 82:
  concept of, 58
  formula for, 58
  percentages (table), 58
annual payments of annuity, 52
annuity:
  basic problems, 51
  compound sum of a $1 annuity (table), 50
  definition of, 49
  determining annual payments, 52
  determining rates of return, 52
  present value formula, 51
  present worth of a $1 annuity (table), 51
  value of, 49
amortization:
  loan payments for, 56
  monthly, 82
  sinking fund plan, 82
appraisal, for tract loan, 105
assignment:
  in lease, covenant against, 126
  of mortgage, 28
  of mortgage with covenant (illus.), 30
  of mortgage with recourse, 31
assumption and release agreement, 11
assumption of existing mortgage:
  assumption statement, 262
  loan assumption and transfer fees, 263
  assumption of loan, statement for (illus.), 264
attorney's fees, mortgage covenant to pay, 23

B

balloon mortgage or note, 147
banks:
  see commercial banks
  see mortgage banking
  see mutual savings banks

basket loan, defined, 133
blanket mortgage, 8; partial release clause in, 8
bonds:
  defined, 42, 152
  mortgage, 152
  treasury, 189
  contractual elements of, 42
  see also notes
bond-type security, 230
break-even, 268
bridge financing, 114
budget mortgage, 7
buyer-lessor, under sale-leaseback, 135
buying money, cost of, 91

C

call second mortgage, 85
carrying charges, calculation of impact of, 106
Chandler Act, 135
Charter Act of 1954, 210
chattel mortgage, 14
clauses:
  escrow provision, 70
  mortgage, 69
  recapture, 118
  subordination, 83
collateral loan, 156
commercial banks:
  assets of (table), 174
  investment policies, 174
  liabilities of (table), 174
  origin of, 172
  regulation and control, 173
  savings flows, 173
  as source of mortgage credit, 172
  structure and operation, 173
commercial financing, 110
commercial real estate loans, 265
common elements, in condominiums, 111
common-law mortgage, 1
completion bond, as protection against liens, 101
Completion Certificate, for second mortgage, 85
compound interest, 44:
  basic problems, 46
  compounding, 45
  compound sum of $1 (table), 45

determining future value, 46
determining investment time periods, 46
determining rates of return, 46
interest factors, 45
compound sum of $1, 45
compound sum of a $1 annuity (table), 50
condemnation proceeding, 127
condominiums, 109:
 common elements, 111
 conventional financing, 114
 converting to, 114
 criteria for, 112
 defined, 111
 FHA financing, 112
 financing, 111
 reasons for, 112
Consolidation and Extenstion Agreement, 279; illustrated, 280–82
construction commitment, cost of, 91
construction financing, 89:
 building loan inspection report (illus.), 97
 feasibility study, 94
 finalizing the loan, 93
 interim, 89
 loan contract (illus.), 94–96
 permanent, 89
 preliminary lending procedure, 90
 proposed site, 93
 site improvements, 89
 variations in, 90
construction loan costs:
 fixed rate, 92
 floating rate, 92
construction loan draw request (illus.), 102
construction loans, 89:
 cost of, 92
 see also construction financing
contract:
 elements of, 21
 option, 73
conventional mortgage, 5
cooperative:
 defined, 109
 FHA financing, 111
 financing, 109
 loan procedure, 110
 proprietary lease, 109
cooperative loan procedure, 110
corporation, effect on financing, 92
covenant against removal, in mortgage, 22
covenant not to assign, in lease, 126
covenant of insurance, in mortgage, 22
covenant to pay attorney's fees, in mortgage, 23
covenant to pay indebtedness, in mortgage, 22
covenant to pay taxes, in mortgage, 23

credit report, for residential loan, 246
credit reputation, for residential loan, 246
credit unions, as source of mortgage funds, 179
crop mortgage, 153

D

debt management, 188
debt payments-to-income ratio, for residential loan, 243
debt service, 81
deed:
 in lieu of foreclosure, 276
 need for delivery of, 62
deed of trust, 31, 40, 61:
 acknowledgment and recording, 27
 action on payment of indebtedness, 40
 defined, 31
 exception to use of, 31
 illustrated, 32
 parties to a transaction, 31
 states used in, 31
 trustor's right of reinstatement, 40
default, 272
deficiency judgments, 275
deficit budget, 188
Demonstration Cities and Metropolitan Development Act of 1966, 239
"demonstration cities" program, 239
direct reduction loan, 82
discount, of future value, 47
discounting, 47:
 creating a second mortgage, 79
 first mortgage, 79
 with a junior lien, 78
discount rate, of Federal Reserve, 185
disintermediation, 162

E

economy:
 see fiscal policy
 see monetary policy
Emergency Home Finance Act of 1970, 211, 223
eminent domain, 127; condemnational proceeding, 127
Employment Act of 1946, 183
employment verification authorization, for residential loan, 246–47
entry, foreclosure by, 275
Equal Credit Opportunity Act, 247
equity of redemption, 272
escalator lease, 119
escrow, defined, 70
escrow provision, Letter of Transmittal, 70
estoppel clause, in mortgage, 24
Extension Agreement, 278

F

"Fannie Mae," *see* Federal National Mortgage Association
Farm Credit System, 234:
  Agricultural Credit Act of 1923, 236
  Federal Farm Loan Act of 1916, 234
  federal intermediate credit banks, 236
  Federal Land Banks and Associations, 234
  Production Credit Associations, 236
  variable interest rate, 235
Farmers Home Administration loans, 249:
  home ownership loans, 249
  rental housing, 250
  rural housing repair loans, 251
  terms of, 250
FDIC (Federal Deposit Insurance Corporation), 173
Federal Farm Loan Act of 1916, 234
federal funds, 185
Federal Home Loan Bank Act of 1932, 207
Federal Home Loan Bank Board, 6, 167
Federal Home Loan Bank System, 167, 207, 223
Federal Home Loan Mortgage Corporation, 5, 211, 223:
  Emergency Home Finance Act of 1970, 211
  forward commitment purchase contract (illus.), 227
  operations of, 224
  Purchase Contract (illus.), 226
  residential loans, 243
  structure and operation, 224
Federal Housing Administration, 208
Federal Intermediate Credit Banks, 236
federal land banks, 9
Federal National Mortgage Association, 209:
  auction market operations, 214
  Charter Act, 209
  competitive offerings, 215
  conventional auction notice (illus.), 218–19
  Emergency Home Finance Act of 1970, 211
  Federal Home Loan Mortgage Corporation mortgage form, 15
  FHA/VA Auction Notice (illus.), 215–17
  Housing and Urban Development Act of 1968, 210
  non-competitive offerings, 215
  structure and organization, 213
  Tandem Programs with GNMA, 229
Federal Reserve Act of 1913, 172, 183
Federal Reserve System:
  discount rate, 185
  establishment of, 183
  Fractional Reserve System, 186

general controls, 184
margin requirements, 187
moral suasion, 186
open-market operations, 186
Regulation Q, 187
Regulation T, 187
Regulation X, 187
relation to commercial banks, 173
selective credit controls, 186
Federal Savings and Loan Insurance Corporation, 167
FHA cooperative financing, 111:
  management type, 111
  sales type, 111
FHA financing, for condominiums, 112
FHA mortgages:
  insured, 3
  loan-to-value ratios permitted, 4
FHLMC, *see* Federal Home Loan Mortgage Corporation
financial institutions, as source of funds, 162
financial projections, pro forma, 266:
  analysis of, 267
  margin and break-even, 268
financing:
  balloon mortgage, 147
  balloon note, 147
  "bridge," 114
  collateral loan, 156
  commercial, 110
  commercial real estate loans, 265
  condominiums, 109
  construction, 89
  conventional, 114
  cooperatives, 109
  credit unions, 179
  crop mortgage, 153
  effect of savings, 159
  Farmers Home Administration loans, 249
  FHA-cooperative, 111
  front money deals, 141
  "gap," 156
  guaranteed trade-in, 157
  high ratio, 131
  housing cycles, 199
  implications for real estate, 196
  by individuals, 180
  interim, 89
  kicker, 145
  land development loans, 104
  through a lease, 120
  life insurance companies, 175
  mortgage banking companies, 177
  mortgage bonds, 152
  mortgage markets, 162
  mortgage on a lease, 152
  mutual savings banks, 170
  noninstitutional mortgage funding, 177
  participations, 146

partnerships, 153
pension funds, 177
permanent, 89
pro forma financial projections, 266
promissory note, 149
property as security, 251
real estate investment trusts, 179
real estate syndicate, 153
residential loans, 242
sale-leaseback, 133
savings and loan associations, 166
sources and use of funds, 159
special purpose, 104
tract loans, 104
truth in lending, 149
wraparound mortgage, 145
fiscal policy, 182:
    debt management, 188
    deficit budget, 188
    economic goals, 183
    economic growth, 183
    emphasis on controlling inflation, 194
    full employment, 183
    international payments balance, 183
    in the 1960s, 190
    price stability, 183
    surplus budget, 188
    U.S. government obligations, 189
fixed rate, for construction loan, 92
flat lease, 117
flexible-payment mortgage, 6
floating rate, for construction loan, 92
FmHA, see Farmers Home Administration
FNMA, see Federal National Mortgage Association
foreclosure, 272:
    alternatives to, 278
    appointment of a receiver, 277
    commencing the action, 273
    completing the action, 273
    deed in lieu of, 276
    default, 272
    deficiency judgments, 275
    by entry and possession, 275
    by exercise of power of sale, 275
    and junior liens, 276
    and land contracts, 277
    lis pendens, 273
    process of, 273
    real estate, 239
    by sale in a judicial process, 274
    Soldiers' and Sailors' Relief Act, 276
    strict, 274
    types of, 274
foreclosure, alternatives to:
    consolidation and extension, 279
    Extension Agreement, 278
    mortgage extension, 278
    spreading mortgages, 282
forfeiture price, paid by mortgage banker, 204

Fractional Reserve System, of Federal Reserve, 184
"Freddie Mac," see Federal Home Loan Mortgage Corporation
Free Market System Auction, 214
front money deals, 141
FSLIC (Federal Savings and Loan Insurance Corporation), 167
funds, money market, sources and uses of, 159, 160
futures market, GNMA, 231
future value, 46; see also compound interest

G

gap financing, 156
general controls, Federal Reserve, 184:
    discount rate, 185
    Fractional Reserve System, 184
    open-market operations, 186
general mortgage clauses, 22
GI Bill of Rights, 205
GI mortgage, 4
"Ginnie Mae," see Government National Mortgage Association
Glass Act of 1933, 173
GNMA, see Government National Mortgage Association
good repair clause, in mortgage, 25
Government National Mortgage Association, 211:
    futures market, 231
    Guaranteed Mortgage-Backed Certificate (illus.), 232–33
    hedging, 231
    Housing and Urban Development Act of 1968, 211
    mortgage-backed security program, 230
    structure and organization, 228
    tandem programs with FNMA, 229
government obligations (U.S.),:
    marketable securities, 189
    nonmarketable issues, 189
    treasury bills, 189
    treasury bonds, 189
    treasury notes, 189
graduated payment mortgage, 7
gross lease, 117
ground lease, 121:
    residential, 124
    subordinated, 121
guaranteed price, for home, 157
guaranteed trade-in, 157

H

hedging, 231:
    long, 231
    short, 234

high ratio financing, 131:
  front money deals, 141
  sale-leaseback, 133
holding funds, for liens, 101
home improvement loans, 85
Home Loan Bank Act, 167
  home ownership loans, by FmHA, 249
Home Owner's Loan Act, 166
Housing and Community Development
    Act of 1974, 4, 87; second mortgages,
    87
Housing and Home Finance Agency, 209,
    237
Housing and Urban Development, 237:
  Demonstration Cities and Metropoli-
    tan Development Act of 1966, 239
  interest subsidy, 238
  "model cities," 239
  New Communities Act of 1968, 239
  real estate foreclosures, 239
  rehabilitation functions, 238
  rental subsidy, 238
  role in mortgage markets, 238
  turnkey programs, 239
  urban renewal, 238
Housing and Urban Development Act of
    1968, 166, 168, 210, 228
housing cycles, factors in influencing,
    199
housing expense-to-income ratio, for res-
    idential loan, 243
housing repair loans, rural, 251
HUD, see Housing and Urban Develop-
    ment

I

improvement, defined, 98
indebtedness:
  action on payment under deed of trust,
    40
  mortgage covenant to pay, 22
index leases, 119
installment land contract, 64:
  builder's option, 73
  common clauses, 69
  effect of judgments on, 72
  escrow provision, 70
  financing, 68
  illustrated, 66–67
  "interest only," 72
  lease with option to buy, 75
  mortgage clause, 69
  recording of, 70
  rolling option, 73
  sale of farms and ranches, 69
  speculator's use of option, 75
  tax deferment, 69
  use of option as financing method, 73
  uses of, 68
  validity of, 64

insurance, mortgage covenant of, 22
insured leases, 124
interest, compound, 44
interest factors, 45
"interest only" land contracts, 72
Interest Rate Adjustment Act, 168
interest rate ceilings, under Regulation
    Q, 187
interim financing, 89; defined, 89
intermediaries, as source of funds, 162
intermediate theory of mortgages, 3;
    states using, 3
intermediation, 162
internal rate of return:
  for investment evaluation, 54
  worksheet for, 55
investment policies:
  of commercial banks, 174
  of mutual savings banks, 171
  of savings and loan associations, 169
investment evaluation:
  internal rate of return method, 54
  methods of, 53
  net present value method, 53
investment time periods, compound in-
    terest, 46

J

"jawbone," policy of Federal Reserve,
    186
joint venture, 141, 153
judicial process, foreclosure by sale in,
    274
juniors lienors, and foreclosures, 276
junior liens, 77:
  discounting, 78
  as financing device, 77
  first mortgages, 79
  major sources of funds, 86
  monthly amortization, 82
  participations, 80
  residential transactions, 77
  second mortgages, 79
  yields, 79
  see also liens
  see also second mortgages

K

kicker, see wraparound mortgage

L

land, sale-leaseback of, 134
land contracts, 277:
  installment, 64
  "interest only," 72
  statute of frauds, 67
land development financing, 104

lease:
    classification of, 117
    classified by method of payment, 117
    common terms, 124
    condemnation, 127
    covenant not to sublet or assign, 126
    defined, 116
    destruction of premises, 129
    eminent domain, 127
    escalator, 119
    financing through, 120
    flat lease, 117
    gross lease, 117
    ground lease, 121
    increasing marketability, 121
    index, 119
    insured, 124
    lessee, 116
    lessee's right to make mortgage payments, 127
    lessor, 116
    long-term, 119
    mortgage on, 152
    net lease, 117
    net-net-net, 118
    option to buy, 75, 124
    option to renew, 125
    percentage, 118
    proprietary, 109
    rent, 116
    residential ground, 124
    revaluation, 119
    reversion, 129
    sale of leaseholds, 129
    short-term, 119
    Statute of Frauds and, 119
    step-up, 119
    stream of income, 129
    subordinated ground, 121
    tax deferment, 120
    unsubordinated leasehold mortgage, 121
    use of premises, 127
leasehold, sale of, 129
leasehold mortgage, unsubordinated, 121
lending, preliminary procedure, 90
lessee, 116; right to make mortgage payments, 127
lessor, 116
leverage, 81:
    defined, 131
    reverse effect of, 132
    second mortgages, 81
    use of, 131
liability, release from, 265
lienor, 100
liens:
    completion bond, 101
    holding funds, 101
    junior, 77
    mechanics, 98
    priority of, 99

    protection against, 100
    use of affidavit, 101
    waiver of, 101
    tax, 278
lien theory of mortgages, 3; states using, 3
life insurance companies:
    assets of (table), 176
    investment policies, 176
    liabilities of (table), 176
    regulation and control, 175
    structure and operation, 175
limited partnerships, 154:
    regulation of, 154
    risks of, 154
    tax effects of, 155
lis pendens, 273
loan amortization payments, 56
loan application, 242
loan assumption and transfer fees, 263
loan closing statement, 270; illustrated, 269
loans:
amortization of, 56
    collateral, 156
    construction, 89
    direct reduction, 82
    home improvement, 85
    participation in, 146
    payment of, 56
    remaining balances, 59
    repayment schedule (table), 57
    statement for assumption of (illus.), 264
    see also financing
loan-to-value ratio:
    defined, 4
    for FHA mortgages, 4
    high ratio financing, 131
long-term lease, 119

M

macro economic environment, 190
macro economic goals, recent developments in, 191
margin, 268
margin requirements, of Federal Reserve, 187
marketability, increasing through leasing, 121
mechanic's lien, 98:
    defined, 98
    lienor, 100
    "New York System" of, 100
    Pennsylvania system, 100
    priority of, 99
    rights between lien and mortgage, 100
    rights between liens, 99
    time in which to file, 99
    time of recording, 99
    see also liens
"model cities" program, 239

monetary policy, 182:
  economic goals, 183
  economic growth, 183
  full employment, 183
  international payments balance, 183
  in the 1960s, 190
  price stability, 183
money:
  advance commitment, 91
  "buying", 90
  cost of, 91
  cost of construction commitment, 91
  cost of construction loan, 92
  front, 141
  M_1 measure of, 194
  as medium of exchange, 182
  prime rate, 92
  time value of, 44
  supply, defined, 185
  usury, 141
money market funds, sources and uses
  of, 159, 160
money supply, M_1, M_2, M_3, 185
moral suasion, use by Federal Reserve,
  186
mortgage:
  annual constant, 82
  assignment of, 28
  assignment with covenant (illus.), 30
  assignment with recourse, 31
  assuming an existing, 262
  assuming the, 10
  balloon, 147
  banking companies, 177
  call second, 85
  chattel, 14
  common-law, 1
  consolidation and extension agree-
    ment, 279
  conventional, 5
  crop, 153
  definition of, 2, 14
  essentials of, 21
  extension agreement, 278
  on a lease, 152
  on a lease (illus.), 136–37
  mortgagee, 2, 14
  mortgagor, 2, 14
  mortuum vadium, 1
  origin of, 1
  purchase money, 61
  purpose of, 1
  release of, 27
  satisfaction of, 27
  satisfaction of (illus.), 29
  theories of real estate, 2
  vivum vadium, 1
mortgage-backed securities, 230:
  bond-type, 230
  pass-through security, 230
mortgage banker, defined, 203

mortgage banking, 202:
  forefeiture price, 204
  forward commitment, 203
  functions of, 203
  mortgage warehousing, 204
  operations of, 203
  recent trends and developments, 204
  standby commitment, 204
  take-out letter, 204
mortgage banking activity, 1970–1975
  (table), 205
mortgage banking companies, 177
mortgage bonds, 152
mortgage broker, 203
mortgage clauses:
general, 22
installment land contract, 69
  purchase money clause, 61
  warrant of title, 62
mortgage clauses, general:
  acceleration clause, 23
  covenant against removal, 22
  covenant of insurance, 22
  covenant to pay indebtedness, 22
  covenant to pay taxes, 23
  warrant of title, 23
mortgage clauses, special:
  covenant to pay attorney's fees, 23
  estoppel clause, 24
  good repair clause, 25
  owner rent clause, 23
  prepayment clause, 26
  receiver clause, 23
  sale in one parcel clause, 25
  trust clause, 25
mortgage clauses and their meanings, 22
mortgaged property:
  assuming the mortgage, 10
  non-assumption clause, 11
  transfer of, 10
  transferred subject to, 10
mortgagee, 2, 14
mortgagee's certificate of reduction
  (illus.), 263
mortgage funds, sources of, 177
Mortgage Guaranteed Insurance Corp.,
  guidelines for underwriting insurance, 5
mortgage loan participations, 204
mortgage market, 162:
  defined, 201
  facilitating function, 201
  primary, 201
  role of Housing and Urban Development, 238
  secondary, 201
  state real estate assistance agencies,
  240
mortgages:
  acknowledgment and recording, 27
  competition for, 159

FHA-insured, 3
financing residential, 162
foreclosure, 272
intermediate theory of, 3
lien theory of, 3
marketability of, 202
mechanics' lien, 100
MGIC guidelines for underwriting insurance, 5
partial release, 64
primary market, 163
redemption, 272
secondary market, 163
special clauses in, 23
spreading agreement, 282
subordination clause, 83
title theory of, 2
total (table), 161
transfers of mortgaged property, 10
types of, 3
uniform FNMA/FHLMC form, 15–21
unsubordinated leasehold, 121
VA, veterans entitled to, 5
VA-guaranteed, 4
variations in, 6
mortgage variations:
    blanket mortgage, 8
    budget mortgage, 7
    flexible-payment mortgage, 6
    graduated payment mortgage, 7
    open-end mortgage, 8
    open mortgage, 8
    package mortgage, 8
    purchase money mortgage, 9
    variable rate mortgage, 9
    wraparound mortgage, 9
mortgage warehousing, 204
mortgagor, 2, 14
mutual savings banks:
    assets of (table), 172
    investment policies, 171
    liabilities of (table), 171
    origin of, 170
    regulation and control, 170
    savings flows, 170
    structure and operation, 170
mortuum vadium, 1

N

National Housing Act of 1934, 4, 167, 208
net lease, 117
net-net-net lease, 118
net present value, 53
net present value method, worksheet for, 54
New Communities Act of 1968, 239
"New York System":
    states using, 100
    of mechanic's lien, 100
non-alienation clause, 11

non-assumption clause, in transferring mortgaged property, 11
non-discrimination, in residential loans, 247
notes:
    balloon, 147
    promissory, 149
    promissory, defined, 40
    promissory (illus.), 41–42
    treasury, 189
    truth in lending, 149
    use of, 40

O

open-end mortgage, 8
open mortgage, 8
opportunity cost, 108
options, 73:
    builders' use of, 73
    to buy, 75
    illustrated, 74
    to purchase, 124
    to renew, 125
    rolling, 73
    seller's financing method, 73
    speculators' use of, 75
option to purchase, in lease, 124
option to renew, in lease, 125
organization of builder, effect on financing, 92
owner rent clause, in mortgage, 25
Ownership Agreement (illus.), 148

P

package mortgage, 8
partial release:
    illustrated, 65
    mortgaged premises, 64
partial release clause, 64; in blanket mortgage, 8
Participation Agreement, 146; illustrated, 148
participations, 80, 146:
    junior, 80
    in the loan, 146
    in the security, 147
    senior, 80
partnerships:
    effect on financing, 92
    joint venture, 153
    limited, 153
    real estate syndicate, 153
pass-through securities, 230:
    modified, 231
    straight, 231
pension funds, as source of mortgage funds, 177
percentage lease, 118; recapture clause, 118
permanent financing, 89; defined, 89

personal property, 14
possession, foreclosure by, 275
pre-construction affidavit, 101; illustrated, 103
prepayment clause, in mortgage, 26
present value:
  basic problems, 48
  determining, 48
  determining investment time periods, 49
  determining rate of return, 49
  formula for, 48
present worth, 47:
  discounted, 47
  of $1 (table), 48
Present Worth of a $1 Annuity (table), 51
primary mortgage market, 163; defined, 201
prime commercial paper, 197
prime rate, 92; defined, 9
Production Act of 1950, 187
Production Credit Associations, 236
promissory note, 40, 149; illustrated, 41–42
property:
  improvement, defined, 98
  personal, 14
  real, 14, 67
  transfer of mortgaged, 10
property as security:
  assuming existing mortgage, 262
  assumption statement, 262
  cost approach of, 251
  economic obsolescence, 252
  FHA Underwriting Report (illus.), 253
  functional obsolescence, 251
  income approach, 252
  loan assumption and transfer fees, 263
  market data approach, 252
  physical deterioration, 251
  release from liability, 265
  tax stamps, 265
  truth in lending, 262
proprietary lease, 109
purchase-leaseback, *see* sale-leaseback
purchase money clause, in mortgage, 61
purchase money mortgage, 9, 24, 61:
  builder's use of, 63
  delivery of, 62
  priority of, 62
  warrant of title clause in, 62

real estate syndicates, 153
real property, 14, 67
recapture clause, in percentage lease, 118
receiver, appointment of, 277
receiver clause, in mortgage, 23
Reconstruction Finance Corporation, 209
recording, of mortgage and deed of trust, 27
redemption, 272; equity of, 272
reduction, mortgagee's certificate of (illus.), 263
Regulation Q, 187
Regulation T, 187
Regulation X, 187
Regulation Z, 149
reinstatement, trustor's right under deed of trust, 40
REITs (Real Estate Investment Trusts), 179
remaining loan balances, 59
removal, mortgage covenant against, 22
rent, 116
rental housing, loans from FmHA, 250
residential ground lease, 124
residential loans, 242:
  application (illus.), 244–45
  borrower's credit reputation, 246
  credit report, 246
  deposit verification, 247
  loan application, 242
  monthly debt payments-to-income ratio, 243
  monthly housing expense-to-income ratio, 243
  non-discrimination, 247
  seller's discounts, 247
  verification of deposit (illus.), 248
  verification of employment, 246
  verification of employment (illus.), 247
residential mortgages, sources of, 165
RESPA, *see* Real Estate Settlement Procedures Act
return:
  determining rates of, 46, 49
  rates for annuity, 52
  rates with compound interest, 46
  rates with present value, 49
revaluation lease, 119
rolling option, 73
rural areas, defined, 249

R

rate of return:
  formula for, 79
  internal, 54
real estate assistance agencies, state, 240
real estate mortgages, theories of, 2
Real Estate Settlement Procedures Act, 254; Settlement Procedures Special Information Booklet, 254

S

sale-buyback, 138; compared to mortgage loan, 140
sale in one parcel clause, in mortgage, 25
sale-leaseback:
  advantages of, 135
  advantages to buyer-lessor, 135
  advantages to seller-lessee, 138
  basket loan, 133

disadvantages of, 135
disadvantages to buyer-lessor, 135
disadvantages to seller-lessee, 138
high ratio financing, 133
of land, 134
partial financing by, 134
purchase-leaseback deal, 133
types of, 133
satisfaction of mortgage, 27; illustrated, 29
savings:
defined, 159
forms of, 159
thrift institutions, 159
savings and loan associations:
assets of (table), 169
investment policies, 168
liabilities of (table), 168
mutual associations, 166
origin of, 166
regulation and control, 167
savings flows, 168
secondary mortgage market, 221
stock associations, 166
structure and operation, 166
savings bonds:
Series E, 189
Series H, 189
savings flows, importance of, 168
second land contract, see junior lien
second mortgage:
call, 85
completion certificate, 85
debt service, 81
home builders' use of, 80
home improvement loans, 85
Housing and Community Development Act of 1974, 87
used to increase leverage, 81
used in land purchases, 83
see also junior lien
secondary mortgage market, 163, 201:
development of, 207
during 1930s and 1940s, 208
during 1950s and 1960s, 209
Emergency Home Finance Act of 1970, 211
Federal National Mortgage Association, 209
Housing and Urban Development Act of 1968, 210
National Housing Act of 1934, 208
need for, 201
recent trends and developments, 211
savings and loan associations, 221
Securities Exchange Act of 1934, 187
security:
participation in, 147
property as, 251
selective credit controls:
Regulation T, 187
Regulation X, 187

sellers' discounts, 247
Servicemen's Readjustment Act of 1944, 4, 205
Settlement Procedures Special Information Booklet, 254:
abstract of title search, title, examination, title insurance binder, 260
additional settlement charges, 261
annual assessments, 260
appraisal fee, 255
assumption fee, 257
attorney's fee, 260
city/county property taxes, 260
commission paid at settlement, 255
credit report fee, 255
division of commission, 254
document preparation, 260
government recording and transfer charges, 261
hazard insurance, 257
hazard insurance premium, 257
interest, 257
items payable in connection with loan, 255
items required by lender to be paid in advance, 257
lender's inspection fee, 255
lender's title insurance, 261
loan discount, 255
loan origination, 255
mortgage insurance, 257
mortgage insurance application fee, 257
mortgage insurance premium, 257
notary fee, 260
owner's title insurance, 261
pest and other inspections, 261
reserves deposited with lenders, 257
sales/broker's commission, 254
settlement or closing fee, 260
survey, 261
title charges, 260
title insurance, 260
total settlement charges, 261
short-term lease, 119
single proprietorship, effect on financing, 92
Sinking Fund Plan, 82
Soldiers' and Sailors' Relief Act, 276
special purpose financing:
"bridge," 114
condominiums, 109
cooperatives, 109
speculators, use of option by, 75
Spreading Agreement, 282
stable monthly income, 243
standby commitment, in mortgage banking, 204
State Real Estate Assistance Agencies, 240
statute of frauds, 67:
charged party, 68

and leases, 119
    real property, 67
step-up lease, 119
strict foreclosure, 274
subject to, use in transferring mortgaged
        property, 10
subletting, covenant against, 126
    subordinated, defined, 121
    subordinated ground lease, 121
Subordination Agreement (illus.), 84
Subordination Agreement of a lease
        (illus.), 122–23
subordination clause, 83
surplus budget, 188
syndicates, real estate, 153

T

take-out letter, in mortgage banking, 204
tax deferment:
    installment land contract, 69
    through lease, 120
taxes:
    for limited partnerships, 155
    mortgage covenant to pay, 23
tax liens, 278
Tax Reform Act of 1976, effect on REITs,
        179
tax stamps, 265
thrift institutions, 159
time value of money, 44
title:
    abstract of, 274
    in mortgage, 23
    warrant in purchase money mortgage,
        62
title theory of mortgages, 2; states using,
        2

tract financing, 104:
    accounting procedures for, 108
    appraisal for, 105
transmittal, letter of (illus.), 71
treasury bills, 189
treasury bonds, 189
treasury notes, 189
trust, deed of, see deed of trust
trust clause, in mortgage, 25
trustor's right of reinstatement, under
        deed of trust, 40
truth in lending, 149, 262
turnkey programs, of HUD, 239

U

uniform mortgage, of FNMA/FHLMC, 15
usury, defined, 141

V

VA-guaranteed mortgage, 4
value, future, 44
VA mortgages:
    GI Bill, 4
    veterans entitled to, 5
variable interest rate, 235
variable rate mortgage, 9
vivum vadium, 1

W

waiver of liens, 101
warrant of title, in mortgage, 23
warrant of title clause, 62
wraparound mortgage, 9, 145

Y

yields, 79; formula for, 79